GREG SCARPA,
LEGENDARY EVIL

THE
MANY
FACES
OF A
MAFIA
KILLER

JONATHAN DYER

WILDBLUE
PRESS

WildBluePress.com

Greg Scarpa, Legendary Evil published by:
WILDBLUE PRESS
P.O. Box 102440
Denver, Colorado 80250

WILDBLUE PRESS is registered at the U.S. Patent and Trademark Offices.

ISBN 978-1-964730-66-0 Hardcover
ISBN 978-1-964730-67-7 Trade Paperback
ISBN 978-1-964730-65-3 eBook

Cover design © 2025 WildBlue Press. All rights reserved.
Author photo courtesy of Vocal Visions

Interior Formatting and Book Cover Design by Elijah Toten
www.totencreative.com

GREG SCARPA,
LEGENDARY EVIL

In Memory Of
Thomas George Dyer, PhD
(1943 – 2013)
Gentleman, Scholar, Teacher, Revered Uncle

CONTENTS

ACKNOWLEDGMENTS

I'll start by thanking two generous men I've known for more years than I care to specify. The first is Joe Poletto, a writing partner on a number of other projects. Joe suggested I write a Greg Scarpa biography. Having never written a book-length piece of nonfiction, I hesitated. To his credit, Joe pushed a bit. Nothing too heavy, just a reminder here and there about what he described as an opportunity. At the end of the day, I'm glad he did, and I'm thankful for the suggestion and push. The second is Pete Farrelly, a friend whose career arc I have admired for years. Pete provided some timely encouragement that got me over the finish line on this book, and for that I'm grateful.

I also want to acknowledge the people at WildBlue Press and thank them for taking a chance on my work even when I wavered. They are hard-working, meticulous, persistent professionals without whom this book would not have come to fruition.

My brother, Peter, and my sister, Pamela, deserve a word of thanks. Their unfailing good humor and support, grounded in our deep, shared history, has buoyed me often. I think about them every day and know I'm lucky to have been born into such fine company.

My daughter, Melanie, has inspired me for years. Her bright, quick mind, her unfailing commitment to decency and fairness, and her sharp sense of humor are all a delight to me, as she will always be.

Finally, my wife, Kerry, deserves more thanks than I can give her. Her patience, understanding, and love enrich my life daily. It is impossible for me to put into words how profoundly grateful I am for our shared life, and it is my inestimable good fortune that she decided to share her life with me.

CHAPTER ONE: WHAT LIES WITHIN HIM

"The more identities a man has, the more they express the person they conceal."

John le Carré, *Tinker, Tailor, Soldier, Spy*

Gregory Scarpa Sr. was a family man, a husband, and a father. He wanted his children to be well educated and insisted on their 100% attendance in school. At home, he taught his eldest son the fundamentals of boxing, and they often did push-ups and sit-ups together. He liked to play touch football and softball. According to his namesake, Gregory Scarpa Jr., no one could hit a softball farther than Greg Scarpa. He was a casual sports fan who liked to root for New York's professional teams. His appearance was important to him: shower and shave every day, a sport coat and dress slacks for work. He was always on time for work, and he insisted that the men who worked for him show up every day, on time, well-dressed, and ready to work.[1] He was, in the words of the man who perhaps knew him best, "a C.E.O."[2] His manner of speaking was often stern, but he eschewed cursing. He liked to dine out, and when he did, his favorite dish was red snapper. He sipped Cutty Sark with dinner, and before he became ill, he smoked Marlboro cigarettes. He wasn't a big movie fan, but he liked the music of Frank Sinatra, Dean Martin, and Barry White.[3] Like most of us, Scarpa had his idiosyncrasies. For instance, every other day for years he went through what is best described as a complex ritualized process, identical every time, to get his hair just right. And he habitually placed his wallet and keys in the same spot whenever he came home, looking down on those who even temporarily misplaced one or the other.[4] In short, in many ways, Greg Scarpa was like millions of other American men of his generation. And in many other ways, he was not.

Greg Scarpa was a killer and a thief, a liar and a con, a traitor and a fraud. His eldest son described him as a "powerful force of nature."[5] His loyal accomplice during his most violent years called him "a vicious, violent animal… unscrupulous and treacherous… a horrible human being."[6] His mistress of more than thirty years, the mother of two of his children, admitted that Scarpa was a cold-blooded killer who left a trail of misery and death in his wake.[7] The life of those around him was one of "misery, death, and nightmares."[8] He was a crass manipulator,[9] a man in love with money more than anything else,[10] a malignant narcissist who committed murder on a whim.[11] According to NYPD Detective Tommy Dades, a man who grew up in Brooklyn and personally knew many of the mobsters he eventually arrested, "'Greg Scarpa had people petrified because of all the murders, the beatings, just a vicious animal.'"[12] A United States District Court judge and Scarpa's closest lieutenant's grandmother both referred to him as the devil.[13] Another federal judge called Scarpa's acts "worse than those of a wild animal."[14]

He was a dangerous criminal for nearly half a century. By the age of twenty-three, he had taken a blood oath of loyalty to the men in what was then America's most vicious and secretive criminal enterprise,[15] and for most of thirty years, he violated that oath by feeding the FBI a steady flow of self-serving information exposing and condemning those same men, leading to arrest and incarceration for many of them. The FBI estimated that by 1970, Scarpa had identified more than 200 Cosa Nostra members in the New York-New Jersey area.[16] In the 1,250 pages of FBI documents relating to Scarpa's activities as a Top Echelon Criminal Informant and the FBI's investigations of Scarpa's criminal activity, there are more than 290 names which Scarpa provided to the FBI. That number is both over- and underinclusive. It is overinclusive in that some of the names, such as Albert Anastasia, Joseph Profaci, Salvatore Scarpa, and Joseph Valachi, were clearly already known to the FBI before Scarpa provided them to his handlers. It is underinclusive in the sense that in many instances, the names Scarpa gave the FBI were redacted from the documents before their release and are thus not available to the general public. Indeed, some of the names may refer to the same person but were simply spelled differently by different special agents. Finally, that number does not contain members or associates who were only mentioned by Scarpa as having been killed.

Given the number of men he exposed for doing precisely what he did for nearly all of his adult life, it is difficult to overstate the scope of his treachery. As he lay dying of AIDS at the age of sixty-six, he committed one final act of perfidy. When given the chance, he failed to absolve the men closest and most loyal to him of any of the heinous sins they committed at his command and on his behalf.[17]

Chronicling a life that in many ways tracked the aspirations and habits of millions of others while filled with treachery, violence, and deceit presents obvious challenges. Sifting through versions of horrific events that have never been subjected to the scrutiny of careful investigation or rigorous cross-examination, of tragic events whose first-hand witnesses are either dead or still living in fear, of shameful events purposely shrouded in secrecy creates significant obstacles when crafting a work of nonfiction. The public's reluctant and usually forced interaction with Greg Scarpa notwithstanding, his life was for the most part private, and the details of that life can vary wildly from one witness to the next despite anyone's best intentions. Unlike those whose fame is earned on a playing field or a movie screen, no legion of journalists reporting on every detail of Greg Scarpa's life followed him around. For an intimate look at the life of a gangster, we have to look to those closest to him. But how does a child provide an objective picture of a parent known as The Grim Reaper? How does a mistress reconcile enduring memories of love, infidelity, and murder? How does an accomplice come to terms with years of betrayal? Beyond that intimate circle lies an official record of society's sporadic and involuntary collisions with this man. But how does a legal system that failed so many for so long repair the damage done by its myopic ineptitude? How can any of the above be rationally explained?

Legends come into being when fact and fiction intersect in a way that explains the seemingly unexplainable. While a good faith effort has been made to separate the fact of Greg Scarpa's life from the fiction surrounding it, that life as described in the following pages is the story of a legend, a story where the line between fact and fiction has been blurred by time, ignored by habit, and erased altogether out of deep emotional need.

CHAPTER TWO:
IMMIGRANTS, INFANTS,
INFORMANTS, AND
INFIDELITY

THE END

The sendoff for a recently departed Mafia big shot is an iconic cultural moment in the world of American organized crime. The funeral of fictional Cosa Nostra boss Vito Corleone in the 1972 movie *The Godfather* is a near-perfect portrayal of what the moment traditionally requires. A hearse is followed by a long line of highly-polished, black limousines crawling through a nearly endless cemetery, its location identified by a glimpse of the George Washington Bridge in the background. Mourners by the dozens—all in black, most wearing sunglasses—assemble in a prearranged pecking order at graveside among large, garish bouquets of flowers further attesting to the importance of the man being laid to rest. The viewer can imagine FBI agents and other members of law enforcement mixed in with the crowd and spying from the perimeter, writing down license plate numbers, noting who is present, where they sit, who talks with whom, and any other information the scene provides to an observant and experienced set of eyes. One by one, flowers are placed on the dead man's coffin by allies and rivals alike, another show of respect at a moment of deep symbolic significance in which powerful men of America's underworld recognize the past and attempt to claim a stake in the future. The scene is so iconic that its portrayal captures our immediate imagination while precisely meeting our cultural expectations. Life and art imitate each other, particularly in the tradition-bound world of the American Mafia.

Fast forward from Puzo's and Coppola's fictional portrayal of Vito Corleone's funeral to the 2002 interment of John Gotti, the Dapper Don, the incarcerated boss of the Gambino family, or borgata, one of the five families of the New York Italian Mafia. After dying of throat cancer in federal prison, Gotti "got a send-off that matched the style and swagger with which he ruthlessly ruled the Gambino crime family… His funeral procession featured 20 limos carrying elaborate flower displays and 21 more filled with family and friends. Weeping mourners screamed 'Goodbye John!' when the hearse passed by Gotti's Bergin Hunt and Fish Club in Ozone Park, Queens."[1] Gotti's importance to the mourners was on full display. As far as the Mafia is concerned, when it comes to a final sendoff for their big men, the bigger the funeral, the better.

Greg Scarpa, for years a big earner and a feared, powerful enforcer in the Colombo family, died on June 8, 1994.[2] Like John Gotti, Scarpa was incarcerated at the time of his death. Like John Gotti, Scarpa's death was neither dramatic nor violent as one might expect. Instead, like Gotti, Scarpa was finally killed by a terminal illness. Unlike John Gotti, Scarpa died a disgraced man, shunned by nearly everyone who knew him best, an outcast among thieves and killers, a rat. "Men who had been in his position customarily have incredible turnouts. Carlo Gambino the old-time boss of the Gambino family had dozens of limos just for the flowers."[3]

With the exception of a few of his closest family members and his long-time mistress, Scarpa's death would be greeted with little more than a disrespectful shrug or a sigh of relief. He died "without a friend to care"[4] eight years after receiving a transfusion of HIV-tainted blood during emergency stomach surgery. His body weight, once noted by the FBI[5] as being 210 pounds,[6] was down to a mere 116 pounds or less,[7] worse than skeletal for a man who stood a full five feet, ten inches. His left eye was gone, having been shot out in December of 1992 in a gun battle while he was under house arrest. He died less than six months after admitting at his sentencing hearing in federal court that he had been an FBI informant.[8] He died one day after signing a sworn statement implicating two men whose unquestioned loyalty during the darkest days of what was known as the third Colombo war resulted in their direct involvement in multiple murders.[9] The way he lived his life rather than the manner of his death was responsible for the disrespect he engendered when that life mercifully came to an end.

Greg Scarpa's funeral was anything but lavish.[10] It bore no resemblance to the fictional burial of Don Vito Corleone or the real-world interment of celebrated Gambino boss John Gotti. There was no line of limos bearing the leaders of New York's Cosa Nostra, no line of respectful mourners waiting patiently for the chance to toss a flower on his casket. Greg Scarpa's final sendoff was attended by a handful of family members, but no friends or former colleagues.[11] The pallbearers, traditionally and symbolically men of consequence who had been close to the deceased, were strangers who had been hired for the day.[12] His confirmed and admitted status as a "rat" for three decades sealed his legacy as a self-serving, violent hypocrite, a legacy that has only grown since his death. He informed on those closest to him in the Colombo family, and on those in the other four Italian Mafia families of New York. He informed on men he barely knew, and men he had known for years. He informed on men above him and men below him in the Mafia hierarchy. As long as the FBI was paying Scarpa for information, everyone he knew and interacted with was fair game.

The man known variously as The Mad Hatter and The Grim Reaper, a man respected by members up and down the Mafia food chain for at least three decades for his status as a big earner, a man feared for his reputation as a ruthless, capricious killer left this earth not with a bang, but a whimper, his treachery and hypocrisy fully exposed. From humble beginnings, typical of millions of children of Italian immigrants during the period of "New Immigration," Greg Scarpa escaped his family's relentless poverty in a way most would never contemplate. And he secured his position of power and prestige within a criminal enterprise by simultaneously aligning himself with the very forces working to destroy that enterprise.

THE BEGINNING: LORENZAGA TO BROOKLYN

Like so many twentieth-century Italian Americans, the story of Gregory Scarpa Sr. starts with his father's journey from a small town in northeastern Italy to America's largest city at a time when millions of Italians were making the same journey in what became known as the First Italian Diaspora. Indeed, by 1900, more Italians lived in New York City than lived in any city in Italy except for Rome.[13]

Salvatore Scarpa was born in 1895. He is reported as having come from the small town of Lorenzaga of the *comune* Motta di Livenza near both Venice and Treviso, in northeast Italy.[14] He came to the United States in 1913, having boarded a ship named the *San Giorgio* in Naples.[15] Salvatore Scarpa's last residence before leaving Italy was listed on the *San Giorgio*'s manifest as Nocero Superiore in southwest Italy. Scarpa, eighteen years old and single at the time, could not have timed his migration from Italy any better. Europe was a powder keg primed to explode during the early years of the twentieth century's second decade. The monarchical heads of too many countries were champing at the bit for a war. Starting in the summer of 1914, they got their war, and then for more than four years they got more than any of them, or their subjects, bargained for. During four-plus years of vicious, modern, large-scale slaughter, Italy alone suffered more than half a million dead and nearly one million wounded combatants. Although Salvatore Scarpa avoided Italy's involvement in the war, according to the 1940 U.S. Census he was an American veteran who served in the "World War," what is now referred to as World War I.[16]

Shortly after the war, the 1918 marriage of Salvatore Scarpa and Maria Palmetta began to produce children. Maria, who went by Mary for most of her adult life, was eight years Salvatore's junior and, like Salvatore, reportedly from Lorenzaga, having emigrated to the United States in 1914 at the age of twelve. The Scarpas' first child, the first of three consecutive daughters, was Teresa.[17] Teresa was followed three years later by Vincenza, who was three years older than their youngest girl, Marie. During the early 1920s, the family lived briefly in or around New London, Connecticut, where Vincenza was born in late 1921.[18] After the family moved back to Brooklyn, the three girls were followed by two sons, Gregory in May of 1928, and finally Salvatore, who was a year younger than and a grade behind his only brother. With the exception of Vincenza, the children were all born in New York City.[19]

As of April of 1940, the seven members of the Scarpa family were still living in Brooklyn, and they were chronically poor. Ten years earlier, the U.S. Census taker noted that the family did not even own a radio, a widespread symbol of modest economic success.[20] The 1940 census lists Salvatore as a laborer with no trade skills and an eighth grade education.[21] When Gregory was two years old, his father's occupation was that of a "laborer tending furnaces."[22] Years later, Scarpa recounted for his mistress what it was like to haul coal with his father when he was only seven years old.[23] Information provided by Mary Scarpa for the 1940 census indicated that her husband somehow managed to earn $400[24] as a laborer in 1939 even though he was unemployed for all fifty-two weeks of the year.[25] Mary earned $600 that same year[26] working as an "operator" in the clothing industry.[27] She self-reported to the census taker as having had no formal education.[28] The $1,000 in income for the Scarpa family in 1939 was the equivalent of approximately $21,824 in 2023, less than half of the federal poverty level for a family of seven that year.[29] The effect of the family's poverty on Gregory Scarpa cannot be stated with any exactitude. However, his mistress of thirty years, Linda Schiro, reported that, not surprisingly, he hated being poor and resolved to lead a better life than the one his parents had.[30] One opportunity in particular began to open up for him in the late 1940s.

FAMILY MAN

Shortly after Gregory Scarpa was finished with high school, he joined the Merchant Marines[31] as the U.S. was demobilizing the enormous military force it had assembled during World War II. Nearly eight million men were in uniform in the U.S. Army when the war ended in the late summer of 1945. Rapid demobilization began immediately.

"Between [Japan's official surrender in early] September and December of 1945, the Army discharged an average of 1.2 million soldiers per month."[32] By July 1, 1947, when demobilization was deemed complete, the Army had discharged more than 7.3 million soldiers.[33] In short, young veterans were flooding the domestic job market just as Scarpa was becoming an adult.

Scarpa returned to Brooklyn after his stint as a merchant marine. Back home, in addition to the flooded job market, another factor worked against his chances of joining the legitimate work force as a young adult: by 1946, he was already being recruited for a life of crime by Calogero "Charlie the Sidge" LoCicero of the Profaci family, one of the five Mafia families of New York.[34] However, even the opportunity for Scarpa to become a member of the Profaci family was potentially doomed from the start. Although both of Scarpa's parents were Italian, a virtual prerequisite for Profaci family membership at the time, he was not Sicilian. Sicilians dominated the five families of New York, and they tended to distrust Italians who were not Sicilian. Profaci, however, welcomed non-Sicilians,[35] and Scarpa soon became a Profaci family associate.

By 1949, Greg Scarpa was doing well enough as a Profaci associate to marry. That year, he and Concetta Farace, who went by Connie Forrest, tied the knot. Connie was leaning out of her bedroom window talking to the girlfriend of one of Scarpa's friends the first time he noticed her. They were soon dating, and their friends saw they were very much in love. Gregory Scarpa Jr. recalled stories of the two of them walking to the movies in the rain together. As fine cars passed them on their way, Scarpa would promise her, "Don't worry, Connie. We will be driving nice cars to the movies very soon."[36]

In 1951, he was a family man in both senses of the word. His daughter, Deborah, turned two years old. He earned his button[37] in the Profaci family that year, and his son Gregory Jr., the second of his four children, the first of his three sons with Concetta and a son who would follow him into the life of a gangster, was born that April.

Scarpa's first decade as a made man in the Profaci family was relatively quiet from a law enforcement point of view. That was at least in part due to the position that J. Edgar Hoover, and thus the entire FBI, was taking on the existence of organized crime in the United States. In short, Hoover's view was that no such thing existed. "Examination of the congressional records for the fifties and early sixties to see what Hoover fed to Congress at appropriations time… reveals nothing about organized crime—for the simple reason that Hoover contended it was a phantom."[38]

Hoover's own words confirmed his position on the possibility of organized crime operating in America. "'No single individual or coalition of racketeers dominates organized crime across this country.'"[39] Even so, by late 1957, the FBI already had regional offices "gather[ing] information on mobsters in their territories" and reporting "regularly to Washington" as part of the so-called Top Hoodlum Program initiated on August 25, 1953.[40] However, it appears that the FBI made little progress during the 1950s in its initial efforts to understand the structure and workings of organized crime, and in particular of the Italian Mafia operating in the U.S. High-profile events like the murder of Albert Anastasia in October of 1957, and the meeting of more than 100 members of the Mafia in Apalachin, New York approximately three weeks later, began to shake Hoover's resolve.

With a few minor exceptions, Gregory Scarpa's own criminal activities as a Profaci wiseguy went largely unnoticed in the

1950s. In 1950, he was arrested under then New York Penal Law section 1897[41] for unlawful possession of a firearm.[42] His next arrest was nine years later for violation of New York's Penal Law Section 722, Sub. 11, which criminalized "(consorting) with others with evil reputations."[43] And in March of 1960, Scarpa was arrested by FBI agents[44] and charged with conspiracy to commit theft of an interstate shipment and possession of goods stolen from an interstate shipment.[45] This arrest proved to be fateful. It is the first known contact the FBI had with Scarpa. And while the results were at first less than satisfactory for the Bureau, a seed was planted that would grow into a thirty-year relationship between Scarpa and the FBI.

The early 1960s marked a turning point in the federal government's attempts to understand and respond to the threat of organized crime in the U.S. As a presidential candidate in 1960, John F. Kennedy emphasized his determination to attack organized crime. In a speech given in Dodgeville, Wisconsin on April 1, 1960, Kennedy said, "there is a highly organized criminal syndicate operating in America today. It is powerful. It is dangerous. And, worst of all, it seems to be growing."[46] The appointment of Robert F. Kennedy as Attorney General by his brother the president ensured that the fight against organized crime in the U.S. would be ramped up at the highest levels. At the retail level, Scarpa's early encounters with the FBI were likely a direct result of this new national emphasis led by Attorney General Kennedy, the Department of Justice, and its principal investigative arm, the FBI.

FINDING COMMON GROUND

Scarpa was released on bond after his March 1960 arrest by federal agents. It was then that the FBI contacted him, hoping to obtain information about his brother Salvatore, who was a suspect in the same case.[47] Scarpa refused to cooperate. President Kennedy was inaugurated in 1961, and from that moment on, a more focused and aggressive approach to Scarpa from the FBI's New York Office is evident.

FBI Special Agents contacted Scarpa a number of times at a social club he was operating in Brooklyn as conflict was erupting in 1961 between the Gallo brothers—Larry, Joey, and Albert—and those loyal to family boss Joseph Profaci in what became variously known as the Gallo-Profaci feud and the first Colombo war. During each contact, Scarpa, while friendly, refused to provide any information to the FBI. In fact, he eventually requested that the agents no longer contact him because of questions people were raising about these limited contacts. The FBI agreed to no longer contact him and informed him that he should feel free to contact them should the need arise. Then, on October 27, 1961, Scarpa phoned the FBI's New York Office and requested to speak with a special agent.[48]

Scarpa's timing, like his father's decision to emigrate, could not have been better, and his relationship with the FBI moved swiftly from that initial call. In November of 1961, the Bureau instituted a new tool to learn about and combat organized crime, the Top Echelon Criminal Informant (TECI) program,[49] a successor offshoot of the earlier, and less well-developed, Top Hoodlum Program. About three weeks after Scarpa's first call to the FBI, he was designated as a "PC"[50] in the TECI program.[51] This original designation, apparently less than a full-fledged Top Echelon Criminal Informant, meant that "contacting agents will merely accept whatever information [Scarpa] desires to furnish."[52] Once the information started, it did not stop for about a dozen years.

A memo dated November 21, 1961, from the FBI's Special Agent in Charge of its New York Office to J. Edgar Hoover, stated that, "GREGORY SCARPA is a current member of the JOSEPH PROFACI group in Brooklyn and is considered to be an individual worthy of concentrated attention in accordance with [the TECI] program."[53] At the same time, some boilerplate language began to appear in the memos about Scarpa that years later would seem incomprehensible to the point of being ridiculous. One was that Scarpa "is considered to be emotionally stable and reliable."[54] Later, he would come to be known as both "The Grim Reaper" and "The Mad Hatter." In spite of that widely-held reputation, the boilerplate language about Scarpa's emotional stability and reliability would be repeated over and over again for years by the FBI. The other bit of boilerplate which also appeared in the FBI's first memo about Scarpa as a potential informant was that Scarpa "has not furnished any information known to be false."[55] Again, this boilerplate contention would be repeated for years during the FBI's now infamous relationship with Scarpa.

It is not possible from the FBI's documents to determine how they initially judged the veracity of Scarpa's information. Frankly, it appears that at the outset of their relationship, and at numerous times thereafter, the Bureau accepted what he said at face value. That acceptance may have been driven by the FBI leadership's pressure for its regional offices to develop TECI contacts. The FBI, like any other organization, goes through stages of institutional emphasis channeling the efforts of those, both inside and out, who are loyal to the institution. The desire to fill the serious gaps in the FBI's knowledge about all aspects of organized crime in the U.S. during the early 1960s would explain, but not excuse, the uncritical eye with which they viewed Scarpa's eventual outpouring of information.

Irrespective of what was driving the FBI and Scarpa to enter into their relationship, it soon proved to be of great value to both of them. The FBI noted early on that Scarpa, then living with his family at 43 Marscher Place on Staten Island, was a "close associate of CHARLES LO CICERO"[56] and had associated with Carmine Persico Jr., Hugh McIntosh, Salvatore Albanese, and Salvatore Scarpa, all "known criminals."[57] In March of 1962, the FBI's New York Office reported its rationale for having Scarpa designated as a Top Echelon Criminal Informant with a "symbol number" indicating his potential high value to the Bureau.[58] As part of their justification, the New York Office provided a detailed recitation of eight separate meetings between Scarpa and the FBI during a slightly more than two-month period starting on October 27, 1961, and ending on January 9, 1962.[59]

Scarpa's newfound willingness to talk fully and frequently to the FBI contrasted with his earlier admonition that they keep away from him. The information, once it started coming from Scarpa, was flowing at an impressive rate. And the FBI found it immensely valuable. None of the details he provided about the Gallo-Profaci feud were otherwise "available to the NYO [New York Office] from an admitted member of the criminal organization."[60] The FBI viewed Scarpa as their sole credible source of information for much of what its agents were learning about New York's Italian Mafia. It is no wonder that his handlers reported almost breathlessly that "[t]he full potential of this informant is yet to be realized...."[61]

Scarpa was not only the primary source for much of their information about the Gallo-Profaci feud, but he also provided the FBI with detailed information regarding the history,[62] structure,[63] membership procedure,[64] customs,[65] and rules, including those pertaining to murder,[66] of the Italian Mafia. Additionally, Scarpa gave the FBI the names of the heads ("bosses") of the five New York families.[67] Collectively, the heads of the five New York families comprised what was then known as the Commission. Scarpa also told the FBI he was a *caporegime*, or capo,[68] in the Profaci family.[69] Scarpa's claim about his rank appears to have been met with some skepticism back at the New York Office. It was noted by the FBI immediately after Scarpa's assertion that an individual whose name was redacted from the files stated, "that informant is at least a button in the PROFACI family."[70] That Scarpa served as a capo in the Profaci family was reported to the FBI by another informant. "Scarpa was made a 'caporegima' [sic] during the early days of the GALLO-PROFACI feud,… but he has not acted in this capacity since the death of JOE PROFACI."[71]

Scarpa provided nearly all of the above detailed information about the New York Mafia in a single interview during the night of June 5, 1962.[72] What Scarpa provided was of such high interest that the New York Office summarized its content in a telephone call to Assistant Director Courtney Allen Evans the next day,[73] and then sent Evans and FBI Director J. Edgar Hoover a lengthy memo detailing the intelligence Scarpa provided in that nighttime interview the following day, June 7, 1962.[74] Scarpa clearly had the FBI's attention, all the way to its highest level.

THE FBI'S SHINY NEW OBJECT

MONEY AND MURDER

Other than the wealth of information provided about the history, personnel, and inner workings of the Italian Mafia in the U.S., several items stand out from these early June 1962 interactions between Scarpa and the FBI. The first item gave the impression that Scarpa was manipulating his new collaborators; the second item may have revealed Scarpa's primary motivation behind his recent, rapid turn; the third item could easily have been Scarpa testing the FBI's limits of tolerable criminal behavior.

The FBI's memo regarding the lengthy interview of Scarpa during the night of June 5, 1962, contained the following paragraph:

"At the time the informant was originally contacted by agents he was in the process of attempting to bring his activities in the organization to a minimum. He stated that he had ceased all activities relating to the organization except those which were absolutely necessary. The informant related that he could not resign from the organization, but that by withdrawing from all but essential activities he could more or less retire."[75]

Scarpa had just turned thirty-four less than one month before he allegedly made the above assertion. The notion that he was trying to extract himself from the Profaci family in 1962 is simply not credible. He was, according to his own statement, a *caporegime*, part of the family's leadership. His relationship with Calogero "Charlie the Sidge" LoCicero, one of the most important and powerful men in the family in 1962, went back to the 1940s. On top of that, "Mafia membership was a lifetime obligation; there were no provisions for resignation or early retirement. 'The only way out is in a box.'"[76] Why would Scarpa claim he had been contemplating retirement and, more importantly, that he had been actively engaged in withdrawing from the organization's activities? The next paragraph in the memo provided a clue.

"During the period of this informant's development by NYO agents, the informant has reactivated his status in the organization in an attempt to be in a position where he could obtain information of greater value to the Bureau. This reactivation process has necessitated that the informant spend more time with other members of the PROFACI group **at considerable expense to himself.** The informant stated that he feels he is now attaining the position where he will be able to furnish information on a continuous basis and will continue to do so as long as the Bureau is desirous of his assistance."[77]

In essence, Scarpa set the stage for a raise. He let the FBI know how much he would love to help them but, he claimed, he simply could not financially afford to continue doing so. In fact, as he had already let them know, he was making preparations to get out of the gangster business altogether, which would have been a shame because he was eager to help America's premier law enforcement agency bring down the New York Italian Mafia, if only his cash flow improved!

Scarpa must have sensed the FBI's enthusiasm for having him as an informant. The attention he was getting would have been a clear indicator of his value to the Bureau. And it is not inconceivable that one special agent or another simply told him how highly valued he was. Scarpa's next move was to let the Bureau know the specific price of his continued cooperation.

"This informant has advised that he is currently heavily in debt in the amount of $3,000 and that he feels that if he can pay off these debts, his income from the organization would pay operating expenses and maintain his position in the organization."[78]

Three grand. That's all it would take to keep the Scarpa pipeline open. And the FBI bought it hook, line, and sinker.

"It was contemplated when the Top Echelon Criminal Informant Program was initiated that situations would arise requiring substantial authorization for payments to high level informants. This informant presents a unique opportunity to fully penetrate the Italian organization in New York."[79]

Apparently, it did not occur to anyone either in the New York Office or in Washington, D.C., to question how a man who was $3,000 in debt to the Italian Mafia was going to survive retiring from the only source of income he had. Scarpa, the master manipulator, played the FBI beautifully from the earliest days of their relationship.

Scarpa's financial probing was not the only test he had for the FBI in 1962. Less than three months after convincing the FBI to pay him $3,000, Scarpa looked to determine the limits of criminal behavior the FBI would tolerate from him. In short, would the FBI turn a blind eye while Scarpa committed murder? He used the credibility of his long-standing relationship with Charlie LoCicero to get the answer to that question.

In a memo marked "URGENT" and dated September 13, 1962,[80] from the Special Agent in Charge (SAC) of the FBI's New York Office to Director J. Edgar Hoover, the SAC reported the remarkable piece of intelligence that Charlie LoCicero had ordered Scarpa to murder Joseph Magliocco.[81] Magliocco considered himself to be the prime candidate to succeed family boss Joseph Profaci, who had passed away from throat cancer on June 6 of that year. The memo went on to state that Scarpa had gone so far as to "case" Magliocco's Long Island home in preparation for the hit.[82] The contents of the memo were so sensational that a follow-up, also marked "URGENT," was sent later that day detailing instructions from the FBI to Scarpa that "under no circumstance can he participate in the murder of Joseph

Magliocco."[83] An additional memo from the FBI's Special Investigative Division in Washington, D.C. confirmed that same day that the New York Office "has instructed the informant and the informant agrees that he must not participate in the execution of Joseph Magliocco."[84]

Murder was clearly off the table in 1962. It is an open question whether LoCicero actually gave Scarpa the order to hit Magliocco. In the memos following the admonition prohibiting the murder of Magliocco, Scarpa reported that LoCicero could not obtain Commission approval for the hit, and it was therefore called off.[85] Scarpa also stated that he believed LoCicero's order to kill Magliocco may have been LoCicero testing Scarpa's loyalty in the ongoing struggle for power after Profaci's death.[86] However, it is just as possible that master manipulator Greg Scarpa was testing the FBI. As FBI Special Agent and Scarpa handler Anthony Villano, who used the alias "Nick Biletti" when referring to Scarpa in his book,[87] noted, Scarpa "seemed to like to test the temperature of the water whenever he contemplated a major crime."[88] Certainly murder qualified as a major crime.

There is no way to confirm Scarpa's version of the kill order or its alleged rescission as reflected in the FBI documents. It is important to remember two things in connection with this sequence. First, the news that Scarpa was ordered to hit Magliocco became known to the FBI either late in the night on September 12 or early in the morning the next day. By the afternoon of September 13, Scarpa had been instructed that he was not to participate in Magliocco's murder. There simply was not enough time to confirm Scarpa's version of events between his reporting and the FBI's admonition given the sensational nature of his information. Second, during the early years of Scarpa's relationship with the FBI, there would have been, in most instances, no way to confirm Scarpa's information. The FBI documents are replete with references to the singular and unique nature of the information Scarpa was providing during the early 1960s. In other words, even if the FBI had felt it had time to check on Scarpa's allegation regarding LoCicero's order, as a practical matter they would have had no means of doing so. Again, it is just as likely that Scarpa, understanding that his information was being accepted almost without question, was testing the FBI about the limits of his behavior or, as Villano suggested, floating a trial balloon before a planned murder, shortly after testing the FBI in specific dollar terms about the value of his information. He received his answer. In no uncertain terms, he was not to participate in murder.

Many years later, FBI Special Agent Lin DeVecchio, Scarpa's last handler, took a less aggressive approach to the question of the limits of Scarpa's criminal activity. As DeVecchio admitted in his book, which is his attempt to exonerate himself of any criminal responsibility for a number of murders committed by Scarpa while DeVecchio was handling him, "[i]n my heart, as Scarpa's handler, of course I knew he was doing hits."[89]

By late 1962, the parameters of Scarpa's relationship with the FBI were coming into clearer focus. First, he would be paid well for his "singular" information. Noted organized crime expert Selwyn Raab estimated that over the course of his career as an informant, Scarpa was paid $158,000 by the FBI.[90] However, there was at least as a matter of policy a line Scarpa was forbidden to cross. As will be seen later, Scarpa not only crossed that line, he obliterated it. Similarly, whatever lines Scarpa may have already established in his personal life began to disappear rapidly in 1962 when he first became involved with Linda Diana.

SCARPA'S SHINY NEW OBJECT

For Scarpa, 1962 was about two new relationships that broke two old promises. His role as a paid informant for America's top law enforcement agency was growing, despite having sworn a blood oath on penalty of death against such involvement. And that summer, he began courting a teenager from Brooklyn named Linda Diana, despite the marriage vows he had taken in 1949.

Words and their meanings matter, and a brief overview of Scarpa's and Diana's status during the years of their relationship is in order. When Scarpa and Diana met, she was seventeen years old. Scarpa, on the other hand, turned thirty-four in May of 1962, the year they first met. She eventually became his mistress, his *gumar*.[91] Their relationship, which did not end until Scarpa's death in 1994, has often been referred to as a common-law marriage.[92] However, the New York State Legislature abolished common-law marriages in 1933.[93] The only exceptions to that rule are common-law marriages established in New York prior to the law's enactment, and common-law marriages formed in states that recognize such unions due to the operation of the Full Faith and Credit clause of the U.S. Constitution.[94] It is likely that referencing Scarpa and Diana as common-law husband and wife represents the use of a familiar phrase, rather than a legal label, to describe their relationship, which included living together for approximately three decades, producing two children together, and holding themselves out as husband and wife for much of that time.

Linda Diana began her relationship with Scarpa as his mistress and continued in that capacity during his two marriages and her only marriage. According to Gregory Scarpa Jr., Scarpa was always a womanizer.[95] His first marriage to Concetta Farace, a union which began in 1949 and resulted in the birth of four children, did not end until they separated without divorcing in 1973. His second marriage was to an Israeli beauty queen named Lily Dajani. That marriage lasted from 1975 to 1983, years that he also spent living with Linda Diana.

Linda Diana's first and only marriage was to Charlie Schiro. It began on March 25, 1968.[96] In 1969, while still married to Schiro, Linda gave birth to a child by Scarpa, their daughter, known as "Little Linda."[97] Linda and Charlie Schiro divorced after Joey, Linda's second child by Scarpa, was born in 1971.[98] It is, however, fair to say that after Scarpa's second marriage was dissolved in 1983, Linda Schiro, as Linda Diana was by then known and as she will be referred to from this point on, was at least Scarpa's partner rather than his mistress.

Greg Scarpa's and Linda Schiro's three-decade relationship, no matter how it is styled, began with a chance encounter in a Brooklyn nightclub, most likely in 1962. There is disagreement as to what year this initial encounter took place. Journalist Peter Lance's meticulously researched and wide-ranging work on Scarpa placed their initial encounter in 1962.[99] Author Sandra Harmon had the year of that meeting as 1964 with some detail about their early relationship that does not appear elsewhere.[100] Linda Scarpa, the daughter of Scarpa and Linda Schiro, stated simply that they met in the early 1960s.[101] If they first met in 1962, Scarpa and his wife, Connie, would have had three children at the time. Their fourth child was not born until 1963. By that time, as Gregory Scarpa Jr. has noted, Scarpa "was dating Linda."[102] Finally, Lance, who had their initial encounter in 1962, incongruously wrote that "Scarpa was thirty-six at the time" he met Linda.[103] Scarpa was born in May of 1928. If Lance is correct about the year they met, Scarpa would have just turned thirty-four. If, as Harmon wrote, they met in 1964, he would have been thirty-six.

Where Scarpa and Linda Schiro met is not in dispute: the Flamingo Lounge at 72nd Street and 13th Avenue in Bensonhurst.[104] By the time they met, Schiro had dropped out of school twice and was working at a clerical job on Wall Street. She first quit school at the age of eleven to take care of her mother, who had been stricken with stomach cancer. She returned to school after her mother's death but dropped out again at the age of sixteen.

Scarpa was not Schiro's first brush with dating a mobster. When Scarpa and Schiro met, she was already involved with a married Gambino wiseguy named Larry Pistone. That involvement did not stop her from dancing with Scarpa the night they met and going to dinner with him and members of his crew at Romano's in Brooklyn a few nights later.

Linda Schiro's familiarity with mobsters and "the life" extended back into her childhood. In fact, her maternal grandmother, with Schiro's assistance, ran numbers.[105] As a teenager, Schiro became a fixture at a pool hall frequented by Colombo and Gambino wiseguys. "'Since I was a kid, I grew up with gangsters in the neighborhood… and I was impressed with them.'"[106] And, as noted above, when Schiro and Scarpa met at the Flamingo Lounge, she was involved with Larry Pistone. An ugly breakup with Pistone after he and Schiro were publicly confronted by Pistone's wife, followed by Schiro's convincing Scarpa not to beat the hell out of Pistone with a bat,[107] paved the way for Scarpa's pursuit of Schiro in the summer of 1962.

During their early courtship, Schiro was aware of some of Scarpa's criminal activity, including burglaries and hijackings.[108] In fact, "her father allowed [Scarpa] to use his apartment to store stolen television sets."[109] Additionally, Scarpa confessed to her that by 1962 he had committed around twenty murders.[110] "I knew what he was. I knew what he did. I was dating gangsters since I was 15."[111] Rather than being put off or frightened by Scarpa's revelations of his life of crime and violence, Schiro has testified that she was "impressed."[112] By the end of 1962, when his wife Connie was pregnant with their fourth child, Scarpa was in a relationship with Linda Schiro that would last until his death almost thirty-two years later.

The changes in Scarpa's personal life in 1962 came at a time when the core elements of his working life were also in flux. His decision to become a paid FBI informant provided federal law enforcement tremendous insight into a world that until then had been well hidden from them. It also provided contemporary and later-day analysts with a detailed look into Scarpa's attempts to understand and influence his personal position in the borgata in the wake of the death of Joseph Profaci, the boss of one of New York's five Cosa Nostra families.

THE CHANGING OF THE GUARD

Joe Profaci died of liver cancer on June 6, 1962, at the age of sixty-four. Coincidentally, Scarpa had been interviewed at length by the FBI the day before Profaci's death.[113] Although "Old Man Profaci," as he was called, had been ill for some time, provision for a smooth transition of the family's leadership via an undisputed succession had not been made, primarily due to an ongoing intrafamily struggle with the Gallo brothers and their supporters. The predictable results of this omission were twofold: an immediate leadership vacuum, and an inevitable contest to fill that vacuum. The information Scarpa provided to the FBI during this period revealed the Profaci family leadership ambitions of Joe and Ambrose Magliocco, the machinations of Scarpa's original Profaci family mentor, Charlie LoCicero, and the effects of both on Greg Scarpa's position within the family.

When Scarpa began his three-decade relationship with the FBI the so-called Profaci/Gallo feud, which later became known as the first Colombo war, was already in full swing. The FBI's files on Scarpa noted that the feud "erupted" in August of 1961.[114] Scarpa was first contacted by the FBI, without success, a number of times in late 1961. His eventual cooperation with the FBI, which began in late October of 1961, included providing his views on events driven by the Profaci/Gallo feud and his shifting predictions as to its potential resolution.

Scarpa's take on the history and conduct of the Profaci/Gallo feud, which he provided to the FBI, placed the blame squarely at the feet of Larry and Joseph Gallo who, after becoming Profaci family members approximately five years earlier, found it impossible to break into the family's most lucrative operations.[115] Per Scarpa, an accumulation of Gallo grievances centering on being frozen out of high-earning activities[116] culminated in the Gallos' leaving the Profaci organization. From there it was all downhill. For instance, Profaci button men Carmine Persico and Salvatore D'Ambrosio attempted to kill Larry Gallo by strangulation on August 20, 1961,[117] and on October 4, 1961, Gallo loyalist Joe Magnasco was murdered by Profaci soldiers who were supposed to kill Joe Gallo.[118] By late fall of 1961, Scarpa believed and reported that the feud, which had escalated into a war, had gone too far for a peaceful reconciliation.[119]

By early 1962, in the middle of the ongoing war with the Gallos, Joe Profaci's health was failing. Within six months, he was dead. The feud with the Gallos did not end with Profaci's death. However, the immediate question was, "Who will succeed Profaci as boss?" The Magliocco brothers, Joe and Ambrose, felt that Joe, who was underboss when Profaci died, was the logical and best choice. Other powerful voices, most notably that of Calogero "Charlie the Sidge" LoCicero and his supporters, were not so sure. And, once again, Scarpa was the sole provider to the FBI of a steady stream of information about all of the above.

As the FBI noted, "none of this information is currently available to the NYO [New York Office] from an admitted member [other than Scarpa,] of the criminal organization."[120] In fact, from the time Scarpa started talking to the FBI on October 27, 1961, through the brief period during which Joe Magliocco was boss of the family, up to April 5, 1964, the date of Joe Colombo's installation as family boss after Magliocco's forced retirement and death, Scarpa and his FBI handler met in person or by telephone at least 112 times.[121] The result is the remarkable view from an insider who was part of the organization's leadership of a nearly two-year contest for power within the Profaci family. For all practical purposes, Scarpa was the FBI's only source for the details of that power struggle,[122] and he was self-reporting that he was a *caporegime*.

It is important to note that whether Scarpa was ever a capo is a subject of disagreement. While Scarpa told the FBI that he was a capo under Joe Profaci, his eldest son, Gregory, has stated that his father was always "a soldier," and that when Gregory Jr. became a capo, he outranked his father.[123] Scarpa's close confidant, Larry Mazza, has stated that Scarpa was a wiseguy for most of his life, but was first made a capo during the early 1990s while the Persico/Orena feud was raging.[124]

FBI Special Agent Lin DeVecchio, whose relationship with Scarpa as his handler spanned more than a decade beginning in 1980, claimed in his memoir that Scarpa was never a capo and was not interested in becoming one because it would have drawn too much attention to him. DeVecchio pointed out that Scarpa was officially part of capo Anthony "Scappi" Scarpati's crew when Carmine Persico was the Colombo family boss.[125] Likewise, Carmine Imbriale, quoting NYPD legend Tommy Dades, claimed, "Scarpa was never a captain. Greg was always a soldier, but of course much more than a soldier."[126] On the other hand, Peter Lance, based on the information that Scarpa provided to the FBI and on Scarpa's own claim, took the position in his book that Scarpa was at one time a capo.[127]

Brooklyn's District Attorney, Charles Hynes, a man who prosecuted a number of mafiosi during the third Colombo war, believed that Scarpa was a capo.[128] Likewise, Michael Franzese, a Colombo family capo and contemporary of Scarpa's, stated that he was close to Scarpa and that Scarpa was a capo.[129] Finally, as already noted, when Scarpa first became an informant, he self-reported that he was a capo in the Profaci family. During Joe Magliocco's brief reign as unofficial family boss, Scarpa did not list himself as a capo in the organizational information he provided to the FBI, nor did he explain his apparent demotion. He did, however, report that Joe Magliocco told him he was "appointing [Scarpa] a Caporegime."[130] That apparently never happened, although according to Scarpa it would have amounted to a *reappointment* given that Joe Profaci had made him a capo in 1961.[131] Scarpa did not list himself as a capo in the Magliocco family or the Colombo family in the organizational information he provided to federal law enforcement.[132]

Gregory Scarpa Jr. has pointed out that his father was not a capo under Joe Colombo, an assertion not inconsistent with Scarpa's *earlier and lapsed* status. Instead, according to Gregory Jr., his father was one of four men who were closest to Colombo and most trusted by him. That status, although officially still that of a soldier, meant that Scarpa answered to no capo, and it gave him more power than the other Colombo family capos.[133] Finally, as noted above, the FBI's Antiracketeering file on Scarpa has the following note: "SCARPA was made a 'caporegima' [sic] during the early days of the GALLO-PROFACI feud in Brooklyn, but that he has not acted in this capacity since the death of JOSEPH PROFACI."[134]

Based on the available evidence, this author's view is that Scarpa was a capo during the waning days of Joe Profaci's reign, and that he expected to be reappointed to that position by Profaci's unofficial and temporary successor Joe Magliocco. The reappointment under Magliocco never happened. However, as will be discussed later, Scarpa was finally elevated to the rank of capo in the early 1990s and remained in that capacity until his death in 1994.

THE MAIN EVENT: MAGLIOCCO V. LOCICERO

Joe Magliocco was nearly sixty-three years old when Joe Profaci died. As underboss of the Profaci family,[135] it was natural for him and his supporters to assume he would succeed Profaci. That process began less than a month after Profaci's death. An "URGENT" FBI memo from July 2, 1962, revealed an intrafamily selection in which Scarpa participated that took place at the Magliocco home the previous morning. During that meeting, Joe Magliocco was

"SELECTED AS BOSS TO REPLACE JOE PROFACI AND SALVATORE MUSSACCHIO [sic] ALSO KNOWN AS SALLY THE SHEIK AS COUNSLERI [sic]. MAGLIOCCO STATED ABOVE NAMES WOULD BE SUBMITTED TO COMMISSION FOR APPROVAL…"[136]

The information in that memo came directly from Scarpa. He attended the meeting and cast three votes for Joe

Magliocco: his own, that of his brother, Salvatore, and that of Profaci soldier Joseph Madelone, both of whom were incarcerated at the time.[137] Charlie LoCicero, who sought the position of boss for himself, was in Italy when the meeting took place.[138] At the same meeting, Salvatore Musacchio was selected as consigliere, and the position of underboss was left open, to be filled by the new boss once he was approved by the Commission.[139]

LoCicero returned from Italy and resolved to fight Joe Magliocco's appointment as family boss. The FBI, for its part, was rooting for LoCicero. "It would appear that such a move, if successful, would place [Scarpa] in the inner circle at the top operational level of one of the most important 'families'..."[140] LoCicero, who had served as consigliere under Joe Profaci, was made to step down from that position in early 1961 and to relinquish all titles except for that of *caporegime*.[141] That move may have accounted for his lingering antipathy toward the Maglioccos. Apparently, the ill-feeling went both ways.[142] Additionally, according to Scarpa, LoCicero was displeased with the way Joe Magliocco's intrafamily selection was handled.[143] At a minimum, LoCicero had his own ambitions, which did not include serving under Joe Magliocco.

LoCicero's attempt to derail Magliocco's selection had four major parts to it. He would allow the Gallos and their followers who had been placed under the protection of the Gambinos during the Profaci/Gallo feud to return to the family.[144] He would engineer a scenario that would result in public humiliation and disrespect from the other New York family bosses for Joe Magliocco.[145] He, along with his supporters, would demand that Magliocco step down.[146] And he, along with Salvatore Badalamenti and Benny D'Alessandro, would complain to the Commission about

Magliocco's leadership.[147] If all else failed, he may have been ready to order Scarpa to kill Magliocco.

As noted above, the relationship between "Charlie the Sidge" LoCicero and Scarpa began when Scarpa was a teenager. When Scarpa first began his working relationship with the FBI, he informed them of his complete loyalty to LoCicero.[148] However, more than a year later, despite LoCicero's clear belief that he had Scarpa's backing in his quest to unseat Magliocco, Scarpa informed the FBI that he told Ambrose Magliocco "he was willing and ready to abide by any instructions received from Magliocco and that his complete loyalty lay with the Maglioccos."[149]

Ultimately, the Commission did not confirm Joe Magliocco as the new family boss. Magliocco resigned on September 3, 1963, citing his poor health.[150] Scarpa told the FBI that in his opinion, Magliocco was told by the Commission to step down and his poor health, which he indeed suffered from, was an excuse used to conceal that fact.[151] Whether it was an excuse or not, Magliocco died less than four months later.

Neither Joe Magliocco's resignation in September nor his death in December cleared the way for Charlie LoCicero. Whether LoCicero was ever a serious contender in the eyes of the Commission or whether he merely overplayed his hand is an open question. As of April 5, 1964, the matter was closed. The FBI's files noted that on April 7, 1964, Scarpa informed them that Joseph Colombo had been installed as family boss two days earlier.[152] Colombo was forty years old at the time. At a minimum, his ascension signaled an end to the family's gerontocracy.[153] In fact, Colombo soon announced that, as a matter of policy, he wished to replace the family's aging set of capos with younger men.[154] This was potentially good news for Scarpa, who was about to turn thirty-six when Colombo was installed.

However, Scarpa, who had been ping-ponged between LoCicero and the Maglioccos for nearly a year, during which time he reported meeting with LoCicero at least thirty-three times and with one or both Magliocco brothers at least twelve times between Joe Profaci's death and Joe Magliocco's resignation,[155] never received a reappointment as capo. Instead, he became a member of Joe Colombo's inner circle and answered only to Colombo, a status accorded only three other men, one that made them more powerful than any Colombo borgata *caporegime*.[156] Furthermore, the conflict between the Gallos and the newly named Colombo family would continue for the rest of the decade and beyond. What neither Scarpa nor anyone else could possibly anticipate was the fact that during Joe Colombo's reign, Scarpa would be thrust into some remarkable and wholly unexpected roles, driven both by his deepening connections to the FBI and the close relationship he cultivated with the new head of the borgata, Joe Colombo.

CHAPTER THREE: GREG SCARPA, CIVIL RIGHTS ICON?

FOUR CASE STUDIES

By April of 1964, the FBI had a clearer picture of the administrative side of the Italian Mafia in the U.S. than it had ever possessed. Scarpa's information about the organization's structure, roles, rules, procedures, and culture was far more thorough than the typical organizational case study in a business or public administration graduate program. Scarpa even gave the FBI a front row seat from which it was able to observe in some detail how an internal power struggle in one of New York's five families arose, proceeded, and was resolved. The shroud of secrecy Cosa Nostra tried to enforce under penalty of death had been removed, never to be restored.

But administrative details alone, while extensive, fascinating, and revealing, were insufficient weapons for law enforcement's battle with organized crime. The FBI needed operational information too. And once again, Scarpa came through. From October 27, 1961, through April 5, 1964, he showered the FBI with often lurid details about crimes committed by the members of all five of New York's Cosa Nostra families. From an event as violent as the botched attempt to assassinate Joe Gallo that resulted in the murder of Joe Magnasco;[1] through acts of arson to hide evidence of tax evasion from the IRS;[2] to extensive reports chronicling the who, what, where, and when of loansharking/shylocking,[3] bookmaking,[4] hijacking,[5] illicit gambling,[6] securities theft,[7] conspiracy to commit murder,[8] attempted murder,[9] and murder;[10] from Buffalo[11] to New Jersey,[12] from Miami[13] to New Orleans,[14] Scarpa provided it all and more.

It is banal to say that the above-noted public offenses are typical of a large-scale organized crime organization. The offenses are serious, but not surprising. And we are now, in part thanks to men like Greg Scarpa, Joe Valachi, and Sammy Gravano, accustomed to the confidential informant or cooperating witness who plays an active part in some or all of those offenses. What Gregory Scarpa is alleged to have done next for the FBI, however, was so atypical and so surprising that the FBI has never acknowledged most of it actually happened, and legitimate questions about the veracity of various accounts, particularly about the events in Mississippi, continue to be left unanswered.

It has been alleged that in 1963, Scarpa solved the murder of Medgar Evers, the NAACP's first Mississippi field officer, using what would today be referred to as enhanced interrogation techniques. It is further claimed that in 1964, Scarpa helped the FBI solve one of the most notorious cases of the civil rights era by acquiring the location of the bodies of three slain civil rights workers in a similar fashion. The third of the Scarpa/civil rights cases has Scarpa traveling once again to Mississippi, this time in 1966, to provide critical assistance to the FBI's investigation of Vernon Dahmer's murder. Finally, Scarpa appears to have faithfully and fully supported family boss Joseph Colombo's sometimes comic, occasionally serious, and ultimately tragic agitation in New

York City for better treatment of Italian Americans by law enforcement, the press, and elected officials through the Italian American Civil Rights League.

So, was Greg Scarpa a staunch defender of civil rights for all Americans who had been historically excluded from full social, economic, and political equality? The accounts of the three Mississippi cases vary widely and at times strain credulity. They are based for the most part on second- and third-hand information, memories of events that happened nearly sixty years ago, conflated descriptions, and purposely incomplete documents. They come from an era before dashcams, cellphones, and GoPros, and they undoubtedly add to the fictional and factual legends of Greg Scarpa. The story of Scarpa's support of Joe Colombo's campaign for better treatment of Italian Americans has a firmer foundation, one grounded in both public action and now public internal FBI memos based on Scarpa's own reporting. It is doubtful, however, that either Scarpa's alleged work in Mississippi or his documented work in New York were manifestations of anything other than a calculation on his part of what was best for Gregory Scarpa.

CASE NUMBER 1 – MEDGAR EVERS

BACKGROUND

Medgar Evers was a World War II veteran and the first NAACP field officer in Mississippi. He was a college graduate who was denied admission to Mississippi's public law school at the University of Mississippi, "Ole Miss," on the basis of his race. His early and often dangerous personal crusade for equality for African Americans included calling for a boycott of gas stations that banned African Americans from their restrooms. As early as 1952, he was distributing bumper stickers in Mississippi that read, "Don't Buy Gas Where You Can't Use the Restroom." Attempts by White supremacists to kill Evers failed until he was assassinated on June 12, 1963, shot by a sniper and left to bleed to death on the front step of his home while his wife and children looked on. The national outcry was immediate, and the FBI came under enormous public and high-level political pressure to bring Evers's killer or killers to justice.[15]

SCARPA'S POSSIBLE ROLE

There are no available contemporaneous first-hand accounts of Scarpa's role, if any, in solving Medgar Evers's murder. Former FBI Agent Anthony Villano, using "Julio" as an alias for Scarpa in his book *Brick Agent*, wrote what purported to be a detailed account of Scarpa's role in obtaining the name of the man who was accused of and, thirty-five years later, finally convicted of shooting and killing Medgar Evers. Villano, then is the only source for what Scarpa did in Mississippi in 1963, if he did anything at all. And Villano's story is second-hand at best.

In the summer of 1963, the FBI's investigation into Evers's murder was not making any inroads with the tight-lipped White supremacy crowd in Mississippi. Villano wrote that Scarpa went south at the Bureau's request to augment their efforts in the Evers case. After driving to Mississippi from Miami, where he had dropped off his girlfriend for some rest and relaxation in the sun, Scarpa assisted in the kidnapping, questioning, threatening, and torture of a man who eventually provided a detailed statement fingering Byron De La Beckwith Jr. as Evers's killer.[16] Scarpa twice interrupted his interrogation to check with eavesdropping FBI agents about whether his victim was being truthful. Twice he was told his "captive" was lying.

"For the third time Julio approached his captive. But now he came on very strong—his pride was hanging by a thread. He took his .38 and stuck it in the mouth of the store manager. 'Listen, prick, this is your last chance. You either tell me the absolute truth or I will blow your head off. I don't have any more time to waste.'"[17]

Villano claimed that as a result of Scarpa's work, Beckwith was arrested. He faced two trials in 1964, both of which resulted in hung juries. He was eventually retried in 1998, convicted of murder, and sentenced to life in prison. Beckwith died in prison in 2001.

Villano's account concluded with the claim that Scarpa was not reimbursed by the FBI, contrary to their agreement, for the $2,300 worth of expenses he had incurred on his trip to Mississippi.[18] As a result, again per Villano, Scarpa stopped working for the FBI. Villano, his handler, tried to get him to change his mind, but Scarpa was resolute.[19]

Linda Scarpa and her co-author Linda Rosencrance came across Villano's account when doing their research for Linda Scarpa's book.[20] For the most part, they repeated Villano's version of the Medgar Evers investigation and outcome. They omitted, however, Villano's allegations about lack of payment and the effect it had on Scarpa's decision to discontinue working for the FBI.[21]

ANALYSIS

Villano's account of the Evers case is likely the most thorough and detailed of any account of the three different Mississippi cases. However, it is second-hand at best, and highly fictionalized at worst. According to his book, Villano "heard the story" from "the agents involved" and then confirmed it with Scarpa, who provided additional details.[22] To his credit, Villano appeared to claim that he heard about Scarpa's trip south shortly after it occurred. However, he also stated that to his knowledge, the facts "never made their way into any official papers"[23] that he was aware of. That assertion runs counter to the FBI's bureaucratic instinct to record all known activities of their TECIs, particularly the content of conversations and debriefings,[24] between TECIs and special agents.

Villano's hearsay version of Scarpa's alleged participation in the Evers case began to unravel when he included details from the 1966 Lawrence Byrd-Vernon Dahmer Sr. case about a TV and appliance store owner.[25] Additionally, Villano's sequence of events surrounding the interrogation of the "store manager" are almost identical to the account of Scapa's alleged interrogation of the "weak link" in the civil rights workers case from reporters Robbins and Capeci as set forth below. Furthermore, the allegation that Scarpa fronted $2,300 of his own money to pay for the trip is also suspect. Frankly, nothing in Scarpa's history points to him behaving in such a manner when it came to money. Also, the idea that Villano tried, unsuccessfully, to talk Scarpa into continuing to work with the FBI after this 1963 mission and that Scarpa refused is not supported by the FBI's own records.

Scarpa's relationship with the FBI continued unabated from the time he first contacted the Bureau in late 1961 until his status as a TECI was initially terminated in 1975. It is also important to remember that Villano was Scarpa's handler in 1963. However, Villano claimed that "two agents who had been talking to [Scarpa] about his interstate flight case" approached Scarpa about helping with the Evers investigation. [26] It is beyond believable that two agents other than Villano would even know Scarpa's identity, let alone independently contact and recruit him for this important mission, and that Scarpa would undertake the mission and return from it having not been paid without Villano having been in the loop on any of the above, and that he would be informed about the entire matter only after the fact. Villano's use of the pseudonym "Julio" for Scarpa in his account of the Evers case further muddied the waters. As soon as Villano concluded his "Julio-solved-the-Medgar-Evers-case" yarn, he began to talk about a man he claimed was another informant, "Nick Biletti."

However, as Peter Lance has pointed out, Nick Biletti is another pseudonym for Scarpa.[27] Villano's clear attempt to protect Scarpa's identity, while he may have felt it was necessary, unfortunately ends up casting additional doubt on the other details of his story about the Evers matter. It is simply impossible to conclude, sixty years after Evers was murdered and forty-six years after Villano's book came out, that Villano's account is accurate. His version of those 1963 events is ultimately too problematic to be taken at face value.

As noted above, Linda Scarpa relies heavily on Villano's book for her account of her father's alleged participation in the Medgar Evers case. However, she also references *The Final Curtain: Burning Mississippi by the FBI*, a self-published book from 2007 by W.O. "Chet" Dillard, a Mississippi lawyer and former judge, as a source that purportedly confirmed her father's assistance to the FBI in the Evers case. That book is no longer available, and Judge Dillard passed away in 2017, making Scarpa's claim about the book's confirmation of the Evers story difficult for this author to assess.[28]

As to others who might have shed some light on Scarpa's alleged involvement in the Medgar Evers case, not one of them provides the sort of information that can rightly be called confirmation. Peter Lance did not mention the Evers case either in his book about Scarpa or in an article he wrote about Scarpa for *The Huffington Post* three years later. In fact, Lance stated in his book that Villano's story about the FBI refusing to pay Scarpa related to Villano's version of the "Lawrence Byrd-Vernon Dahmer mission"[29] rather than the Byron De La Beckwith-Medgar Evers case.[30] Lin DeVecchio also omitted the Evers case from his book, although he did attempt to describe Scarpa's assistance in the 1964 civil rights workers case.[31] Author Sandra Harmon left the Evers case out of her book too.

While it is relatively easy, after a review of the available sources, to cast doubt on the tales of Scarpa's involvement in solving Medgar Evers's 1963 murder, the stories of his assistance in the 1964 civil rights workers case, although not uniformly consistent, rest on a somewhat firmer evidentiary footing.

CASE NUMBER 2 – CIVIL RIGHTS WORKERS

BACKGROUND

By 1964, the modern civil rights movement in the U.S. was ending its first decade. The Supreme Court's decision in *Brown v. Board of Education* in 1954 signaled a potentially radical change in how segregation would be treated at the federal level. Political change[32] was slow to come, however, and the Montgomery Bus Boycott, which followed on the heels of Rosa Parks's arrest in December of 1955 for refusing to give up her seat on a municipal bus to a White passenger, is often seen as the beginning of the popular movement for civil rights.

A core goal for those interested in securing the promise of liberty for all was to remove barriers to registering to vote imposed by Jim Crow laws. Those barriers had been brutally effective. By 1960, only five percent of the eligible Black voters in Mississippi were registered to vote.[33] In 1964, the Council of Federated Organizations (COFO) began training college students from the North to register voters, an effort the Mississippi Freedom Democratic Party had also undertaken. Three of those students, James Chaney, Michael Schwerner, and Andrew Goodman, disappeared on the night of June 21, 1964.[34] They had been shot and killed by members of the local Ku Klux Klan, who then buried their bodies in a recently constructed earthen dam near Philadelphia, Mississippi.[35] Their disappearance sparked a massive manhunt that drew national attention and put tremendous pressure on President Lyndon Johnson's administration, the Department of Justice, and the FBI. On August 4, 1964, "[a]cting on an informant tip," the bodies of the three murdered young men were found.[36]

SCARPA'S POSSIBLE ROLE

The source of the tip that led to the discovery of the civil rights workers' bodies, which has never been officially acknowledged by the FBI,[37] was allegedly Gregory Scarpa. Many facts surrounding the murder of the three students are clear and not reasonably in dispute. Scarpa's participation in the matter is anything but clear. Neither the more than 1,200 pages of FBI documents relating to Scarpa, nor the FBI's 1,049 pages of currently accessible documents relating to the MIBURN (Mississippi Burning) case make any substantive mention of Scarpa's involvement with the FBI in Mississippi. Although Senior District Judge Jack B. Weinstein mentioned Scarpa's participation in the civil rights workers case in his decision in *Orena v. United*

States, the judge recognized that Scarpa's alleged role was "unconfirmed rumor."[38] Finally, there is no contemporaneous first-hand account available of everything that Scarpa did or did not do while in Mississippi. What we do have is Linda Schiro's personal account of making the trip to Mississippi with Scarpa in 1964, the second-hand allegations of the man who planned, but did not otherwise personally participate in, the murder of the civil rights workers, and a report by Tom Robbins and Jerry Capeci that appeared in the *New York Daily News* shortly after Scarpa's death in 1994, thirty years after the alleged incident occurred.[39]

Linda Schiro was most likely romantically involved with Scarpa well before the summer of 1964.[40] Her memory of the civil rights workers event is set forth in some detail in her daughter's book.[41] At a minimum, Schiro provided a first-hand account of a trip to Mississippi with Scarpa. It also appears to be the only trip that Scarpa took to Mississippi of which Schiro has an independent memory. Her account includes details that do not appear in any of the other accounts. Those details lend some realistic contour to an otherwise fantastic story. To begin with, Schiro stated that she was in her "late teens" when she accompanied Scarpa to Mississippi.[42] By the time of the Dahmer case, discussed below, she would have been in her early twenties. However, the civil rights workers case fits her recalled timeline. She also recalled that FBI agents were waiting for the two of them when they arrived at their hotel in Mississippi. After Scarpa and Schiro checked in, one of the agents came to their room and "gave Greg a gun."[43] Before he departed with that agent, Scarpa gave Linda some money and a one-way plane ticket back to New York in case he did not return.[44] At that point in Schiro's narrative, the details allegedly came from Scarpa after his return from his successful mission.[45] Her recall of Scarpa's account of what he had done generally tracks the account of the civil rights workers case provided by Robbins and Capeci in their *New York Daily News* article from 1994, including the presence and role of the ubiquitous TV store owner,[46] as discussed below.

Another participant in the civil rights workers case was Edgar Ray Killen, a Baptist minister and a member of the KKK. Killen was eventually convicted of manslaughter in the slayings. His conviction rests on his having planned the killings and then leaving the dirty work, including the disposal of the workers' bodies, to others while he established an alibi. Killen filed a lawsuit from prison in 2010 claiming that Scarpa, acting at the direction of the FBI, pistol-whipped and otherwise assaulted local citizens other than Killen[47] to locate the bodies of the missing civil rights workers, and that by doing so, Killen's civil rights had been violated. It is worth noting that by 2010, Villano's book and Harmon's book were both available. Additionally, several accounts of the alleged assistance Scarpa gave the FBI in the civil rights workers case were available in print and accessible online by 2010. Killen's lawsuit was dismissed before it came to trial. He died in prison in 2018.

Robbins and Capeci reported in 1994, soon after Scarpa's death, that Scarpa "and a girlfriend flew to Miami and registered at the Fontainebleau Hotel to establish an alibi."[48] According to the article, Scarpa then traveled to Philadelphia, Mississippi via New Orleans, where he connected with two FBI agents.[49] Robbins and Capeci wrote that their story was confirmed by a "high-level federal official who said he knew of the episode"[50] without otherwise identifying that official. Once in the town of Philadelphia, Scarpa connected with an appliance merchant,[51] who was identified by the agents as a Klansman and a "possible weak link in the Klan operation,"[52] to buy a television. When the merchant was putting the TV into the trunk of Scarpa's car, Scarpa knocked him out with a pipe, tied him up, and stuffed him into the trunk of his car.[53] The article does not explain how Scarpa managed to do all of this without attracting any attention or how he managed to conceal the pipe in his hands from the alleged merchant.

Next up in the Robbins and Capeci article is a long drive into the Mississippi woods to a "shanty" where "FBI agents were hidden outside."[54] Scarpa was apparently able to find his way to the shanty without any difficulty. Once he and the appliance merchant were inside, Scarpa tied him to a chair and "demanded to know 'what happened to the three kids.'"[55] The merchant's first two responses were fiction, according to the FBI agents listening to the interrogation from outside. On the third go-around, Scarpa got serious. He "asked one of the agents for his gun and went back inside."[56] The agents later found out from Scarpa that he had "stuck the gun barrel into the Klansman's mouth and demanded the truth." That did the trick, and the merchant gave up the location of the civil rights workers' bodies.[57]

The FBI's MIBURN documents that are available to the public online contain no specific information about Scarpa playing any role in solving the civil rights workers case. There are two items from those documents worth mentioning, however. The first is that the bodies of the three slain civil rights workers were located based on a tip from an informant who was paid between $5,000 and $30,000,[58] a significant sum at either end in 1964. "[I]t was pointed out to [U.S. Attorney General] Katzenbach that we had an informant, that we got information from our informant, and that we paid for it."[59] A debate over whether to release the name of the informant to the public is also memorialized in the same group of documents. Ultimately, the decision was made to protect the informant's identity knowing that otherwise "the source would immediately be killed."[60] The document does not suggest who might do that killing, whether it was the Klan or perhaps the New York Mafia. The second bit of information of interest is more of a lack of information. As noted above, the records of arrests of the suspects in the case do not disclose that any of them owned an appliance store or were appliance merchants.[61]

What Scarpa did in 1964 while in Mississippi depends on who is telling the story. He started by pushing Lawrence Byrd onto the floor of the back seat of his rented car and then shoving a gun in Byrd's ribs while an FBI agent drove the two of them to another location.[62] Or he started by blackjacking[63] Byrd and shoving him into the car. Or he struck an unnamed appliance merchant with a pipe, tied him up, and stuck him in the trunk of a car, which he drove to a shanty in the Mississippi woods[64] with the FBI agents following him in a different car.[65] Then, again depending on who is telling the story, Scarpa, after some questioning, stuck a gun in an unidentified Klansman's mouth and threatened to kill him if he lied to him.[66] Or he threatened to shoot Byrd and cut his penis off if Byrd lied to him,[67] or Scarpa kidnapped the mayor of a local town rather than a TV and radio store owner, and, in succession, put a gun to his head, stuck a gun in his mouth, and finally took out a razor and unzipped the mayor's pants while threatening to cut off his genitals if he did not tell Scarpa the truth.[68] Or just for good measure, Scarpa actually started cutting Lawrence Byrd's penis[69] before his victim, an appliance store owner, or a mayor, or an unidentified Klansman, finally gave up the location of the civil rights workers' bodies.

ANALYSIS

Schiro, as she is quoted in her daughter's book, put Scarpa's alleged interaction with Klansman and appliance store owner Lawrence Byrd of the Vernon Dahmer case in the civil rights workers case.[70] Selwyn Raab does the same thing.

Raab, in his lengthy tome, *The Five Families*, mentioned a third-person account he got from a lawyer who represented mafiosi who knew Scarpa.[71] Harmon's book also conflated facts from the civil rights workers case and the Vernon Dahmer case, as does DeVecchio's book, in particular the information about a TV and appliance store manager.[72] The TV or "appliance merchant" also appears in the Robbins and Capeci story from June of 1994.[73] Similarly, Ewan MacAskill, recounting Schiro's testimony, placed the TV and appliance store owner in the 1964 civil rights workers case. Apparently, if one needed information about murder committed by White supremacists in Mississippi in the 1960s, it was critical to talk to the local TV and appliance store owner.

While the Vernon Dahmer murder case is the only one in which a TV and radio store owner, Lawrence Byrd, conclusively participated, in one form or another he shows up in all three of the stories about Scarpa's alleged missions in Mississippi. Linda Scarpa commented on the coincidence of a TV/appliance store owner being involved in all three. "What's interesting, though, is the information about my father buying a television set from a suspect who owned or managed an appliance store appeared in each and every story." Scarpa did not speculate as to why that was the case, other than to say that it was "interesting," and that "maybe more than one of the three suspects—or even all three—really did sell televisions."[74] Finally, Tom Hays briefly recounted Schiro's testimony about the 1964 civil rights case in his article. He added that during her testimony, Schiro stated that an "unidentified agent" gave Scarpa "a wad of cash" after he had extracted the location of the bodies from the witness.[75] Schiro made a similar claim in Scarpa's book.[76]

In his book, Peter Lance pointed out the problems with Harmon's account but did not do the same with the passages about Scarpa's alleged Mississippi mission for the Evers case in Villano's book. In fact, Lance's 2016 *Huffington Post* article, which came out three years after his book *Deal with the Devil*, did not mention the Evers case. Relying in part on information from Judge Dillard's book, he specifically claimed there were only two cases of Scarpa being used by the FBI to investigate in Mississippi. "In fact, Scarpa Sr.'s mission in what the Bureau dubbed the MISSBURN [sic] case, was actually the first of two civil rights related interrogations he made at the behest of the FBI Director. The second took place in January 1966, following the KKK firebombing and murder of civil rights leader Vernon Dahmer."[77] Why Lance relied on Dillard for certain facts in his book and that article and not others is not clear. One of Dillard's books, *Final Curtain: Burning Mississippi by the FBI*, came out in 2007, well before either Lance's book or his *Huffington Post* article.[78] A press release for *Final Curtain: Burning Mississippi by the FBI* stated it was Dillard's third book and that another was in the works.[79] Linda Scarpa's book, in which she references Villano and Dillard to claim that Scarpa was involved in the Medgar Evers case, was released on January 1, 2016, more than six months before Lance's *Huffington Post* article appeared. Dillard, as noted above, passed away in 2017.[80]

Larry Mazza, in his book *The Life*, did not mention the story of any of the Mississippi trips until he wrote that he heard about the one involving the three civil rights workers after his arrest from accounts that were coming out in the press about Scarpa and the FBI.[81] Gregory Scarpa Jr., in a podcast, said that his father never mentioned the civil rights stories except to say he was traveling.[82] Michael Franzese, a former Colombo capo who knew Scarpa well, confirmed that Scarpa went to Mississippi to track down some Klan murderers. The interviewer did not ask Franzese how he knew that or any additional detail other than to confirm that statement, which Franzese did.[83] Sammy Gravano said that Scarpa was involved in Mississippi Burning without providing any details.[84] Fredric Dannen's reference to the civil rights workers case was limited to recounting Scarpa's claim retold by someone who had visited Scarpa while Scarpa was suffering from AIDS dementia when "he was given to rambling."[85]

CASE NUMBER 3 – VERNON DAHMER

BACKGROUND

Vernon Dahmer was killed by arsonists from the Ku Klux Klan in January of 1966. Dahmer was a Mississippi business owner and farmer who served as president of the Forrest County branch of the National Association for the Advancement of Colored People (NAACP). His work included registering African American voters. He even placed a voter registration booth in his store after passage of the Voting Rights Act in 1965.[86]

On January 10, 1966, two carloads of armed Ku Klux Klan members drove onto Dahmer's property near Hattiesburg, Mississippi, set fire to his store and house, and fired upon both buildings as they burned. While Vernon Dahmer returned their fire, his family fled to safety. Dahmer died later that day from damage to his lungs from the smoke and fire.[87]

One of the men convicted of arson in connection with the case was Lawrence Byrd, a member of the Ku Klux Klan, and the owner of Byrd's Radio and TV Service in Laurel, Mississippi, about thirty minutes from Hattiesburg.[88] Byrd signed a twenty-two-page confession detailing his role in the conspiracy to kill Dahmer and burn his property approximately two months after the fire and Dahmer's death. At his trial, he objected to the introduction of his confession into evidence on the grounds that it was coerced. The Supreme Court of Mississippi upheld Byrd's conviction in 1969. In doing so, it noted, but did not otherwise comment on, the trial court's overruling of Byrd's evidentiary objection.[89]

SCARPA'S POSSIBLE ROLE

Some sources contained elements from the Dahmer case in their descriptions of the other two Mississippi cases, while Peter Lance and Chet Dillard alleged that Scarpa played a specific and pivotal role in solving Dahmer's murder, a point of view shared by Frederic Dannen in his *New Yorker* profile of Scarpa.

Tony Villano wrote that in connection with the Medgar Evers case, Scarpa purchased a TV in Jackson, Mississippi and asked the manager of the store, whom Villano claimed was a known member of the local White Citizens Council, to help him place the TV in the trunk of his rented car.[90] Linda Scarpa, when recounting her version of the civil rights workers case, stated that the "Klansman [Scarpa] had to convince to talk owned a TV store."[91] Sandra Harmon wrote a detailed description of Linda Schiro's and Greg Scarpa's alleged involvement in the civil rights workers case. In that description, Harmon referenced a "Klansman named Byrd" who owned "a small appliance store."[92] As noted above, Lawrence Byrd, a Klansman, owned a TV and radio store in Laurel, Mississippi and was convicted of arson for his involvement in Vernon Dahmer's death. Lin DeVecchio, in retelling an account of the 1964 civil rights workers case wrote that he learned of it "years later... from a confidential source,"[93] and that the "FBI brought Scarpa to the weak link's appliance store, where Scarpa bought a TV."[94] DeVecchio, other than the offhand mention of the ubiquitous and knowledgeable TV store owner, did not mention the Dahmer case in his book.

According to the *New York Daily News*, FBI documents unsealed by court order in May of 1996 "do not mention the 1964 trip but reveal that Scarpa went on a similar mission in 1966 to Hattiesburg, Miss., where the local head of the NAACP had been murdered by Klansmen."[95]

Much of the detail Peter Lance provided regarding Scarpa's involvement in the Dahmer case appears to have come from Chet Dillard's book *Clearburning: Civil Rights and Civil Wrongs*.[96] According to a 2007 press release for Judge Dillard's book *The Final Curtain: Burning Mississippi by the FBI*, now out of print, Byrd's confession about his involvement in the Dahmer case, which formed the factual basis for his conviction, was coerced with the use of force by Scarpa and therefore should not have been admitted into evidence at trial.[97] Lance has more than once agreed with Dillard's view on the matter.[98] Indeed, Byrd objected to his confession's admission at his arson trial on the grounds that it was not obtained voluntarily. However, the trial court judge overruled the objection, and it appears that Byrd did not raise the objection again specifically on appeal, nor did the Supreme Court of Mississippi revisit the issue *sua sponte*. However, as the Supreme Court of Mississippi noted in its decision upholding Byrd's conviction,

> "The Federal Bureau of Investigation obtained a statement from Byrd as to his connection with the matter, which statement consists of twenty-two typewritten pages. When the statement was objected to, a hearing was had by the judge out of the presence of the jury in which it was determined by the judge

that the statement was given voluntarily and not as the result of any threats, force, or other wrongful inferences. The Court therefore overruled the objection to the statement and admitted it into evidence."[99]

In Dannen's Scarpa profile published in *The New Yorker*, the author tells the story of the mobster's alleged participation in solving the murder of Vernon Dahmer. One item of note immediately stands out in Dannen's article. He wrote that on "January 21st, the Jackson, Mississippi, office of the F.B.I. called the New York office and, as recorded in an internal memo, requested the use of informant NY-3461—Gregory Scarpa—for a special assignment."[100] That detail, if accurate, would seem to lend credence to the claim that Scarpa was already familiar to the Jackson FBI office from his earlier assistance in the civil rights worker case. Dannen went on to write the following:

> "One of the immediate suspects in the Dahmer homicide was Lawrence Byrd, the owner of Byrd's Radio & TV Service in Laurel, Mississippi, who held the post of senator in the Klan. One evening in late January, at around nine o'clock, as Byrd was about to close his shop, Scarpa and an F.B.I. agent agreed to buy a television from Byrd and asked him to help carry it to a car parked outside. Byrd was pistol-whipped, shoved into the back seat, forced to lie down, and driven, he believed, to Camp Shelby, a military base built on rural Mississippi swampland. There Scarpa beat a confession out of him."[101]

ANALYSIS

That Scarpa played some role in solving the Vernon Dahmer case is likely. The consistent reference in all three matters to a TV, radio, and/or appliance store owner and manager militates in favor of giving credence to Scarpa's participation in the one case that actually involved such a person. Furthermore, the first-hand, nearly simultaneous claim at trial by Lawrence Byrd that his confession was obtained via threats and force lends additional credibility to the likelihood of Scarpa's involvement. Finally, unlike the other two cases, Scarpa's participation in the Vernon Dahmer case is supported by an available contemporaneous FBI memo that requests "enough money to cover [informant's] expenses for hotel room and transportation for the SA [Special Agent], plus two individuals..."[102] While certainly not a slam dunk, the totality of the evidence supports the conclusion that it is probable that Scarpa, at the request of the FBI in 1966, played a role in solving Vernon Dahmer's murder.

MISSISSIPPI CASES CONCLUSIONS

Of the three Mississippi cases, the following conclusions strike this author as reasonable. First, Scarpa probably played no role in solving the 1963 Medgar Evers case. The main source for the contrary view, Anthony Villano's book, raised more questions than it answered, stated "facts" inconsistent with Villano's role as handler, with Scarpa's character and with his subsequent acts, and relied on allegations drawn from later cases. Second, Scarpa probably played a role in the location of the civil rights workers' bodies. Linda Schiro's first-hand account of the trip she and Scarpa took to Mississippi in 1964 for that purpose, while not error-free, has been solid, as has her recounting of what she was told by Scarpa took place outside of her presence. Third, Scarpa probably played some role in solving Vernon Dahmer's murder. Lawrence Byrd owned a TV and radio store, a fact that appears in some version in all three stories. The repetition of the TV and radio store owner lends strength to the one incident that can be pointed to as actually having had such a store in play. Additionally, if the 1964 civil rights workers case involved Scarpa, the FBI would have had reason to believe Scarpa could repeat that success in 1966. Finally, the Dahmer case includes contemporaneous evidence from Lawrence Byrd's objection to the use of his confession that points to Scarpa's participation.

The three Mississippi cases are studies in how legends grow over time, how the line between fact and fiction becomes blurred, and how stories reflect not only grains of truth, but the needs and points of view of the storytellers. Unlike the Mississippi cases, the availability of real-time documentation of Scarpa's work with Joe Colombo for the Italian American Civil Rights League reduces the chances of self-serving embellishment and outright fabrication.

CASE NUMBER 4 – THE ITALIAN AMERICAN CIVIL RIGHTS LEAGUE

While legitimate questions persist about Scarpa's role, if any, in solving one or more of three cases at the heart of the civil rights movement, it can be said with a high degree of certainty that but for Gregory Scarpa's actions, the Italian American Civil Rights League (IACRL) would never have come into existence. Joseph Colombo Jr., the son of the boss of the Colombo borgata, was an FBI target, thanks to Scarpa, and when the FBI acted on the information Scarpa provided,[103] his father reacted in a way that has been well chronicled but that no one could have predicted.

SCARPA, JOE COLOMBO, AND THE IACRL

Joseph Colombo Jr., the son of the Colombo family boss, was arrested by the FBI on April 29, 1970.[104] He and two associates, Joseph Iannaci and Rocco Miraglia, were charged with violations of the Hobbs Act[105] and laws governing the melting of coins and the fraudulent reselling of the raw metal. When Joe Colombo Sr. heard that his son had been arrested, he went into a rage.[106] As Scarpa reported to the FBI the next day, Colombo immediately ordered Scarpa, on the suggestion of an unnamed associate whom Scarpa characterized as an "imbecile," to assemble his crew for the purpose of picketing the FBI's New York Office that evening.[107] Scarpa did as directed, and he and his crew picketed the office until about 1:00 in the morning.[108]

Colombo then arranged for more picketing, ordered more men to join the line, and added the U.S. Courthouse in Brooklyn as a target.[109] The picketing, with Scarpa present, continued for two months straight.[110] Scarpa's initial take on the picketing was that it was idiotic, that it would anger the other New York Cosa Nostra families by bringing more heat on them, and that it would cause the Colombo borgata to be a laughingstock among the other families.[111]

Throughout this episode, Scarpa, one of Colombo's "choice lieutenants,"[112] "provided extremely valuable intelligence of this important underworld development"[113] to the FBI, and the Bureau continued to pay him regularly for that information.[114] For his part, Joseph Colombo Sr. became focused to the point of obsession. He established the Italian American Civil Rights League (IACRL) to pressure the FBI to curtail what he considered to be their intrusive and unreasonable investigation of him and his associates. He then turned his ire on local and national politicians, and notable cultural figures, demanding they stop using terms like "Mafia" and "Cosa Nostra." He threatened to march on Washington, D.C. He held a "Unity Day" rally attended by tens of thousands. And he held a fundraiser in Madison Square Garden on November 20, 1970, headlined by

Frank Sinatra, who had a close personal relationship with Colombo.[115]

About a month before the fundraiser, Colombo shrewdly recognized an opportunity to add a veneer of legitimacy to the IACRL. A group of tenants of Italian American descent living in the Corona section of Queens found themselves facing eviction in October of 1970 to make way for a new housing project.[116] On Colombo's orders, the IACRL pickets once again swung into action. As Scarpa related to his FBI handler, Colombo saw this round of picketing in support of the tenants as a way "to erase any stigma attached to the IACRL and use the League for a purpose unconnected with the criminal field."[117]

Colombo managed to score some highly publicized successes through the League. He forced *The New York Times* to back down after they falsely claimed they did not use the word "Mafia" in their reporting.[118] U.S. Attorney General John Mitchell agreed to no longer use the term "Mafia" in official Department of Justice publications.[119] And Colombo persuaded the producer of the film version of Mario Puzo's novel *The Godfather* to substitute "family" and "syndicate" in the script for "Mafia" and "Cosa Nostra."[120] In spite of these political and cultural gains, and in spite of his attempt to portray the League as a legitimate defender of a marginalized group's civil rights, he failed to achieve his primary goal of getting the FBI to leave him and his considerable criminal activities alone. In fact, the IACRL tactic backfired; the FBI increased its pressure on Colombo.[121] "The fact of the matter is the Bureau, in the face of Colombo's attack, redoubled its efforts against Colombo…"[122]

The FBI's own memos demonstrated a prickly, self-conscious reaction within the Bureau to Colombo's lengthy agitation campaign, one that signified that Colombo's assessment was correct: there would be no retreat from their all-out assault on the Colombo family and Joe Colombo in particular. They repeatedly referred to Colombo as a "publicity-seeking leader [who]... has led a vociferous smear campaign against the FBI...."[123] The characterization of Colombo as a "publicity-seeking leader" became a standard phrase in subsequent summarizations of Colombo's activities.[124]

Those FBI memos also reveal that while Scarpa was publicly supportive of Colombo's IACRL activities, he was secretly providing the FBI with almost daily updates about those activities. In addition, Scarpa provided remarkably detailed information about Joe Colombo's extensive illegal gambling operations.[125] That information led directly to the arrest of Joe Colombo Sr. and thirty-five others involved in those operations. Indeed, the Special Agent in Charge of the Bureau's New York Office singled Scarpa out for praise in a memo to FBI Director J. Edgar Hoover dated June 16, 1971. "It can be said without equivocation, that informant has materially contributed to every success the NYO [New York Office] has been able to realize against the COLOMBO 'family.'"[126]

The FBI was not alone in its distaste for the IACRL's agitation. Scarpa and other New York Cosa Nostra personnel privately grumbled about Colombo's obsession with the League and his insistence that they support his efforts through activities such as picketing, fundraising, and selling raffle tickets.[127] Even Colombo chafed at the cost of supporting the picket lines on which he insisted. "Informant advised that COLOMBO complained that the demonstration was costing him a great deal of money and that he had discontinued the daily arrival of a food truck."[128] It is not difficult to imagine forced picketers, who were in reality Colombo wiseguys, reacting unfavorably to the disappearance of their daily food truck!

In spite of the external and internal opposition to the IACRL, Colombo drove on. His arrest in the spring of 1971 did nothing to chasten him. If anything, Scarpa reported that as the summer of 1971 approached, Colombo appeared more resolute than ever about making certain that another IACRL Unity Day, scheduled for June 28, 1971, would be a success. About three weeks before that, Colombo passed on to Scarpa the first hint that the day would not go well. And of course, on June 10, 1971, Scarpa passed that same information on to the FBI.

Word had reached Colombo that Joe Gallo, a thorn in Colombo's side since Gallo's release from prison, had become close with a group of African American "hoodlums" while incarcerated.[129] Colombo was also told that early in June, a carload of African Americans was "circling the block many times in the AM hours."[130] Colombo, according to Scarpa, dismissed the news as a clumsy play by Gallo to intimidate him.[131] In that same FBI memo, it was noted that there was "also a significant volume of information that JOSEPH "CRAZY JOE" GALLO is planning to begin hostilities against COLOMBO."[132]

The connection between Colombo's place of business being cased early in the morning and what happened to him at the Unity Day rally is likely nothing more than coincidence. His assailant, Jerome Johnson, was an African American, as was Johnson's female accomplice, but an investigation after the shooting revealed that Johnson's friends were White and, in fact, "detectives were unable to find a single close black friend of his."[133] Whether Johnson and his accomplice ever had any connection to the Gallos has never been satisfactorily established.

What is known is that Johnson shot Colombo three times at almost point-blank range at the Unity Day rally. Colombo collapsed and most of his entourage immediately pounced on Johnson, who was killed instantly by three shots from one of Colombo's bodyguards. Johnson's accomplice, who had hailed Colombo to get him to turn around as Johnson approached him, disappeared in the ensuing mayhem and was never officially identified or found.[134] Scarpa allegedly provided the FBI with a color photograph of a woman suspected of being Jerome Johnson's accomplice. However, at the time, the FBI did not provide the New York City Police Department with a copy of the photograph "as it [was] felt to do so might seriously jeopardize informant's position."[135]

Scarpa gave the FBI a detailed briefing of what he knew about the shooting the next day, including the name of Colombo's bodyguard, which is redacted from the FBI's documents, who pumped three bullets into Johnson.[136] According to Scarpa, another bodyguard whose true name was unknown to Scarpa, took Johnson to the ground while the man Scarpa named repeatedly shot him.[137] Scarpa reported that three men in Colombo's entourage, Nick Bianco, Joe Notch, and Rocco Miraglia, fled when the shooting started.[138] Gregory Scarpa Jr., who was present at the Unity Day Rally and near Joe Colombo when he was shot, questioned the accuracy of that statement. When informed of the allegation about three the men fleeing when Colombo was shot, he responded, "I don't believe it."[139]

Scarpa Sr. went on to describe Johnson as a "would be Black wiseguy" who "often visited social clubs and after hours joints in Brooklyn."[140] Why Johnson tried to kill Colombo and who, if anyone, paid him to do so, has never been established with any certainty. That secret died with Johnson seconds after he shot Colombo on June 28, 1971.

The first iteration of the Italian American Civil Rights League[141] ended with several bangs, all of which were gunshots, and a whimper. Colombo never recovered from his wounds. He spent nearly seven years in a coma before he passed away on May 22, 1978. His assailant was immediately killed by Colombo's bodyguards and his assailant's accomplice disappeared into the crowd. The IACRL's continued operation was of no interest to those Colombo left behind. Its potential assets, however, attracted the likes of Carmine "The Snake" Persico, a man who would become boss of the Colombo family, but his interest in the League was purely financial.[142]

As for Greg Scarpa, when Joseph Colombo went down, Scarpa's taste for acting on behalf of the civil rights of others quickly disappeared, never to return. More importantly, he lost both a prime benefactor within the borgata and a potential source of status and compensation as a Top Echelon Criminal Informant in the eyes of the FBI. His relationship with Colombo's eventual successor Carmine Persico, one that had none of the elements of the trust and close personal contact he enjoyed with Joseph Colombo, would take center stage a few years down the road and for the rest of his life. In the meantime, as a scramble for control of the Colombo family unfolded, Scarpa would be faced with the distinct possibility of long-term incarceration in federal prison, testing his ability to manipulate his relationship with the FBI as it had never been tested before.

CHAPTER FOUR: IT'S WHO YOU KNOW AND WHAT YOU KNOW

Chapter four highlights another internal struggle and two criminal cases at the center of Scarpa's life during the early 1970s. The criminal cases took place while the leadership of the Colombo family was in a state of flux. As with the struggle for control of the family in the wake of Joe Profaci's death, Scarpa was eyewitness to a family succession crisis which reaffirmed his position as a high value FBI informant. Scarpa further enhanced his stature with the FBI and with the Colombo family through the key role he played in solving the second Regina Pacis Crown Jewels case. However, his own criminal activity, in particular his participation in a bungled scheme to print and distribute up to $10,000,000 in phony IBM stock certificates, clouded his future with both the FBI and the Colombo family. Taken together, the events demonstrate Scarpa's remarkable ability to manipulate his ties to the FBI to his own immediate advantage. In both criminal cases, Scarpa's insider relationship with the FBI played a key role. In one case, that relationship received a major boost; in the other, it was tested to the breaking point.

Those who study and write about formal organizations, either from a private business or a public bureaucracy point of view, generally recognize the need for a succession plan for anyone occupying a critical position within an organization. The concept of succession planning is now so routine and mainstream that it has engendered a volume in the "For Dummies" franchise.[1] Additionally, clear, simple guides to successful succession planning are readily available for download off the internet.[2] It is obvious that the position that comes with the most authority within an organization is critical. The boss of a Mafia crime family is such a position. Stripped of its unique nature, a Mafia borgata is in the abstract a hierarchical organization whose primary goal is profit. Of course, it is the unique nature of the organization Joseph Colombo Sr. ruled that removed it from being regarded as just another company or public bureaucracy.

Colombo ascended to the position of family boss in 1964 when he was forty years old. He replaced Joe Magliocco, who stepped down at the age of sixty-five due, ostensibly, to health considerations. As has been noted earlier, Magliocco died four months later, thereby validating his health concerns. Magliocco became the acting boss in 1962 when Joe Profaci's death at age sixty-four left the position of family boss vacant. Calogero "Charlie the Sidge" LoCicero, considered, at least by Charlie, to be a viable candidate to succeed Magliocco, was sixty years old when he was passed over in favor of Joe Colombo. In short, it appears that Colombo's relative youth, and the stability that a long-term reign might bring to the family, was a factor in his being approved as family boss. Furthermore, as also noted above, once Colombo was put in charge, he announced his preference for a younger set of capos as he set about reorganizing what became known as the Colombo family.

In most organizations, an institutional dedication to passing the leadership baton to a younger generation, with or without a viable succession plan, would likely be tested during the extended tenure of whoever was placed in such a critical position. However, most organizations do not count attempted assassination as either an occupational hazard or a routine method of ending a leader's tenure. Indeed, a legal enterprise can even take out insurance, known as Key Person Insurance, to reduce the risk of institutional damage in the event of the sudden demise of an important leader. Not surprisingly, such insurance is not available on the open market to large criminal operations. And even if it were legal to issue such insurance, it seems doubtful any insurance company would take on such a high level of risk.

At the time of the incapacitation of Joe Colombo Sr. by Jerome Johnson, no plan of succession was in place, nor, of course, was the Colombo borgata insured against any financial damage that Colombo's sudden inability to lead might precipitate. Instead, various members of the Colombo family began jockeying for leadership positions. Remarkably, *de facto* leadership ended up in the hands of Carmine "The Snake" Persico, who was effectively running the family from federal prison in spite of Thomas DiBella's appointment as the head of the family. It is difficult to imagine a worse recipe for stable leadership in a large-scale organization.

Indeed, as will be seen in chapters nine and ten, the origins of the family's violent internal struggles of the late 1980s and early 1990s can be traced back to the decisions being made in the wake of the attempted assassination of Joe Colombo. And, as always, Scarpa was in the middle of it all, relaying a steady stream of information to the FBI at great personal risk. A review of how the position of family boss became formally occupied by Thomas DiBella while in fact in the hands of Carmine Persico is in order.

WAR AND PEACE

As of June 28, 1971, Salvatore "Charlie Lemons" Mineo was Joe Colombo's underboss, and Joe "Joe Yak" Yacovelli occupied the third highest position in the family, that of consigliere. As Scarpa noted during a debriefing with the FBI on July 7, 1971, less than two weeks after the attempt on Colombo's life, "it was apparent that JOE COLOMBO had maintained harmony in the family by a very delicate balance of power and had made no provision whatever for any disruption in this balance."[3] In the immediate aftermath of the Colombo hit, it was widely assumed that underboss Mineo would at least assume Colombo's duties so long as Colombo was incapacitated.

Scarpa provided the FBI with the details of a critical leadership succession meeting at Dick Fusco's residence in early July, when the family was still reeling from the Colombo shooting. At that meeting, Mineo, who was then seventy-three years old,[4] declared he would not assume "interim leadership" of the family due to concerns about his age and health. He then voiced his preference for designating forty-three-year-old Joe Yacovelli as acting boss.[5] Scarpa, in the same FBI debriefing, presciently predicted the *de facto* ascendence of Carmine "The Snake" Persico if Yacovelli were to become acting boss. Scarpa's narrative, at least in retrospect, reads more like a warning than anything else. "YACOVELLI would never resist PERSICO,"[6] he opined. In fact, it was Scarpa's view that if Persico managed to "beat his federal case he would undoubtedly kill YACOVELLI and be made boss."[7]

Whoever was calling the shots in the Colombo family by the end of July, it was immediately clear that the most significant issue he would have to navigate was retribution against the Gallos for their assumed role in the Joe Colombo shooting. Even the FBI bought into the idea that Joey Gallo was behind the hit on Colombo, a view that was consistent with their analysis of the danger posed by Gallo to Colombo before the shooting.[8] "The hit on Colombo, detectives theorized, was intended to clear the way for Gallo's comeback."[9]

After the shooting, Scarpa reported rumors among La Cosa Nostra (LCN) groups about the FBI and CIA assisting Gallo in setting up Johnson to assassinate Colombo.[10] And Scarpa preliminarily theorized that Persico was responsible for the hit on Colombo because Yacovelli would name Persico as either underboss or consigliere once Colombo was dead. The fact that Joey Gallo would have been the natural suspect would have, according to Scarpa's theory, given Persico cover.[11] However, a week later, Scarpa concluded that Persico was not involved in the Colombo shooting and Gallo was likely to blame.[12] Not surprisingly then, Colombo's supporters, including commission members Carlo Gambino and Carmine Paul "Mr. Gribbs" Tramunti, initially advised Yacovelli that they wanted Joey and Albert Gallo and their longtime supporter Mooney Cutrone killed.

Cutrone and the two Gallo brothers were already in the crosshairs of the Commission and the Colombo family. Three days before Colombo was shot, Carlo Gambino had approved a contract from Joe Colombo to hit all three of them.[13] Gambino and Tramunti also instructed that, in certain circumstances, "everybody in the GALLO mob should be killed as quickly as possible."[14] The two Commission members even promised to provide financial support and personnel to accomplish the hits.[15] Scarpa, The Grim Reaper, was so impressed he told the FBI, "he had never heard anything so clear cut and ruthless since the days of the GALLO-PROFACI war…"[16] Indeed, this immediate post-Joe Colombo struggle for power has often been referred to as the second Colombo war.

Paranoia understandably dominated the mood among the LCN families in New York for the rest of the summer of 1971. Wiseguys, capos, and associates in the Colombo family, and supporters of Joey and Albert Gallo were all armed to the teeth.[17] The Italian American Civil Rights League headquarters at 84th Street and 17th Avenue in Brooklyn became a virtual armory.[18] Fearing another attempt on Joe Colombo's life, his constant entourage of half-a-dozen bodyguards at Roosevelt Hospital, including Scarpa at times, were also heavily armed.[19] Although the on-again, off-again attempts to make peace with the Gallos were initially ineffective, the killing momentarily stopped due to intense police and FBI pressure. The Colombo family was simply waiting for the right moment to strike.[20] In early September, after numerous arrests of LCN personnel for weapons possession based on information provided by Scarpa,[21] Carlo Gambino instructed the Gallo faction to not take any further action against the Colombo family.[22]

By December, the tension had eased enough for Joey Gallo to seek a peaceful solution to his ongoing and personal feud with the Colombo family. Gallo floated the idea of bringing his crew into the Gambino family.[23] However, at the same time, his close confederate John "Mooney" Cutrone suggested to a group of Colombo capos that the Gallo loyalists should remain in the Colombo family.[24] The Gallo faction was apparently trying to create a rift between Gambino and Colombo's successors by playing one off against the other. Joey Gallo then came up with a specific list of demands for an end to the hostilities. As Scarpa relayed to the FBI, Gallo "proposed that he be made a captain in the COLOMBO family, given authority to 'make' at least ten new members, be given a territory, and all animosity forgotten."[25]

Five days before Christmas of 1971, Gallo's proposal was rejected in its entirety. Gallo's profane response to the rejection was that he would do as he pleased, and he would answer to no one. At that point, Scarpa was "of the opinion that the GALLOs will be killed."[26] That conclusion once again set off alarm bells at the FBI. Scarpa was warned not to participate in any assassinations. He was further instructed to "make every effort to obtain advance information which can be utilized to take appropriate precautionary measures."[27] The FBI repeated their admonition in early March of 1972. Unfortunately for Joey Gallo, Scarpa's cooperation with the FBI did not forestall what by then seemed inevitable.

Meanwhile, the clock ran out on Carmine Persico's attempts to avoid prison through the appeal process for his 1968 conviction in federal court of robbery of merchandise moving in interstate commerce and conspiracy to commit robbery.[28] After a series of unsuccessful appeals and motions, he was ordered by the U.S. District Court to begin serving concurrent prison terms of "fourteen and nine years on each count" on January 27, 1972.[29] Scarpa's prediction that Persico would kill Yacovelli should Persico beat his federal case would not be tested. In spite of his incarceration, Persico "was recognized as the family's leader, his formal anointing only awaiting his parole."[30] Being behind bars barely disrupted Persico's deadly influence.

On April 5, 1972, a Wednesday, Persico's brother Alphonse and Jerry Angella, a bodyguard, visited Carmine in prison in Atlanta.[31] Two days later, the ongoing conflict between the Colombo family on one side and Joseph "Crazy Joey" Gallo, his brother Albert "Kid Blast" Gallo, and their loyal followers on the other, blew wide open. Crazy Joey was murdered in the early morning of Friday, April 7, 1972, slightly more than nine months after Joe Colombo was shot. Greg Scarpa reported to the FBI that Persico's crew, in spite of their leader's imprisonment in Georgia, carried out the revenge killing on instructions from the other LCN families.[32] Two additional murders were ordered by the LCN families. Jerry Ciprio and Richard Grossman, both suspected of being FBI informants, were murdered shortly after Gallo was killed.[33] Joe Yacovelli, fearing for his life after the Gallo hit and a subsequent botched assassination attempt aimed at him, went into hiding, precipitating the end of his brief reign as acting boss of the Colombo family.

The dynamic nature of the relationship between the Colombo family and the Gallos was in full view during April of 1972. On April 12, five days after Joey Gallo was murdered, Colombo capo Charles "Moose" Panarella announced that any Colombo family member was authorized to hit any Gallo loyalist until they were all exterminated.[34] Six days later, Panarella changed his tune, having been informed that the Gallos were "attempting to make peace."[35] Panarella was arrested on April 24 by the FBI on the basis of a tip from Scarpa for possession of a firearm. Panarella erroneously blamed his arrest on the Gallos and once again wanted to kill all of them.[36] However, by May of 1972, it was clear to most in the Colombo family that the only people benefitting from the ongoing feud with the Gallos were the FBI and NYPD.

By the last week in May of 1972, peace appeared within the parties' grasp. The "entire GALLO crew has been granted amnesty and have the option that they could go to any LCN family that they felt they would be comfortable with and… no harm will befall them."[37] And by July 10, Moose Panarella was reporting that the Colombo-Gallo war was about over.[38] In a debriefing a year later, Scarpa reported that a "definite peace [had] been established."[39] Even Mooney Cutrone, who had been marked for death prior to the attempted assassination of Joe Colombo, was seen in the company of Colombo family members bearing him no ill feelings.[40]

The FBI, for its part, was dependent upon and grateful for the information Scarpa, "a prolific source of valuable data,"[41] had been providing during the feud and at least since the attempted assassination of Joe Colombo Sr.[42] Scarpa's attempts to put pressure on Carmine Persico by tying him to the Joey Gallo murder did not yield the results he likely expected. Persico's power in the family was growing, and Scarpa was the target of accusations within the Persico faction that he was an informant,[43] which, of course, he was.[44] The "bad blood" between Scarpa and Persico continued.[45]

When the dust from the Colombo-Gallo war settled, Thomas DiBella was installed as boss of the Colombo family, Anthony Abbatemarco was his underboss, Joe Yacovelli was living in New York City's Little Italy disguised as a hippie and refusing to attend meetings, weddings, or wakes,[46] and Greg Scarpa, who found himself increasingly at odds with Carmine Persico, was not made a capo by the new family leadership as had been assumed.[47] Carmine Persico was in prison, where he would remain until 1979. While Persico was in prison, the FBI noted that "reliable informants [presumably including Scarpa] have described Carmine Persico as a vicious killer who has personally participated in many murders over the years."[48] By many accounts, he was already the *de facto* leader of the family in spite of his incarceration.[49] The leadership contest within the Colombo family that started soon after Jerome Johnson attempted to assassinate Joe Colombo Sr. would plague the family for more than twenty years and would eventually lead to a bloodbath that featured Greg Scarpa and a few trusted members of his inner circle as roaming executioners.

THE FAMILY JEWELS

In 1948, when Gregory Scarpa turned twenty, 65th Street, between 13th and 14th Avenues in the Bensonhurst neighborhood of Brooklyn, began undergoing a major architectural and religious transformation. On October 3 of that year, construction of a votive church "built in the style of the Italianate Renaissance Revival architecture" began.[50] The church was inspired by a request made by Pastor Angelo R. Cioffi in 1942 for donations from the congregation to finance the building of a shrine to the Virgin Mary for the safe return of men from the community, who at the time were overseas fighting in World War II.[51]

Built from Italian marble,[52] the church was completed in the summer of 1951, the same year that Scarpa earned his button in the Profaci borgata. The church, which was originally supposed to cost $1,000,000 to build, ended up costing more than $2,000,000 to complete[53] (more than $23 million in 2023 dollars).[54] As expensive as the undertaking was, the results were impressive. The church's 150-foot steeple dominated the Bensonhurst skyline, and its interior was magnificent. Among the many architectural and artistic features was a massive 60' by 27.5' painting hanging behind the altar. The painting, which was three years in the making, is of the Virgin Mary holding the baby Jesus, and it included a device for hanging a crown on the Virgin Mary,[55] Regina Pacis, the Queen of Peace.

Donations from the congregation were once again solicited, this time for jewelry which would be refashioned into a crown for the Virgin Mary. And the congregation once again responded generously. Churchgoers gave an enormous amount of personal jewelry; so much, in fact, that two crowns were made, one for Mary and one for Jesus.[56] The crowns, which were blessed in Rome by Pope Pius XII in January of 1952,[57] "were estimated to be worth $100,000 and included 600 diamonds, rubies, and sapphires."[58] The two crowns were installed in late May of 1952. Approximately a week later, the church was burglarized and the crowns were stolen.[59]

Several days of frantic searching followed as the story of the stolen crowns attracted local and national media attention.[60] The crowns were not found. They were, however, returned anonymously to the church via "Sunday special delivery mail."[61] Ralph "Bucky" Emmino, a local ne'er-do-well, was quickly fingered as a primary suspect in the theft. Emmino was "a twenty-two-year-old jewel thief with suspected ties to the Mafia" who, shortly after the burglary, "was found shot to death on the side of a road in Bath Beach,"[62] another Brooklyn neighborhood and a popular dumping ground for Mafia victims.

Ralph, his wife Lillian, and their son had lived for a brief period on 66th Street,[63] about two blocks from the church. Ralph, who was in and out of trouble with the criminal justice system from the time he was a teenager, had five brothers,[64] one of whom was eighteen-year-old Vincent Emmino. A notorious photograph was snapped of Vincent being restrained by police after he had viewed his brother's bullet-riddled body. At the scene, Vincent swore revenge on those responsible.[65]

While the bejeweled crowns found their way back to their rightful place, the burglary case and the Emmino murder have never been officially solved. In 1962, Scarpa told the FBI that a goodfellow named "Bucky" stole the crowns and that family boss Joe Profaci, who attended Regina Pacis, ordered that the crowns be returned and that Ralph

"Bucky" Emmino be hit. Ten years after the fact, Scarpa speculated that "Charlie the Sidge" LoCicero could have pulled the trigger, given that Emmino was running numbers for LoCicero back in 1952.[66] Whether Scarpa had it right is open to debate.

Accounts of what happened to the likely thief or thieves vary widely. Anthony Villano claimed that two brothers stole the jewels and that Profaci declared, "'I want one ball from each of those guys brought to me.'"[67] Villano went on to write that "the mutilated bodies of the thieves were found later."[68] Peter Lance stated that the thieves were "reportedly a pair of brothers" and that "they were found dead… strangled with rosary beads."[69] The truth appears to be somewhat less dramatic than either author's version. The only person killed in connection with the theft was Ralph "Bucky" Emmino. He was neither strangled with a rosary, nor was his body mutilated. He was, however, shot twice in the chest and at least once in the head. And while Profaci may have ordered the hit on Emmino for having the temerity to steal from the Catholic Church, nothing in the factual record supports Villano's assertion regarding Ralph Emmino's castration, let alone the castration of two Emmino brothers.

In addition to the confusion about how many thieves were involved, their identities, and their fate, there is some dispute as to Ralph Emmino's age. Some sources refer to him as being thirty-eight years old at the time of his death,[70] whereas others refer to him as twenty-two years old when he was killed.[71] The 1940 U.S. Census lists a Ralph *Emmenio* as living in Brooklyn and being twenty years old as of April of that year, which would have made him thirty-two years old in 1952.[72] That listing, which is of an entire Emmenio family, does not include a younger brother named Vincent, and may, therefore, not be the Ralph *Emmino* who was killed in 1952.[73] It does, however, list a younger brother Jimmie, age five in 1940, which would have made him either seventeen or eighteen in May of 1952. Misspellings of last names, particularly in immigrant families, were not uncommon in U.S. Census forms during the first half of the twentieth century. It is just as likely that the census taker misunderstood Mary Emmenio, Ralph's mother, and noted as the source of the information on the census form, when she told him her youngest son's name. Finally, a list of those incarcerated at the Coxsackie Correctional Facility in Greene County, NY, includes a Ralph Emmino born on January 1, 1920, which would have made him thirty-two years old in early June of 1952.[74] Understandably, neither Villano nor Lance provided any age for either Ralph Emmino or his brother.

In 1952, the comings and goings of small-time thieves, like the Emmino brothers, and Mafia bosses, like Joseph Profaci, was of little interest to the FBI, particularly in a case that did not implicate the violation of any federal laws. It is not unreasonable, therefore, to see no federal law enforcement involvement in the investigation of the Crown Jewels theft or their recovery. However, by 1973, the law enforcement landscape in the borough of Brooklyn was vastly different from what it had been two decades earlier. And it is in that altered context that a second theft of the Crown Jewels took place. And this time, Greg Scarpa would play a central role in its peaceful resolution.

"THOSE WHO CANNOT REMEMBER THE PAST ARE CONDEMNED TO REPEAT IT."[75]

Once again, having a variety of sources leads to conflicting narratives about a crucial moment in Scarpa's life as an FBI Top Echelon Criminal Informant and the facts underlying that moment. Certain facts, however, are not reasonably in dispute. The Regina Pacis Crown Jewels, along with a number of other valuable artifacts, were stolen for a second time at some point between 5:00 p.m. and 6:30 p.m. on Wednesday, January 10, 1973, while the church was open for worshipers.[76] The FBI immediately became interested and just as quickly became involved.[77] Eventually, the Special Agent in Charge of the FBI's New York Office, where Scarpa's handler Anthony Villano worked at the time, wrote a detailed memorandum that served as the rationale for a substantial cash bonus for Scarpa and chronicled the events surrounding the theft, including Scarpa's crucial participation in recovering the stolen articles.[78] Those articles, in addition to the two crowns, included "a ring decorating the Madonna's finger, a cluster of diamonds on her foot, 4 of 12 diamond stars around the heads and shoulders of the Virgin and Child, and possibly jewels that formed a bracelet and part of a necklace on the Madonna."[79] The total value of the pieces stolen was estimated by NYPD at $350,000.[80] The church had the items insured for $100,000.[81]

According to the FBI's detailed memorandum, Scarpa approached the Bureau, presumably Villano, the day after the jewels were stolen.[82] Over the course of the next two days, the FBI, through Scarpa,[83] learned the identity of the thieves. The culprits were Frank Morici and Philip "Philly Boy" Paradiso. Paradiso, a heroin addict for twenty years, eventually became an FBI informant and entered the Witness Protection Program. In 1989, he testified at the murder trial of his older brother, Michael "Mickey Boy" Paradiso, a member of the Gambino crime family. Michael Paradiso was accused of having shot and killed Frank Morici, Philip's partner in the Regina Pacis jewels theft in 1973. Morici was killed when he was shot twice in the head in 1978 for implicating Mickey Boy in a robbery for which Paradiso was sent to prison. Mickey Boy's wife was not impressed with her husband's younger brother Philip or his testimony. "'He's never had an honest job in his life,' she said. 'I can't believe this man. He lived with us. He ate at my house every day. He's a rat and a liar.'"[84] Coincidentally, although the case has never been definitively solved, "Philly Boy" Paradiso may have been the man who shot and killed Greg Scarpa's brother, Salvatore.[85]

Morici and Paradiso were unaware of the non-monetary significance of what they had taken; the thieves had turned the jewels over to Colombo capo Charles "Moose" Panarella, and Panarella and Scarpa were scheduled to meet on January 13 to discuss the disposition of the jewels.[86] During that January 13 meeting, Panarella gave the stolen merchandise to Scarpa and asked him to determine the jewels' value. Apparently, Panarella was in need of some ready cash.[87] Scarpa relayed the substance of the meeting to the FBI the next day, Sunday, January 14. He could not, at that point, risk simply turning the jewels over to the FBI or NYPD. To do so would have raised suspicions that he was cooperating with law enforcement, a potentially suicidal act. Instead, the FBI and Scarpa came up with a plan for the safe return of the jewels. Playing on Alphonse "Allie Boy" Persico's ego and his desire to appear like a bigshot in the LCN world, a special agent whom Persico trusted would phone Persico to let him know of the FBI's interest in the matter and its displeasure with the theft.[88] The wheels were in motion and Scarpa was in the middle of the action.

As a result of the special agent's call to Persico, Scarpa was told to be present at a "sit-down" on Wednesday, January 17, a week after the theft. Scarpa attended and later reported that Persico, Panarella, Benjamin LoCicero, Anthony La Ponzina, and Sal Fusco were also present. Panarella did most of the talking, and what he said consisted largely of what Scarpa, acting on the Bureau's instructions, had told him.[89] Persico decided the jewels needed to be returned to the church and asked Scarpa, who was still in possession of them, if he had any objection. When Scarpa agreed by saying he would do whatever was best for the family, Persico was so grateful that he hugged Scarpa and gave him a kiss![90] Persico then proposed the somewhat melodramatic although subject-appropriate plan to contact a priest who would in turn contact the FBI's Assistant Director in Charge (ADIC) John Malone to arrange for the jewels' return.[91] Malone, a devout Catholic, had been the ADIC of the FBI's New York field office for more than a decade.

While Scarpa was working behind the scenes with the FBI to get the jewels back to the church, NYPD was turning up the heat. That prompted Scarpa to tell Panarella the jewels needed to be turned over to the FBI as soon as possible. In fact, a few days later, Panarella reported that if the jewels were not returned within twenty-four hours, both he and Scarpa would be indicted and arrested by the local authorities.[92] Scarpa gave the jewels back to Panarella on Saturday, January 20. He urged Panarella to turn the jewels over to the FBI rather than NYPD. He even proposed a method: place the jewels in a locker in Grand Central Station and then make an anonymous call to the FBI. Panarella agreed and, after getting the plan approved by Allie Boy Persico, he placed the jewels in a locker and made the phone call. On Sunday, January 21, just before noon, the jewels were recovered by FBI Special Agents led by John Malone.[93]

ANALYSIS

The extensive FBI memo from the Special Agent in Charge to L. Patrick Gray, who was then the FBI's acting director,[94] is arguably the best source for Scarpa's and the FBI's roles and actions in response to the second theft of the Regina

Pacis jewels. It is closer in time to the events than any other detailed memorialization; its author would have had access to the FBI's internal files when creating the memo; it was clearly meant for consumption at the Bureau's highest levels, including by New York's ADIC Malone; and it was the basis for an extraordinary request for money above and beyond what Scarpa was already being paid. When compared to the accounts of Villano and Lance, it appears to be more reliable overall.

Villano's book came out in 1977. As he was preparing his book, presumably he no longer had access to the Bureau's file. So how does *Brick Agent*'s account differ from the FBI's own files? First, as Peter Lance noted, Villano deemphasized Scarpa's role in the entire affair.[95] Villano, using the name Nick Billeti[96] as an alias for Scarpa throughout the book's retelling of the second Crown Jewels caper, clearly felt it was necessary to keep protecting Scarpa's identity. Downplaying Scarpa's role in the matter may have been one more way to do just that. Other particulars in Villano's book account differ from the FBI's internal memorandum account. For instance, Villano alleged in his book that a clandestine meeting in Brooklyn's Prospect Park took place between his boss and Allie Boy Persico to discuss the disposition of the jewels.[97] No such meeting is described in the FBI memo. Villano made no mention in his book of Panarella giving the jewels to Scarpa. And instead of Scarpa learning about the identity of the thieves from Panarella as set forth in the FBI files, Villano wrote that Scarpa learned that the thieves had tried to move them at a "gin mill" Scarpa "occasionally frequented."[98] Villano's book claimed the jewels were eventually placed in a locker in the East Side Airlines Terminal, not Grand Central Station, and that he and a fellow special agent recovered the jewels, not John Malone.[99] Finally, in what admittedly is a nitpick, Villano described the thieves as heroin junkies,[100] whereas the

FBI memorandum had them as "'hop heads' (addicted to pills)."[101]

Villano's portraying the second Regina Pacis jewel case the way he did protected Scarpa's identity, added drama to a narrative to make it more commercially appealing, and overstated his own role for the same purpose. It is, of course, possible that Villano's version is more accurate than that contained in the FBI's files. However, the reasons stated above militate in favor of accepting the FBI's internal version as the more accurate of the two.

Peter Lance, for some reason, after viewing the FBI's file and criticizing Villano's book for downplaying Scarpa's role, returned to that book for much of his depiction of the events surrounding the negotiations and eventual recovery of the jewels.[102] He even characterized the phone tip about the eventual location of the jewels as coming from "a gruff speaking individual"[103] without the benefit of the source of that characterization. Again, the FBI's internal and detailed memorandum, which Lance in part relied upon, appears to be an overall more accurate and complete picture of what took place than Lance's account.

However, the FBI's detailed memorandum begs at least two other questions. Why did the Bureau take such an active interest in a crime that was almost identical to one committed two decades earlier that they ignored? And what accounts for the two cases' distinctly different outcomes? In the 1952 case, a thief was accused and quickly murdered, presumably by the Mafia. In 1973, while two men and a teenaged girl were arrested[104] in connection with the theft and their identities were apparently known to the Colombo family before their arrest, no physical harm came to them for their role in the theft. The FBI's crusade against organized crime and the status of Greg Scarpa as a Top Echelon

Criminal Informant go a long way to explain the disparate treatment and outcome of the two cases.

By 1973, the FBI was taking an active interest in any criminal activity involving organized crime in Brooklyn and had been doing so for about a decade. As noted, Scarpa, one of the Bureau's most active and most productive informants, contacted the Bureau one day after the second theft. Second, the murder of alleged thief Ralph Emmino in 1952 was attributed to Joe Profaci, a Catholic and a Regina Pacis parishioner. In 1973, one of the prime movers in responding to the second theft was also a devout Catholic, but he was the FBI's New York ADIC, John Malone, rather than a Mafia family boss. The 1973 thieves' lives may have depended on that fact. Third, after the attempted murder of Joe Colombo in June of 1971, and the murder of Colombo family rival Joey Gallo less than a year later, the five families of New York were feeling intense pressure from local and federal law enforcement. More random murders would have certainly exacerbated that pressure. Fourth, while the Bureau ignored the 1952 theft, in 1973 the FBI saw the safe return of the jewels as a way to promote its public image. They were right. As Peter Lance noted, it "was a stunning public relations success for the Bureau."[105]

Finally, the central presence of Greg Scarpa, a master manipulator looking to curry favor with Allie Boy Persico, burnish his own credentials with the FBI, and earn a substantial cash bonus in the bargain,[106] cannot be overstated. It was Scarpa who convinced Panarella to forego trying to move the jewels. It was Scarpa, in conversation with the Bureau, who came up with a plan to coax Allie Boy Persico to support the return of the jewels. It was Scarpa who fed Panarella the right lines to convince the egotistical Persico to go along with the plan. And when the heat was on from NYPD to get the jewels back, Scarpa successfully engineered their return to the FBI. All in all, a remarkable record, particularly for a man who was about to face indictment and arrest by the same federal law enforcement institution for the printing and selling of millions of dollars' worth of counterfeit IBM stock certificates.

CATCH ME IF YOU CAN

Scarpa's being handsomely compensated for helping the FBI on one front did not inhibit him from simultaneously violating federal law to otherwise enrich himself on another. In January of 1973, while the FBI's New York Office and Scarpa were working hand-in-hand to resolve the second Regina Pacis Crown Jewels burglary, the FBI's Newark, New Jersey office, through an investigation that began in November of 1972,[107] was developing evidence that would implicate Scarpa in a scheme to produce and sell up to $10,000,000 worth of counterfeit IBM stock certificates. While Scarpa was being praised and rewarded by one FBI field office, he was being investigated by another with, ironically, the assistance of a confidential informant and a cooperating witness. Two rats were ratting on a third rat.

The phony stock scheme began in the summer of 1970. Scarpa, whose time was increasingly occupied with Joe Colombo Sr.'s Italian American Civil Rights League, started working with Louis Astuto in late June or early July to produce fake IBM stock certificates,[108] each one of which would be worth 100 shares of the blue-chip stock.[109] The idea was to sell the certificates at a deep discount of three points[110] to a distributor who would then retail them for twelve points.[111] The end purchasers would convert the certificates to cash by using them as collateral for loans.[112] They would default on the loans and abscond with the cash, leaving the lender with stock certificates that weren't worth the cheap paper they were printed on. Joe De Domenico, aka Joe Brewster, and several others joined the scheme. With the exception of Astuto, De Domenico, and Scarpa, the others involved in and eventually charged for the phony stock scheme have had their names redacted from the set of FBI documents spelling out its investigation into the matter. However, a *New York Times* article from June 8, 1974, listed the additional defendants as Salvatore Cardinale, Edmund L. Graifer, Luke Spann, Nicholas Mainello, and Louis Pergola.[113] Over the course of nearly a year,[114] the plotters argued over money, struggled to find a distributor, blew hot and cold on the project, and stumbled over their own technical incompetence when skill and precision were required. To paraphrase British novelist Thomas Hardy, the plot did not have a propitious beginning, but it did have an ignominious end.

The first technical issue that bedeviled the coconspirators was obtaining paper that contained silk,[115] which was needed for plausible authenticity. De Domenico, who had a sample genuine certificate that would serve as the template for the counterfeits,[116] was in contact with a printer "who was willing to print anything."[117] The paper that Scarpa, et al. ultimately provided to the printer was of poor quality. A succession of issues related to the printing itself followed. For instance, the printer was unable to create a raised seal on the certificates as required by the genuine template. Additionally, the certificates' serial numbers were difficult to duplicate and had to be applied to the back of each certificate by hand, one at a time. In spite of these problems, the coconspirators found a willing distributor for the phony stock so they decided "to go through with the deal."[118] At that point, the printer required $200 to photograph the genuine stock certificate as part of his production process. Scarpa, true to form, "refused to put up the cash"[119] on a deal that the participants thought could mean a six-figure payoff. Eventually, Astuto provided the $200 required by the printer, and the work, which was supposed to take three to four weeks to complete, continued.[120]

The scheme's next stumbling block, at least for Scarpa, was the printer's fee: $2,500 for the completed plates and an additional $2,500 for the completed package of printed counterfeit certificates.[121] Once again conforming to type, Scarpa refused to put up the $2,500.[122] At that point, it appeared that the entire deal would crash and burn. De Domenico loaded up on booze one night and declared he wanted out.[123] The coconspirators' potential distributor turned down the merchandise due to the certificates' poor quality.[124] Scarpa and the others continued to argue about the printer's fee.[125] After being talked out of a cockamamie kidnaping scheme, Scarpa said they should simply destroy the package of fake certificates.[126] In the end, De Domenico, who added phony serial numbers one certificate at a time to the back of each, found someone willing to pay a mere $3,000 for the poor quality counterfeit stock.[127]

The certificates eventually made their way to Philadelphia, most likely through New Jersey and Miami. The scheme quickly unraveled in the City of Brotherly Love. The Secret Service made arrests on May 27, 1971, and on September 22, 1971, indictments were returned charging several locals with federal crimes in connection with eighty-two of the phony stock certificates.[128] By the early summer of 1972, most of those charged in Philadelphia had either pleaded guilty or were found guilty after insisting on going to trial. The remaining defendants, after having been found guilty on April 21, 1972, were sentenced to four years in prison on January 8, 1973.[129]

At that point, for all that Scarpa, Astuto, and De Domenico knew, the matter was concluded. Scarpa's successful and highly lauded assistance with the second Regina Pacis Crown Jewels theft which, coincidentally, began three days after the final sentencing in the Philadelphia case, likely boosted his confidence that he would face no repercussions for his part in the counterfeiting scheme. If so, that confidence was misplaced. In fact, the FBI's Newark office had opened an investigation into the phony stock on November 20, 1972, given that at least some of the certificates had allegedly been sold in New Jersey.[130] Detailed testimony from a cooperating witness[131] and a confidential informant,[132] along with the federal government's physical possession of eighty-two of the phony certificates seized in Philadelphia opened the floodgates. Strike Force attorney Donald McCaffrey decided to bring the matter to a federal grand jury in March of 1973.[133]

The arrest records of Scarpa, at this point containing fourteen entries over two pages, and his coconspirators were forwarded by the FBI's Identification Division to the Newark Strike Force,[134] as were their fingerprints.[135] McCaffrey anticipated that indictments would be forthcoming "sometime before the middle of June 1973."[136] However, in this case, the wheels of justice turned slowly and it would be another year before the federal grand jury returned sealed indictments.

By the fall of 1973, Scarpa's reputation within New York Cosa Nostra circles went well beyond that of a counterfeiter. He and his crew were described by one informant as "'the strength, the shooters' (contract killers) behind the leading figures in the [Colombo] family."[137] A month later, word of the investigation became public knowledge. Then, on October 9, 1973, agents contacted Scarpa, informed him that an indictment in the case was likely, and suggested that he should "provide any further facts or evidence" he had about the case before the indictment came down.[138] Scarpa, angered by the agents' suggestion, "stormed" out of the interview,[139] and then made an atypical unforced error by calling and haranguing the Special Agent in Charge of the FBI's Newark office. During that ill-advised call, he insisted on his own innocence and

> "demanded that something be done to alleviate the situation. SAC, Newark, indicated that Scarpa's remarks were profane, and while specifically denying he was making any threats, were demanding and bordering on being threatening."[140]

In fact, Scarpa "said he is going to reveal everything, scheme and technique, imaginable, pertaining to the FBI."[141] When asked if he was threatening the Newark Special Agent in Charge, Scarpa replied that he "was not making any threat, except to reveal all he knows."[142] The special agent responded by telling Scarpa that "the reason for his contact was not entirely clear, but if it was for the purpose of evading the law, it would not be successful."[143]

Scarpa, recognizing his harangue was a mistake, later called his FBI contact in New York, presumably Anthony Villano, apologized after he "admitted losing his composure," and asked that his apology be conveyed to the SAC, Newark.[144] In that same call to New York, Scarpa relayed his primary concern. If the prosecution were to go forward, he would be forced to plead guilty while facing significant time in prison. If he were able to beat the case, that fact would "lend credence to his fellow mafiosi that he is cooperating with the law."[145] Scarpa went so far as to suggest a polygraph as an alternative to support his claim of innocence.[146] The FBI's Special Investigative Division's note of October 17, 1973 on the matter concluded by stating that "[c]ontact with this outstanding source will be continued until such time as he is the subject of legal proceedings," a position taken five days earlier by the New York Office.[147] In fact, Scarpa was closed as a Top Echelon Criminal Informant about eighteen months later.[148] In the meantime, he would face indictment, arrest, and arraignment for his role in the phony IBM stock scheme. In other words, he became "the subject of legal proceedings."

Strike Force Assistant U.S. Attorney McCaffrey, after more than a year of presenting evidence to a federal grand jury, finally obtained indictments against Scarpa, De Domenico, Astuto, and their coconspirators on June 6, 1974, D-Day.[149] The sealed indictments charged each man with multiple counts of violating sections 2, 371, 1343, and 2314 of Title 18 of the United States Code.[150] The indictments also noted that the counterfeit stock certificates they had allegedly printed and sold had a face value in excess of $4,000,000.[151] Bench warrants were issued for the defendants' arrest. Those warrants were executed by special agents in the FBI's New York Office.[152]

Scarpa and Astuto were arrested the next day (Scarpa at the Parkway Luncheonette in Brooklyn[153] and Astuto at a Brooklyn residence[154]) and brought before a U.S. Magistrate. They both waived extradition. The magistrate set their personal recognizance bonds[155] at $25,000[156] each, and both were ordered to appear in U.S. District Court in Newark when summoned; they were then released.[157] De Domenico turned himself in on June 10 at the FBI's Staten Island Resident Agency.[158] Like Scarpa and Astuto, he was brought before a magistrate, where he waived extradition and was ordered to appear in U.S. District Court in Newark when summoned. He, too, was then released on a $25,000 personal recognizance bond.[159] Scarpa, Astuto, and De Domenico entered not guilty pleas on August 6, 1974, in Newark.[160] A week later, the eighty-two stock certificates, eighty-one of which were in the name of a non-existent business, "Scott-Ford, Incorporated," were "turned over to the custody of the United States Marshals Service, Newark, New Jersey."[161] The lead prosecutor in the case, Joseph

Cranwell, expected a trial to occur in January of 1975 in front of Judge Lawrence A. Whipple.[162]

Again, the wheels of justice turned slowly, coming to a virtual halt for nearly two years. During 1975, the only progress in the case was that two more potential witnesses were interviewed by the FBI. A hearing was then scheduled for January 19, 1976[163] before Judge Whipple, presumably to set a trial date. Instead, on January 6, 1977, almost a year later, two years after the initially anticipated trial date and more than four years after the case was opened in Newark, Judge Whipple dismissed all counts in the indictments as to Scarpa, Astuto, and De Domenico.[164] The reason for the dismissal has been redacted from the FBI's file.[165] Unfortunately, one of their codefendants had already pleaded guilty and still had to be sentenced for the same crimes that were otherwise dismissed.[166] Some guys, including those in Philadelphia, went to prison, and some guys, including Greg Scarpa, got off scot-free.

The public will likely never know why a case supported by witnesses and physical evidence, a case that was solid enough for federal grand jury indictments after presentations by a Strike Force attorney, a case whose underlying facts resulted in the imprisonment of several men, was dismissed as to Greg Scarpa, Louis Astuto, and Joe De Domenico. We know that while all of the above was transpiring, Scarpa made at least one threat to the Special Agent in Charge of the FBI's Newark office to publicly expose and embarrass the FBI if the Department of Justice went forward with its prosecution of the counterfeit IBM stock scheme. We know that in spite of that threat, the FBI continued to use Scarpa as a Top Echelon Criminal Informant for almost eighteen months. We know that criminal proceedings were instituted against Scarpa nearly a year after his one memorialized threat. We know that Scarpa was closed as a Top Echelon

Criminal Informant the next March. And, of course, we know that the case against Scarpa and two others was dismissed in its entirety almost two years later.

One reasonable inference is that when Greg Scarpa let the U.S. government know what his testimony would entail, the FBI simply was not willing to risk having him take the stand in a public trial. Having recently secured a major public relations triumph in the second Regina Pacis Crown Jewels case, perhaps the FBI did not want to allow its image to suffer a blow by risking Scarpa's public testimony. The FBI and the Department of Justice may have decided that the risks of a public trial of Scarpa far outweighed the potential benefit of sending him to prison for a few years, something that in any jury trial is by no means a sure bet. Whatever the reason for the dismissal, Scarpa had to be feeling nearly untouchable at that point. As will be seen, his behavior from the late 1970s on, having just dodged any consequences for violating several federal laws during a months-long conspiracy, was increasingly brazen and increasingly violent.

CHAPTER FIVE: A THIRD FAMILY

Greg Scarpa's life as a mafia wiseguy and an FBI informant was, to say the least, atypical of the lives of most other American men of his generation. It was a life that was not, however, without at least some of the standard trappings other men enjoyed: marriage, children, a family. The union of Greg and Connie Scarpa, which began formally with their marriage in 1949, produced four children, the first of whom, Deborah, was born in 1949 and the last of whom, Frankie, was born in 1963. The Greg and Connie Scarpa family, which was larger than the average U.S. family of 3.67 persons,[1] was by outward appearances, a close, healthy, even robust family not unlike millions of other families in the country in the post-World War II era, the so-called "Baby Boom." Indeed, Gregory Scarpa Jr. described his brothers and sister as happy kids living a solid family life in a big old house on Staten Island.[2] Scarpa, whose income grew steadily during the 1950s, bought the house for Connie so that she could fix it up exactly the way she wanted it for their growing family.[3] By the early 1960s, the Scarpas were, by all outward appearances, a typical, even model family. But the head of that family, of course, was a member of another not-so-typical, not-so-model family.

When Scarpa "earned his button" and became a member of the Profaci borgata in 1951, his second "family" life took on a meaning outside of the middle-class cultural norms of the era. It was a life defined by crime and violence. Two families; two sets of loyalties; two sets of priorities; two sets of values; more than enough for any one person to handle. But Greg Scarpa, always the exception, was not done. In 1962, while still married to Connie, Scarpa's tendency toward womanizing led to his involvement with a teenager named Linda Diana. Within seven years, the two of them would start a family on Linda's idiosyncratic terms. This third "family" of Scarpa's, while once again appearing conventional in many respects, also defied most cultural norms of the era both in its origins and its parallel existence over time to three other marriages, two for Greg and one for Linda, and at least one additional affair for Linda while she was raising the children she had had with Greg during her marriage to another man.

It would be a mistake to assume that Linda Schiro was attracted to Greg Scarpa in spite of his being a gangster. Whenever she has had an opportunity to discuss the origins of their relationship,[4] she has made it clear that she was attracted to Scarpa precisely because he was a gangster. "A middle child raised largely by her father after her mother's death from stomach cancer, she only spent a few months after high school doing legitimate work as a clerk on Wall Street."[5] When the romantic efforts of a few Wall Street types she met had on the job came to naught,[6] she became involved with Larry Pistone, a married Gambino wiseguy. Although she was accustomed to being around gangster types from running numbers for her grandmother or hanging out at a local pool hall, she first experienced the potential for violence that could accompany the gangster life while she was dating Pistone.[7] It was during her relationship with Pistone that she met Greg Scarpa. The contest between Scarpa and Pistone for Linda Diana's affection nearly came to violence. Instead, it was resolved in a fairly unique Mafia manner, through a sit-down attended by Scarpa, Pistone, Joe Colombo, and "somebody from the Gambino family."[8]

Harmon wrote that the sit-down was attended by "the heads of the Gambino and Colombo families..."[9] As noted above, Joe Colombo did not become head of the family until April of 1964. While Colombo may well have been involved in the sit-down, given the timing of Diana's break with Pistone and her committing to Scarpa, Colombo would not then have been the head of the family. Regardless of who attended, the result of the sit-down was clear cut: Pistone was out, Scarpa was in.

Early in their relationship, Scarpa confessed to Linda that he had committed at least twenty murders. Again, she was not put off. "She said she had been around mobsters most of her life, so his boasts that he had been involved in twenty gangland murders didn't frighten her. [para.] 'I was impressed,' she said."[10] "'Greg was a murderer, but we were so much in love. We would have sex, and he would talk. He was so cute.'"[11] The night they consummated their relationship, Linda, who was three months pregnant with Larry Pistone's child, miscarried.[12] Adding children to her relationship with Scarpa would not happen for another seven years.

Not surprisingly, Scarpa's marriage deteriorated when he began seeing Linda Diana on a regular basis. Connie started challenging him about the amount of time he was spending away from home, a trend that continued after the birth of their fourth child in 1963.[13] The two, however, would never divorce. Instead, to simplify matters at least geographically, Scarpa eventually bought his wife a home and horse farm in New Jersey, a place he would visit with some regularity for many years after, while living with Linda in Brooklyn.

The early years of Greg Scarpa and Linda Diana's relationship were characterized by the sorts of ordinary events that nearly all couples share, and by extraordinary events that provided a young woman from Brooklyn with an insider's view of the complex life of a goodfellow who happened to be simultaneously an FBI informant. On the one hand, Linda grew close to Scarpa's mother, Mary, and spent time with his sister Marie and Marie's husband, Tony.[14] Like any suitor, Scarpa brought Linda gifts, including jewelry from an airport heist,[15] and provided assistance when he could. For instance, he arranged a modelling contract for her.[16] On the other hand, although "[h]e was a happy person, caring, giving to those he loved [,]... if you did him wrong, he would kill you."[17] Also, clearly contrary to Mafia tradition and perhaps common sense, he confided in her to a dangerous extent about his double life, confessing to her that he "worked" for the FBI. He regaled her with fantastic stories about "missions" he undertook at the request of the Bureau and the CIA. The "missions" Scarpa claimed to have undertaken included "helping the government frame members of Israel's Mossad; setting up a sting operation for the CIA; and gathering intelligence on Howard Hughes and his connection to the Mafia."[18] Additionally, Linda Diana later testified that Scarpa once "brought back a Colombo associate involved in pornography who was on the lam in Costa Rica."[19] And he introduced her to his first FBI handler, Anthony Villano.[20] He even took her along in 1964 when the FBI asked for his help in locating the three missing Mississippi civil rights workers. Linda also saw first-hand Scarpa's vigorous participation in the Italian American Civil Rights League's anti-FBI public demonstrations orchestrated by Joe Colombo.[21] The ongoing affair in all of its complexity and with all of its contradictions was intoxicating for her. However, six years after their relationship began, she decided she wanted something out of their affair beyond being a Mafia mistress. She wanted to have Scarpa's children.

While Linda Diana's personal code of values was no barrier to having a full-fledged, long-term affair with a murderer[22] who was a married man with four children, she drew the line at having children out of wedlock, fearing it would upset her father and also worrying that such children could not be baptized in the Catholic Church.[23] The year was 1968, Linda was in her early twenties, and the United States was in the middle of a cultural and sexual revolution that would call into question nearly every middle-class custom that had previously formed the foundation of mainstream American life. Unconventional living arrangements between men and women were, if not commonplace, at least on the rise. Linda's unorthodox solution to her personal ethical dilemma puzzled Scarpa. She proposed to marry Charlie Schiro and have Scarpa's children while married to Schiro, who would think the children were his own.[24] In spite of Scarpa's initial misgivings and opposition,[25] Linda Diana[26] married Charlie Schiro on March 25, 1968.[27]

Charlie Schiro, of course, was not privy to his bride's plan to use their marriage as cultural cover for her desire to have the children of a Mafia wiseguy. Linda's scheme soon paid off. While Charlie was at work, Linda and Scarpa would have sex.[28] Linda became pregnant, and Charlie believed the child to be his.[29] When "Little Linda" was born in June of 1969, Scarpa made a cash gift to Linda for the purpose of buying a house for the growing Schiro family. Linda lied to Charlie, again, this time telling him the money had come from her father.[30] Charlie did not question his family's good fortune as he, Linda, and Little Linda settled into their new home on 55th Street between 17th and 18th Avenues in Brooklyn, a place they would all call home for the first few years of Little Linda's life.[31]

Little Linda's recollections of those early years of her life include frequent visits to the Schiro home by Scarpa, whom she referred to as "Greggy" as a child.[32] Given the frequency of Scarpa's visits and the attention he was bestowing on a child that Charlie believed was not Scarpa's, Charlie Schiro finally grew suspicious enough to hire a private investigator.[33] By early 1971, Linda was pregnant again. When the investigator's work confirmed Charlie's suspicions, he confronted his pregnant wife.[34] While Linda did not deny Charlie's accusations, the confrontation did not, as one might reasonably assume, spell an immediate end to the bizarre charade of the Schiro marriage. It was not until after Joey's birth in September of 1971 that Charlie and Linda finally divorced.[35] It appears that the precipitating event was a comment by a nurse who, in the presence of the three adults in this strange triangle, commented on Joey's appearance while she was changing him. "'You know, Mr. Greg, this baby has your eyes and your ears.'"[36] At that point, apparently "two or three months after Joey was born, Charlie left."[37]

Scarpa, whose youngest son by his first wife was eight years old when his only son by his second wife was born, moved in after Charlie moved out.[38] At the age of forty-three, Scarpa would bring his particular brand of parenting skills to another young family.

GROWING UP SCARPA

GREGORY

Greg Scarpa and his first wife, Connie, had four children: Deborah, Gregory Jr., Bart, and Frank. Scarpa and Linda Schiro had two children, Linda and Joey. To understand Scarpa's relationship with the two children of his "third family," it is instructive to look at the upbringing of Gregory Jr., the only Scarpa child who followed his father into "the life" as a goodfellow, and the one who was closest to him as an adult.

Gregory Jr. was born in April of 1951, the second of his parents' four children. The Scarpa family lived in Brooklyn until 1960, when Gregory Jr. was in the third grade.[39] The family of five then moved to a large, five-bedroom house with a swimming pool on Staten Island.[40] As noted above, Connie selected the house after Scarpa urged her to pick out one that she could fix up exactly the way she wanted.[41] From that point on, Gregory was raised on Staten Island while his father worked in Brooklyn.[42] Wanting all of his children to be well-educated, Scarpa stressed attendance at school for Gregory and his brothers and sister.[43]

Gregory Jr. reports that when he, his older sister Deborah, and his younger brother Bart were quite young, their parents got along well and shared parenting duties.[44] Scarpa and Gregory Jr. did pushups and sit-ups together, and over time, Scarpa taught his namesake how to box.[45] Scarpa did not particularly value organized school sports, but he did encourage athleticism in his children. In essence, he "home-schooled" Gregory Jr. in a number of sports.[46] Scarpa's participation in his son's organized athletics outside of school was usually limited to being a spectator, although occasionally he would flash Gregory Jr. signs from the scorer's booth when his son was pitching for his Little League baseball team.[47] Back at home, Scarpa continued to teach his first son how to fight and protect himself. Gregory Jr. showed some talent as a boxer and at the age of fifteen, he "informed his father that he wanted to enter the Golden Gloves Tournament."[48] His fighting ability figured heavily in a pivotal moment in his young life.

While in high school, Gregory Jr. got into a scrape with another student after school one day shortly before his sixteenth birthday. As he recalled, the "other guy" got a good punch in, fair and square, that left a lump the size of a golf ball on his head. That night at home, Scarpa, on seeing what happened to his son, demanded that he beat the boy who gave him the lump the moment he saw him again. Gregory Jr. tried to demur, informing his father it was a fair fight, that it was not a big deal, that the cops broke up the fight, and when they did, he was losing.[49] Scarpa, however, insisted, telling him that if he did not put the boy in the hospital the next day he was not to come home. "My father was my world,"[50] Gregory reflected years later. So, he dutifully obeyed. The next day, as ordered, he beat the young man so badly that he was taken to the hospital for treatment. Not surprisingly, Gregory Jr. was suspended from school and charged with assault. Although the charges were later dropped, he never returned to school.[51] The alternative to continuing with his formal education was for his father to bring him on board, to bring him into "the life."

Gregory Jr. had harbored suspicions about his father's employment for a number of years. As a child, he had run across weapons, stacks of money, and what he later realized were FBI and NYPD documents in the family home.[52] From the age of eight, he had been a frequent visitor to the Wimpy Boys Social Club on 13th Avenue in Brooklyn, the headquarters for Scarpa and his crew.[53] Many of Scarpa's crew members would visit the Scarpa family at their Staten Island home for purely social gatherings.[54] Naturally, Gregory Jr. and his siblings tried to understand just what it was their father did for a living. His sister Deborah confided that she thought their father was in the Mafia. Gregory's response? "Debbie, if he is Mafia, it's a good thing. Don't worry about it."[55]

Scarpa would come home from time to time bearing duffel bags full of jewelry.[56] He told Gregory that if anyone were to ask, he should tell them his father was a jeweler.[57] At one point, when Gregory was quite young and playing with some stolen jewelry his father had brought home, John "Johnny Sap" Saponaro, a member of the Wimpy Boys crew, said to Gregory's mother, "Connie, your son is going to be just like us. He's going to be bad!" Connie was not amused. She snapped back, "Leave him alone, he's going to be a doctor or a lawyer."[58] Unfortunately, Johnny Sap's prediction for Gregory Jr.'s future was more accurate than that of his own mother.

When Gregory Jr. was a teenager, his father confessed to him that he was in the Mafia. Incredibly, he told his son in the same conversation that he also worked for the FBI, that it was his job to tell the Bureau everything he knew about the Mafia.[59] After Gregory's expulsion from high school, Scarpa moved quickly to formally bring his son into "the life." In 1967, on Gregory Jr.'s sixteenth birthday, Scarpa took him to meet Colombo family boss Joe Colombo at Cantalupo Realty on 86th Street in Brooklyn, where Colombo maintained an office. Colombo, who had seen Gregory fight, told him he was a good boxer, but there were better ways for him to make a living than taking shots to the head. Colombo then handed Gregory $500, which Scarpa promptly told him to return. Colombo's response was, "Who's the boss here?" Scarpa quickly changed his tune and told Gregory to put the money in his pocket.[60] It was Gregory Jr.'s first overt lesson in Mafia hierarchy, but it would not be his last.

As if to confirm his earlier confidence to his son about working for the FBI, Scarpa also introduced him to his first FBI handler, Anthony Villano, at a Police Athletic League center while Gregory was still a minor.[61] Gregory's recollection of his meeting with Villano tracks his meeting with Joe Colombo. Villano, like Colombo, praised Gregory Jr.'s fighting skills during the only meeting between the two of them. Villano then told him there was an easier way to make a living. He went on to suggest that he work for the FBI, like his father.[62] Gregory Jr., however, harbored a desire for a path that neither his father nor Special Agent Villano contemplated.

At the height of the Vietnam war, Gregory Jr. gave serious consideration to joining the U.S. Army.[63] Not surprisingly, his father opposed his eldest son's joining the military, and while Scarpa's motivations are unclear, his actions are not. He arranged to have a doctor who apparently never examined his son submit a medical report to the local draft board detailing alleged knee and back problems severe enough to have Gregory declared unfit for service except in the case of national emergency.[64]

Before reaching the age of majority, Gregory dropped boxing and started working full-time as a member of his father's crew. Scarpa turned over a portion of his $10,000 per week numbers business to his son, who proved to be a quick study. Gregory was soon making $2,000 per week on that action.[65] He wasn't only earning cash; he was also earning a reputation as a young man who could take care of himself, who enjoyed the perks of his recently acquired affluence, and who looked the part. He began to dress "like all the guys on 13th Avenue" in Brooklyn and at the age of seventeen, he bought a brand-new Corvette, which he traded in for a Cadillac a year later.[66] By the time he was eighteen, Gregory's adult life was mapped out in its broadest contours. For better or worse, his mother's dream of a legal profession for her eldest son would never be realized, his personal dream of joining the U.S. Army had been stymied, and he would follow his father, the man who was his world, into the life of a Mafia gangster to experience all of the crime, violence, and incarcerated misery that such a life practically guaranteed.

Linda Schiro gave birth to a daughter and namesake on June 21, 1969. As noted above, Charlie Schiro naturally assumed his wife was bearing his child. Charlie would not learn the truth about his children's parentage for another two years: Little Linda would not learn that Greg Scarpa Sr. was her biological father for more than a decade.[67]

The early years of Little Linda's life were otherwise much like those of millions of other American children during the 1970s. Her father, Greg Scarpa, went to work every day. He dressed well, required the same from those who worked for him, was always back at home in time for dinner, watched TV and played video games with his children, and rarely went back out after dinner.[68] Little Linda and her brother Joey would visit Scarpa at work. Sometimes they would get candy at a store across the street. They even got to go to the luncheonette with their father next door to where he worked.[69] And Scarpa, like many wealthy fathers, provided his daughter with a host of material possessions. As Little Linda recalled, she always had the nicest clothes and more possessions than her friends. She had her first fur coat at the age of six.[70] When she was a teenager and learned to drive, she had a Mercedes Benz.[71] She freely admitted that Scarpa spoiled her when she was growing up.[72]

When Linda was about seven years old, the family moved from their home on 55th Street to a new, nicer house on Avenue J in Brooklyn.[73] The trappings of an ordinary family life continued in their new home. Little Linda remembers holiday celebrations, her father making breakfast for friends and coworkers who stopped by, and many parties at a house that was often filled to the brim with people.[74] Like many young children, she and her brother were subject to some strict rules about school, friends, and behavior, but nothing out of the ordinary.[75] As a child living during the week with the man she assumed was her stepfather, Little Linda would often spend Sundays with Charlie Schiro, the man she thought was her biological father.[76] When Linda turned sixteen, Scarpa, her loving, caring, protective, and affectionate[77] father, "beamed" all through an extravagant Sweet Sixteen party he threw for her.[78] Outwardly, then, Scarpa's "third family" was not atypical of other mildly affluent families of the era.

But, of course, behind the façade, Little Linda's family was anything but ordinary. She and her brother never had to pay for the candy they got at the store across the street.[79] Her mother and father weren't married, and her father's wife was living on a horse farm in New Jersey.[80] Unlike most children, for years Linda was unsure what her father did for a living.[81] His office was in the Wimpy Boys Social Club, a place where criminal activity of nearly every stripe was planned and often executed, a place where murder was committed. Few friends attended Linda's Sweet Sixteen party out of fear of her father.[82] His coworkers, those men who came to Little Linda's house for breakfast and parties, were thieves, extortionists, burglars, and murderers who were either made men in the Colombo crime family or associates. Her stepbrother, Gregory Jr., who treated Little Linda with affection as he would treat a little sister, committed his first murder the same year she turned eleven.

As Little Linda grew older, the questions she had about her mother and father naturally became more sophisticated and less likely to be ignored or diverted by less than truthful answers. Like most teenagers, Linda started seeking her own identity and her independence. That search included using pot, which she started at the age of thirteen when she was still subject to a reasonable 9:00 p.m. curfew.[83] Scarpa, whose crew was heavily into dealing drugs on the streets by this time, forbade the presence of any drugs in his house.[84] One night, while Linda was still thirteen, she got so high that she had trouble getting home. She called Larry Mazza for help, and he agreed to give her a ride home.[85] When she arrived home, it was well after curfew and she was still thoroughly stoned.[86] Greg and Linda reacted to her intoxicated state as many parents would. They were angry, and a shouting match between daughter and parents ensued. At one point, after telling her parents she hated them, Linda threatened to go live with the man she still thought was her biological father, Charlie Schiro.[87] It was then that Scarpa and Linda Schiro revealed to their daughter who her biological father was.[88]

The next morning, Little Linda started to understand that violence was her biological father's go-to problem-solving method, a lesson Gregory Jr. learned to his detriment when he was fifteen. However, since the problem Scarpa now wanted to solve involved a daughter rather than a son, Scarpa would be meting out the violence, or ordering his crew to do so, rather than demanding the same of his child. Still boiling over with anger at the sight of his stoned daughter from the night before, Scarpa vowed to find out how she got ahold of the pot she had smoked.[89] True to his vow, he soon discovered the identity of the offending teen, his daughter's close friend Greg Vaca, who was promptly beaten to a pulp for his offense by members of Scarpa's crew.[90] Fortunately, they stopped short of killing him.[91] The pattern of violent retribution would repeat itself when Linda was nearly sixteen years old, although this time Scarpa's penchant for violence took his response to a real threat to her safety and welfare one step further.

When Little Linda was a sophomore at Bishop Ford Central Catholic High School,[92] she and her brother Joey would be driven to school every day by a "Brooklyn car service that her father had hired."[93] On a day that Joey was ill and stayed home, Linda rode to school without him. Her driver, as it was on most days, was José Guzman. Guzman, seeing that Linda was riding alone, suggested she sit up front with him, which she innocently did.[94] After making excuses that he had to pick up another passenger, Guzman, instead of driving Linda directly to school, drove to and parked in a secluded section of Brooklyn's Prospect Park.[95] At that point, he sexually assaulted her. He grabbed her hand and licked it, telling her, "'That's what I'm going to do to you, baby.'"[96] He then ripped Linda's shirt open. Naturally, Linda was in a panic as Guzman continued to grab and kiss her. Linda began to fear for her life. Somehow, something kicked in, and she miraculously regained her composure. She suggested they continue later, that he simply pick her up after school instead, and "we'll go somewhere. I'll make up something to tell my parents."[97] Linda's quick thinking saved her from further molestation and perhaps saved her life. Guzman fell for it. He broke off the attack and drove her to school, believing that the two of them were going to hook up at 2:30 that afternoon to finish what he had started.[98]

Once inside her school, Linda rushed to a payphone and called her mother, begging her to come get her and take her home.[99] When Linda Schiro picked her daughter up at Bishop Ford, she could tell from the shape she was in that she'd been attacked. "My face was flushed. My blouse was all untucked; my shirt was wrinkled. I was a mess."[100] What happened next, while not entirely clear in its particulars, is generally agreed upon in its broad outlines.

Reminiscent of the stories about Scarpa's alleged involvement in three FBI cases in Mississippi during the early 1960s, a number of differing accounts of the Guzman incident and its aftermath are currently in circulation. Linda Scarpa's first-hand account of the assault perpetrated on her by Guzman as summarized above is detailed, thorough, and credible. The facts behind the search for Guzman thereafter, and who undertook it, depend on who is telling the story. One account has Scarpa disguised as an old man gathering information on Guzman's whereabouts.[101] Another account has Linda Schiro going to the car company's offices and threatening the company dispatcher with a butcher knife for that information.[102] A third version, this one from eventual Colombo family consigliere Carmine Sessa, is that after having been told by the car company that Guzman quit, Scarpa "eventually" discovered his home address.[103] After Guzman was located, by whatever means, he was beaten. One account has Scarpa, feigning a limp and carrying a cane, beating Guzman with that cane in "the limo driver's office."[104] Larry Mazza gave a first-hand account in his book of Guzman's "savage beating" by members of Scarpa's crew, including Mazza, between the time the sexual assault occurred and when Guzman was murdered.[105] Mazza's version of the beating Guzman received and who administered it is not inconsistent with Harmon's retelling[106] or Little Linda's recollection.[107]

After Guzman was beaten, however that occurred, Scarpa was not satisfied with the degree of his punishment.[108] According to Mazza, Scarpa said, "'I shoulda' killed dat muttafucker.'"[109] Indeed, his violent response to Guzman's attempted rape of his daughter then escalated from aggravated battery to murder. According to Linda Scarpa, "my father and his crew went back to Guzman's house. They rang the bell. When he opened the door and saw them, he ran. But he didn't get too far. They shot him in the head."[110] Lin DeVecchio alleged in his book that Scarpa claimed he killed Guzman. "'I went back and killed him. I couldn't live with myself.'"[111] Carmine Sessa confessed to participating in Guzman's murder, stating that he and Gregory Scarpa Jr. shot Guzman.[112] That account is somewhat different from the account Larry Mazza alleged in his book, an account which Mazza claimed came from Gregory Jr. on the day Guzman was murdered. According to Mazza, Gregory bragged that he alone shot and killed Guzman.[113] Finally, as if to celebrate, Scarpa openly discussed Guzman's murder in the presence of his mistress, her two children, his eldest son, and Larry Mazza as they all ate dinner together that evening at Romano's, Scarpa's favorite Brooklyn restaurant.[114]

It is clear that the particulars of Scarpa's response to Guzman's attempt to rape Little Linda cannot be stated with certainty. However, what is not reasonably in dispute is that Guzman molested and attempted to rape Scarpa's and Linda Schiro's daughter, that she informed her parents of his attempt, that he was initially beaten for his offense either by Scarpa or on Scarpa's orders, and that he was eventually murdered, again on Scarpa's orders, in retaliation for that offense.[115]

By the time Little Linda Scarpa was eighteen years old, she knew that her biological father was Gregory Scarpa Sr. She knew he was "[o]ne of the most feared hit men in the New York mafia,"[116] and what he did for a living; and she knew he was capable of murder. When Greg Vaca provided Little Linda with pot and when José Guzman sexually molested her, Greg Scarpa's response was violence. Greg Vaca survived; José Guzman did not. In neither case did Scarpa demand that his daughter take matters into her own hands as he had with Gregory Jr. nearly twenty years earlier. Joey, Scarpa's youngest son, would find out that Scarpa's attitude toward responsibility for violent retribution on behalf of his children depended not on the original offender, but on the gender of his offended child.

Linda Schiro and Greg Scarpa's second child, Joey, was born on September 13, 1971. As noted above, Linda's pregnancy had aroused Charlie Schiro's suspicions about Greg and Linda. Those suspicions were confirmed by a private investigator before Joey was born, and shortly after Joey's birth, Charlie Schiro moved out and filed for divorce.

The early years of Joey Scarpa's[117] short life can be characterized in the same terms as those of his sister: the outward trappings of a normal, stable, somewhat affluent family, with the violence and infidelity typical of a dangerous mobster's family never far from the surface. In fact, Joey's life was tied to his criminal and violent future soon after his birth. Joe De Domenico, a well-liked member of Scarpa's crew and, within New York City's Cosa Nostra circles, a widely respected thief, became Joey's godfather.[118] By the time of Joey's baptism, De Domenico, who was commonly known as "Joe Brewster," had an arrest record nearly two pages long with twelve separate entries dating back to 1960.[119] As will be seen later in chapter six, Brewster was murdered on September 16, 1987,[120] shortly after Joey's sixteenth birthday, by Joey's half-brother on orders from Joey's biological father. Such was the reality behind the veneer of Joey Scarpa's life. And that reality kicked in even earlier than it had for his half-brother, Gregory Jr.

The first time Joey was likely cognizant of his father's violent nature occurred when he was four or five years old.[121] Joey came home in tears after being thrown off his bicycle by a local tough guy.[122] Scarpa's response to his youngest son's anguish had two parts to it. First, he gave Joey a bat and instructed him to hit the bully in the head with it.[123] Second, Joey was to tell the bleeding bully to get his father.[124] Joey took the bat from his father, but as any four- or five-year-old might do, he made peace with the errant youngster and ended up playing with him instead.[125]

Like his older sister, Joey spent time at the Wimpy Boys Social Club. Unlike his sister, Joey had to perform for attention and rewards.[126] As a child, Joey was a decent gymnast who was able to easily walk on his hands. Scarpa's crew used to bet on how far Joey could walk on his hands at the club. And, depending on how well he did, the crew members would reward him.[127] Even Scarpa's captain, Anthony "Scappi" Scarpati, delighted in teasing Joey at the club, a habit Scarpa silently resented.[128]

Joey was seven years old when his mother started an affair with Larry Mazza. As Mazza became closer to Scarpa's "third family," he would help Joey with his homework just as he had helped Linda with hers.[129] Mazza also tried to teach Joey karate.[130] When Joey was a young child, Mazza described him as a "cute little kid."[131] Mazza was even Joey's confirmation sponsor, and Joey took Larry's name as his confirmation name.[132]

> "Little Joey looked up to me like a big brother and loved to go places with me. I took him to the movies and ball games. I even had him join karate and Little League. These were things that his father neglected to do for him."[133]

When Joey was a teenager, Scarpa encouraged him to hang out with the Wimpy Boys crew at a time when the crew was increasingly drawn into the lucrative drug trade. In 1986, a mass arrest by the federal Drug Enforcement Agency temporarily decimated that growing segment of Scarpa's illicit economic engine. Nature abhors a vacuum, and by the time Joey was eighteen, he was dealing marijuana and cocaine with Scarpa's full knowledge.[134] The "cute kid" Mazza tutored and taught karate, who did gymnastics tricks for attention and gifts, was "brazen and using steroids to get bigger and bigger." As Mazza noted, Joey was "fueled by the violent reputation his father had."[135]

Six weeks after Joey's eighteenth birthday, he was involved in an altercation that would shape the rest of his life. The night before Halloween of 1989, Joey and some of his friends were pelted with eggs on a street corner near Our Lady of Guadalupe Church on 15th Avenue and 73rd Steet in Brooklyn.[136] The next night, Joey, his closest friend Patrick Porco, along with Ray Aviles and Craig Sobel, decided to roll past the church seeking revenge. Dominick Masseria, a seventeen-year-old, was standing in front of the church at its 15th Avenue entrance. Masseria, according to his family, had not been involved in the egg throwing the night before.[137] Regardless, as Joey, et al. rolled by in a white stretch limousine,[138] someone in the car[139] fired two shotgun blasts that struck Masseria in the head and chest, wounding him fatally.[140] Masseria "died at the scene."[141]

Ray Aviles, who was driving when the hit occurred,[142] turned himself in, gave "a somewhat sketchy account of the incident," and provided the names of the other three men in the car.[143] Joey and Patrick Porco headed for New Jersey to hide on Connie Scarpa's farm until the heat was off.[144] When they returned to Brooklyn less than three weeks later,[145] authorities began questioning Porco about the Masseria killing.[146] Eventually, word got back to Greg Scarpa Sr. that Porco was going to blame Joey for the Masseria killing. It was then that the almost unimaginable occurred. Scarpa, after a botched attempt on Porco's life by one of his crew members,[147] insisted that his eighteen-year-old son kill his own best friend.[148] Joey was ordered to commit murder. Scarpa, in that diabolical moment, ordered a child, his child, to kill his best friend. On May 27, 1990, Joey Scarpa did as ordered, killing his best friend and dumping his body in the street.[149]

Joey Scarpa's deep dive into a life that included dealing narcotics and murder would not last past March 20, 1995. On that date, Vinny Rizzuto ended Joey's life by putting two bullets into the back of his head.[150] Gregory Scarpa Sr. did not live long enough to feel the pain caused by his youngest son's murder, if indeed he was capable of such an emotion. That burden fell to his mistress, Linda Schiro, and Joey's sister, Little Linda, Greg and Linda Schiro's one surviving child.

ENTER LILI & LARRY

One would reasonably assume that being married to one woman who bore four of your children and living with your mistress with whom you had two more children, all the while having sworn a secret oath of loyalty to an extensive crime family, would more than suffice for anyone's relationship commitment needs. But, as has already been noted, enough was never enough for Greg Scarpa. So, when Little Linda Scarpa was almost six years old and her brother Joey was a toddler at about three and a half years, Scarpa officially became what years earlier he had suspected Joe Colombo of being: a bigamist.[151] Without having divorced Connie, and without breaking off his relationship with Linda Schiro, he married Lili Dajani in Las Vegas on February 2, 1975.[152]

Dajani was an Israeli. Her father was a Palestinian dentist; her mother was Jewish. Lili was a beauty contestant who was crowned Miss Jerusalem and went on to be a Miss Israel finalist in 1960.[153] At the time, she was "every Israeli man's dream."[154] She married for the first time in 1961, but the marriage failed.[155] Dajani, whose mother was from Santa Monica, California, eventually made her way to New York where, among other things, she managed an abortion clinic for Dr. Eliezer Shkolnik. Shkolnik, who lost his license to practice medicine in 1976,[156] and Dajani had become romantically involved while she was managing his clinic and, according to at least one source, were briefly married.[157] By the time Scarpa met Dajani at the Diamond Exchange in Manhattan during a meeting to discuss the sale of hot diamonds,[158] her relationship with Shkolnik, to his enduring dissatisfaction, had ended.

After Dajani married Scarpa, she formed a close bond with Gregory Jr., Scarpa's first son from his concurrent wife. Gregory would often visit her at her Manhattan apartment, and she would give him access to, and use of, her personal stretch limousine, all in white with flooring made from mink, at his convenience.[159] Dajani's personal wealth and independence worked to Scarpa's advantage by keeping her relationship with him sufficiently in the background of his marriage to Connie and his ongoing affair with Linda Schiro. Additionally, while he was married to Dajani, Scarpa was cementing his status as a father to Linda Schiro's and his children, Little Linda and Joey. And he continued to visit Connie on a more or less regular basis at the horse farm in Lakewood, New Jersey that he had purchased for her. Before the decade of the 1970s was out, another thread would be added to the growing tangle of Greg Scarpa's relationships. While Scarpa's dance card was arguably full, Linda Schiro's, apparently, was not.

In late 1978, perhaps as a way of evening the infidelity score with Scarpa, Linda sought and received permission from the father of her two children to enter into a sexual relationship with Larry Mazza,[160] a teenaged grocery delivery boy from Brooklyn whom Linda met while she shopped at his place of employment, Danza's Supermarket.[161] Linda, who had been divorced from Charlie Schiro since 1972,[162] was still raising her two children with Scarpa when she met Mazza. Little Linda was nine and Joey was seven when the affair with Mazza began. Linda and Mazza began having sex in Schiro's house regularly once she seduced him.[163] Remarkably, Mazza's presence and activities in the house were known to Scarpa,[164] and, as will be seen, Mazza eventually became Scarpa's closest crew member over the next dozen years. When his affair with Linda started in 1978, however, Mazza was an eighteen-year-old who had just finished high school and was looking forward to following in his father's footsteps by becoming a firefighter. Instead, he found himself thrust into the middle of a complex familial web that consisted of three marriages, two small children, one divorce, and an extramarital affair. The web simplified a bit when Scarpa's marriage to Lili Dajani ended in divorce in 1983,[165] seven years after they tied the knot. Their divorce left Scarpa with a single wife and a mistress, and marked a clean break from a relationship that included the brutal murder of Dajani's former lover and employer, Dr. Eliezer Shkolnik, by Gregory Jr. and Joe Brewster on Scarpa's orders three years earlier.[166]

THE PAST AS PROLOGUE

Although there is much more to follow about how Greg Scarpa conducted his life and the brutal effects that conduct had on those who crossed his path, understanding how he ordered his personal life provides lasting insight into the depths and vigor of his narcissistic depravity. Drawing Gregory Jr. and Joey closer to him ensured that their lives, less than twenty-four years long in Joey's case, would be full of violence and misery, an outcome he viewed with shocking detachment. As if to affirm the path he had chosen as a young man, Scarpa imposed that path on those closest to him regardless of the penalty they would certainly pay.

His family life, to the extent that it exhibited a pattern, was characterized by an upward curve of demands on those around him. He ordered his oldest son at the age of fifteen to beat a young man and put him in the hospital. Incredibly, he ordered his youngest son to do the same when he was only four or five years old. He ordered his oldest son to murder a stranger when he was nearly thirty years old. And he monstrously demanded that his youngest son murder his closest friend when he was only eighteen. His reckless response to Little Linda's typical youthful transgression had the predictable effect of isolating her from an organic system of friendship and support just as she was becoming a young woman. And his fatal response to her being assaulted three years later left no doubt in his daughter's mind about her father's violent capabilities.

Scarpa's gradually accelerating destruction of family members was not limited to his offspring. He had been involved with a mistress for more than a dozen years, and he had fathered six children by two different women when he became a bigamist, realistically just the next level up on the infidelity scale. His cavalier attitude toward the sexual relationship between his mistress, who was raising their two children, and Larry Mazza speaks to his narcissistic view of everyone in his orbit as nothing more than an object. Linda's request that she be allowed to take Mazza to bed can easily be read as a hopeful cry that Scarpa would disapprove, that he would value her enough to reject such a proposal, that his emotional attachment to her after sixteen years during which he would not divorce his wife was real, even profound. When he failed to disapprove, she went at it with gusto, arguably seeking revenge for Scarpa's psychological shrug at her version of infidelity through aggressive sex with a man half her age in the home she built for Scarpa and their children.

It has been said that when you're a hammer, everything looks like a nail. Perhaps it follows that when you're an insatiable, self-absorbed hammer, each nail must be bigger than the last. Gregory Jr.'s description of his father as a "powerful force of nature"[167] expresses a similar idea with an important exception. Scarpa's "wrecking force" was anything but natural. Most, but by no means all, normally functioning humans have a natural regard at the very least for those closest to them, which restrains their worst impulses, which draws out their empathy and compassion. On the surface, Scarpa was often able to imitate those standard familial leanings. But like most imitations, his was a cheap veneer that failed to obscure his self-serving appetites even as they resulted in the ruin of those closest to him. As will be seen, Scarpa's greed and violence, always central to his existence to some degree, became unbounded during the 1980s and beyond, when he was a juggernaut of treachery and murder, acting with virtual impunity until the very last years of his life.

CHAPTER SIX: MY THREE SONS

Children, even those of vicious gangsters, eventually become adults, responsible for their own actions, answerable to society at large rather than the nuclear family which brought them along from the time they were born. As has already been established, two of Gregory Scarpa's biological sons followed him into a life of crime and violence. A third man, Joe De Domenico, aka Joe Brewster, had the dubious honor of being like a son to Scarpa. It is perhaps not surprising that these three men who were as close as anyone to Scarpa had their adult lives ruined or ended by him. One was executed at the age of forty-four on Scarpa's explicit orders. One was incarcerated for nearly thirty-three years beginning at the age of thirty-eight for the crimes he had committed as a Colombo family member, first as a goodfellow and then as a capo; and one was gunned down at the age of twenty-three by rival drug dealers. Adulthood was a brutal experience for all three of them, and a brief experience for two of them.

JOE BREWSTER

Joe Brewster, born Joseph Anthony De Domenico in Brooklyn, New York on October 29, 1942,[1] had been close to Scarpa since 1962.[2] His favored status in Scarpa's orbit was due primarily to his skills as a smart, innovative, and productive thief.[3] Besides being a top-notch thief, he was a "handsome, charming, good-hearted guy,"[4] "a reliable and loyal friend, and a remarkably skilled and efficient killer."[5] He was one of only "two people who knew everything about Scarpa."[6] The two men were so close that Scarpa was the best man at Brewster's wedding.[7] "Scarpa Sr. referred to Brewster as his 'second son.'"[8] Brewster, for his part, was the best man at Gregory Scarpa Jr.'s 1971 wedding to Diane Dimino.[9] In fact, Brewster was so close to Gregory Jr. that he and his girlfriend accompanied the newlyweds on their honeymoon to Hawaii and Las Vegas![10] Scarpa trusted Brewster as much as he trusted his own son.[11] As noted in chapter five, Joe Brewster was godfather to Scarpa's youngest son, Joey, who was born in September of 1971. Brewster would even accompany Linda Schiro and her two children, Little Linda and Joey, on family vacations to Florida.[12] Linda Schiro called Joe Brewster Greg Scarpa's "best friend," and reported that Scarpa said he "loved that guy."[13] Best man, best friend, godfather—the sort of lifelong relationship yearned for in its absence, and treasured during its presence.

A FRIEND IN DEED

However, the foundation of the relationship between Greg Scarpa and Joe Brewster was criminal rather than familial. Brewster was a made man in the Colombo family,[14] and Scarpa was his sponsor.[15] As far back as 1967, when Brewster was arrested on Cape Cod for petty theft from public telephones, Scarpa showed up to bail him out.[16] And as detailed in chapter four above, by the summer of 1970, Scarpa and Brewster were engaged in a scheme to produce and sell counterfeit IBM stock certificates with a face value of $10,000,000. Although the charges were mysteriously dismissed as to both Scarpa and Brewster, it is difficult to come away from reading the FBI's case file without a sense of the close criminal relationship between the two men.

That relationship went well beyond theft and fraud; it included the most heinous of crimes, premeditated murder. Three examples stand out. In 1980, Brewster and Gregory Jr., on Scarpa's orders, murdered Dr. Eliezer Shkolnik, the former lover of Scarpa Sr.'s second wife Lily Dajani.[17] In July of 1982,[18] once again on Scarpa's orders, Joe Brewster and Scarpa murdered Alfred Longobardi, a limo driver who had had the temerity to insult Gregory Jr.[19] And in 1984, Brewster participated in the murder of Mary Bari, the girlfriend of Allie Boy Persico. Persico was in hiding, and he and his brother Carmine were worried that Bari would disclose his location to the FBI. [20] Scarpa personally shot and killed her in Carmine Sessa's social club, Occasions, in Brooklyn. These three killings, which have become relatively infamous, are undoubtedly not the only ones Joe Brewster participated in as a result of his close ties to Greg Scarpa. For instance, Gregory Scarpa Jr. alleged that Brewster executed a crew member whom Scarpa's first handler, Anthony Villano, claimed was ready to become an informant for the FBI,[21] and Linda Scarpa, many years after the fact, became aware that when Joe Brewster accompanied her family on trips to Florida it was for the purpose of killing someone while in Florida.[22]

Any relationship with Greg Scarpa was bound to be unusual and complex. And from the early 1960s on, Scarpa's relationships, the vast majority of which were with men who had chosen a life of crime, were rendered more complex by his status as an FBI informant. His connection to Joe Brewster was no exception. For instance, on November 9, 1970, in a conversation with his FBI handler, Scarpa reported a burglary believed to have been committed by Brewster and Joe "the Mutt" Mutoli. The two men were accused by other Cosa Nostra members of stealing a coin collection from someone close to Carmine Persico, a Colombo *caporegime* at the time who was notorious for being vengeful and violent. Brewster and Mutoli were targeted for execution until family boss Joe Colombo became convinced that Brewster had nothing to do with the burglary, that Mutoli acted on his own and by himself. Persico asked for and received permission to hit Mutoli, who was then murdered for his transgression.[23] Irrespective of whether Brewster was in fact involved in the burglary, it would appear that Scarpa, who was as close as anyone to Joe Colombo, likely went to bat for his close friend in a way that probably saved his life.

At the same time, however, Scarpa had no qualms about including Brewster in a clandestine report to the FBI, clearly a betrayal in the eyes of anyone bound by the Mafia's code of silence. Likewise, in January of 1972, shortly before Scarpa and Brewster would find themselves mutually targeted by federal law enforcement for their clumsy gambit to counterfeit and sell millions of dollars of IBM stock certificates, Scarpa reported to the FBI that Brewster and others in Scarpa's crew were "involved in a counterfeiting deal concerning control of several million dollars of counterfeit ten- and one-hundred-dollar bills with plates."[24] In short, Scarpa gave the FBI potentially inculpating information about a man who had just become his youngest son's godfather. The FBI, for its part, believed Scarpa as it nearly always did, noting in a report two months later once again that "Informant [Scarpa] is considered to be emotionally stable and reliable and has not furnished any information known to be false."[25]

Nothing in the available record indicates any friction between Scarpa and Brewster as of early 1972. The FBI's investigation into the counterfeit IBM stock case had yet to focus on them and would not do so for nearly a year. Although the scheme did not pay off as its participants had hoped, so far as they knew in January of 1972, they were in the clear. For whatever reason, Scarpa's loyalty to a man he claimed to love like a son was not nearly as strong as one might reasonably expect. It did not prevent him from providing the FBI with damaging information about Joe Brewster. It is important to remember that the FBI was then paying Scarpa on a C.O.D. basis. The amount he was paid was a function of the quantity and quality of the information he provided. "Every effort should be made to utilize this informant's services to develop data regarding violations withing the Bureau's jurisdiction. **Payment should be varied in line with the value of his services.**"[26] Scarpa's primary loyalty was always to himself regardless of the expectations of others, even those closest to him. And, as noted above, by his son's own account he was a man in love with money more than anything else.[27] If fattening his paycheck from the FBI called for selling out his dear friend Joe Brewster, so be it.

BANKS AND BULLETS

Brewster's usefulness, however, extended beyond being fodder for Scarpa's enrichment as an FBI informant. He was, by all accounts a skilled burglar,[28] a "bank burglary expert"[29] whose heists over the years made him "one of the top earner's in [Scarpa's] crew."[30] His career as a bank burglar went a long way to account for his value to the Colombo family in general, and to Greg Scarpa in particular. The Scarpa crew "committed more than a dozen bank burglaries."[31] One of Brewster's strategies was ridiculously simple.

> "Brewster, one of the crew's biggest earners, put an employee at a burglar alarm company on the Scarpa's [sic] payroll. Every few months, the 'alarm guy' would disable the alarms at a vulnerable branch bank in Brooklyn or Queens. Once the alarms were off, the crew would burrow into the bank from a nearby vacant house or break through the bank's weakest armored door…"[32]

Scarpa informed the FBI about a similar strategy being used by the New York Mafia, one that involved more risk for the burglary crew but less exposure for the alarm company employee. Crew members would learn about a particular bank's alarm system from the alarm company's employee, enabling the crew to bypass it and enter the bank otherwise undetected.[33] A third approach, more sophisticated than either of the two above, involved buying an alarm system that was used in a particular bank to learn how to disarm it before burglarizing the bank.[34] Finally, another relatively sophisticated strategy, one that Scarpa once again revealed to the FBI, involved purchasing a meter which would shut down an alarm's wiring system without disturbing the remote reading on the other end.[35]

The most consequential of the bank burglaries attempted by Scarpa's crew involving Joe Brewster was a failed second shot at a Dime Savings Bank branch located in a Queens strip mall over Presidents' Day weekend in February of 1984.[36] According to Larry Mazza, a participant in the burglary, all was going well until "more NYPD cars, marked and unmarked, than you would see at an Al Sharpton rally" showed up.[37] Carmine Sessa, Bobby Zambardi, and Joe Brewster were arrested at the scene and spent the rest of the holiday weekend in jail before making bail. Initially, blame for the failed operation fell on Brewster. He had parked his car, a "brand-new Coupe DeVille, with New Jersey plates, right in the [otherwise empty] mall parking lot. It stuck out like a sore thumb and didn't go unnoticed by the law."[38] Scarpa and capo Anthony Scarpati held Brewster personally responsible and had no qualms expressing their severe displeasure.[39] It later became clear that Brewster was not to blame. A suspicious bank officer had a back-up alarm installed without informing either ADT, where the crew's inside man worked, or the bank's president.[40] In Scarpa's mind, however, the operation's failure was due entirely to Brewster's poor parking choice. He never forgave him, and the relationship between Greg Scarpa and Joe Brewster, whether familial or criminal, came to a violent end on September 16, 1987.

Once again, a number of different versions of Joe Brewster's murder exist. However, they all have Gregory Jr. as the trigger man, killing Brewster on his father's orders. The versions diverge when it comes to the details of the hit. Larry Mazza wrote that Brewster was murdered in the front seat of his own 1983 Coupe DeVille.[41] Harmon had Brewster in the back seat of a stolen 1982 Buick Regal.[42] The *New York Daily News* reported that the white Buick Regal Brewster was found dead in was his,[43] a point McGuire made in his book about Carmine Imbriale.[44] Lance and DeVecchio described the killing as taking place in a white Oldsmobile Cutlass.[45] DeVecchio wrote that the Cutlass was stolen.[46] As noted above, Gregory Scarpa Jr., who was riding shotgun while Brewster rode in the back seat, pulled the trigger.[47] He either shot his good friend four times as a forensic pathologist testified twenty years later, once each through his right temple, through one eye, in his mouth, and in his chest,[48] or "twice in the head, twice in the chest,"[49] or "over a dozen times in the head and neck."[50]

Mazza's version of the hit is largely hearsay. McGuire and Imbriale relied on newspaper accounts, Imbriale's personal conversations with Brewster, and sworn testimony from Mario Parlagreco, Carmine Sessa, and a forensic pathologist.[51] Lance relied heavily on DeVecchio and the Brooklyn DA for his account.[52] And while Harmon's version presumably came from an interview with a participant in Brewster's murder, Gregory Scarpa Jr., DeVecchio's detailed account of the murder from beginning to end makes the most sense overall to this author.[53]

According to Linda Schiro, Scarpa was disconsolate over his friend's killing. "Greg suffered over the death of his best friend, but blamed him for signing his own death warrant. "'That fucking guy,' he told Linda late on the night of the murder. 'I don't know why he had to do this. Joe was such a great guy. I loved that guy.'"[54] Incredibly, however, Scarpa met with his FBI handler the day after Brewster's murder and provided the FBI with few details other than the fact of the murder and what Scarpa alleged as the rationale for it.[55] What is jarring is that Scarpa also provided the FBI with other information, some of it routine and some of it about other alleged murders, during the same interview.[56] If Scarpa was somehow shaken by his good friend's murder the day before, either he hid it well during his debriefing the next day, it escaped his handler's notice, or his handler made no note of it in the FBI's files. The entries after Scarpa's description of Brewster's murder are business as usual and the entry about Brewster's murder is itself almost banal.

"On September 17, 1987,[57] source advised that Joe 'Brewster' De Domenico was hit on September 16, 1987 due to his association and narcotics dealing [redacted] Further, Brewster also made a burglary score and failed to cut in his capo, and then denied that he had participated in the burglary. The source said that Junior Persico ordered the hit as a result of the above."[58]

Astonishingly, Scarpa's handler, Special Agent Lindley DeVecchio, does not record anything further regarding Brewster's murder. Presumably DeVecchio was familiar with the relationship between Scarpa and Brewster. DeVecchio's report did not mention that Brewster was a long-time member of Scarpa's Wimpy Boys crew. Although he reported, as he was undoubtedly told by Scarpa, that Carmine Persico had ordered the hit, DeVecchio used the passive voice to report that Brewster "was hit." Nothing indicates DeVecchio asked about the killer's identity. In many instances, Scarpa provided DeVecchio specific information about who pulled the trigger when a fellow Mafioso was hit.[59] In the Brewster case, there is not a word about the killer, nor is there any indication that DeVecchio asked him about that particularly salient point. It is also important to remember that Carmine Persico was incarcerated at the time, a fact DeVecchio would have been aware of, and had no ability to personally confirm the allegations about Brewster's actions. This is not to argue that DeVecchio had a hand in Brewster's murder; it is merely to point out the hands-off approach DeVecchio took with Scarpa, his prized informant, after learning that one of Scarpa's closest associates, a man who was like a son to Scarpa, had been murdered by someone for one reason or another the day after that murder. DeVecchio's lengthy narrative in his book about the murder bears no resemblance to his curt, almost nonchalant FBI file report about Brewster's killing. The best reading of his book's narrative is that it is based on information DeVecchio obtained years after the murder, and that it is a sophisticated attempt to absolve himself of any responsibility for Brewster's death.[60] Whatever DeVecchio's role may or may not have been, there is little question that primary responsibility for Brewster's death lies with Greg Scarpa.

THE WHYS AND WHEREFORES

How Joe Brewster was killed is not nearly as controversial as *why* he was killed. After all, what does it matter what kind of car Brewster was in when he was murdered? It certainly did not matter to him. What difference does it make if he was shot four times or a dozen times at point blank range or where each bullet entered his body? When the shooting stopped, Joe Brewster was dead at the age of forty-four. But the answers to the question "Why was Joe Brewster killed?" vary in ways that are significant in terms of ultimate culpability and, for lack of a better expression, degrees of evil. Why was this man, whose relationship with Greg Scarpa went back nearly twenty-five years to when Brewster was barely twenty years old, a man Scarpa was willing to bail out for a ridiculous petty crime, a man who was as close to Scarpa and his families as anyone could claim, a man who participated with Greg Scarpa in every type of criminal activity imaginable from petty theft to premeditated murder, a man who was willing to kill for Greg Scarpa and did so on several occasions, the target of a hit ordered by Greg Scarpa? Once again, it depends who you ask.

According to Sandra Harmon the trouble started in 1987, when FBI Special Agent Lin DeVecchio reported to Scarpa that Joe Brewster had developed a drug habit.[61] Harmon also wrote that DeVecchio relayed to Scarpa rumors that Brewster was going to start talking to federal law enforcement, a particularly troubling allegation considering it meant that DeVecchio would have been selling out a potential FBI source to an existing one. Harmon continued that Brewster was burglarizing banks without informing Scarpa, a breach in and of itself.[62] However, the more serious implication would be that Brewster was not cutting Scarpa in on the take from those jobs. Harmon added another breach to the list of Brewster missteps by claiming that he refused to commit a murder Scarpa had ordered him to carry out. According to Harmon, Brewster claimed his new girlfriend was a born-again Christian, that he was sharing her "spiritual journey," and, in tears, told Scarpa he could no longer kill.[63] Based on all of the above, Harmon wrote that DeVecchio concluded Brewster could no longer be trusted and had to be killed, the sooner the better.[64] As a result, again according to Harmon, Scarpa and Gregory Jr. agreed that Brewster had to be eliminated and Carmine Persico authorized the hit.[65]

Peter Lance, the author of *Deal with the Devil*, chronicled the Brooklyn DA's and Lin Devecchio's views on what triggered Brewster's murder.

> "Brewster's increased use of cocaine, his refusal to do a murder on Greg, Sr.'s orders, his new-found interest in religion, and his refusal to cut [Scarpa] Senior in on burglary scores he was reportedly doing on his own."[66]

Lance added Linda Schiro's allegation, which she testified to at DeVecchio's trial that "it was Lin's confirmation of Scarpa's suspicions that sealed Brewster's fate."[67] Lance also noted, with a good deal of skepticism, DeVecchio's claim that Scarpa sought, and eventually received, permission to kill Brewster from Carmine Persico via Scarpa's capo, Anthony "Scappi" Scarpati.[68]

Linda Scarpa wrote that at the time of Joe Brewster's murder he was drinking heavily, but the main reason he was killed was that he was a born-again Christian and no longer wanted to be in "the life." According to Linda Scarpa, DeVecchio told her father that Brewster had to go, and he agreed.[69] McGuire and Imbriale put a finer point on what

Lance called Brewster's "new-found interest in religion," claiming that Brewster "'was never a born-again Christian like they said,'" but his recently developed remorse of his own participation in murder led him to "'to start back at church, even [make] a shrine in his house, with saints and candles.'"[70]

Larry Mazza dismissed nearly all of the above-stated reasons for Brewster's murder. Mazza's version of the events leading up to the killing included allegations about Brewster's refusal to murder an unrepentant coke dealer and his sudden religious conversion, presumably at the urging of his latest girlfriend. Mazza was not convinced that Brewster's murder had anything to do with either of those reasons. In fact, he wrote that Brewster's refusal to carry out the ordered hit was simply the result of his not wanting to involve himself in the drug wars of the mid-1980s. Mazza's theory is that "it was all bullshit," that Brewster was killed for one reason only, failing to cut Scarpa and Gregory Jr. in on burglaries Brewster committed on his own that in total "amounted to more than a million dollars."[71] "They were upset they didn't get an end, so they made up a story about Joey [Brewster] refusing to kill. They knew that the Family would okay it that way."[72]

Without alluding to any specific amount of money acquired via burglaries, Carmine Imbriale, a man who worked with and for Brewster for a number of years, echoed Mazza's views on why Brewster was murdered. "'That was all bullshit,' Carmine says. 'Greg was a greedy pig and suspected Joe was not sharing from some of his robberies.'"[73] Mazza alleged he learned the real reason behind Brewster's murder from John Saponaro who, according to Mazza, was "disgusted that he had to be part of the hit," over lunch one day. However, Imbriale and DeVecchio alleged in their accounts that Joe Saponaro,[74] not John, was in on the hit.

According to DeVecchio, Saponaro planted the .38 used by Gregory Jr. to kill Brewster under the passenger seat of the stolen Cutlass. Furthermore, again according to DeVecchio, Joe Saponaro drove the car, a point Carmine Imbriale agreed on, and was thus present during the shooting, and he assisted with disposal of Brewster's body.[75] Of course, it is possible that both Saponaro brothers played some part in Brewster's murder, which would have given them firsthand knowledge of how it occurred.

It is impossible to determine the motivation behind Joe Brewster's murder thirty-six years after the fact. The memories of those who were involved and are still living are tainted by the passage of time and their own bias. Greg Scarpa Sr.'s motive for wanting Joe Brewster dead could have been as simple as greed, as Mazza and Imbriale argued. That motive certainly fits with the portrait of Scarpa that has emerged during this author's research. Its simplicity is also attractive. And it is entirely plausible that Scarpa, a master manipulator, embellished that simple motive to make Brewster's killing more palatable to those involved, at least from a Cosa Nostra point of view. Scarpa's capo, Anthony Scarpati, allegedly said that Brewster's religious conversion was "one step away from being a rat."[76] Carmine Persico, Colombo family boss, similarly quipped, "If he found God, it is time for him to join God."[77] Were all of the other allegations of heavy drinking, narcotics dealing, and disobeying an order to kill simply window dressing? Thirty-six years later, it is impossible to know for certain. What is certain is that Greg Scarpa wanted Joe Brewster dead, and his eldest son, Gregory Scarpa Jr., pulled the trigger when his father ordered him to do so.

GREGORY SCARPA JR.

Joe Brewster's life came to a violent end when he was forty-four years old. Gregory Scarpa Jr., the man who shot Brewster, was indicted two months later in November of 1987, and remained free as a fugitive until he was apprehended in Lakewood, New Jersey at about 2:00 a.m. in the morning on August 29, 1988.[78] At the age of thirty-seven, his life as a free man, as a feared goodfellow and then a capo in the Colombo family, the only life he had known as an adult, came to an end. He would spend more than thirty-two years incarcerated in a variety of institutions until, on November 11, 2020, he was granted a compassionate release while suffering from late-stage nasopharyngeal cancer.[79]

Gregory started working for his father at the age of sixteen. The FBI's files on his father note some minor law enforcement contacts with Gregory Jr. before the age of twenty-two. For instance, a *New York Daily News* article from August 6, 1971, alleges that Gregory knocked down a police officer with his car and then took off speeding. As a result, he was facing a felonious assault on a policeman charge, driving with improper plates, driving without a license, reckless driving, failure to keep to the right, and resisting arrest.[80] The same set of FBI files took note of an article in *The Staten Island Advance* from October 3, 1972, chronicling Gregory's guilty plea to a charge of attempted assault and his conditional release.[81] Those two brief contacts provided little insight into what was in store for Gregory and New York's LCN underworld for the next fifteen years.

Gregory Scarpa Jr. became an official goodfellow, a "made man," in 1977, the year he turned twenty-six. According to Larry Mazza, Gregory Jr. was a legitimate tough guy who, unlike others in Mazza's experience, did not hide behind the fact that he was a made man in one of New York's five families.[82] Gregory was eventually elevated to the position of capo, in charge of his own crew, in the Colombo family.[83] He married three times, fathered at least four children, owned a night club, conspired to commit or personally committed at least six, and possibly more[84] murders, and made a small fortune as a drug dealer.[85]

Scarpa Sr.'s genetic legacy to his eldest son was his physique. Gregory Scarpa Sr., prior to becoming ill in 1986, was "a robust five feet ten, with the compact body of a 200-pound wrestler."[86] Gregory Jr. was "five feet ten inches, with massive arms, [and] a powerful chest."[87] Scarpa Sr.'s adulterous tendencies were passed on to Gregory Jr. the way many behaviors are passed from one generation to the next, by way of example. As part of his career legacy to his son, Scarpa purposefully taught him how to visit violence on his fellow human beings, up to and including murder. During the 1980s, Gregory Jr. added drug abuse to an already dangerous mix of character traits, and the results were personally tragic.

LOVE AND MARRIAGE

Gregory Sr.'s status as a role model for personal relationships, particularly those with women, was unconventional, to say the least, as has been chronicled above. By the time Gregory Jr. was a teenager, his father was intimately and regularly involved with Linda Schiro while continuing to be married to his first wife, Connie, Gregory's mother. Before Gregory's first foray into marriage, his father and Linda Schiro had a daughter together and another child, this time a son, was on the way. And of course, Scarpa Sr. was still married to Connie. They never divorced. Gregory Jr. and his first wife, Diane Dimino, had two daughters, Kori and Diane.[88] Their marriage ended shortly after their second daughter's birth.[89] Gregory's adultery and his suspicions that his wife was similarly engaged were major factors in his first marriage's failure.[90] In the meantime, Gregory's father committed bigamy by marrying for a second time while still married to Connie, all the while continuing his relationship with Linda Schiro and their two children. Two more marriages for Gregory Jr.—Lillian[91] and Maria—and two more children—Gregory III with Lillian and Maria with Maria—jealousies stemming from at least one blended family, more adultery and suspicion, and at times heavy cocaine by one spouse or the other or both proved to be the limit for Gregory Jr.[92]

DEADLY BUSINESS

BAPTISM BY FIRE

In 1980, when Gregory Scarpa Jr. turned twenty-nine, he had no illusions about the violent world he inhabited as a member of the Colombo crime family. However, he had yet to kill anyone. That was about to change.

As noted in chapter four, Dr. Eliezer Shkolnik never got over losing Israeli beauty queen Lili Dajani to Greg Scarpa Sr. His continuing infatuation with his former business partner and lover, even after her marriage to the man known as The Grim Reaper, prompted a series of poorly-considered actions that ultimately cost Shkolnik his life. As Shkolnik's discontent continued to gnaw at him, he attempted to even the playing field. He allegedly contacted an old friend, a Genovese family goodfellow, hoping to enlist his help in getting Scarpa to stay away from Dajani. His friend wisely told him he should drop the matter.[93] Instead, Shkolnik foolishly pressed on. He either threatened to go to the FBI about Scarpa[94] or started providing the IRS with information about Dajani and Scarpa.[95] Either way, Shkolnik's active refusal to accept the status quo sealed his fate.

Word got back to Scarpa that Shkolnik was making waves that implicated one or more offices of the federal government. Scarpa's go-to solution to the risk Shkolnik's continued existence posed was, of course, murder. This time, he sent his eldest son on his first hit to take care of the festering Dr. Shkolnik problem.[96] Gregory Jr., accompanied and assisted by Joe Brewster, shot and killed Dr. Shkolnik on December 3, 1980, in the lobby of Shkolnik's parents' Forest Hills apartment.[97] Gregory's entry into the dark world his father inhabited was complete. However, his first murder would not be the last he committed at his father's command, even when his distorted conscience urged him to disobey.

WHO'S THE BOSS?

As tough and as ruthless as Gregory was, he was still no match for his father, even though he eventually rose above him in the Colombo family hierarchy. "Although it's true that I was a capo and Dad was just a 'soldier,' my father was meaner than anyone I've ever met. I always knew that if I disrespected him in any way, or crossed him in any way, no matter how long it took him, he would have found a way to make sure I would one day be found dead."[98] Indeed, the murder of Alfred Longobardi in July of 1982 was a deadly replay of Scarpa's insistence that his eldest son take overwhelming violent revenge on a high school classmate fifteen years earlier.

The circumstances leading to the Longobardi hit, once again, depend on who is doing the telling. In the summer of 1981, Longobardi was either a Staten Island mobster who did not appreciate the fact that Gregory was running a successful nightclub, On the Rocks, in his territory.[99] Or he was a limousine driver who got drunk one night and threatened[100] or insulted Gregory at that same nightclub.[101] Or he was a Staten Island tough guy with a reputation for violence and a big mouth who shot Gregory in the ass outside of On the Rocks after an exchange of words inside the nightclub.[102] Whether Longobardi fired off an insult, a threat, or a round from a .38, the incident cost him his life. Who ordered the hit is also in dispute. Either Scarpa Sr. "put a contract out on Longobardi's life for disrespecting Gregory,"[103] or Gregory, at least initially, "planned to kill Longobardi personally."[104] The most interesting version of how the hit was ordered comes from Larry Mazza, whose version indicates he was present for the exchange between Gregory and his father.

According to Mazza, Longobardi, after some "[w]ords were exchanged," followed by some "pushing and shoving," shot Gregory in his posterior.[105] Gregory, who was not seriously injured, downplayed and tried to diffuse the entire matter. He told his father, "it's no big deal."[106] But Scarpa, feeling that his son had been seriously disrespected, insisted on Longobardi's death. "'NO BIG DEAL!' Senior exploded... 'You're a Goodfella, for crying out loud... You're not supposed to get shot... in the fuckin' ass!'"[107] As with the incident that resulted in Gregory's expulsion from high school, Scarpa's will overpowered that of his son. Longobardi was hit a year later, and Gregory would ultimately be charged with his murder.[108] Longobardi's face was shot away by his killer or killers. "[t]o send a message about 'respect.'"[109] When Alfred Longobardi's family came for his body, they could only identify him through his tattoos.[110]

As ruthless as the Brewster and Longobardi murders were, the murder of Mary Bari stands alone for its cold-blooded brutality.

THE GATES OF HELL

Unlike so many of the other moments that comprised Greg Scarpa Sr.'s life, there seems to be general agreement about what happened to Mary Bari. Perhaps the unvarnished truth is so shocking that adding something to the story of her killing to make it more sensational is simply not possible. That does not mean no one tried. For instance, shortly after the murder, Carmine Sessa's wife, Annie, told Linda Schiro that Mary Bari's ear had been shot off, and that a small dog she brought to the "interview" with her found the ear, with an earring still in it, and brought it to Scarpa Sr. Scarpa, the story went, took the ear from the dog, removed the earring, and put that in his pocket. None of that happened. The story was Scarpa Sr.'s idea of a joke to play on his mistress.[111]

Mary Bari was the girlfriend of Alphonse "Allie Boy" Persico, Carmine "The Snake" Persico's brother. They met in 1969, when Mary was about to turn sixteen and Allie Boy, then a married man, was close to twice her age. Soon after they met, they began a relationship that lasted for nearly a dozen years. In 1980, facing the prospect of significant prison time on a loansharking and extortion conviction, Allie Boy disappeared, and the family cut Mary off.[112]

By 1984, rumors were circulating about Mary's willingness to cooperate with law enforcement. The rumors included accusations that she was "an informant" who was "being targeted to cooperate,"[113] or that she may have talked to the FBI,[114] or that she, in fact, had been communicating with federal law enforcement officers,[115] or that she knew where Allie Boy was hiding and was going to talk to the police,[116] or that she was dating a police officer and might let Allie Boy's hideout slip,[117] or, finally, that she was considering dating an FBI agent.[118] In DeVecchio's far-fetched account of the entire Mary Bari matter, which often included her personal thoughts, even about Greg Scarpa's "animal magnetism" and "charisma,"[119] he offered an unsourced account of an alleged conversation Bari had with Junior Persico in which she admitted to going on a single, platonic date with a police officer to see a preview of the movie *Once Upon a Time in America*.[120] The primary thread of concern running throughout the various versions of suspicions about Mary Bari was that she might reveal Allie Boy's whereabouts, leading to his arrest.

FBI Special Agent Lin DeVecchio was one alleged source of the information Scarpa received about the possibility that Bari had been talking to law enforcement.[121] The allegation included DeVecchio's advice to Scarpa in light of Bari's law enforcement contacts. Referring to the possibility of Bari giving up Allie Boy's location, Linda Schiro testified that DeVecchio told Scarpa Sr., "'You have to take care of this.'"[122] For his part, Gregory Jr. did not believe that Mary Bari had or would provide any information to law enforcement. "'Mary Bari was a stand-up girl. There was no way she was going to cooperate.'"[123]

NYPD Detective Tommy Dades, a Brooklyn native who had known Mary Bari and her family for years, interviewed Gregory Scarpa Jr. a number of times as he prepared for his testimony in the 2007 trial of DeVecchio.[124] During one of those interviews, Gregory corroborated Schiro's testimony that DeVecchio provided Scarpa Sr. with information alleging Bari was an informant. However, Gregory did not relate a conversation between DeVecchio and Scarpa in which DeVecchio allegedly stated that Scarpa had to "take care of" the Bari problem. According to Dades, that proposition came to Gregory Jr. from Scarpa Sr.[125] Of course, it is possible that Schiro was testifying about a conversation between Scarpa Sr. and DeVecchio for which Gregory was not present. However, the allegation that DeVecchio advised Scarpa Sr. that Bari had to be taken care of makes little sense. Why would DeVecchio, who had a personal and professional relationship with Scarpa Sr., want to prevent Alphonse Persico, a fugitive since 1980, from being apprehended?

Nothing in the record indicates that Persico's apprehension would have had negative consequences for Scarpa that DeVecchio was anxious to prevent. The only way the allegation makes sense is if one accepts that by 1984, DeVecchio was so far gone in terms of his loyalty to not only Scarpa specifically, but to the Colombo family in general, that he would have suggested it was necessary to kill Alphonse Persico's former girlfriend before she could reveal his whereabouts if she indeed possessed that information. Furthermore, if DeVecchio's assertions about his sophisticated understanding of mob life which run throughout his book are at all credible, he would have known there would be no need to make such a suggestion to Scarpa. Telling him that Bari was talking to the FBI would have sufficed. There would have been no need for him to gild that lily. In short, the allegation that DeVecchio suggested killing Bari to Scarpa Sr. strains credulity.

Additionally, nothing in his history indicates that Scarpa would care if Allie Boy Persico were found and apprehended. Recall that Scarpa willingly provided information to the FBI that led to the arrest of both family boss Joe Colombo Sr. and his son, Joe Colombo Jr. That information was in Scarpa's TECI file a decade before Bari's murder. DeVecchio would have, or at the very least should have, been familiar with that information. Hindsight is not necessary to reach the reasonable conclusion that a potential arrest of Alphonse Persico would not have been of any concern to Scarpa. Hindsight, however, does buttress that conclusion. As will be shown below, Scarpa also fed the FBI a steady stream of information attempting to tie Carmine Persico, Colombo's eventual successor as family boss, to multiple murders.

Regardless of the thin basis of the rumors about her, Scarpa Sr. "demanded the Bari execution." Moving Allie Boy, who was apprehended in 1987 in West Hartford, Connecticut,[126] rather than executing Mary Bari does not appear to have been discussed as a reasonable solution to the rumored dilemma. The hit happened on September 25, 1984,[127] at Carmine Sessa's club, Occasions.[128] Anthony "Tony Muscles" Frezza picked Mary up and drove her to Sessa's club.[129] She thought she was going to an interview with Sessa for a cocktail waitress job at his Bay Ridge nightclub and she dressed accordingly.[130] When she got to Sessa's club, she went inside. It was over quickly. Sessa and the two Scarpas were there to meet her. Both DeVecchio and Lance also placed Joe Brewster at Sessa's club for the murder.[131] Additionally, Lance included Bobby Zambardi in his version of the murder.[132] Larry Mazza, who was not present, did not place either Brewster or Zambardi at the hit. According to Mazza, Scarpa Sr., who provided him with the details of Bari's murder after the fact, claimed he had purposely kept Larry out of the hit and did not include Bobby Zambardi because "Bobby loves people too much."[133]

After a few standard social exchanges with Mary and some meaningless compliments from those present, Scarpa Jr., who was charged with Bari's murder as an underlying offense supporting the second Racketeer Influenced and Corrupt Organizations Act (RICO) prosecution the federal government brought against him,[134] put his arm around her and suddenly pulled her to the floor. Scarpa Sr. pulled out his .38 revolver and shot her three times in the face while his son held her down.[135] She died instantly.

Scarpa Sr. later told Larry Mazza that he had to be the shooter because "'he was the only one that... had the stomach for it.'"[136] The men at the club then wrapped her body up in "movers' blankets,"[137] or "'in a blanket or tarp'"[138] or "in canvas,"[139] and placed it in the trunk of Scarpa Sr.'s car.[140] He and Sessa eventually dumped her body on McDonald Avenue in Brooklyn, a couple of blocks from Scarpa Sr.'s house.[141] Her face was so disfigured that she could only be identified by her tattoo, that of a peach, a nickname Allie Boy had for her.[142]

When speaking about the Bari murder, Colombo capo Anthony "Scappi" Scarpati is alleged to have said, "We're probably going to go to hell for this."[143] If the men who plotted and killed Mary Bari were not already headed for hell, there can be little doubt that her execution put them on the fast track.

GATEWAY DRUGS

At one time, selling drugs was not only frowned upon by the Italian Mafia in the United States, it was strictly forbidden. Indeed, in January of 1963, Scarpa Sr. advised the FBI "that he has heard that the death penalty will be imposed for any member who is engaged in counterfeiting activities or in narcotics traffic."[144] That prohibition held for the rest of the decade. On December 17, 1969, Scarpa reported on a meeting between Joe Colombo and a small group of important family members during which Colombo "was surprised at all the 'heat' being brought on his family stating that 'they' should be grateful at the way his 'family' behaves, noting that he would not tolerate narcotics, prostitution, or disrespect in general."[145]

Joe Colombo's position regarding narcotics did not end with his shooting and incapacitation. The general prohibition regarding handling narcotics was echoed by Charles "Moose" Panarella at a meeting in May of 1973. "PANARELLA again instructed that the COLOMBO 'family' should not engage in prostitution, narcotics, counterfeiting or securities...."[146] The prohibition was not well enforced, and by 1974 Scarpa was aware of, and reported to the FBI the Gallos' involvement with "Cubans and South Americans in the narcotics trade...."[147] The Gallos were not alone in their quest for the easy money that trafficking narcotics could generate. By early 1981, Scarpa was reporting that the Genovese family "controls a major portion of the illegal narcotics activity in the New York city area."[148]

In spite of the increased narcotics activity by the New York LCN families, as of the summer of 1981, the bosses of the five families were still at least outwardly opposed to family members handling narcotics. Indeed, according to Scarpa Sr., Collie Di Pietro of the Genevese family was killed for dealing "large quantities of cocaine... as an example to other members of the Genovese family not to deal in narcotics, noting that the bosses of the five New York LCN families have recently reiterated their opposition to family members handling narcotics."[149] And as late as December 21, 1988, Scarpa Sr. was reporting that "the Colombo family has taken a new hard line on narcotics."[150] It is worth recalling that one of the reasons given by Scarpa for Joe Brewster's 1987 murder was Brewster's involvement with narcotics.

Irrespective of what the Colombo family's or the Commission's stated stance on dealing narcotics may have been at any one moment, eventually the amount of money to be made in drug dealing was too attractive for Gregory Scarpa Jr. and his crew to ignore. However, Gregory's drug use predated his drug trafficking by a number of years. As noted above, cocaine abuse was at the center of the failure of at least one of his three marriages.[151] Additionally, as Larry Mazza has chronicled, Scarpa Jr. and most, if not all, of his crew were using cocaine heavily at Junior's club, On the Rocks, as early as 1981 when the trouble with Alfred

Longobardi started.[152] Personal use led to drugs as a business, a lucrative source of income. The first time Gregory was indicted for racketeering, the criminal behavior supporting the racketeering counts was drug trafficking.

> "[T]he Scarpa Crew first became involved in marijuana distribution in the summer of 1985 when they ousted two dealers, Scotty Brennan and Peter Crupi,... from a location adjacent to Staten Island College (the "college spot"). The operation at the college spot proved highly lucrative, so the Scarpa Crew also established spots at Wolf's Pond Park on Staten Island, and at 13th Avenue and 73rd Street, and 20th Avenue and 81st Street, both in Brooklyn."[153]

Another indication of the growth in the importance of narcotics trafficking to the New York LCN is the fact that the subject of "narcotics" appears around half a dozen times in the first four sets of FBI documents on Scarpa's informant activities covering 1961 through 1975 in 725 pages. By contrast, there are at least twenty-one references to narcotics in the 240 pages of sets five and six covering 1980 through 1992.

Not long after the takeover of Brennan's and Crupi's operation, a Drug Enforcement Task Force made up of Drug Enforcement Administration (DEA) agents and New York Police Department (NYPD) officers investigating "mafia drug trafficking"[154] began to target Gregory's crew's drug trafficking having "stumbled onto Scarpa's marijuana mart at Staten Island College."[155] The Task Force's investigation led to the indictment in November of 1987[156] of Gregory and nearly his entire crew. Officials alleged, among other things, that the crew was selling $10,000 worth of marijuana each day at the Staten Island location.[157] However, the Scarpa crew's operation was not simply a matter of selling marijuana to an established market of college students, an offense that would seem tame by today's standards. The criminal complaint revealed the vicious characteristics of the organized crime effort involved in the operation. It included accusations of bribery, extortion, distribution of heroin and cocaine, intimidation, and murder.[158] Before any arrests occurred, however, Gregory "disappeared, almost as if he had been tipped off."[159] He was, in fact, tipped off. His crew was arrested; he was not, at least not initially.

Larry Mazza speculated that Gregory was able to flee ahead of arrest with, perhaps, "some help from his dad's mole."[160] Linda Schiro claimed she was present when FBI Special Agent Lin DeVecchio provided Gregory's father with a list of men who were about to be arrested on drug trafficking charges.[161] Assistant U.S. Attorney Valerie Caproni suspected DeVecchio of tipping off Scarpa Sr. about his son's pending arrest.[162] According to Gregory Jr., there were two lists DeVecchio shared with Scarpa Sr. The first list, which Scarpa Sr. also showed to Gregory, did not have his or his father's name on it.[163] The second list, one that Scarpa Sr. once again shared with Gregory, had Junior's name on it.[164] DeVecchio, naturally, denied having supplied Scarpa Sr. or anyone else with the information about Gregory's impending arrest. In his book, DeVecchio concludes, after some mental gymnastics, that the record demonstrates that Scarpa Sr. was receiving his law enforcement information from Anthony "Gaspipe" Casso, who was getting his information from NYPD Detectives Louis Eppolito and Stephen Caracappa, the so-called "Mafia Cops."[165]

For Gregory Jr., regardless of who the source was, the problem the tip presented was a simple one: get lost or get arrested. Gregory got lost. He, his third wife Maria, and their daughter spent time hiding from law enforcement in the Poconos,[166] Florida, and New Jersey. Gregory, while still a fugitive, even visited his father from time to time in

Brooklyn.[167] Scarpa Sr. let the FBI know on December 3, 1987, that Gregory's crew, such as it was at that point, was placed temporarily under the control of Benny Aloi until Gregory's expected return.[168]

Gregory's last "hideout" was a small motel near his mother's house in Lakewood, New Jersey. He was apprehended at the motel at about 2:00 in the morning, on August 29, 1988, [169] and his adult life as a free man came to an end for more than three decades. His arrest was accomplished without fanfare or violence. In fact, he engaged in a casual, even friendly, conversation during his in-custody transport from the Lakewood Township jail to the federal courthouse in Camden, New Jersey, with DEA Agent John Gilbride and Deputy U.S. Marshal Dominick A. Cama the morning after Gilbride arrested him.[170]

INCARCERATION AND RELEASE

In February of 1989, after being convicted on seven counts, including racketeering, in the first case the federal government brought against him, Gregory Scarpa Jr. was sentenced to 240 months in federal prison.[171] "In late 1998, a jury returned a verdict finding him guilty on all six counts of a [new] indictment including extortionate extensions of credit… and RICO conspiracy.… Among the racketeering acts the jury found proven were Scarpa Jr.'s conspiracies to murder four individuals.…"[172] He was sentenced to an additional 482 months in prison.[173]

After Gregory Jr.'s arrest on the first racketeering case, his father cut off support for his wife Maria and his other wives and children.[174] Gregory's last discussion of Colombo family business came when Gregory, angered by his father's decision to discontinue support of Gregory's families, told his father he was "through with the mob and that it had brought me nothing but misery."[175] Scarpa never again discussed Colombo family business with Gregory. Instead, he told Gregory's brother Frankie that anyone who did so was a dead man.[176] Scarpa followed up by cutting off any financial support for his eldest son in 1989.[177]

Gregory Scarpa Jr. was forty-three years old when his father died in a prison hospital on June 8, 1994. By the time Gregory Jr.'s compassionate release was ordered in November of 2020, he had been incarcerated for more than thirty-two years, four years of which he had spent in solitary confinement.[178] In 2012, conflicting emotions were still evident when Gregory reflected on his father's impact on him and others. "This guy was just out for himself."[179]

"This man ruined my life and the lives of my brothers and sisters, and he put a mark on my name that I'll have to live with forever. He was The Grim Reaper, but he was still my father. Would I follow him again? Never. Would I break the law for him? Absolutely not. Do I pray each day for the people he killed and the bodies he had buried? You bet. He got to renounce this life at sentencing, and I renounced it a long time ago.[180] I carry around a huge amount of remorse.... I admire him the way you might stand back and look at a tornado or a hurricane—some really powerful force of nature. Do you want it in your life? No. Do you feel bad for the bodies it leaves behind? Damn right. But hating my father would be like hating an earthquake or a tidal wave. When you see something like that coming, you just have to get out of its way."[181]

Gregory, Greg Scarpa Sr.'s eldest son, was thirty-eight years old when he was arrested for the last time, and nearly seventy when his compassionate release was granted in 2020. The years he missed as a free adult can be stated with certainty. And Scarpa Sr. did not live long enough to see

Joey, his youngest son, killed. Joey, who was shot twice in the back of the head at the age of twenty-three, barely made it to adulthood.

JOEY SCARPA

There is tragically little to say about an adult life that began and ended in murder and that lasted for less than six years. Such was the life of Joey Scarpa when he was no longer a minor. As noted in chapter five, Scarpa ordered his youngest son, who was then eighteen years old, to kill his best friend. Joey complied on May 27, 1990. Joey Scarpa was murdered a little less than five years later, on March 20, 1995.[182] As veteran organized crime reporter Jerry Capeci stated when reporting about the murder, little was publicly known about Joey Scarpa at the time of his death.[183]

Predictably, private memories diverge about what kind of young man Joey Scarpa was. Within the Scarpa family, he was also known for playing a minor but crucial role in the feud between the Persico and Orena factions during the so-called third Colombo war. However, his public notoriety, if any, stemmed from his participation in a murder in 1990, and a gun battle on December 29, 1992, in which one of his father's eyes was shot out.

HIS FATHER'S SON

The portrait that emerges of Joey Scarpa from those he left behind varies widely. On the one hand, he was conflicted, not unlike many young adults, between intense loyalty to his father and a desire for independence and his own identity.[184] He was sociable and, when he and his older sister, Linda, were growing up, he generally had more friends than she did.[185] He was "burdened by... an innate sensitivity."[186]

When his father was dying in a prison hospital in Rochester, Minnesota, Joey could only bring himself to visit him once in spite of Scarpa's asking for him.[187] Joey's widow, speaking at the sentencing hearing of the man who murdered Joey, "talked about how Joey loved to spend all the time he had with their daughter—loving her, playing with her, teaching her to walk and talk."[188] On the other hand, Larry Mazza, who thought Joey was a "cute little kid," watched with disdain as Joey dropped out of high school and became involved in the drug trade.[189] Joey got caught up in the "fast money" to be made dealing drugs.[190] Mazza watched Joey grow into a man "fueled by the violent reputation his father had,"[191] who, like his father, "had become a loose cannon."[192] He was, in Mazza's words, "a chip off the old block."[193] And his greed knew no bounds. After Mazza was arrested, Joey tried to collect on a $800 weekly loan shark payment Mazza owed by harassing Larry's mother and father.[194] Finally, as noted above, when it came to committing murder, he found himself, like his half-brother, unable to overcome the malignant will of his father.

HIS FATHER'S HELPER

During the early 1990s, two factions of the Colombo family engaged in a shooting war conducted for the most part on the streets of Brooklyn. The primary events and participants in that war will be discussed at length and in detail in chapter ten. However, one allegation in particular deserves attention here, given that it provides additional contour to the relationship between Scarpa and his youngest son, Joey. The allegation comes from the sworn testimony and written statements of Gregory Scarpa Jr. Although Gregory was incarcerated when the alleged events occurred, he has testified that his father informed him of Lin DeVecchio's and Joey's roles in Scarpa Sr.'s attempt to frame Vic Orena.[195]

Vittorio "Little Vic" Orena[196] was the leader of one of the two Colombo family factions vying for family supremacy in the early 1990s. Greg Scarpa Sr. was heading up the effort of the other faction, the so-called "Persico faction." During the spring of 1992, Orena was in hiding at the home of Gina Reale, his girlfriend, in Valley Stream, Long Island.[197] On April 1, law enforcement raided the house,[198] arrested Orena on suspicion of murder, and found, among other things, a plastic bag of weapons—four semiautomatic pistols, two revolvers, and two magazines—under the house's deck.[199] According to Gregory Jr., his father told him the bag was planted by Joey Scarpa, as directed by Scarpa Sr., while Lin DeVecchio acted as lookout.[200]

While the courts have not allowed Gregory's testimony about how the bag of guns came to be under the deck of Vic Orena's girlfriend's house into evidence[201] and Lin DeVecchio has specifically denied Gregory's allegations,[202] the portion of the story regarding Scarpa's direction to Joey rings true. After all, this is a man who introduced Gregory Jr. and Joey to "the life" while they were both still teenagers. And this is a man who insisted they both commit murder. It does not take a great leap of faith, based on what is undisputed about the relationship Greg Scarpa had with his sons, to believe he would order Joey to plant incriminating evidence.

Harmon claimed the guns were planted to "help frame Orena and [Pasquale "Patty"] Amato for the Grancio murder."[203] That seems unlikely. As will be shown in chapter ten, in January of 1992, four months before the search of Reale's home and Orena's arrest, "Nicky Black" Grancio was killed by Larry Mazza using a double-barreled shotgun, a fact Greg Scarpa Sr., who was present when Grancio was murdered, would have known. Planting a bag of pistols and conventional ammunition would not connect Orena or anyone else to the Grancio killing. While Orena's sentence included "ten years for illegal possession of a firearm,"[204] of the twelve firearms seized in the search,[205] several were discovered *in* the house in addition to those discovered *under* the house. Harmon may have been referring to the totality of weapons found during the search, which included "four loaded shotguns and two assault rifles."[206] However, according to the U.S. District Court, the search of Gina Reale's home produced "fully loaded shotguns in each of the three basement closets.... On the main floor of the house agents found a fully-loaded pistol-grip shotgun and an ammunition belt holding numerous shotgun shells."[207] In other words, the bag found *under* the house did not contain any weapons that might have linked Orena to the Grancio murder.

Given what Scarpa had up to that point demanded of both Gregory Jr. and Joey, requiring one of them to plant some evidence on a Colombo family rival, for whatever reason, appears on its face credible and, frankly, rather tame. However, what Scarpa demanded of Joey eight months later would have fatal consequences.

HIS FATHER'S OBSESSION

When Scarpa Sr. determined that his eldest son had been disrespected by Alfred Longobardi, the penalty for Longobardi, despite Gregory Jr.'s objections, was death. When Joey told his father about some trouble he had with a pair of Lucchese family drug dealers,[208] Scarpa, less than two years away from dying of AIDS, led an immediate manhunt with the dealers' execution as his goal.

Two days before New Year's Eve of 1992, Joey complained to his father that he had been insulted by rival drug dealers Ronald "Messy Marvin" Moran and Michael "Mikey

Flattop" DeRosa.[209] Scarpa, who was under house arrest at the time, was wearing an ankle monitor. However, rather than staying home and insisting, as he had in the past, that twenty-one-year-old Joey take care of the matter on his own, an enraged Scarpa[210] led the charge, hell-bent on revenge for the culprits' perceived disrespect of his youngest son. Once again, Joey tried to talk his father out of taking any action.[211] Linda Schiro suggested that Scarpa let Larry Mazza and Scarpa's crew handle the matter.[212] Scarpa, however, was resolute, perhaps owing to being "juiced up from the AIDS drugs and the steroids" in addition to smoking "street weed."[213]

With Scarpa at the wheel of Joey's Ford Escort, and with Joey and his friend Joseph Randazzo in the back, the hunt was on.[214] Scarpa's ankle monitor went off, but he ignored it.[215] When they found their targets, a gun battle ensued after it appeared that the matter had been peacefully resolved. As Michael DeRosa was walking away from the car carrying Greg and Joey Scarpa and Joseph Randazzo, Greg Scarpa opened fire, hitting DeRosa. Moran returned fire. Greg was shot in the face, Randazzo was hit in the head, and Joey, thinking both men were dead, fled on foot.[216]

DeRosa, who was wounded in the shootout, gave Linda Scarpa a slightly different, and more detailed version of what led up to the shootout as well as the shootout itself. His version and Linda Scarpa's recollection of Joey's version both have Greg Scarpa firing the first shot at DeRosa as DeRosa walked away from the car. DeRosa related his account to Linda Scarpa a number of years after the shootout.[217] Another account, from the day after the shootout, came from veteran organized crime reporter and author Selwyn Raab. In a *New York Times* article, Raab described the shootout as an "ambush" of Scarpa and, citing "federal and city law-enforcement experts on organized crime," understandably but inaccurately surmised the shootout was part of the ongoing feud between the Persico and Orena factions.[218]

Randazzo died two days later.[219] Scarpa lost his left eye.[220] And Joey, for the time being, survived, shaken but physically unscathed. He would not be so lucky in his next encounter with drug dealers and bullets. Joey Scarpa would survive his father by less than nine months.

On March 20, 1995, without his father's advice to dissuade him, without his father's reputation to protect him, Joey got into a car with Vinny Rizzuto, a fellow drug dealer. As Joey sat in the car, for the moment parked on Brown Street in Brooklyn's Sheepshead Bay neighborhood,[221] Rizzuto shot him twice in the back of the head, killing him instantly. Joey's last moments, sadly and predictably, were spent in the company of a murderous narcotics dealer.

Scarpa's youngest son was dead at the age of twenty-three, his eldest son was incarcerated for more than three decades beginning at the age of thirty-eight, and a man so close to Scarpa that he was like a son to him was killed on Scarpa's orders at the age of forty-four. Scarpa's propensity to ruin the lives of those men closest to him claimed at least one more victim, Larry Mazza, a middle-class kid just out of high school with dreams of following in his father's footsteps by becoming a firefighter. Instead, he was, by his own admission, seduced at first by Scarpa's mistress and ultimately by the riches to be had leading the gangster life. The path he chose led to personal ruin and ten years in federal prison.

CHAPTER SEVEN: THE MAZZA, SCHIRO, SCARPA TRIANGLE

On March 4, 1982, Judge Charles Sifton of the U.S. District Court for the Eastern District of New York issued an order in the case of *Berkman v. City of New York*, effectively freezing the hiring of firefighters in New York City, except on a showing of "compelling necessity," on the grounds that FDNY's physical test discriminated against women in violation of Title VII of the Civil Rights Act of 1964.[1]

LIVING THE DREAM

Larry Mazza, the second of three children of Lawrence Sr. and Joan Mazza, was born in Brooklyn Hospital on Kings Highway on February 21, 1961.[2] Larry's father was a firefighter who rose to the rank of lieutenant in New York City's fire department, the FDNY.[3] His mother worked in a bank when Larry was young, but she eventually "became a stay-at-home mom."[4] Larry and his two siblings grew up in a brick house on Avenue U in the Gravesend section of Brooklyn. The two-story house "had a double lot, which served as a makeshift playground for the local kids."[5] Given his family's traditional connection to the Catholic Church,[6] Larry attended Our Lady of Grace Elementary School, a local K-8 Catholic school, finishing in the spring of 1974. When it came time to attend high school, after two days at Nazareth High, another Catholic school, Larry opted for the local public high school, Lincoln High, instead. "It wasn't the nuns and the piety that convinced me that Catholic high school wasn't for me. It was the commute.... It took me ninety minutes to get there."[7]

Sports was a focus for Mazza and his tight circle of friends as they grew up, particularly during high school. Larry eventually became interested in kickboxing. He was good at it, and he enjoyed the notoriety that came with some success in local kickboxing tournaments.[8] At the age of sixteen, he discovered the thrill of betting on sports, horseracing in particular, a passion that would serve him well when he came under Greg Scarpa's influence.[9]

The mob was never too far in the background of Mazza's idyllic early years. "The Life was all around us,"[10] he recalled. For instance, before Mazza learned how to "take care of himself" under the tutelage of martial arts legend and former world kickboxing champion Louis Neglia,[11] he was a skinny kid who was picked on by the son of "a capo in Coney Island who was later murdered."[12] And his mother's brother, Albert Maniscalco, was a Colombo associate, a bookmaker. It was Uncle Albert, a man who later arguably saved Larry's life, who first introduced Mazza to horseracing and sports betting at Monticello Raceway during a family vacation at a dude ranch in the Catskills.[13]

When Mazza was growing up, he naturally assumed he would follow in his father's footsteps and join the Fire Department of New York City. Although Larry was a capable student, his ambivalent attitude toward academics convinced his father that "he wasn't college material."[14] But his father did have ambitions for his son that went beyond his joining the fire department. He encouraged his namesake to become an FBI agent.[15] To that end, Larry enrolled in New York's John Jay College and began taking courses in police and fire science.[16] For his part, Larry continued to focus on becoming a firefighter, perhaps even an arson investigator one day. He studied for and took the fire department's written exam as soon as he turned eighteen in 1979,[17] scoring 99 out of 100 on it. That score made him eligible to take the physical portion of the exam. Mazza aced that as well, scoring 95 out of 100.[18] His performance on the two tests meant that he was placed on the fire department's hiring eligibility list. At that point, it was simply a matter of working, going to school, and waiting for the call. Before the call came, two unrelated events converged to derail the dreams of both son and father, and both events involved women.

COLLATERAL DAMAGE

As Mazza was preparing to graduate from Lincoln High School, and as Linda Schiro was contemplating seducing a grocery store delivery boy, Brenda Berkman, a law student at NYU,[19] was filing a complaint with the Equal Employment Opportunity Commission.[20] Berkman, along with eighty-seven other women who had already passed the FDNY written test, took the physical portion of the test between February 15 and April 30 of 1978. None of the women passed that portion of the test.[21] Berkman's complaint alleged that the physical test violated the prohibition against sex-based discrimination contained in Title VII of the Civil Rights Act of 1964. The case, a class-action lawsuit, made its way to Judge Charles Sifton's federal district courtroom in the Eastern District of New York. *Brenda Berkman v. City of New York, et al.,* was tried in late 1981 without a jury. The judge's forty-one-page decision, issued on March 4, 1982, was a victory for the plaintiffs. The injunction the class of plaintiffs sought, one that prohibited New York from using the eligibility list generated from the 1978 written and physical tests for purposes of offering employment to Fire Department of New York applicants, was granted by Judge Sifton.[22]

Whether the decision ultimately had any impact on Mazza's life arc is debatable. As Mazza has admitted, "[b]y the time a decision was made, by a Judge Sifton, I'd embarked on a completely different path that didn't include the fire department."[23] However, in the next paragraph, Mazza wrote about the personal import of the court's decision in *Berkman*. "There would be no fire department in my future. Those dreams, like the dreams of my father, were about to go up in smoke."[24] To the extent that Larry Mazza still harbored a desire to become a New York firefighter, Judge Sifton's decision put a final nail in that dream's coffin. However, that dream had begun dying as early as three years before the judgment in the *Berkman* case. In late 1978, Linda Schiro, with a decisive assist later from Greg Scarpa, put Larry Mazza on a significantly different career path. And for Mazza, there was no turning back.

THE COUGAR'S PREY

Before graduating from high school, Mazza worked for Danza's Supermarket during the summer. The "Danza family owned ten or twelve stores that were all over Brooklyn at the time."[25] Larry's part-time job involved assisting drivers who were delivering groceries to local customers. When he got his driver's license at the age of seventeen, Mazza started driving and delivering Danza's groceries on his own.[26] His presence at Danza's was noticed by at least one steady customer, Greg Scarpa's mistress, Linda Schiro, who by then was in her early thirties.[27]

As Schiro has testified, she "developed a crush" on Mazza, and soon afterward told Scarpa she wanted "to go to bed with Larry." His response? According to Schiro, Scarpa replied, "'whatever makes you happy.'"[28] Her targeting of Mazza unfolded over his several visits to her house to deliver groceries. "I'd get excited every time I saw her, but I never expected anything to happen."[29] And then it did.

One day in late 1978, Linda called Larry at his gym and asked him to stop by her house. This time, she wasn't ordering groceries. Larry "had a feeling that things were going to be different."[30] When he arrived at her house, she was ready for him. Soft music, the lights down low, a bottle of wine and two glasses, and a joint in the ashtray. Mazza took a pass on the joint, letting her know he did not smoke anything.[31] Other than that, he was all in.

Mazza enjoyed the tenor of his new relationship, the basis of which initially was frequent sex with an attractive, experienced partner. "Having sex with Linda was magical."[32] However, the details of her personal life were for the most part a mystery to Mazza. He knew, from their conversations, that she was a mother of two children,[33] and he assumed she was married. In fact, Mazza was still in grammar school when Schiro's only marriage ended in the early 1970s.[34] Larry was initially indifferent to Schiro's vague references to her "husband."[35] "I figured the guy was a schlub… who wasn't packing enough heat to satisfy his insatiable wife."[36] His assumptions about both the existence of a husband and her putative husband's character proved to be entirely inaccurate.

Mazza's first real hint that his relationship with Linda was oddly unconventional came in 1979, when she suggested he meet her husband. "She told me her husband was a prominent guy and that she wanted me to meet him."[37] Mazza thought meeting Linda's husband was more than a bad idea; it struck him as "weird."[38] His misgivings about meeting the husband of the woman he was spending four nights a week with were compounded the first time he saw him.

> "[I]t felt as though I was watching a film in slow motion. I saw this tough looking guy, about fifty but in very good shape, get out of a big, black Caddy. He was dressed in a sharp sports jacket and wearing a ton of jewelry and sunglasses, even though it was dark out. As I was watching this guy walk assertively towards Linda's front door, I said to myself, *"If I had to draw a picture of a gangster in my mind, this would be it."*[39]

Mazza's next hint came when he learned the name of the man who was the very "picture of a gangster," Greg Scarpa. He had always assumed Linda's husband's last name was Schiro. As discussed earlier, that was the name of the man Linda married to give respectable cover to her having children with Scarpa.

LINDA WAS THE BAIT; MONEY WAS THE HOOK

Learning Scarpa's name initially made little impression on Mazza other than to add to his mild confusion about the details of his paramour's life. Unaware of Scarpa's status as a particularly infamous and brutal goodfellow in the Colombo crime family, Mazza did not even connect him to organized crime. Larry was further taken in when Linda's representation that her "husband" was a man who could offer Larry a job proved to be more than idle boasting. Indeed, at the first meeting between Mazza and Scarpa, over dinner at Sorrento's,[40] a local Brooklyn restaurant, Scarpa offered Larry a job as a salesman.[41] His job was to sign local stores up for having their fire extinguishers serviced by a company Scarpa and some others were building.[42] Larry would sell those same stores "paper products, like toilet paper, paper towels, and cleaning materials."[43] Mazza, whose future was rapidly taking on a different shape than what he had imagined for himself, jumped at the opportunity. He was soon working for Scarpa, and he learned he was a good salesman "making a few hundred a week" and "the business was growing."[44]

Mazza still had little idea who Greg Scarpa was, and while his family had some misgivings, for the most part they were glad to see Larry finding his way after high school in spite of what was happening with the fire department. Schiro and Scarpa, through what can be best described as a charm offensive, cultivated a relationship with Larry's parents, which included get-togethers at the Mazza house and dinners out. Lawrence Sr. recalled that "'Scarpa came off like he loved Larry like a son. And he was a personable guy.'"[45] Likewise, Larry's mother remembered that "'I knew he (Scarpa) was in The Life… and I was assured that my son wasn't going to be doing anything wrong with him. He assured us of that.'"[46] Not every member of the family was buying Scarpa's act. Josephine Maniscalco, Larry's maternal grandmother, warned, "'Keep your son away from him. He's the devil.'"[47] And when Larry's Uncle Albert, the Colombo family associate, heard that Larry was working for Scarpa, he told Larry's parents that Scarpa "'was a bad guy. But by then it was too late.'"[48]

Mazza soon found himself at a crossroads. The sales job imploded in less than a year due, apparently, to either issues between Scarpa and his partners,[49] or the fact that the company's warehouse burned to the ground.[50] Mazza had "dropped out of John Jay [College], the fire department was on ice, and [he] had turned down a job with the NYPD."[51] Instead of taking the opportunity to extricate himself from an impossible relationship with a mother of two who was twice his age, a woman who was the mistress of a man Mazza now understood was a powerful Mafia gangster,[52] he took his first steps into the illegal world his manipulative mentor inhabited.

His early assignments from Scarpa included getting into the numbers racket,[53] followed by collecting on gambling tickets in stores and bars throughout Brooklyn.[54] Collecting gambling slips involved Mazza's first personal taste of the Mafia's world of violence. Whether it was giving someone a flat tire or a beating, people who did not pay had to be hurt.[55] Mazza soon became acclimated to the violence. He quickly graduated from collecting on gambling tickets to bookmaking, partnering eventually with Gregory Scarpa Jr.[56] When he moved up to bookmaking, the money, like the gangster's mistress, was seductive. "Even though there were a lot of hands in the pot, there were weeks when we were splitting thousands of dollars."[57]

Meanwhile, Mazza's misgivings and trepidation about his ongoing affair with his boss's mistress continued to mount. Learning who Greg Scarpa was, Larry understood that the game he was playing was potentially deadly. A reckoning was due, and it came.

Mazza's transition to a contributing member of Greg Scarpa's crew included adhering to a few basic work requirements followed by all the "Wimpy Boys." As noted above, Scarpa required the men who worked for him show up on time every day, well-dressed, and ready to work. No exceptions. Mazza made the mistake of showing up in swimming trunks one day after spending a morning at the beach. Scarpa told him to go home and change, that showing up for work in such garb was not acceptable, and that he was never to come to work dressed like that again.[58]

Upon arriving to work at the Wimpy Boys Social Club one morning, Mazza, properly dressed, was led by Scarpa to the club's back office, the exclusive province of the boss, for a private meeting. Scarpa sat behind his desk. Mazza, as Scarpa directed, sat down in a chair directly in front of the desk facing Scarpa. The night before, Scarpa had told Larry he needed a ride to see Anthony "Scappi" Scarpati, Scarpa's capo. By then, Larry was convinced Scarpa knew about his relationship with Linda and that he was going to kill Mazza that night, so he was a no-show.[59] Remarkably, Mazza went to the Wimpy Boys Social Club the next day as if it were business as usual. It wasn't.

Mazza and Scarpa, having shown up early, were the only ones in the club. Scarpa was in an unusual, almost jovial mood. After the two of them wandered to Scarpa's back office and sat down, it became obvious to Mazza that Scarpa was about to confront him with his relationship with Linda. Scarpa insisted that Mazza sit in "a particular chair in [the] office where Greg would have people sit if they were going to get whacked."[60] As their conversation unfolded, Mazza became convinced he was a dead man. As he wondered where the shot would come from,[61] he briefly contemplated escape. Scarpa took the lead. "I know that when Linda cares for someone, there's nothing she won't do for them. I know she cares a lot for you... and it's pretty obvious that you feel the same way about her."[62] Instead of running, Mazza stayed put. After a moment's reflection, he responded to Scarpa's oddly gentle accusation in a way that may have saved his life. "I knew you knew."[63] He then continued. "I always respected you... and feel you're a smart guy... certainly not a fool and only a fool couldn't see it."[64]

Scarpa's response to Linda's and Larry's affair was to put Mazza at ease and to swear him to secrecy. He told Mazza that if word got out, they would both be killed.[65] By reacting the way he had, by agreeing to share their mutual secret, Scarpa drew Mazza closer to him. At the same time, Scarpa made Mazza both grateful for not killing him, and dependent on him for his life. It was a brilliant stroke by a master manipulator.[66] As much as Mazza may have wanted to leave "the life" behind over the next dozen years, his personal loyalty to The Grim Reaper, solidified at that crucial moment of confrontation, made such a move effectively impossible. The trap that had been set by Linda Schiro was closed by Greg Scarpa.

THE SUM OF ITS PARTS

The broad outlines of the relationship between Larry Mazza, Linda Schiro, and Greg Scarpa were firmly in place by 1980, and they read like a Hollywood logline for a Greek or Elizabethan tragedy. "Underworld father and apprentice adoptive son share avaricious mistress." Like the classic tragic forms, given that its creation was mired in multiple layers of deceit and nourished by years of crime, their unorthodox relationship could only end in ruin. Any other outcome would be dismissed by an even mildly sentient audience. Once the relationship was confirmed and, indeed, approved of by all participants, at least two questions remained to be answered: "What depths will the three participants in this triangle plumb?" and "How will their inevitable fall occur?"

SCHIRO-MAZZA

Mazza's memoir is quite frank, and at times graphic, about the sexual education he received from Linda. By his own account, he had slept with a few girls before meeting Linda,[67] but what he encountered with her was akin to going from being a high school football special-teams guy to a starting quarterback in the NFL overnight.

Sexually, there was almost no bottom for Linda Schiro and Larry Mazza. Nearly every moment they could steal was filled with physically satisfying themselves. Scarpa often spent weekends in New Jersey with his first wife, Connie,[68] or nights in Manhattan with his other wife, Lili Dajani.[69] And rumors persisted about another mistress, this one living on 13th Avenue in Brooklyn, who from time to time had sex with Scarpa in his office.[70] Spending time with this second mistress added to Scarpa's already significant time away from the home he and Linda Schiro otherwise shared. Schiro and Mazza took full advantage of Scarpa's absences. However, even when Scarpa was out of the house and not likely to return for some time, an additional factor complicated their nearly insatiable desire for each other: the presence of Linda's two children, Little Linda and Joey. Little Linda would frequently spend the night at a friend's house, but Joey "was always around" during the school year. Schiro and Mazza "even started calling him Joe Mannix, after the old TV detective."[71] He came close to "catching [Linda and Larry] in some very compromising positions."[72]

After Scarpa gave his blessing to their affair, Schiro and Mazza became increasingly brazen. They began having sex when Scarpa was in the house. For instance, Mazza would stop by the house most mornings before heading to the club. He and Linda would not hesitate to have sex during those mornings as long as Scarpa was engaged in one of his meticulously timed showers. Greg's habitual forty minutes in the shower followed by ten minutes of grooming with the blow dryer provided Schiro and Mazza with, apparently, just enough time to satisfy their morning urges.[73] And they had sex in the house at night when Scarpa was asleep. As Mazza has confessed, "I prayed he was a heavy sleeper."[74]

While Mazza was surrounded by infidelity, he at least kept his relationship with Linda monogamous.[75] And to keep that relationship secret, as he had promised Scarpa, he avoided being seen with her in public. He was so fastidious about both avoiding other women and not being seen in public with Linda that he started worrying about how his fellow crew members would perceive his sexuality.[76] The solution (or perhaps the rationale for starting to move away from Linda) was to start dating other women. Scarpa agreed. Linda did not.[77]

Mazza's on again, off again, attempts to distance himself emotionally from Linda culminated in a relationship that resulted in marriage[78] and, eventually, fatherhood.[79] Predictably, as Larry sought other female companionship, Linda froze him out of her life. Their affair was over, and, at least for a while, Linda refused to have anything to do with him.[80]

In spite of the emotional distance between Larry and Linda resulting from his dating and subsequent marriage, he remained, incredibly, an integral part of the Scarpa/Schiro family, and was often called upon to assist when the family or its members were in dire need. When José Guzman sexually assaulted Little Linda, Mazza was part of the crew that gave Guzman a non-lethal "savage beating."[81] When Scarpa suddenly began bleeding internally from severe stomach ulcers, Mazza was called upon to get him to the hospital.[82] He "took him back and forth from one hospital to another, from one specialist to another."[83] When Little Linda was so stoned that she couldn't find her way home, she called Mazza, who picked her up and gave her a ride.[84] When Joey had some trouble with a couple of drug dealers, Linda suggested that Greg let Larry and the crew take care of it. When Scarpa's eye was shot out in the ensuing gun battle with those same drug dealers, Mazza once again was called upon to drive him to a hospital.[85] Even years after Linda's and Larry's sexual escapades had come to an end, the family's default in times of extreme family need was to reach out to Larry. And he always came through.

His loyalty was unshakeable right up until that moment in December of 1993 when, while incarcerated at the Metropolitan Correctional Center in Manhattan, he was convinced by one-time Colombo family acting boss Vic Orena, who read a newspaper account of Scarpa's sentencing hearing to him, that Greg Scarpa had been an FBI informant for nearly three decades.[86]

SCARPA-MAZZA

When Larry Mazza first encountered Linda Schiro, and by extension Greg Scarpa, the most serious breaches of the law he had been involved with were limited to some typical underage drinking[87] and underage betting. Given his family's close ties to the Catholic church, Mazza claimed he would have been an altar boy if it had not been "impossible for [him] to wake up early in the morning." [88] While he missed out on being an altar boy, he found other ways to help his church and community. For instance, as a teenager he belonged to a group run by the local parish priest referred to as "God's Squad." The "Squad" was made up of Mazza and half a dozen other teenagers from the church who "supervised younger kids at a youth center."[89]

> "We ran the center for two years, did a lot of sports, and were positive role models for the kids. Father Ronnie thought the world of me, still does even with all that I've done."[90]

Mazza's mother recalled, "He was a very good little boy. He was very good. He was good in school. I didn't have any problems with him. And he was a very kind person, a very kind little boy."[91] Mazza's childhood friend Tommy Dades, a tough kid, a little rough around the edges, who grew up to be a police officer, once reflected, "In police work… where you see a sweetheart like Larry Mazza become a killer, you realize that anything can happen."[92]

By contrast, Scarpa's world from at least the early 1950s, when he earned his button in the Profaci family, to the moment he met Larry Mazza was defined by a wide range of criminal conduct. As already noted, although it is impossible to assess the veracity of the claim, Linda Schiro stated that when she first met Scarpa in the early 1960s, he reported having committed at least twenty murders by 1962.[93] Schiro has also stated that early in their relationship, she became aware of Scarpa's involvement in burglaries, the numbers racket, and hijackings.[94] By 1979, the year Scarpa and Mazza met, Scarpa's criminal record included arrests for illegal possession of firearms, conspiracy to commit theft of an interstate shipment, possession of stolen goods from an interstate shipment, bookmaking, running a numbers racket, petty larceny, assault, attempted grand larceny, possession of stolen mail, conspiracy to commit an offense against or to defraud the U.S., fraud by wire, radio, or television, and transportation of stolen goods, securities, moneys, fraudulent State tax stamps, or articles used in counterfeiting.[95] Of course, the above represent only those offenses for which Scarpa was arrested or which others have been willing to discuss. It is reasonable to assume that a big earner like Scarpa was also involved in the Colombo family's other highly profitable criminal activities, such as gambling and loan sharking,[96] during the 1950s through the 1970s.

In short, Mazza, who was barely an adult when he found himself in the constant company of Linda Schiro and Greg Scarpa, was completely out of his depth. Recall that Schiro had already conned a man into marriage and then compounded the con by deceiving him about who the father of their two children was. And recall that by 1979, Scarpa had already manipulated a federal law enforcement bureau full of college-educated men and women to his own advantage for more than a decade. By the time he started working for Greg Scarpa, the odds against Larry Mazza, in spite of his solid upbringing, were long indeed. And they were about to get longer.

In the summer of 1980, Mazza's violence tutorials, which had consisted primarily of vandalism and assault, took a gruesome leap forward when, according to his public accounts, he witnessed Scarpa murder Dominick "Big Donny" Somma[97] in the back office of the Wimpy Boys Club. In Mazza's version of events, he, Robert "Bobby Zam" Zambardi, Carmine Sessa, and Gregory Jr. were gathered in that office with Scarpa, who was sitting at his desk. Somma dropped by the club to deliver some money he had collected. Mazza, who was sitting in the chair across from Greg Sr., got up to let Somma sit down. Mazza stood near the office door watching Somma give his money to Scarpa, who counted it and wrote down the amount collected. When Scarpa was finished with this bit of accounting, he asked Somma about a rumor he had been hearing that Somma was calling Scarpa a rat, i.e., an informant. Somma's face turned white as a sheet. When he managed to speak, he failed to expressly deny the rumor. Instead, he claimed that he had been drinking and popping off and that whatever he said did not mean a thing. Scarpa asked Somma if he had any "paperwork," for the accusation, i.e., proof that Scarpa was an informant. Somma responded saying that he had none and again pleaded his case. To no avail. Scarpa pulled a revolver out of his desk drawer and shot him point blank in the head, killing him instantly.[98] After shooting Somma in the face, Scarpa "put one behind the ear."[99] Somma's body was then rolled up in the office's dark brown rug[100] and removed from the club.

Carmine Sessa's versions of the reason for Somma's murder and who was present during the execution[101] differ from Mazza's on some important points. Sessa stated that Somma was killed by Scarpa for being openly critical of Gregory Jr.'s performance during an aborted bank burglary. According to Sessa, Allie Boy Persico had already ordered that Somma be hit for dealing drugs.[102] Sessa claimed that Scarpa, hearing that the hit order was going to be withdrawn, decided to kill Somma anyway for having criticized his son. Scarpa "summoned" Somma to the Wimpy Boys Club where the murder took place.[103] Sessa's testimony did not place Mazza at the scene. According to Sessa, he, Gus Farace, Joe Brewster, and Bobby Zambardi were in Scarpa's office and witnessed the murder, while the Saponaro brothers, Joe and John, played cards in the club's front room. When Somma entered, per Sessa, Scarpa immediately shot him in the head. As in the Mazza version, Somma's body was rolled up in the office's rug. Sessa added that it was then dumped in Staten Island's aptly named Fresh Kills landfill.[104]

Harmon's book provided additional detail about Somma's complaint about Gregory Jr.'s performance during the bank burglary, claiming that he lodged it with Scarpa's capo, Anthony Scarpati.[105] Months later, again per Harmon,[106] Carmine Persico ordered Somma killed for being "involved in drug deals with the Gambino family—without seeking permission from the Colombo bosses."[107] According to Harmon, "a few days after Greg Sr. was let off with probation on the credit card conviction,"[108] Gregory Jr. was in the Wimpy Boys Club office along with John Saponaro,

Carmine Sessa, and Joe Brewster. Scarpa was at his desk. He phoned Somma telling him to come to the club. Later, when Somma walked into the office, the usual joking and bullshitting ensued.

> "As the noise increased, Greg Sr. casually reached into the bottom drawer of his desk, withdrew a handgun, pointed it at Donnie's head, and pulled the trigger.... Greg Sr. pushed back from his desk, walked over to the fallen form... and shot him in the head once more."[109]

Harmon's account included wrapping Somma's body in the office rug and dumping it "on the side of a service road" in Staten Island.[110]

Special Agent Lin DeVecchio made only a passing mention of the Somma murder in his book. He managed to omit most salient facts while botching the murder's timing.

> "Once a member of Scarpa's crew complained about his son Gregory Jr.'s lackluster performance during a bypass bank burglary and Scarpa responded to the complaint by drilling the man on the spot and having him buried."[111]

DeVecchio's book, unlike his report of November 6, 1980,[112] named Scarpa as the shooter and provided the alleged rationale for the shooting. Furthermore, for some reason, DeVecchio omitted the victim's name in his book, a detail included in his report.[113]

Regardless of which version of the details of Greg Scarpa Sr.'s murder of Dominick Somma is accurate, and each is likely flawed in some respect, the following conclusions are more than reasonable from all of the above. By August of 1980, slightly more than two years after graduating from high school, and less than two years after first hooking up with Linda Schiro, Larry Mazza was a Wimpy Boys Club regular. He was by then involved in a variety of criminal activities under the guidance and at the direction of Greg Scarpa. And by that time, Mazza knew that Scarpa was a powerful Mafia gangster and a cold-blooded killer. Larry Mazza, unfortunately, failed to beat the long odds against him. And he had Linda Schiro and Greg Scarpa, and to no small extent himself, to blame.

SCARPA-SCHIRO

Linda Schiro's sex life, which one would assume to have been at a minimum an embarrassment to Scarpa, a man routinely referred to as her "common law" husband, had no effect on his otherwise unwavering loyalty to her. And as far as can be determined, Scarpa's additional marriage and rumored additional affair or affairs likewise had no effect on Schiro's unwavering loyalty to him. By 1980, what had started as an extramarital affair in 1962 between a man in his thirties and a teenager had managed to survive through two additional marriages, one for each of them, the birth of two children, at least one additional affair which may have produced another child,[114] and a long-term, unconventional sexual relationship between the teenager, by then a woman in her thirties, and a young man barely out of high school. By the mid-1980s, Scarpa was still married to his first wife but divorced from his second wife,[115] the affair between Schiro and Mazza was over, and Scarpa and Schiro had two fairly typical and somewhat problematic teenaged children at home. How the evolving dynamic of their relationship might have otherwise turned out is impossible to say because in 1986, Scarpa received a transfusion of HIV-positive blood. That moment understandably altered their lives and relationship in a way no one could have foreseen.

What did each of them get from the other that was incentive enough to maintain what to an outsider would seem to be an impossible and enervating bond? As with most long-term relationships, the answer varies over the course of that relationship. The life that Greg Scarpa and Linda Schiro shared arguably went through three distinct phases. Phase one began in 1962 when they met and ended in 1975 when Scarpa became a bigamist ushering in phase two. Phase two ended in 1986 when Scarpa needed emergency surgery for his severely bleeding ulcer. And finally, phase three lasted for eight years until Scarpa's death in a prison hospital in 1994.

PHASE ONE

As chronicled in some detail in chapters two and five above, Linda Schiro's involvement with and attraction to gangsters did not begin when she met Greg Scarpa. Scarpa, however, proved to be a perfect match for her, providing her with the attention, material possessions, and experiences she coveted most. Although hardly a neophyte when she became involved with him, her experiences did not extend far beyond her Brooklyn neighborhood. Scapa soon introduced her to a world she could not previously access. For example, before she and Scarpa traveled to Mississippi and then Miami together in 1964, Linda had never been on a plane.[116] She loved the life that Scarpa provided; she loved the money.[117] "Being with Scarpa made her feel safe. It was exciting and it was dangerous, which was right up Linda's alley."[118] From the time "she was 18 years old, everything had come easy to her. She married [sic] a rich and powerful man who gave her everything."[119] And although the two of them never did marry, contrary to Mazza's assertion, Linda enjoyed the role of Mafia wife as a keeper of secrets.[120] Scarpa "told me about everything—committing burglaries, the numbers racket, murders."[121] For instance, with Schiro and her two children present, Scarpa spoke openly about the killing of José Guzman.[122] He also revealed to Schiro the rationale behind his ordering the murder of Joe Brewster.[123] "This talk of murder and treachery was very normal to her now. It became the only life she knew."[124]

Scarpa confirmed his confidence in Schiro when he told his lawyer, Lou Diamond, that he did not keep any secrets from her.[125] Although she met Scarpa's two primary FBI handlers, Anthony Villano[126] and Lin DeVecchio,[127] Scarpa was not entirely forthcoming about the scope and substance of his work on behalf of the FBI.[128] Finally, as detailed above, Schiro sought and relished the central role of motherhood, "a unique and important role in the furtherance of the [Cosa Nostra] organization."[129]

Scarpa also provided Schiro with a constant stream of gifts. That was especially true early in their relationship.[130] And he was not above giving Schiro stolen goods, jewelry in particular, as gifts.[131] "After a score, he and his crew would lay out all the jewelry on Schiro's dining room table and he would tell her, 'Pick something you want.'"[132] Even after the birth of their two children, the illicit gifts continued. For her part, Schiro was fully aware of the origin of some of Scarpa's largesse but chose to ignore its provenance because she "loved the way he treated her."[133] The gifts included a new car every year,[134] a house for her after her marriage to Charlie Schiro,[135] and another new house for her and their two children after Charlie divorced her.[136] "What a life Linda had. All the luxuries money could buy."[137]

Their early years together were not defined entirely by materiality. The emotional bond between Scarpa and Schiro, while unconventional, was strong during this first phase. "There was no one tougher than Greg. Yet there was an outside to him and an inside to him. Inside, strangely enough, he was truly sensitive."[138] Schiro's description of their relationship contained some standard hallmarks of close affection. According to Schiro, she and Scarpa "enjoyed 'a beautiful sex life.'"[139] "[W]e were so much in love."[140] And, "in contrast to his reputation as a cold-blooded killer, Greg always showed a human side at home."[141] Furthermore,

> "Greg and Linda enjoyed a relatively 'normal' life of marital convenience and companionship. On a typical day the couple would wake at 7:00 a.m. and have coffee together. They would chat until 9:30 a.m., when. . . Scarpa would whip up pancakes or scrambled eggs for the whole family.[142] Greg Sr. liked this domestic routine...."[143]

As close as they might have been, as much in love as Schiro claimed they were, Scarpa's appetite for more continued to govern his personal behavior. There seems to be little doubt that during the early years of his relationship with Schiro, and during her childbearing and their child-rearing years, Scarpa was not monogamous. He was still visiting his wife in New Jersey on a regular basis,[144] and those close to him have reported that Scarpa had an active sex life outside of his relationship with Schiro.[145] Indeed, Larry Mazza, employing a bit of common phallic imagery, referred to Scarpa as a "swordsman."[146] Gregory Jr. confirmed his father's reputation when he stated that his father "was always a womanizer."[147] As discussed above, he even chose to marry again in 1975, cementing an affair that began after a meeting in Manhattan to discuss the sale of stolen diamonds.[148] His marriage to Lili Dajani, who was apparently aware of Scarpa's existing marriage and his relationship with Schiro,[149] was known to Schiro,[150] and it signaled a change in their relationship that would last for more than a decade.

During this first phase of their more than three decades together, Scarpa provided Schiro with security, excitement, luxury, and love, whereas Schiro provided Scarpa with the prestige among his Mafioso peers that came with keeping a young, attractive *gumar*, a practical requirement for a powerful Cosa Nostra man.[151] They provided each other with a biological family, her first, his second, at least. And while they both received something they valued, their relationship fostered Schiro's dependence on Scarpa. She may have been able to acquire the material goods and excitement she craved elsewhere, but Scarpa was also able to provide security and love and, after a fashion, respectability and stability. As will be shown below, their roles of provider and dependent were largely reversed in the final phase of their years together. Before that happened, however, Schiro managed to flip an important part of the script on Scarpa by inviting a man half her age into her bed in phase two of their relationship.

PHASE TWO

In 1962, Greg Scarpa, a father and husband in his early thirties, pursued Linda Diana, a single woman half his age. In 1978, Linda Diana, by then Linda Schiro, a mother and Mafia *gumar* in her early thirties, pursued Larry Mazza, a single man half her age. Her motive? We can only speculate. Any number of things may have moved her to seduce Larry Mazza. Revenge for Greg's marriage to Lili Dajani. Physical and emotional boredom in her relationship with Scarpa. By effectively recreating the origins of her involvement with Scarpa, perhaps she sought to recapture whatever excitement those early years provided her. Or, as she has repeatedly claimed, she simply indulged an attraction to a considerably younger sexual partner. "'[Y]ou know how sometimes you'll watch a movie and you'll see [somebody] who might turn you on? That's how it was with Larry. He was really so cute.'"[152]

Perhaps her motivation was a combination of two or more of the above, or something else entirely.[153] Assuming that

Larry Mazza's account of the physicality of his relationship with Linda Schiro is for the most part accurate, it is not unreasonable to conclude that at some point Scarpa was no longer satisfying Schiro emotionally or sexually.[154] Indeed, Schiro has not disputed Mazza's account of their sex life and has rather affirmatively confirmed portions of it. For instance, as noted above, Mazza wrote about having sex with Schiro at her home while Scarpa was in the house. Schiro confirmed that seemingly dangerous habit during an interview with Peter Lance.

> "According to Schiro, [Scarpa] was often at home when she and Larry had sex. 'Larry would come and we would make love and either Greg was in another room or he was down in the basement and that's how it went, but Larry didn't know that Greg was in the house.'"[155]

Likewise, assuming the various accounts of Scarpa's marriage to Lili Dajani and his apparent ambivalence about his mistress's affair with Mazza are for the most part accurate, it is not unreasonable to conclude that Schiro was no longer satisfying Scarpa emotionally or sexually. Indeed, Scarpa remarkably thanked Mazza for "helping out Linda."[156] It is important to recall that Scarpa was aware from the outset of the relationship between Mazza and Schiro that they were having sex. That of course, begs the question, "What did Scarpa mean when he thanked Mazza for 'helping out Linda'?" Scarpa may have been referring to Mazza's help with Little Linda and Joey. As noted above, Mazza would help both of them with their homework and took a particular interest in helping Joey with martial arts instruction. Beyond that, it is difficult to discern from the available sources anything else Mazza was providing Linda with other than emotional and sexual gratification.

Regardless of the bizarre nature of the above circumstances and the participants' attitudes, it certainly is not uncommon for couples with small children who have been together for the better part of fifteen years to experience emotional distancing. Greg Scarpa and Linda Schiro may have simply lost interest in each other and sought to fill the resulting void. Divorce, for this unmarried couple, was not possible. Nor, as far as can be determined, was separation ever discussed. Mazza has claimed that Schiro floated the idea of running away with him as an option. "Let's go to Hawaii. I have a million dollars. We can live on that."[157] However, it does not appear they ever seriously contemplated such drastic action. Scarpa, meanwhile, seemed to continue to regard Schiro with genuine, if sporadic, affection, and he did not alter his close relationship with their children. From all outside appearances, the affair between Mazza and Schiro had little effect on his day-to-day life and its routines.

As to the continued relationship between Scarpa and Schiro, this second phase of their lives together was grounded not in physical intimacy but in the acquisition of personal and material possessions. Larry Mazza, who had a front row seat for most of phase two, wrote,

> "Linda was as crazy and as happy as she had ever been. After all, she had it all—an older rich guy to take care of her, a sugar daddy, and a young, good-looking, athletic boyfriend. Her boy toy. At the time I believed Greg truly cared for her. But in time, I came to realize she was just another one of his many possessions. His feelings for her were nothing like mine. He treated her like a queen by showering her with gift after gift."[158]

Those material possessions were piling up. Scarpa "particularly enjoyed boasting about the jewelry he got for Linda" using fake credit cards.[159] The Scarpa/Schiro family even moved to the more upscale Brooklyn neighborhood of Dyker Heights.[160] As Steve Dunleavy cogently noted in 2007, Schiro was "a petite beauty who was spoiled rotten by 'the life' that owned her."[161] While Mazza eventually understood that Schiro was just another possession for Scarpa, he also seemed to understand on some level that he was just another possession for Schiro. In his memoir, he twice referred to himself by the less than flattering sobriquet of Schiro's "boy toy."[162]

Besides the material possessions that were symbols of an opulent lifestyle, Schiro possessed two men, both of whom were living a life she found exciting, and both of whom provided her with whatever status she had in the dangerous gangster world. She also possessed, by virtue of those two relationships, a vicarious pride she was not above displaying. For instance, as Scarpa and Mazza discussed, over dinner with Schiro at Romano's, the murder of Alfred Longobardi planned for later that night, she "was sitting there as proud as a peacock. She even seemed a bit excited knowing that Greg would be shooting someone to death and that [Mazza] would have a minor role in the hit."[163]

This second phase of the Scarpa/Schiro relationship might have continued for many years. However, Larry Mazza slowly distanced himself from Linda Schiro as he was getting closer to the middle of Greg Scarpa's inner circle, a position he would occupy until 1993. At about the same time, Scarpa divorced Lili Dajani, a move that might have precipitated a return to the sort of relationship he had enjoyed with Schiro years earlier. Whatever life Schiro and Scarpa had remaining as a couple, Scarpa's sudden illness in the summer of 1986 changed his and her worlds in ways that neither of them could have anticipated. During the last phase of their relationship, their lives were, perhaps for the first time, affected by forces neither one of them could control.

PHASE THREE

Schiro's decision to mirror Scarpa's original pursuit of her by seducing Larry Mazza was followed by a similar but necessary role reversal that began in 1986. Linda, who over the years found herself dependent on Greg for her long-term financial and personal safety, became Greg's primary caregiver starting in late 1986 as his health entered a long, slow decline until his death from AIDS in 1994.

The early 1980s, which were the early years of the AIDS epidemic, were a time of confusion, misinformation, and fear where the disease was concerned. Some of the early misinformation, even that which may have been well-intentioned, gained a foothold relegating those who had the misfortune to become HIV positive to the status of outcasts who brought the disease on themselves through their own same-sex promiscuity. In 1981, and continuing through much of 1982, terms such as "Gay Men's Pneumonia," "Gay Cancer" and "Gay-Related Immune deficiency" or "GRID" were used "to describe the new epidemic."[164] It was not until September of 1982 that the Center for Disease Control (CDC) first coined the neutral, more accurate, and less judgmental term, "acquired immunodeficiency syndrome," or AIDS.[165] Still, in a 1983 article, the CDC noted that "AIDS is most prevalent 'among gay men with multiple sexual partners, people who inject drugs, Haitians, and people with hemophilia.'"[166] In 1984, misconceptions about a study in the *American Journal of Medicine* gave "rise to the myth of Patient Zero, a promiscuous or even malicious gay man who single-handedly and knowingly touched off the AIDS pandemic in the United States."[167] By 1986, the American public's view that AIDS was primarily, and in many people's minds exclusively, a disease contracted by promiscuous gay men was nearly as rampant as the disease itself.[168] And 1986 is the year that Greg Scarpa become HIV positive as a result of a transfusion needed to treat a nearly fatal bleeding ulcer.

By the time Scarpa turned fifty-eight, he had been popping aspirin on a daily basis for years, perhaps since his early twenties.[169] On the one hand, he took aspirin as a preventative measure to avoid potential hangovers that resulted from his habit of drinking hard liquor—scotch on the rocks or a vodka martini—in the evening.[170] His aspirin-popping habit was likely reinforced and augmented by the need to alleviate chronic back pain.[171] Lin DeVecchio wrote that Scarpa's "alleged reason for taking them was to stave off a heart attack, but I understand he was addicted."[172] Scarpa testified at one point that he had been taking "'four to six aspirin a day'"[173] for pain resulting from back surgery in the late 1970s.[174] Whatever the reason, Scarpa's alcohol intake combined with his aspirin habit[175] was slowly taking its toll on his stomach. In August of 1986, the dam broke, requiring Scarpa to undergo an "emergency hiatus [sic] hernia operation."[176]

As noted above, Larry Mazza got the call when Scarpa fell ill. Scarpa had been to see his personal physician, who recommended he be hospitalized.[177] He was bleeding internally[178] and his daughter Linda told Mazza when she called him that Scarpa had collapsed.[179] Mazza took him to Victory Memorial Hospital,[180] which was only about four blocks from Scarpa's Brooklyn home.[181] Scarpa's condition worsened[182] as he went in and out of consciousness.[183] He was losing blood at an alarming rate and emergency surgery was required.[184] Between the loss of blood and the surgery, which resulted in the removal of much of his stomach,[185] Scarpa was also in dire need of a blood transfusion. Scarpa, however, did not trust the hospital to provide blood that was not HIV-tainted.

His reason or reasons for not trusting the hospital's blood supply vary from one writer to the next. Mazza, in a podcast interview, implied that Scarpa's primary concern was the sexuality of an unknown donor, and that he "knew his men weren't gay."[186] Harmon attributes Scarpa's rejecting of the hospital's screened blood to his being "at once naturally suspicious and racist to the core..."[187] Linda Schiro called the rumors that Scarpa had an aversion to blood from African Americans false.[188] Scarpa testified that he rejected the hospital's blood "because Linda was told by nurses at Victory Memorial that 'she would be putting [Greg] at risk by getting hospital blood.'"[189] DeVecchio simply stated that Scarpa "was given blood donated by his family and criminal associates, the only blood he would trust," without providing a rationale for that mistrust.[190] As an alternative to a transfusion of blood from Victory Hospital's supply, members of the Wimpy Boys crew were called to the hospital and tested for a possible match. Paul Mele, whom Scarpa had known since Mele was seventeen,[191] was one suitable donor.

Mele was a weightlifter who, it is speculated, used shared hypodermic needles to inject steroids. Even before providing blood for Scarpa's transfusion, questions about Mele's health were common among the Wimpy Boys crew members.[192] Indeed, Mele was likely suffering from AIDS at the time of the transfusion without being aware of it.[193] Not long after providing blood for Scarpa, Mele died of AIDS.[194]

After three surgeries, the last of which was at Mt. Sinai Hospital, and "two months in intensive care," Scarpa returned home. However, his health and ego took another blow when his personal physician informed him that it had been determined he had received HIV-tainted blood.[195] That diagnosis cemented Linda Schiro's new role as caregiver and advocate that she had temporarily taken on during Scarpa's prolonged medical emergency. And while Scarpa went on to live for another eight years, some of it filled with the most vicious moments of his lifetime of crime, with each passing day he became more dependent on Schiro to provide him with the care he needed and to guard his newest and arguably most devastating secret. Her new roles predictably took their toll.

"She was only about 40 at the time Greg had entered the hospital. She was still very youthful and attractive. But the fact that she had to be a 24-hour nurse made her age right before my eyes. By the time the secret was out, she was a wreck." [196]

In the short term, Scarpa's drastically evolving personal health barely slowed him down. Overall, the 1980s were perhaps the most openly violent of Scarpa's criminal career to that point. Other than altering the fundamental dynamics of his relationship with Linda Schiro as they both were compelled to transition to this third and final phase of their lives together, the events of 1986 did little to alter his behavior. As already noted, Scarpa ordered the murder of Joe Brewster, a man who was like a son to him, in 1987. And as will be seen in chapters nine and ten, the last years of his life as a free man featured an unthinkable degree of violence and death.

CHAPTER EIGHT: A GRIM HARVEST

The homicide rate in New York City in 1970 was 14.15 per 100,000. By 1980, that rate had almost doubled to 25.62 per 100,000.[1] The following decade, the 1980s, provided little to no relief, and by 1990, when the murder rate in New York City reached 30.7 per 100,00,[2] the city "notched a modern-era record 2,245 murders,"[3] a remarkable increase of 17.8 percent in just one year.[4] By contrast, the number of murders in New York City in 2022, the last year for which statistics were available at the time of this writing, was 433, a rate of 5 per 100,000[5] or less than 1/5 the rate at the beginning of the 1980s, and less than 1/6 the rate of 1990. As a *New York Post* headline on December 23, 2017, stated, "Murder was king of New York in the '80s and '90s."[6] If murder was king for twenty years, then for thirteen of those years Greg Scarpa was the Lord High Executioner, dishing up death in New York at an astonishing rate through the end of 1992, when he was finally incarcerated for good.[7] As for the 1980s, Greg Scarpa's human harvest was indeed grim.

CLOSING SCARPA

Scarpa was closed as an FBI Top Echelon Criminal Informant after March 1, 1975. A memo from the FBI's New

York Office Special Agent in Charge to the Director of the FBI dated May 5, 1975, regarding the New York Office's letter to Bureau headquarters in D.C. dated March 1, 1975, stated in its entirety, "Above captioned source is presently being closed by New York Office."[8] The letter of March 1 referenced in the May 5 memo included the following:

> "On October 31, 1974, source advised regarding the body found buried alongside DOMINCK SCIALO last month that he heard the following story from very reliable sources: [para.] The individual murdered was named (First Name Unknown) (FNU) COCCHIO, a kid who was murdered about 10 years ago at the request of JUNIOR PERSICO to JOE COLOMBO who ordered the hit. Source heard that COCCHIO had apparently killed a relative of PERSICO in a bar fight. COCCHIO was grabbed off the street in Bay Ridge by NICK BIANCO and GREGORY SCARPA who administered a severe beating to COCCHIO. COCCHIO was then taken to the garage adjacent to JOE IANNACI'S residence on Bay 10th Street, Brooklyn, where source heard he was killed by DUKE SANTORO with one bullet in the head. The body was put back in BIANCO'S car and delivered to PERSICO'S crew downtown, who in turn apparently buried the body in the basement of the social club. (New York City Police Department (NYCPD) advised of the identity of the body.)"[9]

It is entirely possible that this entry precipitated the closing of Scarpa as a TECI. The entry clearly connects him to a murder in 1964, too early for the reference to have been to Gregory Scarpa Jr., who turned thirteen that year. And, as discussed in chapter two, the FBI told Scarpa as early as September of 1962 in no uncertain terms that he could not be involved in murder. If the above entry is accurate,

Cocchio's murder took place about two years after that warning. Furthermore, even though the information about Cocchio's murder was made available to an FBI handler in October of 1974, the memo memorializing Scarpa's participation in the murder was not circulated until March 1, 1975. That same day, Scarpa's closing appears to have been initiated. Whether Scarpa's participation in Cocchio's murder was the rationale for his being dropped as a TECI is impossible to tell conclusively from the documents the FBI has made public, but it is a distinct possibility given the timeline set forth above.

Scarpa's threats during the IBM counterfeit stock investigation may have also played a part in the FBI's decision to drop him. It is worth recalling that the FBI took the position during that investigation that contact with Scarpa in his role as an informant would continue until such time as he became a subject of legal proceedings. On June 6, 1974, less than ten months before his closing was initialized, Scarpa indeed became the subject of a federal grand jury indictment.

Peter Lance theorized that Scarpa simply lost interest in supplying the FBI with valuable information after the death of J. Edgar Hoover in 1972 and the retirement of Anthony Villano in 1973. Scarpa, per Lance, had lost two major advocates in the Bureau. Hoover's successor, L. Patrick Gray, was not nearly as interested in fighting organized crime as Hoover had been, again according to Lance. Furthermore, with Anthony Villano's retirement, the theory goes, Scarpa lost the inside contact who had helped him receive insurance kickbacks on stolen goods recovered through information Scarpa had provided. After 1973, again per Lance, Scarpa was merely providing the FBI with "what amounted to low-level Mafia gossip."[10] According to Lance, both sides of the Scarpa/FBI relationship had lost interest in continuing, and the relationship was terminated in 1975.

Finally, DeVecchio claimed in his book, without the benefit of providing the source of his information, that it was Scarpa who broke off the relationship in 1975 "because he thought he was owed money that a supervisor wouldn't sign off on."[11] Nothing in the FBI's documents that have been made public supports that allegation.

Whatever the reason for Scarpa's being closed as an FBI informant, it was not until FBI Special Agent Lin DeVecchio moved to reopen Scarpa in 1980 that he once again started providing the FBI with information about the New York area Cosa Nostra. It would be the beginning of a most memorable eight-year run.

REOPENING THE GRIM REAPER

DeVecchio, both in his book and in the FBI documents, described the process he went through that led to Scarpa's reopening. Those two descriptions are not in sync. For instance, in the FBI documents, DeVecchio stated, "It is noted that approximately six months have been required to discreetly re-contact the source and to persuade him to resume furnishing information which is of extremely high quality and unobtainable from any other current NYO source."[12] The first "discreet" contact noted in DeVecchio's book is when, "on a beautiful sunny June day in 1980,"[13] he staked out Scarpa's Bensonhurst home, watched Scarpa get into his car, and blocked his driveway so Scarpa could not back his car into the street. DeVecchio, according to his book, introduced himself, referenced his relationship with Anthony Villano, and gave Scarpa his phone number, telling him he wanted to learn "more about the ways of the life."[14] Two weeks later, on June 26, he was in Scarpa's house getting information from Scarpa on the Colombo family's members and organization as noted in his report of July 1, 1980.[15] Whether the process of reopening Scarpa as a TECI took two weeks or six months, by the summer of 1980, Scarpa was back at it, manipulating the FBI to his advantage every chance he got, and committing or ordering murder while he did it.

1980

On August 26, 1980, during the fourth meeting between Scarpa and DeVecchio, the manipulation began in earnest. During that meeting, Scarpa revealed that Donnie Somma, a Colombo family member, had been killed "on a contract approved by Carmine Persico."[16] Understandably, Scarpa did not tell DeVecchio that he had killed Somma by shooting him point blank in the face,[17] nor does it appear that DeVecchio inquired and Scarpa refused to provide information about Somma's killer. For reasons that likely died with Scarpa, ten and a half years later, he reported to DeVecchio that "Dominic [sic] Somma" was one of seven Colombo family members who were "deceased."[18] Of course, Scarpa once again made no mention of his role in Somma's decade-old demise. The omissions are particularly glaring given that on August 12, 1980, exactly two weeks earlier, Scarpa reported on the murder of two Colombo family members, Ralph and Shorty Spero, and included the identity of their murderer, Jerry Pappa, a Genovese family member.[19] According to Carmine Imbriale, Pappa killed Ralph Spero that year and, "[s]everal months later Shorty Spero disappeared."[20] As to Jerry Pappa, he "had his head blown off by a Colombo hit team" in July of 1980.[21]

Scarpa's lack of interest in providing the name of Somma's killer is understandable; DeVecchio's apparent willingness to ignore that salient omission is not. Interestingly,

DeVecchio's book, as it recounted the information Scarpa provided in those summer of 1980 meetings, made no mention of the Somma murder. Instead, the book relied on that later murder, without actually naming Somma as the victim, to demonstrate that DeVecchio was aware that Scarpa was a cold-blooded killer.[22] Since Scarpa never publicly admitted to killing Somma,[23] the question is, when did DeVecchio become aware of the identity of Somma's killer? Either DeVecchio committed malfeasance when he failed to report in August of 1980 that Scarpa had admitted committing murder earlier that summer, or he was incompetent when he did nothing during his debriefing of Scarpa or afterward to follow up on the revelation that Somma had been murdered by someone, since the law of murder generally requires human agency. Take your pick. In other words, less than two months after he reopened Scarpa, DeVecchio got played.

As the 1980 holiday season rolled around, Scarpa had another killing on his mind. This time, instead of being the shooter, he did what any self-respecting "C.E.O." would have done: he delegated that task. As noted above, the assignment to kill Dr. Eliezer Shkolnik fell to Gregory Scarpa Jr., with assistance provided by Joe Brewster. On December 3, 1980, Gregory Scarpa Jr. obeyed his father and committed his first murder by gunning down Dr. Shkolnik in the lobby of his parents' Forest Hills apartment. Scarpa made no mention of Shkolnik's murder when he was debriefed by the FBI on December 12, 1980, and January 7, 1981. He did, however, reveal five hits approved by Genovese family boss Frank "Funzi" Tieri,[24] and that Carmine Persico ordered the murder of Nick Prospero, the owner of Prospero's Funeral Home, for his "increasing dislike for the Colombo Family influence in his funeral home."[25] Unlike his revelation that Dominick Somma had been killed, Scarpa did not bother to mention the shooting death of Dr. Shkolnik. Based on

DeVecchio's apparent failure to press Scarpa about the details of the Somma murder, Scarpa's reticence to disclose the fact of the Shkolnik murder in December of 1980 seems to have been misplaced.

1981

Set five of the FBI's files relating to Scarpa includes nineteen pages of reporting dated December 11, 1981.[26] Those pages are divided into four sections, all of which contain notes from meetings between Scarpa and his handler, presumably Lin DeVecchio. The earliest date of the meetings covered in the nineteen pages is January 27, 1981. The last date of the meetings covered is November 19, 1981. During the period covered by this report, Scarpa provided information to the FBI during meetings on eleven different dates: January 27, February 10, March 4 and 24, April 7, May 12, July 14 and 28, September17 and 21, and November 19. During those eleven meetings, Scarpa referenced five different New York area LCN killings.

On May 12, 1981, Scarpa reported that Alphonse "Sonny Red" Indelicato, Dominick "Big Trin" Trinchera, and Phil "Phil Lucky" Giaccone of the Bonanno family had been killed on orders from Bonanno family boss Philip "Rusty" Rastelli.[27] On July 14, 1981, Scarpa reported that Colombo capo John "Irish" Matera had been hit "on authorization from Colombo family boss Carmine Persico during the past week."[28] And on July 28, 1981, Scarpa reported that Genovese family member Carlo "Collie" Di Pietro was killed.[29] What Scarpa failed to mention at any time during those eleven meetings is that in July of 1981, his son, Gregory Jr., shot and killed thirty-four-year-old Robert "Bucky" DiLeonardo,[30] a member of Scarpa's crew, on his orders.

According to Peter Lance, Scarpa Sr. ordered the hit on DiLeonardo because he had been bragging about taking part in bank jobs pulled by Scarpa's crew.[31] Lance's version of the rationale for the shooting appears to have been based on a debriefing of Carmine Sessa,[32] who, according to both Lance and John Kroger, participated in the killing.[33] Kroger, however, likely conflating the story behind Donnie Somma's murder with that of DiLeonardo, wrote that Bucky was shot because "he complained loudly about Scarpa's faulty lookout work on a bungled bank burglary."[34] Both authors noted that DiLeonardo was killed in his own car, and that Gregory Scarpa Jr. did the shooting. In fact, Gregory Jr. was ultimately charged with DiLeonardo's murder in connection with a second RICO prosecution brought against him on the basis of a twice-amended indictment filed in the first instance in June of 1995.[35]

The basic facts of DiLeonardo's murder are not in dispute. In July of 1981, Scarpa Sr. ordered the murder of Robert "Bucky" DiLeonardo, and his eldest son pulled the trigger. And although Scarpa reported the Somma murder to his FBI handler in 1980, a year later, Scarpa developed an understandable reticence when it came to reporting murders he had ordered. As a side note, Scarpa Sr. was never charged for his involvement in DiLeonardo's murder.

1982

A drop in the overall crime rate in New York City in 1982 included a decline in the number of murders from 1,826 in 1981[36] to 1,675 for the following year.[37] Scarpa was personally responsible for at least one of those 1982 killings.

As detailed in chapter six, Alfred Longobardi was murdered on Scarpa's orders in July of 1982. The information Scarpa provided to the FBI that year is set forth in reports beginning at page twenty-five of the fifth set of FBI files. The first of those reports is dated September 9, 1982, and it contains notes from meetings between Scarpa and his handler, which took place between January 5, 1982, and August 10, 1982. Reports for the remaining 1982 meetings, the last of which was on December 16, 1982,[38] end on page fifty-nine of FBI file set five. While Scarpa's recently acquired hesitance to mention murders that he committed continued in 1982, that did not prevent him from informing the FBI about murders committed by other LCN members. The reports of the meetings in 1982 between Scarpa and his FBI handler contain accounts of four successful killings and two attempted killings committed that year.

One of the murders was that of Angelo Mazzola. As Scarpa reported, Mazzola's murder was "not an LCN sanctioned hit but was done by young punks who had an argument with Mazzola and killed him."[39] The same file entry goes on to indicate that Mazzola may have been responsible for the attempted murder of someone who was dealing in narcotics and whose name has been redacted from the FBI's Scarpa files.[40]

Scarpa also provided information about the murder of Joe Peraino Jr. and the attempted hit on his father, Joe Peraino Sr. Both occurred on January 4, 1982, and, according to Scarpa, both were carried out by Andrew Russo's crew on orders from Carmine Persico. Persico had a number of complaints about the Perainos, including the allegation that they were dealing in both narcotics and pornography. Additionally, Joe Peraino Sr. was said to have refused to carry out a hit ordered by Gambino family boss Paul Castellano.[41] The transgressions cost Joe Jr. his life just as 1982 was getting underway.

According to Scarpa, about two months later, Joseph Rizzo was murdered as the result of a dispute with Charles

"Moose" Panarella, once again on orders from Carmine Persico. The hit was carried out by the crew of Carmine Persico's son, Little Allie Boy, possibly by Jackie DeRoss.[42] Scarpa also informed the FBI of a potential hit on a person whose name was redacted from the FBI's files. The redacted target of that hit gave a beating to an LCN member close to Jackie DeRoss and was to be killed for having administered that beating.[43] If that murder took place in 1982, Scarpa either did not know about it or simply did not report it as no further mention is made of it in any of his 1982 debriefings.

Finally, in October of 1982, Scarpa reported on another Colombo family hit. Scarpa informed his handler that Nicholas "Nicky Black" Grancio was in on the murder of John Aratico, who was shot and killed in front of his Brooklyn house in April of 1982.[44] Per Scarpa, Grancio's nephew, Joe Tolino, at the time a Colombo family associate, was also in on the Aratico murder.[45]

In all of those pages developed from debriefings conducted over the course of twelve months of meetings, either Scarpa did not mention the hit on Longobardi, or if he did, his handler failed to record what Scarpa said about it. As noted above, while the circumstances leading to the murder of Alfred Longobardi are the subject of some disagreement, ultimately, he was shot and killed in July of 1982. His wounds were so intentionally severe that his family could only identify him by his tattoos. His killing, therefore, was not a secret or unknown event among New York law enforcement circles. At a minimum, NYPD was notified about the killing. Additionally, according to Peter Lance, the police developed a clue potentially linking the killing to Joe Brewster. Furthermore, Longobardi was "the first husband of Scarpa crew member Carmine Imbriale's wife."[46] Either the FBI deliberately ignored Longobardi's murder, one that was clearly linked to their prized Top Echelon Criminal Informant, or they were so oblivious as to be negligent.

While Scarpa was feeding Lin DeVecchio a steady stream of information about murders committed, ordered, attempted, or contemplated by others in New York's LCN families, he had been, by the end of 1982, personally involved in four murders in less than two years. Predictably, with an apparent lack of external restraints, he would add to that number in 1983.

1983

In 1983, the number of homicides in New York City dropped again, to 1,622 for the year, which was equal to a rate of 22.8 homicides per 100,000 population.[47] For his part, Scarpa may have picked up the pace a bit, recording at least one, and perhaps two, homicides for the year as opposed to the single confirmed murder he had ordered the year before.

For reasons unknown, Scarpa's recorded contacts with his handler Lin DeVecchio dropped off slightly in 1983.[48] The FBI's files that have been made public note ten meetings between Scarpa and DeVecchio during the year, three each in March and September, two in April, one possibly in June, and one in August. All of the meetings are recorded in a single report dated November 16, 1983.[49] Of course, it is possible that more meetings occurred that DeVecchio did not feel warranted reporting due to a lack of information passed by Scarpa. Or it could be that there are other documents relative to meetings between Scarpa and DeVecchio in 1983 that the FBI has not released to the public. At any rate, in only one of those ten chronicled meetings did Scarpa discuss a murder, that of a man he knew as Charlie Champagne.

According to Scarpa, Champagne was involved in dealing narcotics with Little Allie Boy Persico. When Persico was arrested on a narcotics charge, Charlie Champagne became a target of suspicion in LCN circles for his alleged cooperation with law enforcement. On September 13, 1983, Scarpa reported that Charlie Champagne had been killed about two weeks earlier, that "the body was disposed of, and there [was] probably no report of Champagne being missing at this time."[50]

Scarpa did not pass along anything of note, if he met at all with DeVecchio, in January and February of 1983, despite the fact that in January of 1983, he ordered and witnessed the murder of Sal "The Hammerhead" Cardaci. Although Carmine Sessa, who had yet to earn his button with the Colombo family,[51] pulled the trigger of the .357 magnum that killed Cardaci, it was Scarpa who ordered the hit. Cardaci was suspected of leaking information to NYPD about auto thefts committed by Scarpa crew member Billy Meli.[52] Cardaci, who was also a car thief, [53] was in the restroom of Mike's Candy Store when he was murdered by Sessa as Scarpa looked on. Cardaci's body was then stripped and buried in the basement of the candy store which, fortuitously, was owned by Scarpa. Another participant in Cardaci's murder, Mario Parlagreco, years later tearfully recounted his role in the hit. Parlagreco, who had an emotional distaste for pulling the trigger, instead "cleaned up Cardaci's blood and brains in the bathroom of Mike's Candy Store."[54] It would not be the last murder Parlagreco was ordered to sanitize. At Gregory Jr.'s direction, Parlagreco made his garage available for wiping down the car that was the scene of Joe Brewster's murder in 1987.[55] Parlagreco assisted with clean up after the hit. Cardaci's murder, like those of Somma, Longobardi, and DiLeonardo, was later included in the charged underlying offenses supporting the second RICO action brought against Gregory Scarpa Jr.[56]

The gruesome murder of Sal Cardaci in January of 1983 was followed by the killing of Albie Variale in July of the same year. The available evidence pointing to Scarpa as being responsible for the Variale murder is admittedly thin. In fact, Peter Lance, after including the killing of Variale in a list of "seventeen murders directly attributed to Gregory Scarpa Sr." during the 1980s, noted that the only official source he was able to rely on for his claim that Scarpa was involved in that murder was the Second Circuit's opinion in *United States v. Sessa, et al*. In that case, the Court of Appeals affirmed the District Court's overruling of Gregory Scarpa Jr.'s challenge to his second RICO prosecution on double jeopardy grounds.[57] In its published opinion, the Second Circuit listed the murder of Albie Variale in July of 1983 as having been allegedly committed by Gregory Scarpa Jr. "and others." Given that Gegory Scarpa Jr. had committed murder on orders from his father in the past, it is not inconceivable that Scarpa Sr. ordered Variale's murder, and that he was among "the others" the court referenced.

The only other references to Variale's murder this author was able to locate were online.[58] The first is from an article posted on the Gangsters Inc. website and purportedly written by "Puparo," which is Italian for "puppeteer." In that article, under the heading of "Gregory Scarpa sr [sic] and Greg jr" [sic], it is noted without attribution that "Scarpa jr [sic] killed in July 1983 Albie Variale."[59] The second reference is from an article written by Ed Scarpo and posted on the Cosa Nostra News website. Scarpo's article claimed that Kevin Granato, one of Scarpa Jr.'s crew members and a codefendant in the first RICO action brought against Gregory Jr., et al.[60] was responsible for the Variale killing. Quoting a source who "agreed to speak only if allowed anonymity," Scarpo wrote that "one of Granato's murders was Albert (Alby) Variale's, who was killed on 86th Street and 20th Avenue in front of hundreds of witnesses...."[61]

Whatever doubts might reasonably exist about Scarpa's direct or indirect participation in the murder of Albie Variale in 1983, his role in the contemptable murder of Mary Bari in 1984 is well documented and unassailable. If Scarpa had committed no other crimes during his life, killing Mary Bari would have easily justified, at a minimum, his spending the rest of his years behind bars.

1984

By 1984, a year in which New York City's total number of homicides once again fell slightly to 1,450, or a mere 20.4 murders per 100,000 residents,[62] Scarpa had explicitly credited at least five murders in four years to either direct orders from, or as being authorized by, Carmine Persico: Donnie Somma, Nick Prospero, John "Irish" Matera, Joseph Rizzo, and Joe Peraino Jr. Scarpa's willingness to inform the FBI on the criminal activity of the de facto boss of the Colombo family did not, however, extend to mentioning Persico's, or anyone else's, role in the brutal murder of Mary Bari. In fact, the FBI files released to the public regarding Scarpa's role as a Top Echelon Criminal Informant contain no evidence of any debriefings or meetings with his handler in 1984. Although DeVecchio cited a 209 report, an FBI form which records information provided by a TECI, of his having met with Scarpa on November 21, 1984, in his book,[63] for some reason that report is not included in the Scarpa files the FBI has made available online. As it turned out, in 1984 Scarpa did not seek authorization from his family boss to kill Mary Bari. He acted on his own. As Peter Lance put it, "[h]e'd committed other homicides on the FBI's watch and he had reason to be confident that he could get away with this one."[64] In other words, Greg Scarpa, who liked to tell his daughter Linda and his son Joey that he was like James Bond,[65] for all intents and purposes, had a license to kill.

As noted above, Mary Bari and Alphonse "Allie Boy" Persico, Carmine "The Snake" Persico's brother, began their relationship in 1969. That relationship effectively ended when Allie Boy became a fugitive in 1980 to avoid the prospect of prison time on a loansharking and extortion conviction. The Colombo family, as was fairly routine, did not support Mary in Allie Boy's absence.[66] Thereafter, rumors of various stripes began to wind their way through the Colombo family that Mary Bari, who was struggling to make ends meet, was contemplating giving up Allie Boy's location, and possibly more, to the FBI.

The inconsistent and unfounded rumors circulating by 1984 about Bari allegedly caught Greg Scarpa's attention. Irrespective of the rumors' lack of foundation and consistency, Scarpa quickly fell back on a tried-and-true solution to what he perceived to be a potential threat: violent death. He acted on that default solution, and on September 25, 1984, Mary Bari's short life came to a quick and brutal end.

Whether Scarpa was working on a tip and/or advice from Lin DeVecchio about the possibility that Mary Bari might reveal Allie Boy's whereabouts has been the object of much speculation. As noted above, that proposition's validity, in this author's view, is dubious. Another possibility exists, one that perhaps makes more sense: Scarpa learned that Mary Bari was an FBI informant, and he used her previous connection to Allie Boy as a cover story to justify her killing.

Victor Oboyski, a deputy U.S. Marshal, participated in the seven-year search for Allie Boy Persico, Mary's boyfriend, after Persico failed to show up for his presentencing hearing in 1980. Allie Boy was eventually arrested in West Hartford,

Connecticut three years after Mary Bari was executed by Greg Scarpa. Persico had managed to evade capture for seven years thanks to the Rhode Island Patriarca crime family's elaborate "underground railroad" for mobsters on the lam, which provided him with "funds and phony identification papers."[67] Oboyski's take, which he related to Jerry Capeci, was that Bari was killed because Scarpa found out she was an FBI informant. According to Oboyski, Bari had no idea where Persico was and had had no contact with him for years. In fact, again according to Oboyski, Persico's family did not know where he was. If she had been asked by law enforcement where Persico was hiding, Bari would have had nothing to offer. However, Oboyski claimed that Bari was an FBI informant, a conclusion he reached after a conversation with an unnamed FBI agent in the early 1980s.

> "'They [the FBI] came to us. They wanted pictures of the Saugerties farm [which the Persico family owned] and they wanted info that we had developed about the farm during our investigation. At some point, I said to the agent, "We're very interested in talking to Mary Bari." He said, "We'd appreciate it if you didn't. We have a special relationship with her." So we just dropped it.' Mr. Oboyski said. [para.] 'It was troubling when she was killed, and even more troubling when I learned that she was killed by Scarpa, another informant,' said Mr. Oboyski. 'The case has always bothered me.'"[68]

How Scarpa learned that Bari was an informant has never been the object of a serious inquiry, so far as can be determined from existing public sources. The story that Scarpa fed Carmine Sessa and the other participants in Bari's murder about her potentially giving away Allie Boy Persico's location has been widely retold and generally accepted. And, indeed, it may be true. Before Oboyski's allegations can be tied to Scarpa, some evidence linking Scarpa to the allegation about Bari's status as an informant is required. So far as this author has been able to determine, that evidence has not been developed. Perhaps it does not exist. Once again, trying to determine the accuracy of conflicting accounts of events that took place nearly four decades ago is problematic to say the least, particularly in the context of persons sworn to secrecy and a tight-lipped bureaucracy. What can be said with certainty is that on September 25, 1984, Gregory Scarpa and his son brutally murdered Mary Bari in Carmine Sessa's club. It was the only murder known to have been committed by Scarpa that year. Scarpa's having dropped off the pace in 1984 did not signify that he was mellowing with age as he headed into his late fifties. He instead followed up that effort with a banner year that yielded more killings in spite of a drop in the overall murder rate in New York City by 4.6 percent to a total of 1,384 people killed in 1985.[69]

1985

The FBI's Scarpa files for 1985 do not record any activity between Scarpa and his handler until after November 5, 1985, the day Scarpa was arrested by the Secret Service for credit card fraud. One of the remarkable entries in 1985, which is dated March 1, summarized the value of the information provided by Scarpa since his reopening in 1980, and claimed, "The above represents a small portion of the quantity of the significant information provided, which if fully documented would require a lengthy summary report."[70] Apparently, the higher-ups in D.C. were expected to simply take the FBI New York Office's word for it without "a lengthy summary report." And apparently, they did.

In the same vein, on September 20, 1985, a request by the FBI's New York Office to FBI headquarters for payment to

Scarpa, which was granted, was accompanied by another generic statement that "this source has furnished information of value in furtherance of one or more FBI investigations or on matters of investigative interest to other federal, state, or local authorities...."[71] It is reasonable to conclude from the above entries and the lack of entries for 1984 and much of 1985, that either the substance of the contacts with Scarpa was no longer being recorded with any sort of regularity, or that Scarpa and DeVecchio simply did not meet for more than a year and a half. The former seems more likely than the latter.

Of course, a third possibility exists. It could be that Scarpa and his handler met, that those meetings were duly chronicled, and the FBI has not made the reports of the contacts during that time period public. Whatever the case, resumption of more or less regular written reports about regular contacts between the two appears to have been prompted by Scarpa's November 5, 1985, arrest for credit card fraud, which was first noted in a teletype to FBI headquarters on November 19, 1985.[72]

Scarpa had been producing and selling fake credit cards— counterfeit access devices[73] in law enforcement parlance— for a number of years.[74] The cards were used for everything from free dinners[75] to purchasing high-end merchandise which was then resold for cash.[76] According to Larry Mazza, who was no fan of the fake credit card scheme,[77] in 1985, Scarpa had been approached by a regular buyer who was "interested in buying the fake cards by the bundle."[78] What Scarpa did not know was that the buyer was cooperating with the Secret Service as a result of his having recently been arrested in Atlantic City.[79] After some initial contacts, an undercover Secret Service agent "met with Scarpa at the Wimpy Boys Club and sold him three hundred blank cards—150 Visas and 150 Master Cards—for $9,000."[80]

"[Scarpa's arrest] by Secret Service was the result of Secret Service UCA [undercover agent] and a cooperating witness sent into the source in an attempt to sell credit card blanks. The source agreed to look at samples on the day of the arrest, and in fact was arrested in his vehicle with the UCA. This operation appears to have started four to six weeks prior to the arrest, and was not related to any assignment as an FBI source."[81]

The FBI's New York Office immediately went into full damage control mode to both protect Scarpa's identity and to justify his continued use as an informant, which would naturally require his staying out of prison. To buttress the claim of Scarpa's importance to fighting organized crime, specific reports about contacts between Scarpa and his handler began reappearing regularly again in the files. Astonishingly, the suggestion to the FBI that Scarpa redouble his informant efforts came from his appointed counsel William Kelleher.[82]

"Kelleher believes that further contact will assist the source against a possible indictment, and through efforts of the NYO with respect to organized crime investigations beneficial to the EDNY, would remove any further threat of prosecution. Kelleher also believes that the current case against source is weak, and not worthy of prosecution compared to the value of the source to the government."[83]

Kelleher's point of view coincided nicely with the FBI's, and the contacts and reports resumed in earnest. The first of those reports stated quite candidly that the information was provided by Scarpa after his arrest on November 5, 1985.[84] For the rest of 1985, Scarpa met with his FBI handler on December 5, 11, 16, and 17.[85] Remarkably, given what he was then facing, Scarpa reported on December 5, 1985, that

"Colombo member Joseph "Lefty" San Georgio is heavily involved in the use and sale of fraudulent credit cards, and is in business with Vincent Caputo [and]... that Rocky Riccobone, a Colombo family associate, currently has possession of the machine used to emboss the blank credit cards."[86]

Scarpa's habit of projecting did not apply solely to credit card fraud. As will be seen below, while he continued to commit murder in 1985, he simultaneously continued to report about murder committed by other LCN members. For instance, on December 17, Scarpa reported that the hit on Gambino boss Paul Castellano and Gambino capo Thomas Bilotti the previous day[87] was "set up by John Gotti and Frank DeCicco."[88]

Scarpa kept the freshly-motivated flow of information coming in the new year by meeting with his handler on January 2, and February 5, 10, and 26.[89] As almost an afterthought, on July 11, 1986, the FBI's New York Office reported that Scarpa also provided information on October 1, 1985, November 1, 1985, and December 5, 1985, updating the probable cause required in a T-III [wiretap] case.[90] In short, ten meetings were chronicled in the space of just over four months when none had been reported during all of 1984 and the first nine months of 1985. It is reasonable to conclude that one or more persons who were anxious to demonstrate Scarpa's continued value to the federal government in spite of his arrest by the Secret Service wholly agreed with the strategy proposed by Scarpa's counsel William Kelleher.

In the meantime, the federal government still had to work out what to do with one of its most valued informants, given he was about to be the subject of a public prosecution for credit card fraud. The negotiations about the potential disposition of the Secret Service's case against Scarpa began as soon as Scarpa mentioned after his arrest that he was an FBI informant to Ed McDonald, Chief of the Eastern District of New York's (EDNY) Strike Force.[91] From that moment on, the FBI's New York Office (NYO) "worked out details with EDNY to afford NYO continued contact with source, without jeopardizing [the] code of federal regulations."[92] McDonald, who was not willing to give Scarpa "'a pass in this case,'" offered him, in exchange for his cooperation and testimony, entry into the witness protection program."[93]

Scarpa turned down the offer, which McDonald duly reported to the Secret Service. Discussions ensued between the FBI and McDonald, which at one point included Assistant U.S. Attorney Norman Bloch, and the Secret Service agents.[94] The FBI's primary stated concern was Scarpa's personal safety.[95] That concern extended to the safety of his brother Sal and son Gregory Jr.[96] Beyond worrying about Scarpa's safety, the FBI did not want to lose their valuable informant to a prison sentence. For its part, FBI headquarters in Washington, D.C., wanted it both ways.

> "The New York Division is advised to take no action to effect [sic] the outcome of prosecutive action by the Eastern District of New York (EDNY) without prior FBIHQ approval. However, New York may furnish general information to Ed McDonald, Strike Force Chief, EDNY, as to the value of this informant to the FBI."[97]

McDonald wanted to prosecute. Scarpa refused to cooperate. The FBI wanted their prized TECI to continue in that role, but it also wanted to appear neutral about the EDNY's case. Any public trial would make that impossible and would threaten Scarpa's life. But if Scarpa were able simply to walk away from the arrest, his status as an FBI informant would be confirmed and he would likewise be as good as dead. The solution? After a federal grand jury returned a four-count indictment on May 15, 1986, Scarpa, as he offered, would take a plea[98] and his sentence would consist of five years' probation and a $10,000 fine. That sentence, after a good word from SA Lin DeVecchio,[99] was imposed by Judge Leo Glasser on February 6, 1987.[100] Frankly, it was less than a slap on the wrist for a man who continued to murder people at will. Scarpa's remarkable string of successful manipulation of the FBI continued unabated even in the face of arrest by the Secret Service and potential prosecution by Eastern District of New York's Strike Force. He avoided prison time, he was not summarily executed by the mob for being an informant, and he continued his lucrative second career as a mole for the FBI.

Not everyone was fooled by the federal government's light touch in Scarpa's credit card case. Carmine Imbriale, a former Colombo family associate who received a three-year sentence in federal prison for possession of three fake credit cards, smelled a rat.

> "'I get pinched with just three credit cards and do time,' Carmine says. 'I get out. I'm eating dinner with Carmine [Sessa]. I ask him, "How the hell did Greg get caught with hundreds of cards *and* testimony from a Secret Service agent, and *nothing* happens? Come on now."' [para.] Sessa shut the conversation down. 'He stopped me cold, warned me to never ever say anything like that about Greg to anyone unless I could prove it, and even then, I was better off keeping my mouth shut. *Or else*.'"[101]

Scarpa would do no jail time for a federal offense that generated a four-count indictment from a federal grand jury, and that could have resulted in a seven-and-a-half-year prison sentence and a $250,000 fine.[102] For all intents and purposes, he emerged, more than a year after his arrest, unscathed. In 1985, in addition to committing fraud with practical impunity, he once again got away with murder.

As detailed above, José Guzman was murdered in 1985.[103] While the accounts of Guzman's murder vary, there can be little doubt that it was ordered by Greg Scarpa after Guzman was viciously beaten by members of Scarpa's crew. The most interesting point in all of the accounts lies in DeVecchio's book where he stated the following:

> "Scarpa got a cane and walked into the limo driver's office limping, as if he were relying on the cane. The driver assumed Scarpa needed a limo because of some injury. Scarpa limped up to the driver and bopped him over the head with the cane, then whipped him with it. [para.] 'I told him he was fired. He couldn't drive my daughter to school no more.' [para.] What happened after that? [para.] 'I went back and killed him. I couldn't live with myself.'"[104]

The source of DeVecchio's version of events surrounding Guzman's murder is not clear. It bears no resemblance to Linda Scarpa's recollection. And, given the assistance putting her book together that Linda Scarpa received from her mother, Linda Schiro, it would appear Schiro could not have been the source for DeVecchio's allegations. Likewise, there is little in common between DeVecchio's story and those of Mazza, Gregory Jr., and Carmine Sessa. It could be that DeVecchio simply fabricated the exchange with Scarpa as he apparently fabricated much of his lengthy narrative about the run-up to Mary Bari's murder. Or Scarpa could have confessed to DeVecchio at some point. Nothing in DeVecchio's version of the Guzman murder indicates when he received it or who gave it to him, and it is likely we will never know.

We do know that Tony "Muscles" Frezza was also murdered in 1985.[105] We know why he was murdered. And we know who murdered him. Frezza, who drove Mary Bari to Carmine Sessa's club the night she was murdered, killed a Gambino family man by the name of Joey DiAngelo. Frezza was a Colombo associate who had had a few too many one night in Tali's Restaurant and Cocktail Lounge on 18th Avenue in Brooklyn.[106] Frezza started popping off and eventually DiAngelo had him removed from the bar. Tony went home, grabbed a gun, returned to the bar, and "blew Joey DiAngelo away right in front of a host of witnesses."[107]

Tony's impulsive execution of a Gambino goodfellow resulted in his own death sentence. The Gambino family insisted that Frezza, who was under Colombo capo Anthony Scarpati, be killed. Scarpa's crew, after some negotiations between Scarpati and the Gambino, was given the work.[108] The task fell to Gregory Scarpa Jr., Kevin Granato, and Mario Parlagreco.[109] At this point, the two detailed accounts of Frezza's murder diverged. According to Mazza, Parlagreco related the following to Scarpa Sr. about the hit the morning after it took place. Frezza was told they were all going to a party at Greg Jr.'s house on Staten Island to celebrate Frezza's coming out of hiding. He had been in Florida and returned to New York when Scarpati told him everything had been worked out with the Gambinos.[110] The four men drove out to Staten Island, stopping to get some cocaine on the way. When they reached their destination, Frezza was shot and killed as they walked from the driveway to the house. His body was buried in a shallow grave in the woods across from Wood's Pond along Staten Island's Hyland Avenue. The attempt to conceal Frezza's body failed, and it was found the next day.[111]

According to Kroger, Frezza and Scarpa walked into Scarpa's house and Scarpa "then shot him in the heart at his own kitchen table."[112] Kroger added that Scarpa Jr. "showed the body to the Gambinos, to prove the killing had been done."[113] Then Scarpa and his crew buried Frezza's body "on Staten Island's New Dorp Beach,"[114] which is about an eighteen-minute drive from Wolf's Pond, where Mazza alleged the body was buried. Of course, as already noted, so far as can be determined from the records the FBI has released, Scarpa did not report the murder of Tony Frezza to DeVecchio.

Peter Lance referenced two other murders connected to Scarpa that were committed in 1985. Peter Crupi, who was gunned down on August 2, and Albert Nocha, who was shot three times in the head and once in the chest, all at close range and whose body was found on December 10, were both Staten Island drug dealers whose lucrative territories the Scarpas coveted.

In the first RICO case filed against Gregory Scarpa Jr. and several members of his crew in 1988, the government originally included an allegation that Peter Crupi was murdered by Scarpa's codefendant Nunzio DeCarlo as one of the underlying offenses supporting the racketeering count. However, the federal prosecutor moved to strike that allegation from the indictment before trial.[115] It was, therefore, no longer part of the federal government's case and was not adjudicated. Larry Mazza, who personally witnessed the burgeoning drug trade that captured the greedy imagination of both Scarpas, wrote that he eventually concluded, based on all he had learned over the years, that Crupi was killed by Gregory Jr.[116] Even if Gregory Jr. pulled the trigger as Mazza surmised, Scarpa Sr. was clearly in charge of the Wimpy Boys' efforts in the illicit narcotics trade.[117] As Lance put it, "Greg Scarpa Sr. was raking in millions from his own narcotics activity."[118] It is not unreasonable to conclude, then, that the killing of Peter Crupi was ordered by Greg Scarpa Sr. as the Scarpas moved heavily into dealing narcotics, particularly on Staten Island, in the mid-1980s.

As to the killing of Albert Nocha, while four of Scarpa's codefendants in the same case, Kevin Granato, Cosmo Catanzano, Mario Parlagreco, and Nunzio DeCarlo, all of whom had been previously identified as associates of Greg Scarpa Sr.,[119] were charged with Nocha's murder as an underlying offense supporting the first RICO count in the indictment, only DeCarlo was convicted on the basis of Nocha's murder.[120] At trial, testimony was introduced that included DeCarlo's twice confessing to killing Nocha, who had been selling marijuana not far from where the Scarpa crew was operating. Nocha was warned once by Eric Leon, another Scarpa associate, and once by DeCarlo, to stop selling at that location, but he ignored the warnings. Word got back to Gregory Scarpa Jr. about Nocha's sales and his refusal to move. What happened next was sadly predictable.

"On December 10, 1985, Albert Nocha was found shot to death in Clove Lake Park. He had approximately $400 in small bills in his pocket and a paper bag containing marijuana in his hand. An autopsy revealed that he had been shot once in the chest and three times in the head at point-blank range. Evidence at trial, including Leon's testimony that DeCarlo told Leon that DeCarlo had killed Nocha, tied DeCarlo to the shooting."[121]

Once again, given that Nunzio DeCarlo was an associate of Greg Scarpa Sr., who was running the Wimpy Boys' narcotics dealing operation, it is reasonable to conclude that Scarpa Sr. ordered the killing of Albert Nocha, a competitor who refused to relocate after being told twice to do so.

While 1985 was a busy year for Scarpa in terms of homicide with as many as four murders to his credit, 1986, the year in which he spent a considerable amount of time bedridden after emergency surgery on his bleeding ulcer, was an otherwise quiet year by comparison for The Grim Reaper.

Citywide, the number of homicides for 1986 was 1,598,[122] reversing a trend of slight decreases that began in 1982.

1986

The only credible reference to homicides potentially committed or ordered by Scarpa Sr. in 1986 comes to us from a Second Circuit U.S. Court of Appeals decision handed down in 1997. As noted above, in that decision the Court of Appeals affirmed the District Court's overruling of Gregory Scarpa Jr.'s challenge to his second RICO prosecution on double jeopardy grounds.[123] The court's opinion included the murders of "Michael Yodice and Jose Lopez in December 1986" as having been allegedly committed by Gregory Scarpa Jr. "and others."[124] As has been stated a number of times, Gregory Scarpa Jr. committed murder more than once on orders from his father. It is, therefore, plausible that Scarpa Sr. ordered the murder of Yodice or Lopez or both of them. Unfortunately, no further information about those killings was located during the production of this book.

Likewise, Scarpa was for the most part mum about other LCN killings during his fourteen meetings[125] with his FBI handler in 1986. The only mention of a murder was during his February 5 debriefing, when he provided the name of a proposed Gambino family member who "may have been one of the shooters of Paul Castellano."[126] While the FBI was hoping Scarpa would be able to provide information about the murder via car bomb of Gambino underboss Frank DeCicco[127] on April 13,[128] nothing in the Scarpa records that the FBI has made public indicates that Scarpa was able to meet that expectation.

The information provided to the FBI by Scarpa during 1986 was, overall, routine and revolved primarily around less than lethal criminal activity of various LCN members and changes in LCN family leadership and membership. However, what Scarpa had provided over the years, by the FBI's reckoning, led directly to the indictments on October 24, 1984,[129] and the convictions in federal court on June 13, 1986, of Colombo family boss Carmine Persico, his son, "Little Allie Boy" Persico, Colombo underboss Jerry Langella, Colombo capos Jackie DeRoss, Andrew Russo, and Anthony Scarpati, Colombo goodfellow Dominic Cataldo, and Colombo associates Frank Falanga and Hugh McIntosh.[130] As Rudolph Giuliani, then the U.S. Attorney for the Southern District of New York, said, "The jury had 'crushed the top leadership of the Colombo Mafia family.'"[131] As will be seen in chapters nine and ten, those convictions, a bloodbath of a different sort directly precipitated by Scarpa's role as an FBI Top Echelon Criminal Informant, created a leadership vacuum that went a long way to contributing to the violence in Brooklyn over the next six years.

While Scarpa's surgery in August of 1986 and his slow recovery, coupled with the news that he was HIV-positive from a tainted blood transfusion, may have blunted his taste for killing in 1986, he was fully back in the saddle in 1987. He ordered at least two more murders, one of which was of Joe Brewster, and he is suspected by some of having participated in the murder of Salvatore Scarpa, his only brother.

1987

The number of murders in New York City in 1987 increased again over the previous year, coming in at 1,691[132] for the year in which Greg Scarpa turned fifty-nine. By then, much of his stomach had been removed and his blood was HIV-positive. While he was not yet suffering from full-blown AIDS, the general perception in the U.S. in 1987 was that becoming HIV-positive was a death sentence. Understandably, many have speculated about the effect Scarpa's health had on his behavior during the last years of his life. Generally, the analytical tendency is to try to attribute what some view as Scarpa's increasing recklessness and violence to his grim personal prognosis. Whether he was undergoing a transformative change in character due to his health, or he simply never stopped being "The Grim Reaper" or "The Mad Hatter," is best left to those who would venture to psychoanalyze the dead. For 1987, at any rate, Scarpa's willingness to commit horrific acts of violence, even directed at those closest to him, was a core characteristic of his personality he had long since established.

On January 14, 1987, Greg Scarpa's only brother, Salvatore Scarpa, was murdered. His murder has never been solved, and some have concluded that Greg either ordered his brother killed or did the killing himself. The Scarpa brothers had a strained relationship for much of their adult lives. Given the discrepancies in the various sources, a note about the birth order of Scarpa and his siblings is in order.

It is commonly, and correctly, reported that Salvatore Sr. and Mary Scarpa had five children, three girls and two boys. In Linda Scarpa's book, Linda Schiro claimed that Greg was the second of five children.[133] Larry Mazza referred to Sal as "older than Greg" and "not nearly as respected as his kid brother."[134] Likewise, Peter Lance called Sal "Gregory Scarpa's older brother."[135] Fredric Dannen wrote that Scarpa "appears to have been drawn into the Colombo family—then called the Profaci family—by his older brother, Salvatore, who died in a shooting in 1987."[136] Other than the fact that Scarpa had four siblings, those descriptions are all inaccurate.

According to the United States census of 1940, Salvatore and Mary Scarpa had five children. The first three were girls, Teresa, Vince (Vincenza), and Marie in birth order. Teresa was twenty, Vincenza was seventeen, and Marie was fourteen on April 3, 1940, the date the census was taken. The next two children were boys, Gregory and Salvatore, again in birth order. The form states that Gregory was eleven and in the fifth grade, and that Salvatore was ten and in the fourth grade on the date the census was taken. The census taker noted on the form that the information about the Scarpa family came from wife and mother Mary Scarpa, who was thirty-seven years old at the time.[137] In this author's view, the census is dispositive on the issue of the birth order of Greg Scarpa and his siblings. Simply put, Sal was younger than Greg, and both of them were younger than their three sisters.[138]

The two Scarpa brothers shared more than just a last name. They were both made men, and it is likely that Sal preceded his brother Greg into "the life."[139] Furthermore, Sal is credited by some with bringing Scarpa into the Profaci family.[140] It was not unusual for a number of years for them to work together. Sal shows up early in the FBI's files recording the Bureau's contacts with Scarpa. In fact, the FBI's original contact with Scarpa came about as the Bureau sought information about Sal's participation in an interstate transportation theft that Scarpa had been arrested for in March of 1960. Sal was an additional suspect in that case. Sal is also listed as a relative and a "criminal associate" of Scarpa's in the first report of the FBI's attempts to turn Scarpa into an informant.[141] Scarpa refused to assist the FBI with its search for his brother,[142] just as he initially refused to provide any information to the FBI. The close working relationship between the Scarpa brothers did not last.

Joey "Brains" Ambrosino, who initially worked for Sal Scarpa before eventually becoming part of the Wimpy Boys crew, said in 1994 that the Scarpa brothers "had a love/hate relationship."[143] Linda Schiro reported that the relationship between the two men was not good. According to Schiro, Greg and his brother Sal used to "always butt heads. [Greg] loved Sal, but Sal was a thickhead and never listened to Greg."[144] By the mid-1980s, when Greg was dealing in counterfeit credit cards, their relationship was defined by money more than anything else. At one point, Sal came to the Wimpy Boys Club to "see Greg about purchasing some [phony] cards." [145] Sal owed Greg $100 and Greg refused to sell Sal any more credit cards until he paid off the debt. The two exchanged words and Sal "ran out in aggravation."[146] Money was always thicker than blood for Greg Scarpa.

Sal was shot and killed two weeks into the new year in 1987 while in his Dyker Heights social club on 74th Street.[147] The murder was initially reported as having been committed during the course of a robbery of those in the club by five men. However, "'Sal's watch, a gold pendant and his wallet with $313 in cash in it were found beside his body. The gunmen may have stolen the belongings of the other people in the club to make it look like a robbery, but that was all bullshit. It was a hit on Sal, and they never found out who killed him.'"[148] Angela Clemente, "the forensic investigator responsible for the release of the FBI Scarpa files," eventually concluded that Sal was killed by Philip "Philly Boy" Paradiso, who was acting on orders from Greg Scarpa.[149] According to Clemente, Greg had his brother killed because he believed Sal was going to expose him as an FBI informant.[150] Linda Scarpa also believed her father was responsible for her Uncle Sal's death. "'It was like growing up with a serial killer,' [said] Schiro, who believes her father's murder victims included Scarpa's own brother, Sal, her uncle."[151]

Sal Scarpa's murder remains officially unsolved. Unofficially, however, Angela Clemente's conclusions after her careful and thorough analysis may indeed be accurate. However, Scarpa was never charged with his brother's murder, nor was Philip Paradiso. While questions remain about the degree of Scarpa's involvement in the murder of his only brother, as detailed previously, there is no question about his role in the murder of Joe Brewster in September of 1987.

Brewster's killing may have had an outsized negative effect on the Colombo borgata, coming as it did on the heels of the decimation of the family's leadership in federal court. Brewster "was a straight-up gangster, an armed robber, and a cold-blooded murderer."[152] In spite of the fact that he was a murderer and a thief who preyed on legitimate businesses and the people who owned them, or perhaps because of that, Brewster was well-liked among those who knew him best. Larry Mazza was sickened by not only Brewster's death but also the mendacious rationalizing of it. "Another dear friend was killed by our own."[153]

When Carmine Imbriale, a man who was particularly close to Brewster for years, read about Brewster's murder, he "remember[ed] feeling overwhelmed by sadness, helplessness... and clarity."[154] Carmine Sessa testified that he "was very upset about the murder of Joe Brewster,"[155] and added he thought "that murder, Joe Brewster, was a turning point for a lot of guys on the Avenue."[156] As will be seen in chapters nine and ten, a heightened sense of paranoia pervaded the ranks of the Colombo family in the late 1980s and early 1990s. That paranoia, coupled with a lack of definition in the family's leadership that drove an insidious and deadly competition, resulted in a violent internal struggle that brought ruin to the borgata. Brewster's murder may well have been an inflection point, as Sessa surmised.[157]

Finally, although the timing is murky, in 1987, Scarpa arguably triggered a conspiracy to kill one of his own crew members, Cosmo Catanzano, [158] who was involved in the crew's lucrative drug trade on Staten Island. A variety of sources have repeated some form of the allegation, so it is worth examining. The overall arc of the story is that Catanzano was to be executed on Scarpa's orders, but his arrest saved him. A review of the facts at play is helpful.

As the story goes, at some point in the summer or fall of 1987 Scarpa became convinced that Catanzano was going to become an FBI informant if he were arrested.[159] Scarpa allegedly found this out as the DEA was preparing to arrest nearly everyone, including Catanzano, in Gregory Jr.'s crew for their drug dealing and related activities such as assault and extortion.[160] Scarpa Sr., having been informed of the pending arrests, is said to have forbidden anyone about to be arrested from going "on the lam." Additionally, he is supposed to have ordered Catanzano's murder, since he believed Catanzano was a "weak link" and would talk if arrested.[161] Billy Meli, who was also targeted by the DEA for arrest, was given the job of killing Catanzano. Pre-execution preparation included digging a grave,[162] which, the story continues, Meli and Kevin Granato dutifully did along Staten Island's Arthur Kill Road.[163] However, on November 10, 1987, before Meli could kill Catanzano, they and most of the other members of Junior's crew were arrested.[164] Here is where the story begins to fall apart. The fact is that Catanzano, Kevin Granato, and Anthony DeBiase had been arrested eight months earlier, on March 20, 1987. The three of them, facing charges related to their drug dealing activities, were tried and convicted on October 8, 1987. [165]

In a U.S. District Court opinion from 2011 in the case of *United States v. Michael Sessa*, the court stated that the significant arrest in the Catanzano caper, the one that allegedly spared Catanzano's life, was that of Billy Meli rather than of Catanzano. Meli, according to the court, failed to carry out the execution of Catanzano before his own arrest.[166] But Meli's arrest in November could not have been the reason Catanzano, who would have been incarcerated at the latest upon his October conviction, was not killed. And, given that Catanzano was arrested in March and Scarpa did not learn until months later about concerns that Catanzano would become an informant if arrested, Catanzano's arrest could not have been the reason his murder did not take place, as some others have claimed.[167]

The next time Catanzano *might* have been arrested would have been in November of 1987, when Meli and the rest of Scarpa's crew were rounded up. But Catanzano would have already been incarcerated by the time Meli was arrested, given his own arrest eight months earlier and his conviction in October. And if Catanzano were somehow free after his October conviction and subsequently arrested in November, an unlikely proposition, Granato could not have helped Meli dig Catanzano's grave since Granato, as reported in *The New York Times*, was already incarcerated before the November 10, 1987, arrests.[168] Simply put, the various pieces of the somewhat colorful story do not fit together.[169]

The story likely has some elements of truth to it that can no longer be separated from the ensuing embellishments. Thirty-six years later, it is difficult to sort out exactly what happened with the Scarpa/Meli/Catanzano matter. For whatever reason, Catanzano was not murdered, nor did he ever become an FBI informant or any other kind of informant. Instead, he served his time in federal prison and was eventually released.[170]

For all of 1987, the FBI's files record fourteen meetings between Scarpa and his handler.[171] Scarpa disclosed three killings in two of those meetings. As covered previously, Scarpa briefly referenced the murder of Joe Brewster during the meeting of September 17, 1987, without detailing his own role in the killing.[172] Additionally, three days earlier, he disclosed what he assumed was the retaliatory murder of local barber Vito Scaglione, indicating that to his knowledge the person charged with the murder did not commit it.[173] Finally, the FBI files for 1987 record one more murder discussed by Scarpa on September 17, 1987, the same day he provided information about the Brewster hit. At that meeting, Scarpa also noted the "recent" murder of an unnamed man from Staten Island. The murder, per Scarpa, was committed by someone whose name has been redacted and who was in partnership with the victim. According to Scarpa, the two got into a dispute over a narcotics deal, leading to the unnamed man's death. Based on the available documentation, Scarpa may have been referencing the murder of Ray Shapiro.

According to the Second Circuit Court of Appeals, Shapiro was murdered in September of 1987 by Gregory Scarpa Jr. "and others." Shapiro's murder was charged in connection with the considerable narcotics dealing activities of Scarpa's crew in Staten Island.[174] Although it is impossible to say definitively that Scarpa was referencing Shapiro's murder on September 17, 1987, the circumstances and timing involved in that killing fit with the killing Scarpa described.

From 1980 through 1987, there were a total of 13,073 homicides in New York City, an appalling waste of human life. For his part during the same period, Greg Scarpa Sr. killed or ordered the murder of at least eight men, and possibly five more, and one woman. He also ordered the murder of at least one more man that, for reasons which are not entirely clear, was never implemented. Remarkably, as will be seen in chapters ten and eleven, Scarpa was never indicted, arrested, or tried for any of those murders. He was never sentenced to a single day in jail on the basis of any of those murders. While it is a cliché, in retrospect, one cannot help but conclude that Scarpa's presumed value to the FBI allowed him to get away with murder. That fact no doubt emboldened him as the darkest days of the Colombo family's third internecine struggle in three decades began to cast a deadly pall over Brooklyn.

CHAPTER NINE: A STORM GROWS IN BROOKLYN

Nature abhors a vacuum. The vacuum created by the prosecution and long-term incarceration of the Colombo family leadership, while an admirable law enforcement aim and result, had practical consequences that brought more death and misery to Brooklyn. While Scarpa was killing or ordering the deaths of fellow mafiosi with impunity during the 1980s, he continued to provide the FBI with information that would decimate the leadership of his own borgata and that of the other New York LCN families through prosecution and incarceration. And while more than a dozen men went to prison as a direct result of the information Scarpa provided, the record leaves little doubt that the primary target of Scarpa's perfidy was Carmine Persico, the man he had already connected to at least eight murders.[1]

THE OTHER SIDE OF THE SAME COIN

Carmine Persico's incarceration did not prevent him from continuing to control the Colombo family, either as a matter of fact or as a matter of title, in the years following Jerome Johnson's attempt to assassinate Joe Colombo Sr. After a series of mistrials, retrials, and appeals, Persico was finally convicted in federal court in 1971 of charges stemming from a 1959 hijacking. As noted previously, Persico began serving concurrent terms on that conviction of "fourteen and nine years on each count" in federal prison as ordered by the U.S. District Court on January 27, 1972.[2] While Thomas DiBella was officially the Colombo family boss during Joe Colombo's lingering incapacitation, "[b]y the late 1970s, although still behind bars, [Carmine Persico] was recognized as the [Colombo] family's leader, his formal anointing only awaiting his parole."[3] In effect, Persico was running the Colombo family from prison through DiBella.[4]

Persico was released on parole in 1979,[5] but the *de facto* Colombo boss's legal jeopardy did not end. While in federal prison in 1977, Persico, and others acting on his behalf, had attempted to bribe an Internal Revenue Service Special Agent so that Persico could be moved from the United States Penitentiary in Atlanta to the Metropolitan Correctional Center in Manhattan, closer to his home base of operations.[6] Rather than endure another jury trial, Persico pleaded guilty in 1981 to conspiring to bribe a public official and was sentenced to the maximum term of five years.[7] Additionally, in May of that year, Persico had been arrested for violating the terms of his parole by "associating with reputed organized crime members."[8] His parole was revoked and he was ordered to serve the four years remaining from his 1971 federal conviction concurrently with his sentence for conspiring to bribe a public official.[9] Although Persico was released from prison in March of 1984,[10] his troubles with the law, especially with the FBI and the Department of Justice, once again were far from over.

During the early- and mid-1980s, the FBI conducted two extensive investigations, with significant assistance from Greg Scarpa, that had long-term consequences for the viability and tenuous stability of New York's Colombo crime family. One, codenamed "Star Quest," was aimed specifically at the Colombo family leadership, and those close to its leaders. The operation was a success and the indictment of the family's leadership, including Carmine Persico, was announced on October 24, 1984.[11] The other operation, codenamed "Five Star,"[12] cast a broader net and encompassed the leadership of all five of New York's Mafia families, the so-called "Commission."[13]

Those investigations triggered two of "the most significant prosecutions of organized crime in the NYO [New York Office], and are considered to be [among] the premier organized crime prosecutions in the U.S."[14] All told, both investigations resulted in high-profile indictments, trials, and convictions that, in the short term, added to the deadly chaos on the streets of Brooklyn. According to the FBI, the information Scarpa provided over the years was "the major supplier of probable cause for" those matters.[15] Scarpa's treachery was bounded only by his greed.

STAR QUEST

The jury trial of the Colombo family leadership in the Star Quest case began on October 5, 1985. The defendants in the consolidated case were family boss Carmine Persico, underboss Gennaro Langella, Carmine Persico's son Alphonse Persico, family capos John J. DeRoss, Andrew Russo, and Anthony Scarpati, who had been acting as "street boss" while Carmine Persico was incarcerated,[16] Colombo soldier Dominick Cataldo, and Colombo family associate Hugh McIntosh.[17] The jury was finally given the case on June 2, 1986, and returned convictions eleven days later.[18] "The jury found that the defendants were members of, or associated with, the Colombo Family of La Cosa Nostra, a criminal enterprise that systematically engaged in a wide-range of criminal activities."[19] The court, in denying defendants' motion for a new trial, stated that a "review of the record of the twelve straight days of jury deliberation, during which the jury was sequestered, irrefutably demonstrates that the jury carefully examined the evidence before returning its discriminating and thoughtful verdict."[20]

On November 18, 1986, the Star Quest case concluded when Carmine Persico was sentenced to thirty-nine years in federal prison while his son "Little Allie Boy" was given a lighter sentence of only twelve years.[21] The lighter sentence for Carmine Persico's son had the unintended effect of prolonging the in-absentia leadership of the Colombo family and thus the chaos on the streets of Brooklyn. Carmine would continue to rule the family from prison with the goal of Little Allie Boy, who would be eligible for parole in eight years, succeeding him when he was released, thereby maintaining the Persicos' operational and, more importantly, economic dominance of the Colombo family.[22] The FBI, for its part, specifically cited the "continuous flow of extremely singular information" Scarpa provided "for the past several years" as having led to the successful prosecution of the Colombo family leadership in the Star Quest case.[23] Anthony Daniels, Deputy Assistant Director of the FBI's Criminal Investigative Division appeared before the United States Senate's Committee on Governmental Affairs' Subcommittee on Investigations on April 11, 1988. In his prepared statement he reported that

> "The family enterprise investigation of the Colombo family, codenamed 'Starquest,' took four years to complete, during which time 17 court-authorized electronic surveillances and 60 extensions of those court orders to permit monitoring beyond the initial 30-day authorization were utilized."[24]

That portion of Deputy Assistant Director Daniels's statement closely tracks the language used in the FBI's files regarding Scarpa's contributions to the Star Quest investigation and prosecutions.

> "For the past several years [Scarpa] has provided a continuous flow of extremely singular information which led to 17 Title III intercepts and 50 reauthorizations forming the basis for the prosecution of the hierarchy of the Colombo family."[25]

Since Scarpa, as of April 1988, was still a Top Echelon Criminal Informant whose identity was a closely guarded secret, nowhere in the 1,261-page document generated by the Senate Subcommittee's hearings is Scarpa credited by name with providing the information leading to the wiretaps as he was in the FBI's own files. However, the FBI's files and the Senate's clear use of the information in those files leave little doubt about Scarpa's "singular" contributions.

FIVE STAR

The trial resulting from operation Five Star brought more bad news for Carmine Persico. Indictments in the so-called "Commission Case" were initially filed on February 25, 1985.[26] Although the heads of the other New York families were named in those indictments, Persico, who was incarcerated at the time, was not initially included among them. On June 25, 1985, a federal grand jury for the Southern District of New York returned a sealed superseding indictment adding Persico and Stefano Cannone, then consigliere of the Bonanno family, to the Five Star/Commission case.[27] Trial of the sensational case began in federal district court on September 8, 1986,[28] and lasted until November 19, 1986, when guilty verdicts against Persico and several of his codefendants were returned by the jury.[29] The guilty defendants were sentenced on January 13, 1987, by U.S. District Court Judge Richard Owen. Persico was sentenced to 100 years in prison and ordered to pay a fine of $240,000.[30] Absent the unlikely success of an appeal or the granting of parole, Carmine Persico was likely to "'die in prison,'"[31] which he did in 2019.[32]

Remarkably, Persico's violent and sometimes deadly influence from behind prison bars continued after his Star Quest and Five Star convictions. As has already been noted, Persico likely approved the murder of Joe Brewster.[33] Furthermore, on July 17, 1987, Scarpa reported on a beating ordered by Persico of a man whose name has been redacted from the FBI files.[34] Additionally, as will be discussed below, the murder of Jimmy Angelina in November of 1988, who became acting consigliere of the Colombo family after his brief incarceration, as reported by Scarpa on the 29th of that month,[35] would most likely have been ordered by Persico or at least approved by him, a supposition confirmed by Scarpa six months after Angelina's murder.[36] Scarpa's habit of connecting murders to Carmine Persico continued unabated.

In retrospect, the Five Star/Commission case "demonstrated that after decades of law enforcement neglect, the mafia had become sloppy and vulnerable."[37] More importantly, however, looking forward, the two ground-breaking 1986 trials of New York's Mafia and the sentences handed down to Carmine Persico and his son Alphonse set the stage for a protracted and deadly struggle for control of the Colombo family on the streets of Brooklyn. Separately, with the ranks of the New York Mafia Commission decimated, the FBI eagerly envisioned another potential prize: a mole on the Commission, a seat at the table of the highest LCN leadership level for its star Top Echelon Criminal Informant, Greg Scarpa.[38]

REARRANGING THE DECK
CHAIRS ON THE TITANIC

Greg Scarpa had predicted back on June 6, 1986, that if Carmine Persico and Anthony Scarpati were convicted and imprisoned, as they both were, then Joseph "Joe T" Tomasello and Jimmy Angelina would run the day-to-day operations of the Colombo family.[39] Scarpa's prediction proved to be prescient. As of December 15, 1986, when Scarpa had recovered from his emergency surgery sufficiently to resume providing the FBI with information about his fellow gangsters and a month after the sentences were handed down in the Star Quest case, a three-man committee, comprised of Tomasello, Angelina, and Benny Aloi, was tasked with running the Colombo crime family[40] of nearly 100 members and approximately 500 associates.[41] According to Scarpa, those men were receiving their orders from Carmine Persico via his brother, Teddy, since Carmine's son, Little Allie Boy, was also incarcerated.[42] Little Allie Boy's crew, meanwhile, was given to acting capo Victor Orena.[43]

The decision to have a three-man committee run the day-to-day operations of the family began to unravel as early as July of 1987. On July 17, Scarpa revealed that Joe Tomasello, while still a capo, was "no longer acting as one of the three members running the street operations." Carmine Persico had demoted Tomasello due to Tomasello's absences from capo meetings that indicated he was "unwilling to assume responsibility."[44] Tomasello was eventually demoted from his capo position too and replaced by Joel "Joe Waverly" Cacace.[45] Scarpa added on July 17 that Vincent "Jimmy" Angelina[46] was acting boss of the Colombo family, but that the family would be run by Benny Aloi, Jo Jo Russo, and Vic Orena if Angelina went to prison, which he did. While Angelina was in prison, his crew was given to Pasquale

"Patty" Amato as Scarpa had, once again, predicted.[47] Scarpa's information about Genovese family boss Vincent "Chin" Gigante's disapproval of the three-man committee being used by not only the Colombo family, but also the Lucchese and Bonanno families while their bosses were incarcerated was perhaps most important. Gigante preferred creating another Commission with a single representative from each family.[48]

The Colombo family response, which was less than satisfactory, was that "the three man [sic] structure should be viewed as retaining the traditional boss, underboss, and consigliere, and that any of these individuals in the 'acting' capacity is capable of sitting in on 'commission' meetings."[49] Eventually, added pressure from Gambino family boss John Gotti resulted in the demise of the three-man committee in favor of naming an "acting" boss, underboss, and consigliere with "full power to run the family."[50]

In the meantime, the rapid and startling ascension of Carmine Sessa through the ranks of the Colombo family was underway. Before March 11, 1987, Sessa was a Colombo associate. On that date, according to Scarpa, Sessa earned his button and, as an official member, was placed in the crew of capo Vic Orena.[51] Less than eighteen months later, Sessa was elevated to the position of capo and given his own crew. [52] Although Scarpa initially reported that Sessa had taken over Teddy Persico's former crew,[53] he corrected himself about a month later when he noted that John Saponaro was the only member in Sessa's crew and that Teddy Persico, who had not been replaced by Sessa, was becoming "more active in the Colombo family business on the instructions of [Teddy's brother] Carmine Persico."[54] As astonishing as Sessa's rapid rise to capo was, his becoming consigliere in June of 1990 was even more remarkable.[55]

The position of consigliere in the Colombo family had been vacant since Jimmy Angelina's murder in late 1988. A consigliere is "the counselor or advisor on family matters and on relations and disputes with other Mafia groups."[56] He's a "skilled counselor or diplomat [who] iron[s] out problems inside the family and resolve[s] feuds with other borgatas."[57] The consigliere is considered the number three man in the family leadership. The position of consigliere is one "that demanded experience, wisdom, tact and even charm. The capos are all supposed to admire and respect the consigliere as a friend."[58] According to Mazza, "Carmine [Sessa] had none of these attributes. He was way too young and naïve."[59] Sessa may have been aware of his own lack of skills and experience required to properly carry out the duties of his new position. As Scarpa reported to the FBI on June 13, 1989, Sessa had sold his house in Brooklyn and moved to Long Island to be closer to Vic Orena. Sessa was becoming increasingly close to Orena, and not just geographically. The result was that he was also becoming a major power in the family just two years after first earning his button.[60]

The position of consigliere was not alone when it came to the rapidly revolving leadership merry-go-round of the Colombo family in the late 1980s. On April 8, 1988, Scarpa reported that in addition to Jimmy Angelina being named acting consigliere, Vic Orena was named acting boss, and Benny Aloi became the acting underboss.[61] Tomasello was out, Orena was in, within seven months Angelina would be dead, and an unprepared, thirty-seven-year-old Carmine Sessa would take over as consigliere. Additionally, the Colombo family was quickly elevating members to the position of capo. Scarpa reported on May 3, 1988, that Richard Fusco had been made a Colombo capo, and Anthony "Chucky" Russo and William "Wild Bill" Cutolo had been named acting capos.[62] The promotions continued, and on April 17, 1989, Scarpa revealed that Thomas Petrizzo and Ralph Scopo's son Joseph had both been made capos,[63] while by November 15, 1989, Scarpa was reporting that Cutolo was the family's underboss.[64] On the flip side, as of June 6, 1988, Joe Tomasello, who two years earlier sat on the three-man committee running the Colombo borgata, had been forced into retirement, and Joel "Joe Waverly" Cacace was no longer a capo. Instead, Cacace was given the amorphous assignment of handling "matters concerning the boss, underboss, and consigliere."[65]

New leaders were not the only additions to the family after sentences were handed down in the Five Star/Commission case. New members were also being brought into the borgata in spite of an edict from the other families that the books were "closed,"[66] i.e., that new members could not be admitted. Carmine Persico had bestowed upon acting boss Vic Orena the power to name new members,[67] and Orena went at it with gusto. Robert "Bobby Zam" Zambardi and Dennis Guzzardo were both made goodfellows on March 11, 1987, the date on which Carmine Sessa got his button.[68] Five new button men were added to the Colombo family on July 28, 1987, including Vic Orena Jr., Jimmy Randazzo, Aurelio Cagno, and Benny Aloi's brother Vincenzo.[69] On October 30 of that year, Scarpa claimed that another eight members would soon be added to the rolls of the Colombo family.[70] Finally, over the course of two weeks in December of 1988, eleven new goodfellows were added to the borgata, one of whom was Carmine Sessa's brother Michael.[71]

Not only were men being added to the Colombo family roster at an astonishing clip, but the additions exposed a rift that would fester and eventually explode. As Larry Mazza noted, the newly made men "were all from Queens. They were all close to Vic or 'his' captains. And they all got their buttons quickly. The Brooklyn men, however, were held back."[72]

The simple result of the extraordinary personnel transitions, which Scarpa dutifully reported to the FBI every step of the way,[73] was that the ranks of the Colombo family were swelling with untested leaders and inexperienced followers, a dangerous recipe for any large-scale enterprise. Furthermore, the men being promoted or coming into the borgata were overwhelmingly loyal to one man, Little Vic Orena. Carmine Persico's attempt to control the borgata from prison a second time around was in serious jeopardy as the 1980s were coming to a close. By October of 1989, Persico realized the family's instability was growing. He believed the solution was "older, experienced leadership,"[74] so he brought sixty-five-year-old Charles "Moose" Panarella back to New York from Las Vegas. Persico's control on the family was slipping, and unlike Persico's earlier incarceration for a finite period that was shortened by his having been paroled, this time around it was clear the only way Persico would be getting out of prison would be in a casket. That simple fact likely emboldened a number of Colombo family leaders and members who sought a greater piece of the family's considerable economic pie for themselves as the disruptive changes in leadership and membership continued into the next decade.

THREE FUNERALS AND A WEDDING

The significance of certain events leading up to November of 1991, and who was the prime mover behind those events are subjects of considerable disagreement. On the one hand, years of litigation have persuaded neither the apparently objective nor certain clearly biased individuals and institutions of the federal government that their basic interpretation of the run-up to the third Colombo war and where responsibility for initiating that conflict lies is flawed. On the other hand, a collection of characters that includes self-interested, habitual liars and their well-meaning advocates, and earnest, respected, and well-intentioned chroniclers both inside and outside of the Colombo family continue to insist their version of the facts and motivations that resulted in that war is both reasonable and persuasive. Stepping into such a minefield of competing visions is a task likely to anger at least one, and possibly both of those factions.

Choosing an analysis that jettisons instructive abstractions in favor of assumptions about the limits of action based on perceived character traits results in a caricature that explains and buttresses a predetermined narrative rather than in a nuanced analysis. Vic Orena was a smart, money-focused man who eschewed personal involvement in the sort of violence that was typical of Greg Scarpa's conduct. Greg Scarpa was a smart, manipulative man for whom being a killer was a tool for achieving his personal goals of prosperity and security. Both descriptions are accurate; they are not, however, exhaustive or even profound. If they are treated as complete, allegations of actions outside of those parameters are dismissed. However, if each man is viewed as a human being whose behavior wanders outside of facile generalities, then actions otherwise dismissed as inconsistent with those generalities become imaginable. The wellsprings of human conduct are as varied as they are mysterious, and we are daily astonished at the behavior of our fellow man. To insist that anyone is incapable of a certain type of behavior is irrational and contrary to experience. No man is a murderer, until he is.

The events following the sentencing of Carmine Persico and his son Little Allie Boy that led to the destructive shooting war in the Colombo family began with the murder of acting consigliere Jimmy Angelina.

THE JIMMY ANGELINA HIT

As noted earlier, when Carmine "Junior" Persico was sentenced to 139 years in prison, Angelina was on the three-man committee appointed to run the family in Persico's absence. Orena, who was an acting capo at the time,[75] was not on that committee. Seven months later, in July of 1987, Scarpa reported that Angelina would effectively be the acting boss of the family until he went to prison for a brief sentence. The three-man committee eventually proved to be unworkable. In its place, an "acting" boss, Vic Orena, an acting underboss, Benny Aloi, and an acting consigliere, Jimmy Angelina on his release from prison, had been appointed as of Scarpa's debriefing of April 8, 1988. If Scarpa correctly reported Angelina's earlier status as effectively that of acting boss, then his appointment as acting consigliere was an effective demotion. It is not unreasonable to believe at that point that Orena viewed Angelina as a competitor who needed to be eliminated.

With the new acting leadership structure in place, Angelina was soon instructed by Orena to poll the Colombo family capos on the issue of their level of support for Carmine Persico as family boss.[76] According to Larry Mazza, Orena then claimed that rather than conducting a poll on his behalf, Angelina was "approaching the captains with a plan to take over."[77] Orena peddled that claim to Junior Persico to get permission to kill Angelina.[78] Even without that permission, Orena took the position, according to Lucchese family acting boss Alphonse D'Arco, "that he had the power to 'make members or kill guys' unless explicitly instructed otherwise by Persico, authority that only could be vested in a Boss or Acting Boss."[79]

Killing a consigliere is no small matter, even in an organization known to use murder to handle personnel matters. As Larry Mazza wrote, at one point, "Jimmy Angelina was officially declared 'gone' by the family. No one took credit or even admitted any knowledge of the almost certain assassination."[80] Two decades after Angelina's murder, Rocco Cagno testified at the trial of his brother, Aurelio Cagno, that they, along with Jimmy Randazzo, Carmine Sessa, and Bill Cutolo murdered Angelina "[i]n or about November 1988."[81]

> "Rocco's home was selected as the site because it could be accessed through the garage without anybody being seen from the driveway. It was decided that Carmine Sessa and Billy Cutolo would do the shooting from the top of the steps because they were capos and Angellino [sic], the intended victim, was an acting consigliere. Defendant, who was armed, was instructed to hide and be ready as a back-up to the shooters. [Jimmy] Randazzo brought Angellino to Rocco's house. Rocco, who had stashed his gun in the basement, opened the garage door for them. The lights went out and Rocco heard shots. When the lights went on, 'Angellino was in a corner on the bottom of the steps.'"[82]

Seven men, most likely including two Persico brothers, conspired to murder the Colombo family's acting consigliere. As it turned out, Carmine Sessa, one of the two shooters on the Angelina hit,[83] would be Angelina's successor. In fact, Sessa was the second choice for the position after Carmine Persico vetoed acting boss Vic Orena's first choice, Nicholas "Nicky Black" Grancio.[84] Appointment as an LCN consigliere is an appointment for life, which, as Jimmy Angelina found out, is no guarantee. The hit, according to Sessa, was his second attempt to kill

Angelina.[85] As for a funeral, Angelina's body "was put into a body bag that Randazzo had brought and was placed in the trunk of Randazzo's car."[86]

For his part, Scarpa's intelligence on the Angelina hit evolved over time. On November 29, 1988, Scarpa reported Angelina's murder but professed ignorance as to why he was killed. He did, however, accuse Carmine Persico of ordering the hit.[87] That accusation is consistent with Mazza's version of events noted above, a version that may have come, of course, from Mazza's close mentor, Greg Scarpa. By May of 1989, Scarpa was reporting that Angelina had been killed because he refused to step down as consigliere in favor of Benny Aloi, another indication that Orena may have viewed Angelina as a competitor for the family's top job. Scarpa once again claimed that the hit order came directly from Carmine Persico, adding that it had been relayed by Persico's brother Teddy.[88]

At a minimum, Carmine Sessa's ascension to the position of acting consigliere came about as a direct result of Jimmy Angelina's murder. That murder may have been tied to an order from Vic Orena, an order which he later misrepresented, that Angelina poll the Colombo capos about Carmine Persico's continued leadership of the family during his incarceration. At any rate, a contest for the top spot in the Colombo borgata was clearly brewing. A year later, at least one of the contestants could not get out of his own way.

THE OCERA MURDER

On October 5, 1989, after almost three years of Carmine Persico's attempts to maintain control of the Colombo family from prison through reorganization of its key personnel, an isolated event that would have enormous consequences took place on Long Island. The Suffolk County Police Department executed a search warrant of The Manor Restaurant in Merrick and seized the Colombo family loansharking records maintained by, and entrusted to, Tommy Ocera.[89] That seizure set in motion a chain of events that, three years later, led to the end of the third Colombo war, a "cycle of violence that erupted in 1991,"[90] which resulted in more than three life sentences for Vic Orena and a virtual death sentence for Greg Scarpa. Parsing the consequences of that seizure begins with understanding who Tommy Ocera was.

Gaetano "Tommy" Ocera was either a Colombo family associate,[91] or a Colombo family member/soldier,[92] or a Colombo capo.[93] Regardless of his actual rank within the Colombo family, there is general agreement that Ocera was, among other things, a loan shark,[94] or at least a "collector" for Orena's loansharking business.[95] Ocera operated, and may have been part owner of The Manor, a Merrick, Long Island restaurant.[96] In late 1989, he was involved with Diane Montesano,[97] who was managing The Manor at the time.[98] In addition to operating The Manor, Ocera ran a pair of gambling clubs.[99] In short, as Peter Lance observed, in late 1989, Tommy Ocera appeared to have it made.[100]

Within the Colombo family, it was Ocera's responsibility to look after some detailed loansharking records. Those records, which Colombo capo Pasquale Amato conceded at his trial were authentic, "listed the names of Colombo family members and payment amounts."[101] For instance, the records reflected "regular payments to 'Patty,' 'Pat,' and 'Pat A,' diminutives of Pasquale Amato."[102] The trial judge in Victor "Little Vic" Orena's trial[103] personally inspected the seized records "which included names and numbers with notations such as 'collect,' 'paid,' and 'balance.'"[104] Furthermore, at Pasquale Amato's trial the evidence revealed that Amato and Tommy Ocera had frequent, early morning meetings.[105] Likewise, at Orena's trial the evidence showed that "Orena and Ocera met regularly to discuss Colombo Family business at Ocera's restaurant."[106] In short, the seized records were thorough, meticulous, and damning, and the testimony at both trials connected Vic Orena and Pasquale Amato to Ocera and the loansharking records.

Ocera failed to adequately discharge his obligation to keep those records out of the wrong hands when the Suffolk County P.D. seized them from The Manor. Once law enforcement had possession of those records, Orena and Amato were both in legal jeopardy, particularly if Ocera could be called to testify as to the contents of the records. Because of his failure to properly safeguard those books, Ocera was rightly convinced he was marked for death.

Vittorio "Little Vic" Orena,

> "as a soldier[,]… had ducked out of violent tasks, but he knew which 'cowboys' to choose for dangerous work. In fact, after taking charge of Little Allie Boy's crew as a capo, he often instructed soldiers and wannabes assigned to murders that he preferred a traditional Sicilian method known as *lupara bianca* (literally, 'white shotgun' but meaning 'white death'), the euphemism for making certain the corpse is not found."[107]

Ocera, immediately recognizing his personal peril, attempted to retrieve the Colombo family's seized loansharking records from the Suffolk County P.D.[108] However, rather than making the desperate plea himself, he sent his girlfriend, Diane Montesano, to do the heavy lifting.[109] When she returned empty-handed, Ocera became despondent and, "uncharacteristically," hit the booze and hit it hard.[110] He had little more than a month to live. In the meantime, he "received two anonymous phone calls, one informing him that he was 'dead,' the other instructing him to run."[111] He should have taken that piece of advice to heart.

During the fourth week of October in 1989, Ocera survived what may have been an attempt on his life. He and Diane Montesano closed The Manor, as usual, about 1:30 a.m. on October 22.[112] They then left the restaurant in separate cars. Ocera, who had followed Montesano to her car because she was carrying the day's receipts,[113] left the parking lot first. Montesano noticed two cars with tinted windows and no license plates parked at the train station across from The Manor.[114] Concerned that the restaurant might get burglarized, she drove to the train station and approached the parked cars.[115] On her way home, she encountered one of those cars. It "veered directly at her, head-on. She managed to avoid a collision, and the car disappeared. Montesano was able to make out the profile of one of the drivers, testifying that it might have resembled Gregory Scarpa."[116]

The next night at the restaurant, Vic Orena "had evidenced to her that he was aware of an attempted ambush of Ocera the night preceding the discussion."[117] He told her "he heard she was a good driver and that she had 'done a great job the night before.'"[118] However, it is important to note that Montesano later testified her conversation with Orena occurred after Orena had heard about her encounter from Tommy Ocera.[119]

Although Ocera had managed to survive for more than a month after his loansharking records were seized, on November 13, 1989, his luck ran out. Earlier that month, Orena ordered Giachino "Jack" Leale to kill Ocera, primarily for failing to retrieve the loansharking records,[120] and for skimming money from loansharking[121] and gambling operations.[122] As the court noted in *Orena v. United States*, "Orena, as Acting Boss, directed subordinates to murder

Ocera. One of these subordinates was Scarpa"[123] At that point, the execution of Tommy Ocera was inevitable and imminent.

As Ocera headed for The Manor on Monday morning, November 13,[124] he stopped off at Patty Amato's house in Merrick, apparently having been lured there by Jack Leale.[125] When Ocera arrived, Amato threw him to the ground and Leale garroted him with a piece of metal wire.[126] Ocera's body was then dumped into the trunk of a car belonging to Leale's brother-in-law and Colombo associate Harry Bonfiglio, which Leale had borrowed. That night, Bonfiglio, Michael Maffatore, who was another Colombo associate as well as Leale's driver, and Leale buried Ocera's body in Forest Park, Queens.[127] Bonfiglio later testified that he did not know at the time that Amato and "Leale had killed Ocera; a few weeks later, Leale told him that 'Patty' [Amato] held down Ocera while Leale garroted him."[128] At a dinner one month after Ocera was murdered, Vic Orena bragged to Alphonse D'Arco, who was then the acting boss of the Lucchese crime family, that "'we whacked Tommy Ocera. We gave him a *luparo bianco*,' [sic] meaning that they made his body disappear."[129] Orena's boast turned out to be an empty one. Tommy Ocera's body was located about two years later with the wire used to garrot him still around his neck.[130]

Less than a week after Tommy Ocera was murdered, Scarpa once again updated the FBI on the state of the Colombo family's leadership. During that November 19, 1989, debriefing, Scarpa reiterated that Orena, Cutolo, and Aloi occupied the three top spots of boss, underboss, and consigliere, respectively, in the Colombo family.[131] A note of outward stability appeared when the same personnel were reported by Scarpa as occupying the same positions about six months later.[132] In that debriefing, Scarpa, almost as an aside, revealed what would be at the heart of the coming contest for power. When referencing Orena, Cutolo, and Aloi, he reported that "all three share in the proceeds generated by the Colombo family through its illegal activities to include gambling, loansharking, labor racketeering, extortion, and murder."[133] Who was going to be on top came down to, as it so often does, a question of money. By the fall of 1991, that defining issue would be out in the open. In the meantime, however, Carmine Persico continued his ongoing efforts to firm up control of the family until Little Allie Boy could assume the position of boss on his release from prison in 1993. With Carmine Sessa in the position of acting consigliere, by June of 1990, Persico had replaced Cutolo, a man Persico feared was becoming too powerful,[134] as underboss by giving Benny Aloi the number two job.[135]

PETER ORENA'S WEDDING

As of June 5, 1991, Scarpa was reporting that Carmine Sessa was still the Colombo family's acting consigliere,[136] having lasted considerably longer in that role than his murdered predecessor, Jimmy Angelina. Sessa, having participated in Angelina's murder, had to know his title did not guarantee his personal safety. Meanwhile, the chess game between Carmine Persico and Vic Orena continued. In early 1991, "Carmine Persico announced that 'Allie Boy,' upon his anticipated release from prison in June 1993, would become Boss of the Colombos."[137] While not entirely unexpected, "[t]he announcement raised tensions between Colombo family members loyal to Orena and those loyal to Persico."[138] Time was running out for Vic Orena if he was determined to replace Persico as the family's official, rather than acting, boss. Making a move before Little Allie Boy's release would be critical.

"By the spring of 1991, Orena was tired of Persico's intrusions and told his hatchet men that Carmine was out of touch, obstructing the family's profits, and that he, rather than Little Allie Boy, deserved the title and recognition as boss."[139]

On June 14, 1991, Peter Orena, one of Little Vic's sons who was not in "the life," got married. His father decided to use the occasion to determine the level of support he had for replacing Persico among the family's capos. He instructed Sessa to poll the family's captains at the event.[140] "Orena cajoled Sessa to label the elder Persico a 'rat' who should be 'knocked down.'"[141] Sessa, recalling how the end came for Jimmy Angelina, became understandably concerned about Orena's directive and where it might be heading. However, he complied with the order, to a degree. One of the wedding guests was Teddy Persico, Carmine's surviving brother.[142] After Sessa revealed to Teddy that Orena "advocated that CARMINE PERSICO should be removed,"[143] Teddy Persico told Sessa to finish taking the poll, which Sessa apparently did.[144] According to Larry Mazza, the poll produced a "50/50 split" among the capos, a fact which "perturbed" Orena.[145] Sessa, again mindful of Jimmy Angelina's fate and his own role in it, took matters into his own hands less than a week later. And he made a dog's breakfast of it.

THE GANG THAT COULDN'T SHOOT

After Peter Orena's wedding, Carmine Sessa was convinced Vic Orena would order him to be killed. Sessa learned from capo Richie Fusco that Orena planned to strike at an induction ceremony adding new members to the Colombo family ranks "at Joe Waverly's club in the Gravesend area of Brooklyn."[146] Carmine decided to launch a preemptive strike.[147] Mazza characterized the plan to hit Orena as a "simple one."[148] Find Vic; kill Vic. While part of the plan, the portion Mazza was apparently aware of, was arguably simple, the entire plan was not. Three separate teams were involved: two hit teams and a surveillance team. In addition to taking out Orena, Sessa and his cohorts planned to kill underboss Joe Scopo. The plan's timing was dependent on two men, Orena and Scopo, doing exactly what Sessa and his coconspirators predicted and hoped they would do. The hit was planned for June 20, 1991,[149] a Thursday. They assumed Scopo would spend Thursday evening at Turquoise, a club in Brooklyn, as was his custom. They further assumed they would be able to easily locate Vic Orena using an unarmed surveillance team. Once that team located Orena, according to the plan, they would keep tabs on him until Scopo left the club. Then the two teams of shooters would simultaneously kill Scopo and Orena.[150]

The plan was destined to fail. It had too many moving parts and was based on too many assumptions of actions beyond the conspirators' control. And fail it did. Scopo never showed up at the club,[151] and Orena surprised the surveillance team, after they had been searching for him for nearly five hours, by pulling up alongside them at a traffic light. When the light turned green, the surveillance team went left, hoping Orena had not recognized them. Orena, having recognized the thinly disguised crew for what it was,[152] went straight home. Not a shot was fired at either target, and the entire operation went bust.[153]

Scarpa reported some of the details of the failed hit to the FBI on July 8. In that same debriefing, he outlined the membership of the Colombo family's two opposing factions. Scarpa also incorrectly predicted that "this dispute will be settled soon, with the assistance of another LCN family who will act as a mediator and insure [sic] protection of all parties."[154] For the Orenas and their supporters, the attempted hit on Orena and Scopo "'was Pearl Harbor.'"[155] Larry Mazza took a similar view. "The war had begun. The two factions had no idea how bad it was going to get. We had no idea of the tragedies that would take place in the year to come."[156]

However, unlike Pearl Harbor, it would be another five months before any shots were fired. In the meantime, the parties made at least a showing of wanting to avoid the bloodshed of a third internal war in the Colombo family in thirty years. To that end, the botched Orena/Scopo assassination was followed by a series of meetings, the first of which took place at the funeral of Joseph "Joe Sap" Saponaro a month after Sessa's failed coup d'etat.

JOE SAP'S WAKE

For John and Joseph, the brothers Saponaro, 1991 was a rough year. On March 26, 1991, Scarpa reported to his FBI handler that John Saponaro had died three days earlier, on March 23.[157] After years in "the life," his passing, at the relatively young age of fifty-five, was nonviolent. "He fell to a massive heart attack while out to dinner with his wife."[158] Joe, who was four years younger than his deceased brother, took John's death as a wakeup call. He started working out, lifting weights as he had in the past. But he went at it too soon, too hard, and too fast, and "ruptured a blood vessel in his brain."[159] He was fifty-one years old when he died, about a month after the botched attempt on the lives of Vic Orena and Joe Scopo. His funeral, like that of his brother John, would likely have gone unnoticed by those outside of his immediate circle had it not been the occasion for a meeting of representatives from two sides of a vicious crime family about to engage in a deadly shooting war on the streets of Brooklyn.

Joe Saponaro's wake was held at the Sessa Funeral Home in Bay Ridge.[160] The wake was well attended, attesting to Saponaro's popularity. Carmine Imbriale recalled the "viewing area jammed with dozens of Colombos."[161] Scarpa and Orena were both present at some point, and Imbriale's recollection is that Carmine Sessa and many of the Wimpy Boys attended, all of which was duly noted by FBI agents surveilling the scene.[162] According to Larry Mazza, who also attended the wake, Carmine Sessa, Robert "Bobby Zam" Zambardi, who was in on the failed attempt to hit Orena and Scopo, and Anthony "Chucky" Russo, who had been Joe Saponaro's capo, did not make an appearance. As Mazza stated, "Unlike his older brother's earlier wake, none of the old friends were there. None of the Persicos, Russos, or their men showed up."[163]

Of course, between the two Saponaro funerals, Carmine Sessa had tried to kill Vic Orena, which may explain Sessa's absence. However, it is worth remembering that a typical wake can last for hours, and few, if any, attendees, other than closest family members, will sit for the entire thing. Attendees will come and go and may have no occasion to encounter each other. The fact that Mazza and Imbriale provided divergent accounts of the same event may have been a result of when they and others attended that event. In short, the men Mazza encountered at the wake may have been different from those encountered by Imbriale at some other point during the wake, and both of their accounts could be entirely accurate.

For his part, Orena used the wake to conduct a meeting in a private room on the second floor of the funeral home.[164] During that meeting, he repeated his accusation that Carmine Persico was a rat, he related the story of the attempt on his life a few weeks earlier, and "he denounced his consigliere [Carmine Sessa] for turning on him."[165] Orena, after pointing out that Scarpa was in attendance, leveled a threat aimed at those in the family opposed to his leadership. "'I'll give them two weeks [to come in] or they're dead.'"[166]

Joseph "Joey Brains" Ambrosino, who was also present for the meeting at Joe Sap's wake, interpreted Orena's request for members "to come in" as a conciliatory gesture rather than a threat.[167] To Mazza, at that moment it was clear that "the split in the Colombo family" was real and officially in the open.[168] Scarpa, who attended the meeting, refused to show his hand, hoping to create the impression that he supported Orena[169] while planning "to pledge his loyalty to Junior [Persico] and Chucky [Russo]."[170] Scarpa played the room beautifully. He used the moment to assure Orena loyalist acting underboss Vinnie Aloi of his intentions, after which he reported to Mazza, "'Yeah, we're in good shape over here.'"[171]

The meeting at Joe Sap's wake was the first of many over the next few months between the two Colombo family factions. Those meetings ranged from symbolic gestures of strength, to intransigent demands and threats, to arbitrated attempts to find a peaceful path forward. If a shooting war was to be avoided, either Carmine Persico or Vic Orena would have to blink.

ON THE HOMEFRONT

By the fall of 1991, Scarpa's health was in steady and obvious decline. While he would not tell Little Linda and Joey about his HIV-infected transfusion until 1992, Linda Schiro and Larry Mazza, among others, were aware of the source and nature of his illness. It is likely that others beyond the small circle Scarpa confided in knew as well. As Ben Franklin wrote in *Poor Richard's Almanack*, "Three may keep a secret, if two of them are dead."

Scarpa's attempts to deal secretly with his advancing disease had consequences for his status as a Colombo wiseguy. As Little Linda recalled, Carmine Sessa provided a great deal of care for Scarpa when he finally got out of the hospital in late 1986. Sessa knew Scarpa was HIV-positive, but he would dress Scarpa's "open wounds in his stomach."[172] Scarpa felt as if he had the plague and was amazed and gratified by the care Sessa showed for him and gave him.[173] Additionally, Morris "Moe" Terzi, the husband of Linda Schiro's older sister, Maryann, became particularly close to Scarpa after his hospitalization. As Little Linda explained, Terzi was not in "the life" and, as a long-time friend of Scarpa's, was one of Scarpa's few solid connections to the non-gangster world. Terzi, like Sessa, did a great deal to take care of Scarpa when he was ill. When Terzi died of cancer, he arguably took Scarpa's strongest link to a normal life with him.[174]

Scarpa's physical deterioration was visible, and its cause was perhaps the worst-kept secret in Brooklyn. Greogry Jr. stated that his father's weight loss and resulting change in appearance affected his self-confidence.[175] He could not help feeling that people were judging him.[176] Little Linda wrote that Scarpa, who by 1991 was contemplating retiring, felt he had to participate in the Colombo war or he would be viewed as soft and washed up because of AIDS.[177] Scarpa's physical deterioration was accompanied by a slow mental deterioration, both from the disease and from how he was treating it through both prescribed medication and self-prescribed marijuana.[178] Although he quit smoking cigarettes after his hospitalization, he made heavy use of "street weed" as part of his treatment.[179] The drugs, prescribed and otherwise, together with the disease's progression, seriously affected his judgment and acuity. In short, on the eve of the third Colombo war, Scarpa was in his early sixties and in a state of serious physical and mental decline. Life at home was of little comfort.

His two children with Linda Schiro were both adults. Little Linda was living back at home after a failed marriage that had lasted less than a year.[180] Sensing his soon-to-be son-in-law was not the man for his daughter, Scarpa warned her a week before their marriage in 1990 that her fiancé would make her miserable.[181] Scarpa and Little Linda were both sick at her wedding, she with morning sickness, he from AIDS.[182] Indeed, in retrospect, his daughter recalled that the groom already knew that Scarpa was suffering from AIDS on their wedding day.[183] Linda, however, clung to the belief that her father's deterioration was due to cancer as her parents had told her.[184]

Little Linda's marriage was doomed from the start, and the birth of a son a few months later did nothing to bring the newlyweds, by then living on Staten Island, closer together.[185] Little Linda's relationship with her husband had grown so acrimonious that at one point, Scarpa asked his daughter for permission to kill her husband. Horrified, she refused.[186] Instead, they divorced and Little Linda and her young son moved back into Scarpa and Linda Schiro's Brooklyn home on 82nd Street.

Linda Schiro never flinched. She continued to take care of Scarpa during his decline. Their lives were no longer characterized by physical intimacy due to his HIV-positive status, which eventually became full-blown AIDS,[187] but her loyalty and tenacity, if anything, increased. As already noted above, during this period of their relationship, which lasted nearly eight years, she steadfastly assumed the roles of caregiver, advocate, and protector. And as will be seen below, she continued in those roles despite Scarpa's increasingly erratic and dangerous behavior in the early 1990s until his death at the age of sixty-six in 1994.

TAKE A MEETING

After Joe Saponaro's funeral, Carmine Persico had to view his ability to dominate the Colombo family and ensure the wealth being generated by its vast illegal activities flowed primarily to the Persicos as being in serious jeopardy. Over the course of a week, beginning on August 13, 1991, Scarpa reported once again to the FBI that Vic Orena was intent on wresting control of the family from Junior Persico.[188] Understandably, Orena had already removed Carmine Sessa, who clumsily tried to assassinate him, as acting consigliere in favor of Vinnie Aloi, while moving loyal capo Joe Scopo into the slot of underboss.[189] According to Scarpa, Carmine Persico's response was to declare from prison that "Vic Orena is being removed as acting boss, and will be replaced by Carmine Sessa."[190] Such a move represented another attempt to maintain the Persicos' power and influence pending Little Allie Boy's release from prison in 1993. It was also a slap in the face to Orena, given Sessa's recent attempt on his life. Scarpa, who had to know he was the primary if not sole source of the FBI's information regarding the Colombo family's internal conflict, then somewhat disingenuously added that "reaction to this is unknown at this time, but some problems could arise from those loyal to Orena."[191] As he had been doing for some time, Scarpa continued to frame Orena's position as the catalyst for conflict between the two factions. Furthermore, Scarpa offered the FBI a solution to the likely shooting war: "Carmine Persico has already put out the order to have Vic Orena hit. [Scarpa] said the logical move would be to take out Vic Orena and Benny and Vinnie Aloi..."[192] Orena's supporters came to a different conclusion.

A season of meetings followed Joe Saponaro's funeral. Three major themes were apparent from those meetings. First, both groups were intransigent. Orena wanted Persico to step aside in his favor; Persico wanted to maintain the title of boss and the economic privileges flowing from that title. Second, both groups wanted to control the greater share of the Colombo family's substantial money-generating activities. Third, Greg Scarpa, in spite of his advancing age and deteriorating health, was a major threat to Orena and his supporters. The first two items could not be resolved by direct negotiation or outside arbitration from the other LCN families. The third item could only be resolved by Scarpa's retirement or death.

ORENA/PERSICO TWO-STEP

Carmine Imbriale and Larry Mazza were both present for a meeting at Stella's Restaurant on Long Island in the fall of 1991.[193] The restaurant was owned by Tommy Petrizzo, a capo under Vic Orena. This was "one of several meetings held to broker terms for peace."[194] The gathered group was relatively small. The primary actors were Vic Orena Sr. and Carmine Sessa. Imbriale and Mazza were along as muscle since the two sides had agreed that firearms would not be permitted at the meeting. Orena, citing the obvious problems flowing from absent leadership, made his case for a change in his favor, given Persico's effective life-sentence. He did not hesitate to ask for Sessa's backing. Sessa, predictably, reiterated his support for Persico. Neither side budged.[195] The meeting, conducted without outward acrimony, ended in a stalemate with clarity in the opposing factions' positions the only real outcome.

The other New York LCN families fared no better in resolving the Colombos' intrafamily dispute. During the summer of 1991, three of the other families—Gambino, Lucchese, and Genovese—established an ad hoc committee to try to arbitrate the dispute between the Persico and Orena factions of the Colombo family.[196] The "committee's efforts to keep the peace were directed primarily at Orena, since he controlled a majority of the Colombo soldiers and seemed eager to open hostilities."[197] While unable to mediate a resolution, at a minimum the other LCN families "demanded that no side start shooting."[198] Furthermore, they declared that all four families would turn against whichever side broke the uneasy truce.[199] Carmine Sessa agreed that "'all the families would attack anyone who broke the truce.'"[200]

Scarpa reported to the FBI on the other LCN families' efforts to avoid open warfare. In Scarpa's view, Orena had expected the other families to back his takeover attempt.[201] However, as Scarpa pointed out, the other family bosses were unlikely to depose a jailed boss since, as a result of the Commission case, virtually all of the other family bosses were in jail.[202] In short, the Commission case reduced, if not entirely eliminated, the effectiveness of an important restraint on the actions of the New York LCN families.

Scarpa kept up a steady stream of reporting on the families' reaction to the split during the fall of 1991. He noted at one point that the Genovese family was unofficially backing Carmine Persico while officially not taking sides in the matter.[203] It is not clear from the documents how the Genovese family was hoping to walk that tightrope. Furthermore, John Gotti, per Scarpa, was taking a hardline against the Persico group by circulating a list of about twenty-five "Colombo members loyal to Carmine Persico, and advised all Gambino members to have no contact in business or otherwise with" them.[204] Finally, on October 23, Scarpa reported that mediators from the other LCN families, unable to resolve the dispute, had stopped meeting with the two sides.[205] As will be seen in chapter ten, the tenuous truce held for less than a month after that report.

Before the shooting started, two other meetings that fall focused on the issue that was at the heart of the entire dispute: money. One of those meetings, summarized by Scarpa for his FBI handler, took place on October 6, 1991.[206] The Orena group was represented by Benny Aloi, Nicky Grancio, Billy Cutolo, Funzi D'Ambrosio, Joel Cacace, and Joe Legrano. The Persicos were represented by Richie Fusco, Jo Jo Russo, Teddy Persico, and Joe Monte.[207] According to Scarpa, Teddy Persico opened the meeting by asking Benny Aloi if Orena's backers recognized his brother Carmine as Colombo family boss.[208] Aloi's response, which was unsatisfactory to Teddy Persico, was that Persico was boss, but Orena spoke for the Colombo family. Teddy, after reiterating that his brother was the official boss, demanded all the money the Persicos should have gotten over the past several years that went to Orena. Although the Orena group appeared to want to discuss specific issues relating to the intrafamily dispute, Teddy Persico cut off any further discussion absent a recognition of Carmine Persico's formal position as family boss.[209] Additionally, Teddy Persico announced that Vic Orena was no longer the family's acting boss. Scarpa's take was that he "expected serious trouble" once Carmine Persico was informed of the meeting.[210]

Another meeting was called, this one for Bill Cutolo's club on 11th Avenue,[211] and it had all the appearances of an ambush. Scarpa, Mazza, and a handful of their men were greatly outnumbered and outgunned, so much so that it nearly unnerved the otherwise steady Larry Mazza. The numbers on the Orena side approached 100 heavily armed men including rooftop snipers, two men with Uzis in full view, and a machine gun sitting on top of "Wild Bill" Cutolo's Lincoln and leveled squarely at Scarpa's crew.[212] Scarpa strode confidently into Cutolo's club, which was teeming with Orena loyalists, while Mazza and his small group remained outside fully expecting to be lit up at any minute. And they were seriously underprepared. "We had shit that Dillinger must have used and bulletproof vests that were probably second-hand."[213] For lack of a better plan, Mazza ordered his men to spread out and told them, "just take cover and find a place to run."[214]

The standoff lasted for ninety minutes while Scarpa, surrounded by Orena loyalists, met with Orena underboss Joe Scopo. At issue, at least on the surface, was the disposition of the late Joe Sap's numbers action, "one of the largest numbers businesses in the state."[215] More importantly, however, both sides were trying to gauge the other's commitment to conflict. On both counts, Scarpa prevailed. He secured, at least for the time being, the rights to Joe Sap's numbers action, and he almost single-handedly won the battle of nerves. Mazza learned the next day that many of Orena's men were so terrified of The Grim Reaper that a number of them panicked and ran off when Scarpa appeared. [216] And when Scarpa and his crew arrived, "Wild Bill" Cutolo reportedly jumped "around frantically saying, 'Don't let him in… don't let him in!'"[217]

Shortly after the standoff at Cutolo's club, another incident illustrated Scarpa's effect on the readiness of Orena's supporters to engage in violent conflict. Salvatore "Big Sal" Miciotta, who had been under Andrew Russo, split off and joined the Orena faction as a way to avoid paying a debt of nearly $400,000 he owed the Russos.[218] When Miciotta found out that a couple of numbers runners were turning their work in to Scarpa, he "ordered them to meet him at Snaps Candy Store on Fort Hamilton Parkway," which had been owned by the late Joe Saponaro. Presumably, Miciotta was going to demand that the runners turn their numbers proceeds over to him. Mazza, Scarpa, and about a dozen other crew members got to the store thirty minutes before Miciotta was due. As Miciotta pulled up, Mazza let Scarpa, who was waiting inside, know of his arrival. Scarpa came out of the store. Miciotta, who had three men with him, bolted, driving away as soon as he spotted Scarpa. According to Mazza, "[t]hey wanted no part of us."[219]

The crucial lesson for Orena to draw from the standoff at Cutolo's club and Miciotta's unwillingness to engage with Scarpa a week later was simple: Scarpa was a powerful symbol who had to be eliminated. Orena's men, no matter their superior numbers and firepower, were overmatched and nearly paralyzed by Scarpa's reputation as a vicious killer. Orena would have to make a move against Scarpa if he hoped to prevail in his ongoing chess match with Carmine Persico.

 By Halloween of 1991, there appeared to be little on which the two sides could agree. Unfortunately for Jack Leale, that was not entirely the case. Leale, who together with Pasquale Amato had murdered Tommy Ocera, made the mistake of relying on a couple of amateurs to dispose of Ocera's body. Orena had wanted the body to disappear.[220] Instead, it was found in late September of 1991 with the cooperation of Michael Maffatore, one of the men given the task of disposing of it. Law enforcement's recovery of Ocera's body meant that Leale's days were numbered. On October 31, Leale's body was "found dead in a Long Island hotel parking lot."[221] When Scarpa reported the hit to the FBI four days later he included his surmise that both sides in the brewing Colombo conflict wanted Leale dead.[222] If so, it would be the last thing they would agree on until the third Colombo war ended.

CHAPTER TEN: WAR!

"In the early 1990s the Colombo family was torn apart by a violent struggle to see who would replace boss Carmine "The Snake" Persico, who had been imprisoned for life in the Commission case. Two-thirds of the family backed the powerful Long Island capo Vic Orena... The remainder, including the Scarpa crew, backed Alphonse "Allie Boy" Persico, Carmine's son. From 1991 to 1993 the two sides shot it out in what became known as the Colombo Family War, the last great mob war in history. By the time it was over ten men had been shot dead."[1]

"Persico loyalists included... most notably, Greg Scarpa Sr."[2]

"[A] man described by the police as a capo aligned with Mr. Persico, Gregory Scarpa Sr."[3]

"In 1991, Mr. Orena tried to assume permanent control of the Colombo family as its new boss. Investigators said that Mr. Persico, confined at the Federal Penitentiary in Lompoc, Calif., directed his loyalists to eliminate Mr. Orena and his supporters."[4]

"He is the highest-ranking leader in the family to become a casualty in a Colombo war that erupted in June 1991 between Mr. Scarpa's faction, which is loyal to Carmine Persico, the imprisoned boss of the family..."[5]

"Gregory Scarpa, Sr., a sixty-three-year-old mobster, immediately took command of the armed faction loyal to Persico."[6]

"He said Mr. Orena was a central figure in an internecine power struggle that had crippled the Colombo family in recent months, with one faction loyal to Mr. Orena and the other to the group's boss, Carmine Persico, who is in prison."[7]

"Mr. Scarpa was a battle commander for the Persico group."[8]

"Scarpa was the Persicos' best killing machine."[9]

"Colombo defectors testified that a war over the succession erupted in 1991 and that Mr. Scarpa sided with the smaller Persico faction."[10]

It is impossible to read the existing exposition on the third Colombo war and not conclude that Greg Scarpa Sr. was a fierce Carmine Persico loyalist who killed repeatedly on his behalf. Scarpa personally reinforced that perception. As will be seen, he even claimed that he declared, "This one's for Carmine!" during the hit on Nicky Black. However, Larry Mazza, the man who actually shot Nicky Black as Scarpa fumbled with his rifle, said Scarpa's statement was "embellishment" that Scarpa reported to Carmine Sessa after the hit.[11] In short, it never happened.

A review of Scarpa's entire history, and not simply the last three years of his life, controverts the portrayal of Scarpa as a Persico loyalist. Scarpa was always a Scarpa loyalist. When Joe Profaci died, Scarpa variously pledged his loyalty to Charlie LoCicero and the Magliocco brothers, first one then the other. When Joe Colombo became family boss, Scarpa, who was given a position of trust by Colombo few other men shared, gave the FBI enough information to arrest Colombo. When it was clear that Carmine Persico would dominate the family in the wake of the power struggle after Joe Colombo's incapacitation, Scarpa, once again true to form, provided the FBI with a steady stream of accusations linking Persico to several murders. His contest with Vic Orena was simply more of the same.

That contest has been labeled variously the third Colombo war, the Colombo Family War, and the Persico/Orena feud. It is more accurately the first rather than the last. As Orena became more powerful in the family while Persico struggled to maintain control from behind prison walls, Scarpa duped his contacts in the FBI and, as will be seen, made use of his virtual license to kill to have Orena taken off the streets by the federal government. With Persico in prison for life, Scarpa's competition/target became Vic Orena when Orena was anointed with the title of acting boss. Orena made it easy for Scarpa when he decided he wanted to be the actual rather than acting boss. His decision gave Scarpa cover; Scarpa could claim loyalty to Carmine "The Snake" Persico, the man he had tied to multiple murders in reports to the FBI, as he tried to stop the shift of power and thus wealth that was accruing in Orena's favor. For Scarpa, that financial end justified his violent means.

Those who pursue violent conflict, either individually or collectively, often do so when internal pressure to alter external influences renders other solutions untenable or, if previously attempted without success, no longer relevant. The pursuit seems rational if the desired outcome appears attainable at an acceptable cost. Of course, that calculus may be based on faulty reasoning or inaccurate information. Furthermore, navigating a conflict's path will likely be fraught with tactical and strategic error. The so-called "fog of war" obscures a conflict's events in a manner most accept as inevitable. Trying to sort fact from fiction either during or after a conflict is so heavily dependent on point of view that we often look to apparently neutral voices whose perspective reassures us of objectivity via physical and temporal distance. And so it is with the roots of a conflict. As we shed our bias for one competitor or the other, we have the opportunity to come to a clearer understanding of "why" and not just "what." But first we must agree on the "what."

THE OPENING SALVO

General agreement exists on the point that the first shots in the third Colombo war were fired on November 18, 1991. However, in addition to Carmine Sessa's failed attempt on Orena and Scopo noted above, it is likely that Scarpa and his crew had previously begun hunting Orena loyalists, in particular "Wild Bill" Cutolo, earlier that fall.[12] When the actual shooting started, however, the target was Greg Scarpa.

In 1991, Colombo family members loyal to Vic Orena often met at Joe Scopo's social club, Cafe on N.[13] At some point that year, John Rosatti, who sided with Orena and was a member of Pasquale "Patty" Amato's crew,[14] "came to Cafe on N to speak to Orena."[15] Rosatti complained to Orena that Scarpa had abused one of his employees, and he wanted Scarpa killed for the transgression. As noted earlier, Orena believed "he had the power to 'make members or kill guys' unless explicitly instructed otherwise by Persico."[16] Rosatti's request led to the attack on Scarpa in front of his home on November 18, 1991.[17]

According to Linda Scarpa, her father's driver that day was Ilario "Fat Larry" Sessa, who was driving his Lincoln. Joseph "Joe Fish" Marra was in the car with Sessa and Scarpa.[18] Linda Scarpa and her eight-month-old son[19] nearly got caught in the crossfire. She survived and has provided a first-person account of the event.

Two weeks before the ambush, Scarpa reported to the FBI that he considered himself a likely target should the standoff between the two factions erupt into a shooting war.[20] He did not, however, alter his routine in view of that perceived risk. His daughter, Linda, who was twenty-two years old in November of 1991, reported that Scarpa left their house on 82nd Street the same time every day between 11:00 a.m. and noon.[21] On November 18, she, carrying her son Freddy, and Scarpa left their house simultaneously which she stated was unusual.[22] After Scarpa helped his daughter get her son into her Mercedes Benz, he kissed her goodbye and climbed into the Lincoln, which was parked in the driveway with Larry Sessa behind the wheel.[23]

The attempted hit featured three vehicles besides the two carrying Scarpa and his crew and Linda and her son. One of the three other vehicles, a white truck, pulled into the intersection of 82nd Street and 12th Avenue, northwest from Scarpa's house, and stopped to block Scarpa's potential escape route.[24] A second vehicle, a van, came speeding up 82nd Street from the southeast heading for Scarpa's car, which was by now at the stop sign of the blocked intersection.[25] The van had Scarpa's vehicle in sight, but it was blocked by Little Linda in her Mercedes Benz as she pulled into the street from the curb in front of the Scarpa house. At this point, Little Linda was right behind Scarpa at the blocked intersection.[26] A third vehicle, a car with Vincent Fusaro at the wheel, blocked any escape to the southeast when Fusaro parked it at the intersection of 13th Avenue and 82nd Street.[27] Scarpa, his crew, his daughter, and his grandson were boxed in and set up for an ambush.

Several armed men wearing ski masks jumped out of the van behind Little Linda and started shooting.[28] They fired at both Scarpa's car and his daughter's car.[29] Little Linda reported they were armed with handguns with silencers.[30] She also saw a man on the sidewalk with a walkie-talkie.[31] Lin DeVecchio wrote that the assailants were armed with shotguns.[32] Larry Mazza's account had four men armed with shotguns perpetrating the attack.[33] Mazza wrote that the men in Scarpa's car, including Scarpa, jumped out to return fire.[34] Their ability to engage was impeded by the presence of Linda's car between them and their attackers.[35] Linda Scarpa claims that Joe Fish was the only man to get out of the car and return fire.[36] She further recalls that a bullet passed through Joe's hair,[37] and, according to Mazza, Fish was also "grazed in the right shin by a [shotgun] pellet."[38] Linda thought she saw her father go down.[39]

Once everyone was back in the Lincoln, Larry Sessa sped off, squeezing past the white truck at the intersection by driving up onto the sidewalk.[40] The shooters returned to the van and gave chase, but the van was too large to get through the intersection past the parked white truck.[41] The men in the van jumped out of it and into a waiting getaway car driven by the driver of the white truck.[42] As Scarpa's crew members made their escape, Scarpa screamed at Sessa to stop the car so he could get back to his daughter and grandson.[43]

By this time, Little Linda had thrown her car into reverse to return to the Scarpa house. She thought her father was dead. His car had so many bullet holes in it that it "looked like Swiss cheese."[44] She backed into the driveway, parked her car, which had also been hit by gunfire, grabbed her son, and ran up to the front door of the Scarpa home, right past the man with the walkie-talkie. The front door was locked. She banged on the door, screaming and pleading with her mother to open it. When Linda Schiro unlocked the door, Linda Scarpa bolted inside. She handed her son to her mother and nearly collapsed, still screaming, telling her mother that her father was dead.[45] Moments later, Scarpa walked into the house, unharmed.[46]

Other than the slight injury to Joe Fish, no one had been hit in the attack. Scarpa credited Little Linda with saving his life and the life of everyone in the Lincoln by blocking the van filled with the hit men.[47] Relieved that his daughter and grandson were unhurt, he fumed, "They're all fucking dead. They're going to die, starting tonight."[48]

When law enforcement showed up on the scene, Scarpa tried to convince them that his daughter had been caught in the crossfire of rival drug dealing gangs and that he had not even been present during the shootout.[49] However, Scarpa immediately reported the attempted assassination to his FBI handler Lin DeVecchio. In his report, he pinned blame for the attack squarely on "members of the 'Vic Orena' faction."[50] Linda Scarpa alleged that her father provided DeVecchio "the license plate number of one of the trucks used in the shooting" and that DeVecchio later reported to Scarpa "the truck belonged to William 'Wild Bill' Cutolo,"[51] one of Orena's top men.

Larry Mazza added some details in his book *The Life* about the hit and its aftermath that he learned sometime later. According to Mazza, the driver of the white truck that blocked the intersection was an "old-time Persico guy" who "always liked and respected Greg, so he purposely left space" for Scarpa's car to get by.[52] Mazza also stated that Sal Miciotta told him that Nicky Black and Joe Tolino, both Orena loyalists, were among the shooters that day, which, according to Carmine Imbriale, included Chickie

DeMartino.[53] Another Orena supporter, Vincent "Vinnie Venus" Fusaro, the man blocking the intersection of 13th Street and 82nd Avenue, cruised by Mazza's poolroom later on November 18. Larry Sessa was out in front as Fusaro drove by. Apparently believing the hit on Scarpa had been a success, Fusaro came to a stop, rolled down his window, took a big puff on his cigar, and gave Sessa the finger.[54]

Finally, Mazza has also alleged that while the shootout on 82nd Street was underway, an attempt on Gregory Scarpa Jr.'s life was unfolding in Lewisburg Prison.[55] The attempted hit resulted in two serious knife wounds to Gregory Jr., who nonetheless survived. "He was hit in the neck and lower back. If it hadn't been for a friend's warning at the last second, Junior would not have been able to block the likely fatal blow."[56] The assailant reportedly told Scarpa crew member Kevin Granato later he had been paid $10,000 for the hit.[57] According to Mazza, the attempt on Gregory Jr.'s life was engineered by Ralph Scopo, a fellow Lewisburg inmate of Gregory's and the father of Joey Scopo,[58] Vic Orena's underboss and a potential victim of Carmine Sessa's botched hit on Orena and Scopo back in June.

The Orenas, Pasquale Amato, and their advocates in federal court have offered an alternative theory about what happened in front of Greg Scarpa's house on November 18, 1991. Once the relationship between Scarpa and DeVecchio was out in the open, the Orenas and Amato sought to reframe the generally accepted narrative about the origins of the third Colombo war. That reframing included inferring from the impropriety of DeVecchio's dealings with Scarpa that the shootout on November 18, 1991, "could have been more easily understood by the jury as a hoax by Scarpa than as a product of an Orena directive."[59] In *Orena v. United States*, a case in which Vic Orena and Amato moved for either a dismissal of their indictments or new trials, the court reviewed in detail the evidence offered at their trials and considered at length their proffered arguments and inferences based on DeVecchio's alleged misconduct. The court, after referring to Orena's and Amato's "bizarre, but not entirely implausible, contention,"[60] ultimately rejected "so fantastic a theory."[61]

Given the totality of the circumstances, it appears unlikely to this author that Scarpa would have risked injury or death to his daughter and grandson in such a grandiose fashion simply to portray Orena as the aggressor in their ongoing dispute. As Scarpa was evidently aware, the FBI and in particular, Lin DeVecchio, had been willing for some time to accept Scarpa's version of events and relationships within the Colombo family as gospel. As of the date of the shooting, DeVecchio was still touting Scarpa's information about the Colombo family feud as "singular."[62] To assume that Scarpa fabricated, in a recklessly dangerous fashion, an ambush on himself, members of his crew, his daughter, and his grandson to demonstrate Orena's position in his feud with Scarpa and Persico's supporters is beyond the pale, even for Scarpa.

For better or for worse, regardless of one or more Colombo family member's contrary point of view, the official version of the third Colombo war settled on November 18 as an attack on Scarpa by the Orena faction and the war's violent starting point. Robert McFadden's reporting for *The New York Times* was typical. "Officials said the war, unfolding mostly in Bay Ridge and Sheepshead Bay, began Nov. 18 with shots fired at a Persico soldier, Gregory Scarpa, who was not hit."[63]

Once started, the conflict escalated immediately, from a shooting war to a killing war. Before the month of November was out, three plots to kill had either failed or were aborted, an impromptu attempt to kill a Persico loyalist resulted in the wounding of four innocent bystanders with no harm coming to the intended target, and one man had been killed. December brought more blood to the streets of Brooklyn as teams from both factions hunted their human prey, with lethal effect.

A FITFUL START

Not long after the ambush of Scarpa in front of his home, Larry Mazza was targeted by the Orena faction. He quickly learned that the streets he had grown up on and the neighborhoods he had roamed for nearly thirty years were no longer safe, that being caught out alone could be a fatal mistake.

Driving his father-in-law's car, Mazza pulled away from home at his usual time on the day the Orena faction targeted him for execution.[64] With an appointment in Manhattan as his destination, he headed for the MTA's F Train stop on 20th Avenue between 63rd and 64th Streets. At a stop sign on the way, Mazza noticed a car behind him with four men in it: Vincent "Chickie" DeMartino[65] and Frank "Frankie Notch" Iannaci in the front, both Orena loyalists, and two more Mazza could not identify in the back. A yellow van joined the parade, and Mazza quickly realized both vehicles were following him. He was without his bulletproof vest and was carrying nothing more than a .38 for defense.[66]

Outmanned and outgunned, he went for broke. He pulled his car into a gas station, parked it, and jumped out, his pistol drawn. DeMartino and company stopped when Mazza was no more than ten feet away from their car with his pistol pointed directly at Frankie Notch's head. The windows of DeMartino's car were still rolled up. As Mazza noted, "[t] hey had lost the element of surprise."[67] After a standoff of about five seconds, DeMartino "did the smart thing and took off."[68] For Mazza, the confrontation highlighted the deadly reality of the feud.

> "The war was getting much more serious to me now. It was hitting much closer to home. First Greg, now me. I didn't like the feeling of being hunted. I didn't like the feeling of knowing how close I had come to being killed."[69]

Mazza reported the attempt on his life to Scarpa when he returned from Manhattan that night. He let Scarpa know he was angry, tired of feeling like a target, and ready to strike back. "We gotta send some bullets their way to let them know that we ain't scared."[70] Scarpa's resolute response was simply, "You're right. You are 100 percent right."[71]

For the moment, Mazza survived unscathed. However, his friend Hank "The Bank" Smurra would not be so lucky. Smurra's fate may have been sealed by a third failed hit in less than a week. This time, the hunters were the Wimpy Boys. Their intended victim was Little Vic Orena. The date was November 23, 1991, and the plan, which was put together on a moment's notice, was, coincidentally, to hit Orena in Queens in front of a funeral parlor.

Two separate crews were employed for the hit. The first crew consisted of Carmine Sessa, his brother Michael, and Joseph "Joey Brains" Ambrosino. A second crew was instructed to bring the equipment, "machine guns, handguns, [and] bulletproof vests," necessary for the hit. That group consisted of John Pate, Bobby Zambardi, and "Jerry Boy" Chiara. The plan was to link up at a local diner and go from there to hit Orena, Joe Scopo, and Thomas Petrizzo. The second crew was late. By the time they showed up, Orena and company were gone. However, word got out about the botched attempt which, it turned out, was the likely catalyst for the move on Hank Smurra the next day.[72]

FIRST BLOOD

Hank "The Bank" Smurra was a former Genovese associate who was released to the Colombo family by Genovese boss Vincent "Chin" Gigante. While Smurra was in Carmine Sessa's crew, he earned his button.[73] Depending on who is doing the telling, Smurra was either a "fat, jolly and lovable guy, always joking around and happy to see you. Hank couldn't do enough for you. I don't think he had an enemy in the world."[74]

> "But he also had a problem staying awake. The man could fall asleep anywhere and at any time. He once fell asleep in Pastels, the hottest disco in Brooklyn. The music was blasting, the broads were all around us, flashing lights and all. He just conked out on the barstool. We were poking him, tickling him and even making the girls kiss him on the cheek. One even rubbed his dick. The man didn't move." [75]

Or Hank Smurra was a man who did not deserve to be a goodfellow.[76] He was a "jerkoff," a "coward" who was supposed to drive a getaway car for a jewelry store robbery pulled by Carmine Imbriale and Anthony "Bird" Coluccio. Instead, he got "spooked" for no reason and left the two men after they robbed the store and "beat the shit out of the owner."[77] He was a guy who ran "away in the middle of a job, when there [was] not even a threat."[78] Whatever Smurra was before November 24, 1991, he was the first fatality[79] in the third Colombo war thereafter.

Carmine Sessa had tasked Smurra with locating possible safe houses, either in Sheepshead Bay[80] or on Staten Island,[81] as the war was heating up. On Sunday, November 24, after checking out an apartment with Michael "Black Mike" Calla, Smurra stopped at a Dunkin' Donuts in Sheepshead Bay.[82] Black Mike jumped out of the car to make a phone call. Mazza surmised that Smurra, as was his habit, simply fell asleep while sitting in the car waiting for Calla to return.[83] If he was taking a nap, it would be his last one. Before Calla was done with his phone call, Smurra was shot in the head[84] at point-blank range anywhere from three[85] to six[86] times as he sat or snoozed behind the wheel of his 1988 Continental.[87] Calla saw the hit from start to finish and was able to identify the shooter as Vincent "Chickie" DeMartino,[88] one of the alleged gunmen in front of Scarpa's home less than a week earlier.[89] The third Colombo war, as of November 24, 1991, was officially deadly. A response to Smurra's execution was in order, yet the plan Scarpa devised for revenge was so bizarre as to be comical.

DRESSED TO KILL BILL

Between November 24 and November 28, all was relatively quiet in the Colombo war. Behind the scenes, however, another plot to kill "Wild Bill" Cutolo was brewing. Scarpa learned that Cutolo would be spending Thanksgiving with his girlfriend.[90] Either she or her grandmother[91] lived in a heavily Hasidic section of Brooklyn, most likely Borough Park.[92] Her family, along with Wild Bill, would be celebrating the holiday together there.[93] The plan was for Scarpa and a couple of his crew members to dress as Hasidim, wait for Cutolo to either arrive or leave, and ambush him when he did.[94] The disguises were necessary, the reasoning went, to allow Scarpa and his crew to get close to Cutolo without being recognized.[95] According to Larry Mazza, Linda Schiro's brother-in-law was to be the source of the disguises.[96] However, Joey "Brains" Ambrosino testified that the costumes came from Larry Fiorenza's girlfriend and were picked up and delivered by Anthony "the Arab" Sayegh.[97] Mazza wrote that Scarpa, Jimmy Delmasto,[98] and he were slated to don the outfits and carry out the bizarre mission.[99]

The image of those three men trying to credibly pass themselves off as Orthodox Jews in traditional garb is laughable to the point of pathetic. One can surely imagine the pretense collapsing at the first "Shalom, motherfucker!" uttered by one or more of the three to passersby. Fortunately for the prospective undercover killers, their ability to assume a wholly unfamiliar persona for the purpose of committing murder was never tested. Their farcical mission was canceled when an article appeared in *The New York Post* that same day claiming that Scarpa was an FBI informant.[100] Although the article was retracted about a week later,[101] Scarpa, rather than carrying out the Cutolo hit, had to go into damage control mode[102] as members of the Colombo family worried that if he were "a snitch, they might be in jeopardy."[103]

The day after Scarpa and his minions were busy preparing for and then canceling, for the third time, his ridiculous scheme targeting the Orena leadership, a fellow crew member found himself scrambling for his life on the streets of Brooklyn.

Ilario Sessa was a big man. He was not merely big, he was also heavy, hence the nickname "Fat Larry." Larry Mazza estimated that Sessa, who stood a full six feet two inches tall, weighed 370 pounds.[104] As noted above, he was Scarpa's driver when he was ambushed in front of his house on November 18. Eleven days later,[105] Sessa made the mistake of spending too much time in the middle of the day at a hair salon frequented by a number of Colombo wiseguys, including Bill Cutolo.[106] Sessa was there to make a collection after which he hung around waiting to hear back from another customer he had paged using the payphone in the salon.[107] Unfortunately for Sessa, Chickie

DeMartino had seen him enter the salon. Chickie started making calls from a pizza parlor down the street, putting a hit team together on the spot.[108]

When Larry came out of the salon about twenty minutes after entering, he immediately saw the hit team DeMartino had put together—four shooters from Cutolo's crew—crossing the street toward him.[109] Larry was armed with an impressive, large caliber handgun, which he quickly deployed. For a moment, the entire hit team froze when they saw Sessa's weapon. They quickly regained their nerve and started shooting.[110] Larry bolted, as only a man who weighed in at more than 370 pounds could. As he ran down 86th Street[111] bobbing and weaving, bullets flying, four shooters giving chase, a car driven by Sessa's friend and fellow crew member Ronnie Calder pulled up and the door flung open. Larry dove in.[112] Calder hit the gas, and together they headed straight for the shooters. Ronnie Calder took a round in the shoulder as he ducked during the melee, and another round hit him in the hand.[113]

The hit team jumped into their car, and a wild chase through the Christmas shopping crowd ensued. At one point, Calder lost control of his car and jumped the curb, seriously injuring at least two pedestrians,[114] "including a four-year-old girl,"[115] before getting the car back into the street. Sessa and Calder sped past a police station and a squad car pulled out after them.[116] Larry threw his weapon out of the car window and told Calder to pull over for the squad car, realizing that was the easiest way to shake the hit team.[117]

Both Calder and Sessa were immediately arrested. Calder was taken to a hospital and treated before being released a few days later. Whatever charges were filed against the two men were eventually dropped.[118] Miraculously, Larry Sessa was unscathed, untouched by any of the rounds the four-man hit team fired at him as he fled first on foot and then by car. A month later, at Scarpa's annual Christmas party, Sessa regaled the attendees with his colorful retelling of the entire incident, capping his story off with, "'That's the gang that couldn't shoot straight.... How the fuck did they miss ME?'"[119]

THE HIT PARADE

Fewer misses and more hits characterized the Colombo family's feud during early December of 1991. The lesson from the murder of Hank Smurra and the attack on Larry Sessa was clear: the streets of Brooklyn were not safe. Scarpa sought revenge, so he, along with Mazza, Delmasto, and Joe Fish started hunting for Orena loyalists every day. Their route would take them past Lolly's Luncheonette, a popular lunch site for "the Avenue U crew,"[120] before cruising by Nicholas "Nicky Black" Grancio's club and then Alphonse "Funzi" D'Ambrosio's club. They would then check out D'Ambrosio's bar and his home before moving on to "Fat Patty's"[121] club on Avenue U. Next up was Joel "Joe Waverly" Cacace's[122] club on the corner of Avenue U and East 14th Street. They would continue down Avenue U, past Benjamin "Benny the Sidge" LoCicero's "pizzeria... café, and home."[123] They repeated this routine several times a day, adding in clubs and homes as they obtained tips and addresses. For days on end, they came up empty-handed.

At least once, sometime after Hank Smurra was killed, Scarpa's twenty-year-old son Joey accompanied the Scarpa hit team in a macabre rendition of "take-your-son-to-work" day. As Larry Mazza recalled, Joey would pepper his father with questions about killing someone, anyone, as they drove around the streets of Brooklyn.[124] At one point, Scarpa, irritated by his son's relentless pestering, responded. "All right, Joey. Ya' want me ta' shoot that woman crossing the street?" Joey's response was nervous laughter "which just irked his father all the more."[125] Still, they continued to hunt, often to no avail. The "Orena soldiers had changed their routines," which added to the frustration of Scarpa and his hit team. "All this driving around seemed to be one big waste of time. We didn't spot anyone and we were getting desperate. [para.] Then we got our break."[126]

What happened next, as has often been the case in the Scarpa saga, is subject to some dispute in the details, but is otherwise well-chronicled. On the morning of December 3, a Tuesday, Jimmy Delmasto was at the wheel of the van Scarpa had tricked out for "hunting." Joe Fish rode shotgun, Scarpa was in the second row of seats by himself, and Mazza sat all the way in the back, in the third row of seats. A crash car with four other crew members as back-up shooters followed the van.[127] Mazza's first-hand account stated they saw Joe Tolino driving past Funzi D'Ambrosio's bar, The Wrong Number, on Avenue T while they were cruising. They surmised he was on his way to open "the club," presumably the club of his uncle "Nicky Black" Grancio, the Mother Cabrini social club on McDonald Avenue, as Peter Lance wrote. The McDonald Avenue club location noted by Lance coincides with the information in George James's near-contemporaneous December 6 article in *The New York Times* mentioning the hit.[128] Contrary to Mazza's version, Lance wrote that when Scarpa and his crew saw Tolino, Scarpa initially thought he was Nicky Black.[129]

Joe Tolino reached the club and stopped to talk to two men in the doorway, Funzi D'Ambrosio and Gaetano "Tommy Scars" Amato.[130] As the van approached the club, three of the men in the van, Fish, Scarpa, and Mazza, opened fire. Fish emptied an eight-round clip from his automatic pistol before the van stopped in front of the club's entrance. Scarpa fired a .38 without opening the van's sliding door and blew out a van window. Mazza fired a single shot through the hole Scarpa's shooting had made in the window.

Amato "fell like a tree struck by lightning,"[131] Tolino was hit in the left foot,[132] and D'Ambrosio escaped injury by diving in through the club's front door.[133] The only fatality, Amato, was a seventy-eight-year-old semiretired Genovese soldier.[134] The two Colombo men, Tolino and D'Ambrosio, survived.

Scarpa and his crew were proud of the work they had done until it became apparent that no Colombo rivals had been killed, that they had gunned down an aging Genovese wiseguy but had failed to take out either of the two Orena loyalists on scene. To add to their humiliation, they were immediately being referred to in local radio news reports as "the gang that couldn't shoot straight."[135] And when Carmine Sessa learned that the hit team had killed a Genovese soldier, he feared that Genovese boss Vincent "Chin" Gigante would seek revenge or at least throw his considerable influence Vic Orena's way. Gigante, however, was indifferent to the old gangster's fate.[136] "'Tommy was a big boy and he shoulda' known better than to be in a Colombo club.'"[137]

Mazza recalled a similar reaction to Amato's murder from Scarpa who said, frankly, "Well, he shouldn't have been there."[138] Linda Scarpa saw her father's reaction in a different light. She wrote that Scarpa "was pissed off and aggravated" that he had killed Amato, that "Tommy was a nice guy... a family man, and he didn't mean to hurt him."[139] Linda went on to note that she "had never seen [her] father show remorse before."[140] It is, of course, possible that both recollections are accurate and that Scarpa presented one face to his crew members and another face to his daughter.

For a war that started, at the latest, on November 18, 1991, neither side could claim any significant success as of sundown on December 3. There had been one deliberate fatality, Hank Smurra; one unintended fatality, Gaetano Amato; three minor wounds, Joe Fish, Ronnie Calder, and Joe Tolino; two complete misses, Greg Scarpa and Larry Sessa; at least two injured bystanders; and countless stray bullets. Less than impressive. With the exception of the injuries suffered by some bystanders when Ronnie Calder lost control of his vehicle during the escape from Larry Sessa's attackers, there was little reason as of December 3 for the authorities to care about the low-level and mostly inept conflict. However, the next week's activity would force law enforcement's hand, as the level and frequency of effective violence increased, and an innocent bystander was brutally executed.

FATAL ESCALATION

According to Lin DeVecchio, on Thursday, December 5, two days after Scarpa, et al. killed Tommy Scars Amato and wounded Joe Tolino, Scarpa reported that Teddy Persico and Chuckie Russo had met with Carmine Persico at the United States Penitentiary in Lompoc, California.[141] During that visit, Carmine gave them instructions about who should be killed on the Orena side.[142] Of course, Orena's loyal followers did not have to travel to California for their marching orders. And so, hours before Scarpa checked in with DeVecchio, the Orena faction struck again. The victim this time was another septuagenarian, seventy-nine-year-old Rosario "Black Sam" Nastasi,[143] a Colombo bookmaker.[144] Nastasi "was shot five times in the head and once in the torso as he played cards inside a social club he operated on 63rd St. near 10th Ave., Bay Ridge."[145] Nastasi's girlfriend was also wounded in the attack,[146] having been shot in the chest trying to protect Sam.[147] The man who shot the aging gangster five times in the head was once again believed to have been Chickie DeMartino using the same weapon he had used to kill Hank Smurra.[148]

Nastasi was an unlikely target. Lin DeVecchio referred to him dismissively as "an extremely low-level Persico cohort."[149] The elderly Nastasi, who could barely lift a pistol out of his desk drawer,[150] was certainly no longer a strategic or operational threat to Orena or his followers. His symbolic value as a target might be explained by the fact that Scarpa and Nastasi had been close friends for decades. Nastasi had been "straightened out at the very same induction ceremony as Greg"[151] back in the early 1950s. Now he and Hank Smurra, two men on the Persico side of the feud, were dead. And Scarpa's crew had yet to register a kill of an Orena follower in the deadly chess game being played out on the streets of Brooklyn. That was about to change.

Scarpa, Mazza, and Delmasto were, as was their habit, cruising and looking for Orena targets on Friday, December 6. They had company that day. Delmasto was at the wheel of a full van. Scarpa was in the second row. Joe Fish and Mazza were in the last row of seats.[152] They found a target at 3:55[153] in the late afternoon. Vincent "Vinnie Venus" Fusaro, the night manager of the Venus II diner at 9316 4th Avenue in Bay Ridge,[154] was stringing up Christmas lights with his wife on the door of their home at 310 Bay 11th Street in Bath Beach.[155] While other men in the van were armed,[156] Greg Scarpa was the lone gunman on this hit. He fired three shots from his rifle.[157] His first shot hit Fusaro in the back of the head,[158] just as he was hanging his wreath,[159] killing him. Scarpa, however, pumped two more rounds into him, one in the neck and one in the torso.[160] Fusaro was thirty years old[161] when he was murdered in front of his wife. And he was the first Orena man to be killed in the Colombo war.

An unintended victim of the Fusaro hit was the Venus II diner where Fusaro was the night manager. It had been a popular spot among organized crime figures,[162] but it closed after Fusaro was murdered and never reopened. Immediately after the hit, "one owner fled to Greece and a foreclosure ensued."[163]

As of December 6, Brooklyn District Attorney Charles Hynes and Police Commissioner Lee P. Brown would not "classify the shootings as a part of mob war."[164] However, the killing of eighteen-year-old Matteo Speranza on Sunday, December 8, forced law enforcement's hand to take action to reduce the violence plaguing the streets of Brooklyn, irrespective of its origins, once that violence had claimed the life of an innocent bystander.

KEROSENE ON THE FIRE

Pearl Harbor Day fell on a Saturday in 1991. Unlike its historic antecedent, it was a quiet day on the streets of Brooklyn, where the rival factions of the Colombo family were concerned. That brief respite from the violence of the Colombo war was broken on Sunday, December 8, by the shooting of James Malpeso, the son of Colombo soldier Louis "Bobo" Malpeso, who was then dropped off at Coney Island Hospital[165] with a non-fatal chest wound.[166] The attempted murder of the younger Malpeso was followed by the brutal execution of Matteo Speranza, an innocent bystander who was classically in the wrong place at the wrong time.

Speranza's murder had its origins in the news of Vincent Fusaro's killing two days earlier. Christopher Libertore, who had just turned twenty years old,[167] and Louis "Bobo" Malpeso were celebrating their birthdays at Joe Scopo's Cafe on N when word came that Fusaro had been killed.[168] In response, Pasquale Amato and Malpeso put together a plan to kill Persico loyalists Frank Guerra and Anthony Ferrara the next day.[169] The plan was a bust. Five men, including Malpeso and Libertore, in three cars searched for Guerra and Ferrara in vain.[170] One of the places they looked for the two men was the Wanna Bagel shop[171] at 8905 Third Avenue in Bay Ridge[172] that Guerra and Ferrara owned.[173] Neither man was at the shop. Eventually, the hunt was called off and Libertore and Malpeso returned to Malpeso's apartment.[174] While there, they received the news that Malpeso's son James had been shot in the chest and dropped off at Coney Island Hospital.[175] Malpeso, convinced that Guerra and Ferrara were responsible, instructed Libertore to "go find Anthony [Ferrara] and [Guerra]," and "go kill the guys in the bagel store."[176]

Libertore and his father, Anthony Libertore, who both later pleaded guilty to Speranza's murder,[177] carried out the order. After failing to find Guerra or Ferrara at home, they drove to the Wanna Bagel shop.[178] Christopher, wearing a black leather coat,[179] waited until a customer left the shop and went inside,[180] a mere twenty minutes after a wounded James Malpeso was left at Coney Island Hospital.[181] Matteo Speranza, a teenager,[182] was working behind the counter.[183] Christopher Libertore asked Speranza where Guerra and Ferrara were.[184] After asking Libertore why he was looking for them,[185] Speranza either leaned under the counter[186] or reached under the counter.[187] Libertore, who testified to shooting Speranza "four or five or six times,"[188] put six shots[189] into Speranza. He "shot Speranza in the head and watched him slide down the wall. He then shot him in the back and chest and walked out."[190] Speranza died at 10:05 a.m. at Lutheran Hospital.[191] Like the Venus II diner, the Wanna Bagel never reopened after the killing.[192]

Linda Scarpa wrote that in the wake of the Speranza murder, her father "was pissed... He was really going nuts about this poor kid, who was completely and totally innocent, getting killed."[193] As angry as Scarpa may have appeared to his daughter, the Speranza killing did nothing to dissuade him from continuing the violence. The death toll would continue to climb with the end of the war still months away. However, the "Speranza killing exploded in the media,"[194] and that brutal murder of an innocent bystander, a teenager working on his high school G.E.D.,[195] forced law enforcement out of its indifferent slumber. "'When Matteo Speranza got killed, it really turned up the pressure,' recalls NYPD Detective Thomas Dades."[196] Carmine Imbriale concurred. "'When they killed that poor kid, everybody knew it was a mistake, all a big mix up... But that one shooting really put the heat on.'"[197]

Both the FBI and Kings County District Attorney Charles "Joe" Hynes felt the heat. They had to do something to rein in the violence plaguing the streets of Brooklyn and threatening the lives of innocent bystanders. The FBI, for its part, finally opened an investigation on December 9, the day after Speranza was murdered.[198] NYPD "'got involved very deeply as a conduit to the FBI, because [they] had extensive knowledge of the players.'"[199] And "[i]n an attempt to stop the current bloodletting, [Brooklyn DA Joe[200]] Hynes... issued subpoenas to more than 90 reputed Colombo men."[201]

> "District Attorney Joe Hynes had his Organized Crime Task Force turn up the heat. He was furious over the latest innocent bystanders who were hurt. In the days that followed, there were more raids and arrests than the families were accustomed to and the D.A.'s plan worked. The other Families finally ordered a truce."[202]

As Behar noted, and as D.A. Hynes pointed out in his 1991 interview with Charlie Rose, New York law, which made "immunity automatic unless the individual agrees to waive it,"[203] hampered the DA's investigation. "Since mid-December, more than thirty camera-shy wiseguys—many donning upturned collars, oversize hats and dark sunglasses—have strolled in and out of Brooklyn's courthouse without admitting anything."[204] Hynes wanted the subpoenaed "camera-shy wiseguys" to waive immunity. Not surprisingly, for the moment, he was out of luck.

The public and law enforcement reactions to the shocking murder of Matteo Speranza did precipitate a temporary halt to the Colombo family violence.[205] The shooting on the streets of Brooklyn abated for the rest of the year. However, by January 2, 1992, the war was on again in earnest with Scarpa, Mazza, and Delmasto taking a poorly executed shot at Joel "Joe Waverly" Cacace, a man Scarpa had despised for years.[206] The attempt started with a stakeout of a club Cacace ran on East 3rd Street.[207] The three-man hit team did not have to wait for long. Shortly after the stakeout began, Cacace emerged from the club and headed for his car, which was parked out front.[208] Jimmy Delmasto was driving for the hit team. "As we pulled up, [Waverly] was just putting his key in the ignition. [para.] Jimmy perfectly positioned our car's passenger side to Waverly's driver's side. We were so close we could have shaken hands."[209] Scarpa, with his thirty-round Tech-9 inches away from Cacace's head, pulled the trigger.[210] His weapon jammed. Mazza got off a single shot from his Walther PPK before it, too, jammed.[211] Cacace was not hit, and he managed to return fire as the Scarpa crew fled.[212]

The only casualty of the inept attempt was the car Mazza had rented from Avis for the occasion. Cacace had managed to put several bullet holes in it and to blow out one of its windows when returning fire.[213] As the hit team made its getaway, Mazza had to laugh at the sight of Scarpa picking pieces of broken safety glass out of his thinning hair.[214] Other than that, no one on either side sustained any injury. In short, the "hit" was another dangerous waste of time.

Scarpa's activity in late December of 1991 and early January of 1992 was not limited to cruising the streets of Brooklyn looking for possible targets. When the opportunity arose, he continued to manipulate FBI Special Agent Lin DeVecchio. On either December 10 or December 11, 1991, DeVecchio, along with FBI Special Agent Ray Andjich, paid Scarpa a visit at his home.[215] With Andjich parked in front of Scarpa's living room TV so he could not hear their conversation, Scarpa and DeVecchio met "in the privacy of [Scarpa's] kitchen."[216] According to DeVecchio's 302 report, an FBI form which records information from a cooperating witness, Scarpa denied any knowledge of the Colombo family war.[217] However, in a 209 DeVecchio filed the next day, he reported that Scarpa claimed the attempt on Larry Sessa's life, the ambush on Scarpa at his home, and the murders of Hank Smurra and Rosario Nastasi were all carried out by members of Wild Bill Cutolo's crew. Scarpa went on to state that the Persico faction had killed Gaetano Amato and Vincent Fusaro and had attempted to kill Joel Cacace.[218] As was always the case, Scarpa made no mention of his own role in the murders of Amato and Fusaro or the attempted murder of Cacace.

Nothing in either the 302 or the 209 from that meeting indicated that DeVecchio made any attempt to discover who in the Persico faction was responsible for the Amato and Fusaro murders or the attempted murder of Cacace. On December 30, the manipulation continued. Scarpa told DeVecchio "that an arrest of VIC ORENA would temporarily halt the shooting war."[219] Apparently, DeVecchio, who claimed "[i]n my heart, as Scarpa's handler, of course, I knew he was doing hits,"[220] never seriously considered the effect that arresting Scarpa, his prized TECI, might have on the shooting war.

Another important development in the ongoing conflict, one that was both administrative and symbolic, took place shortly after the 1991-1992 holiday season ended. Those in the Colombo family who were at least nominally loyal to Carmine Persico gathered at the Sheraton "next to the Meadowlands Racetrack in New Jersey across from Giant [sic] Stadium,"[221] and recognized a number of important promotions. Joe Tomasello was named acting boss; Jo Jo Russo was named acting underboss; Larry Mazza and Jimmy Delmasto were both sworn in as made men; and Greg Scarpa was named an acting capo.[222] The promotion of Joe Tomasello to acting boss had been suggested by Scarpa[223] as a way to weaken the ranks of the Orena faction. Tomasello was generally well-respected and well-liked, and Scarpa thought his promotion might cause some Orena men to defect.[224] While the move did not have the decisive effect some might have hoped for, it did cause some defections that eroded the strength of Orena's support. Furthermore, both the Bonanno and Genovese families "recognized Joe [Tomasello] and the new administration,[225] while the Lucchese family remained split, and the Gambinos continued to back Orena, although their ranks did not unanimously support him."[226]

The decision to elevate Scarpa to acting capo was driven in large measure by the desire to keep the Scarpa, Mazza, Delmasto hit team together. Once Mazza and Delmasto were made, they had to be assigned to a captain, which would have removed them from Scarpa's immediate control. However, by making Scarpa an acting capo, Mazza and Delmasto could be assigned to him as members,[227] thereby preserving what until then, and for the rest of the war, was the most effective killing team on the Persico side.

Although Scarpa's presence on the streets of Brooklyn in January of 1992 as a capo, along with newly-made members Mazza and Delmasto, failed to have a decisive effect on Joel Cacace, the same cannot be said for Nicholas "Nicky Black" Grancio.

TOO CLOSE FOR COMFORT

Scarpa had been providing the FBI with information about Joe Tolino's uncle, Nicholas "Nicky Black" Grancio, since at least 1982. In October of that year, Scarpa informed DeVecchio that Grancio, who at the time was in Dominick Montemarano's crew,[228] "was in on the hit of John Aratico, who had been shot in front of his house on 21st Avenue, Brooklyn, N.Y., in April of 1982."[229] Scarpa also provided the FBI with his views on Grancio's level of activity within the Colombo family, and his involvement with the Teamsters.[230] When Grancio became a capo, Scarpa passed that information on to DeVecchio.[231] And Scarpa twice told DeVecchio that Grancio had sided with the Orena faction.[232] It was general knowledge within the Colombo family that Grancio and Vic Orena were "very close friends."[233] Finally, according to Vic Orena Jr., Grancio was "fiercely loyal to his father."[234]

Scarpa likely regarded Grancio as a competitor and rival,[235] which may have marked him for elimination. However, a conversation that Grancio had with Albert Maniscalco, Joan Mazza's oldest brother and thus Larry Mazza's uncle, may have had more to do with Grancio's murder than how Scarpa viewed him. Grancio told Maniscalco that "he should convince [Mazza] to come over to his side. 'If he doesn't, I'm gonna kill him.'"[236] Word of Grancio's threat quickly got back to Mazza via Carmine Sessa.[237] Grancio lived for another two days. As Mazza stated, "It had become very personal for me with Nicky Black."[238]

Nicholas "Nicky Black" Grancio was killed on January 7, 1992, at about 3:15 in the afternoon.[239] He was sixty-two years old.[240] He was shot in the head as he sat in the front seat of his SUV "at the intersection of McDonald Avenue and Avenue U in Gravesend."[241] A second man, Anthony Bianco, who was twenty-six years old at the time, suffered a slight wound to his head and survived.[242] He had just walked up to Grancio's car when the attack occurred. Mazza alleged that Bianco was handing an envelope to Nicky Black that had $15,000 in it, but the envelope was never found.[243] Joe Tolino, Grancio's nephew, was in the car, a Toyota Land Cruiser, and he "was lucky to escape with just a few grazes,"[244] but "'he ended up with brain matter all over him.'" The men involved in Grancio's killing were Greg Scarpa, Larry Mazza, and Jimmy Delmasto.[245] The vehicle they were in was disguised to look "like a police surveillance vehicle."[246] The disguise included "a fake siren light on the windshield,"[247] "'a big walkie-talkie,'"[248] "coffee cups on the dashboard,"[249] and binoculars,[250] which Mazza used to spot Grancio, like "cops on a stakeout."[251]

During the investigation into the killing, according to detective Joe Simone, NYPD "'recovered one of Nicky's teeth from the wall of a house fifteen feet away.'"[252] The above facts are generally agreed upon by the participants in Grancio's murder, by law enforcement, and by those who have reported on the killing. Accounts of the events immediately before Grancio's murder and how he was murdered are not, however, uniformly in agreement.

The primary and crucial point of contention regarding the moments leading up to Grancio's death is whether law enforcement surveillance, which by its very presence was providing de facto protection for Grancio, was unexpectedly and purposefully removed, thereby leaving Grancio exposed to assassination by his Colombo family rivals. Peter Lance's thorough and rigorous examination of the subject revealed the difficulty of conclusively stating that Scarpa and the FBI, in particular Special Agent Lin DeVecchio, conspired to leave Grancio vulnerable to Scarpa's hit team. As Lance noted, NYPD and the FBI were conducting surveillance on Grancio on the afternoon of January 7. As NYPD Detective Joe Simone told Lance, "'We knew the heat was on Nicky [Grancio], so we were keeping him under virtual round-the-clock surveillance.'"[253] At 1:30, the FBI and NYPD surveillance teams were instructed to go to 26 Federal Plaza [in Manhattan] for a meeting with FBI Special Agent Chris Favo.[254] The instruction was "unusual" since meetings of that sort usually occurred "at the end of the day."[255]

Peter Lance, in typical thorough fashion, wrote that Larry Mazza testified under oath "'he didn't notice any surveillance on Nick Grancio that day.'" He further testified that "'from the moment [he] first saw Mr. Grancio till the moment he was killed, there was no time to make any calls.'"[256] However, according to both defense attorney Flora Edwards and the late Dr. Stephen Dresch, Mazza told them in separate interviews that when they first spotted Nicky Black, there was a law enforcement surveillance presence in the area. Scarpa then called "Del," his "law enforcement source," and in essence told his source to call off the surveillance.[257]

Linda Schiro claimed that Mazza, Delmasto, and Scarpa were in the Scarpa home when Scarpa called DeVecchio about surveillance surrounding Nicky Black. After that call, according to Schiro, "the surveillance wasn't there anymore."[258] Quoting her mother, Linda Scarpa wrote,

> "'Larry came to the house with Jimmy and told Greg he had just seen Nicky on Avenue U, but there was police surveillance around. Then Greg got on the phone and got in touch with Lin, and then the surveillance wasn't

there anymore. So when Greg, Larry, and Jimmy went back to Avenue U, there was nobody around, and that's why they had the opportunity to kill Nicky Black.'"[259]

There is no doubt that Grancio was under NYPD surveillance on the day he was murdered. There is also no doubt that the surveillance was withdrawn due to an unusual call from FBI Special Agent Chris Favo for those conducting the surveillance to come to 26 Federal Plaza in Lower Manhattan for a meeting. DeVecchio refers to the call from Favo to withdraw the surveillance as little more than a "known and reported unhappy coincidence"[260] that left Grancio exposed "hours before Scarpa's crew ever came across Nicky Black."[261] Recall that the order to withdraw came at 1:30 p.m., and Black was not killed until 3:15 p.m. Whether Favo's call had a more sinister origin, as suggested by Schiro, Edwards, and Dresch, will likely never be definitively known. Once again, the conflicting accounts of an event that took place more than thirty years ago underscore how difficult crafting an accurate narrative of that event can be.

As to the moment of Grancio's death, the primary points of disagreement are about who pulled the trigger and whether Greg Scarpa said anything in the immediate aftermath of the killing. Mazza's first-hand account is almost tragically comic. Scarpa, whose physical and mental faculties were in decline from the effects of AIDS, the medication he was taking, and the "street pot" he was smoking to alleviate some of his symptoms, was prepared to kill Grancio with his rifle. When he went to take the safety off, he instead released the rifle's clip.[262] As he fumbled with the clip, trying to reload his weapon, which already had a round chambered, Mazza fired a blast point-blank at the back of Grancio's head from a riot control shotgun, "which had 12-gauge double buck pellets in the chamber,"[263] killing him instantly. Mazza has also said that Scarpa may have discharged a round from his rifle when Mazza fired, but the noise from the shotgun made it impossible for him to distinguish one weapon's sound from the other.[264] Peter Lance quoted Mazza as saying in an interview that "Scarpa 'got one shot off and then the clip fell out [of the M1].'"[265] Mazza then rolled down his window and killed Grancio with his shotgun.[266] It is not surprising that Mazza's recollection of an event as traumatic as Grancio's murder is neither precise nor entirely consistent, particularly with the passage of time. He has, however, been consistent about the immediate aftermath of the murder during which Scarpa is alleged by a number of sources to have said, "This one's for Carmine!"[267] As noted above, Larry Mazza has attributed the quote to Scarpa's after-the-fact embellishment. In other words, it never happened.

The significance of Nicky Black's gruesome death was not lost on the participants in the third Colombo war. "Nicky Black was the first significant kill by Scarpa's side and he was the only capo killed by either side."[268] Linda Schiro has said that after the hit, Scarpa came home and "got on the phone with Lin [DeVecchio] and told him, 'This was the big one.'"[269] Some of Orena's men started wondering what they had gotten themselves into as they "watched the awesome scene surrounding Nicky Black's corpse."[270] "Little Vic and Nicky had been very close friends. Yet Vic refused to give in."[271] Orena's alleged response was to order his hit teams "to focus on the Scarpa crew."[272] At the FBI's New York Office, DeVecchio was advised, one day after the hit, that "GRANCIO was the main go-between for VIC ORENA and was a very influential ally of ORENA's."[273]

As to Scarpa's claim that he killed Nicky Black for Carmine Persico, it is hard to imagine that Scarpa felt a need to burnish his credentials as a cold-blooded killer with Persico or anyone else by January of 1992. It may be that with his health in a serious state of decline, he felt no constraints on his actions, legal or otherwise. There is little doubt that he continued to be an active participant in the violence plaguing the streets of Brooklyn, and there seemed to be nothing from either side of the law standing in his way.

The District Attorney's use of subpoenas to coerce one or more Colombo members or associates into turning on the rest of them was not having its intended effect. Law enforcement, therefore, changed tactics. Knowing that scores of Colombo men were armed nearly every waking moment, the DA and the FBI devised a strategy to achieve arrests and to remove some of the lethal hardware from the streets. "One of the major goals of the Colombo Family Strike Force (CFSF)[274] was to quell the violence of the shooting war within the Colombo Family by taking 'guns out of circulation whenever possible.'"[275] The strategy proved to be effective. During early 1992, the arrests began to mount. "In an effort to slow what was proving to be a particularly bloody struggle, the F.B.I. focused on stopping hit teams before they engaged in shooting.... As a result, thirty-five of the first thirty-seven arrests were for possession of firearms. Over 100 guns were seized during the course of the fray."[276]

"Over the course of this fratricidal bloodletting the F.B.I., with the aid of the New York City Police Department, made 123 arrests of Colombo Family members. By September 1992, twenty-four of the fifty-four arrested were Persicos. All told, by War's end, sixty-one of those arrested were on the Orena side; sixty were on the Persico side, which was one-third the size of its rival faction.[277]

Scarpa likely assumed his relationship with the FBI as a Top Echelon Criminal Informant would shield him from law enforcement's new strategy as well as it had in the past. For the moment, that was certainly the case. As the winter of 1991-1992 dragged on, Scarpa continued his unabated hunt for Orena supporters, usually with Larry Mazza and Jimmy Delmasto. On February 26, the trio struck again. Their victim that day was a familiar one, Joel "Joe Waverly" Cacace. In fact, this would be their third attempt to kill Cacace. During the second attempt, not long after Nicky Black's funeral, Scarpa, Mazza, and Delmasto were wrapping up their day when they happened to spot Cacace with about eight other men in front of Cacace's club, The Party Room Social Club, on East 14th Street at about 3:30 in the afternoon.[278] Scarpa and Mazza both fired from Scarpa's black Mercedes Benz[279] at the group of men who variously dove, scattered, or ran back into the doorway of the club.[280] No injuries were reported. Cacace would not be so lucky the third time around.

On the morning of February 26, Scarpa, Mazza, and Delmasto were once again on the hunt, looking for victims. This time they were in a white station wagon that was loaded to the gills with weapons. They cruised by Cacace's club on East 14th Street and spotted him "walking back towards his club with grocery bags and his dry cleaning."[281] Cacace saw the hit team, dropped his bags, pulled out an automatic Glock, and started firing. Scarpa fired at Cacace with his M1 rifle, and Mazza fired as well. Together, they unleashed at least fourteen rounds as they tried, for a third time, to kill Joel "Joe Waverly" Cacace. Cacace was hit in the "stomach and the groin."[282] He did not go down without a fight, as evidenced by the six huge bullet holes in the hit team's station wagon.[283] Cacace's injuries were not fatal. He underwent surgery at Kings County Hospital and was listed in fair condition the day after the shooting.[284]

Having survived three attempts on his life by Scarpa and his crew, Cacace decided he had had enough of the conflict. The appointment by Carmine Persico of Joe Tomasello as acting boss, after having been nominated for the position by Scarpa,[285] likely sealed the deal. As Larry Mazza noted, Cacace had "been with Joe T for many years and Waverly had a lot of respect for him."[286] In effect, Cacace withdrew from the Colombo war by going "underground in the wake of the last attempt on his life."[287] He "eventually moved out of New York."[288] He was quoted as saying, "'I don't need this shit no more.'"[289]

A remarkable turn of events followed immediately after Scarpa and his crew sent Joel Cacace to the hospital. FBI Special Agent Lin DeVecchio was ordered by his superiors to close Scarpa. He would no longer serve as a Top Echelon Criminal Informant. By memo dated March 3, 1992, from the FBI's New York Office to the Director of the FBI, Scarpa's potential involvement in a conspiracy to commit murder was disclosed to FBI headquarters in D.C. The basis of the allegation was a February 25 report from DeVecchio that clearly implicated Scarpa's giving a contract to Joe "Fish" Marra to kill Frankie "The Bug" Sciortino.[290]

In addition, Carmine Imbriale, who had been arrested on February 27, 1992, agreed to become a cooperating witness and to wear a wire.[291] He disclosed the substance of a statement Scarpa made at dinner about the recent attempt on Joel Cacace's life. According to Imbriale, Scarpa said, "This is one for the good guys" while toasting Cacace's shooting.[292] Imbriale was wearing a wire during the meeting,[293] and from the information gathered via that wire, the FBI knew that "Scarpa was committing new acts of violence during the war."[294] As a result of all of the above, Scarpa was closed "until such time that NY can prove the reliability of the information with respect to captioned source's possible involvement into the reported contract, this source will be placed in a closed status [para.] If, at a future time, the NYO can show that the information is unreliable or inconclusive with respect to captioned source's involvement in the conspiracy, this source will be reopened."[295]

Incredibly, Scarpa was not being closed for his involvement in the recent, highly-publicized murders of Gaetano Amato, Vincent Fusaro, or Nicky Black, or for the three attempts on Joel Cacace's life, all of which took place within less than three months of the closing memo. Equally remarkable is the fact that DeVecchio wrote in his book that it was not until a March 6 disclosure from Scarpa about a contract on him "'in view of the recent hits on ORENA faction members'"[296] that Scarpa's sometimes deadly participation in the Colombo war was confirmed to DeVecchio's satisfaction.[297] In spite of the disclosure of an alleged conspiracy to commit murder, and in spite of DeVecchio's being convinced as of March 6 that Scarpa was killing members of the Orena faction, DeVecchio fought Scarpa's closure as a TECI. Meanwhile, the killings in the third Colombo war continued.

On March 25, 1992, Colombo capo and Orena loyalist John Minerva and his bodyguard[298] Michael Imbergamo were murdered in front of a cafe/pastry shop Minerva owned in North Massapequa, Long Island.[299] Nine men, including Scarpa, have been implicated over the years in this double homicide that became known as the "Pastry Shop" murders. First, Scarpa telephoned Lin DeVecchio on March 31, 1992, and told him that the Minerva and Imbergamo murders were "handled by Jo Jo and Chuckie RUSSO'S people."[300] The Russos, along with Joseph "Joe Monte" Monteleone Sr., were convicted of the murders. And while the trial court granted them a new trial based on the government's failure to disclose the DeVecchio/Scarpa relationship,[301] that order was appealed by the government and reversed in 1998 by the Second Circuit. Ultimately, their convictions were affirmed on appeal in 2001.[302]

Then, in 2004, ten years after his father's death, Gregory Scarpa Jr. testified that his father told him that he "and a 'kid' named Eric Curcio" killed Minerva and Imbergamo.[303] Next, in 2008, Thomas "Tommy Shots" Gioeli was arrested and charged with the Pastry Shop murders.[304] At his trial in 2012, he was convicted on the single racketeering count in the indictment based in part on the Minerva and Imbergamo murders. But, oddly, he was acquitted of the murders themselves.[305] At Gioeli's trial, Robert Ventriglia testified that he, on orders from Eric Curcio, and Anthony Calandria "opened fire on Minerva and Imbergamo."[306] And finally, at least as of this writing, in 2017, Dino Calabro admitted that he "took part in the murders of John Minerva and Michael Imbergamo, two Colombo members who were fatally shot in a car outside a diner on Long Island."[307] Irrespective of who actually plotted, took part in, conspired, and/or pulled the trigger, two more Orena loyalists were killed by Persico followers in the third Colombo war near the end of March in 1992.

One day after Lin DeVecchio was told by Scarpa that the Pastry Shop murders of two Orena loyalists had been carried out by Persico supporters, Vic Orena was arrested, a move Scarpa had been encouraging for months, a move he claimed would bring about an end to the third Colombo war violence. However, as will be shown below, Scarpa personally planned and participated in another killing of an alleged Orena supporter after Orena's arrest. In other words, once again, Scarpa manipulated an entire federal bureaucracy of formally educated and experienced men and women.

The arrest of Vic Orena and two of his sons, Andrew and John, took place at the Long Island house of Little Vic's girlfriend Gina Reale on April 1, 1992.[308] Orena was arrested for the murder of Tommy Ocera.[309] Along with the arrests, a search of the premises turned up

> "...an arsenal. There were fully loaded shotguns in each of the three basement closets. Extra ammunition was stored with the shotguns, including hollow-point bullets, shotgun shells, and a 16-round, 9 millimeter clip. On the main floor of the house agents found a fully-loaded pistol-grip shotgun and an ammunition belt holding numerous shotgun shells. In the crawl-space under the backyard wooden deck, they retrieved a black plastic garbage bag containing six loaded operable handguns and two extra clips.[310] [para.] Aside from the weaponry, the search uncovered a bullet-proof vest and three sets of mobile phones and beepers. Orena's briefcase was found in the second floor bathroom. It contained $55,000 in cash."[311]

After Orena's arrest,[312] as if to justify his own prediction, Scarpa made an immediate phone call to Lin DeVecchio claiming that three Orena supporters were about to defect.[313] Two weeks later, he made another call to DeVecchio. This time he warned that the Persico faction, at the express direction of Carmine Persico, was going to kill additional Orena supporters with an eye toward creating more defections.[314] At that point, by his own admission, DeVecchio knew that Scarpa was committing murder, or more accurately murders, in the context of the third Colombo war. Under those circumstances it is impossible to read Scarpa's second April 1992 phone call to DeVecchio as anything less than a threat to murder again. However, instead of arresting Scarpa, the FBI's New York Office, at

DeVecchio's urging, took the extraordinary position that Scarpa should be reinstated as a TECI.

FOOL ME THRICE

One week after the Pastry Shop murders, the New York Office sent the FBI director a request to reopen Scarpa.[315] In fact, that request was made on the same day of the first of Scarpa's two phone calls to Lin DeVecchio about potential Orena defections. The request was granted in less than a week on the basis that "the allegations set forth in [your teletype] dated March 3, 1992, regarding the CI's possible involvement in a contract murder were unsubstantiated."[316] The teletype reopening Scarpa, which was dated April 7, 1992, went on to state that "[i]n view of the CI's historical relationship with the New York Office, coupled with the fact that the CI is a made member of the LCN, the CI is authorized to maintain Top Echelon (TE) status."[317] DeVecchio wrote in his book that Scarpa was reopened on April 22 rather than on April 7.[318] If that was the case, then Scarpa was reopened after his April 14 phone call to DeVecchio, which was little more than a direct threat to continue murdering Orena supporters.

In either case, Scarpa was designated as a Top Echelon Criminal Informant by the FBI for the third time in thirty years. His special relationship with the FBI was once again restored in spite of the fact that his handler, at long last, was convinced he was committing murder, and had done so recently. It would take four more months and one more murder for agents from the FBI's New York Office to finally arrest Greg Scarpa, The Grim Reaper, for conspiracy to commit murder, and for the FBI to end Scarpa's privileged status as a Top Echelon Criminal Informant for good.[319] But Scarpa's arrest proved to be too late for Larry Lampasi.

About a month after Scarpa was reopened as a TECI, he committed his last murder in the third Colombo war. The unfortunate victim was Lorenzo "Larry Lamps" Lampasi. The "sixty-six-year-old wiseguy"[320] was killed "in his Kensington, Brooklyn driveway."[321] Unlike the Pastry Shop murders, there is no controversy over who killed Lampasi.[322] Once again, Scarpa, Mazza, and Delmasto were the executioners. Mazza's first-hand account is graphic and specific. The morning of the shooting, the trio rolled up on Lampasi as he was getting out of his car to lock the gate to the lot next to his apartment building where he parked his car every night.[323] All three men jumped out of the car as soon as it was stopped. Scarpa took the first shot with his rifle, hitting Lampasi in the back.[324] Larry Lamps collapsed and tried to crawl back to his car.[325] He did not get far. As the three men approached, Lampasi looked up and said, "Do it."[326] Mazza fired his "shotgun blowing up his body like Sonny Corleone in the tollbooth."[327] Mazza "fired again and Jimmy knelt beside him and fired one right behind his ear."[328] The results were intentionally gruesome. As Mazza wrote, "[w]e were getting to where we didn't want to just kill an Orena soldier, but make a mess of him. Splatter him so much that others on the enemy side would cringe. We wanted to send a message."[329]

As with Nicky Black's murder, Scarpa immediately began to embellish the circumstances of the hit, "saying that Lampesi [sic] asked, 'What did I do wrong?' and Greg had answered, 'You picked the wrong side.'" [para.] But he had never asked that and Greg's response was also untrue, just like the comment on Nicky Black about 'this is for Carmine' never happened."[330] As others have pointed out, Scarpa's alleged comment fit the general narrative of the Colombo family killings all being tied to the ongoing struggle between supporters of Carmine Persico and those of Vic Orena. Scarpa's lie about Larry Lampasi's final conversation placed his killing squarely within that accepted narrative. The context of Lampasi's murder drove a conclusion about why he was killed in contemporaneous press accounts,[331] in reporting subsequent to the third Colombo war,[332] and in relevant case law.[333] That conclusion was straightforward: Lampasi was an Orena loyalist killed by Persico supporters. It was also a conclusion disputed by those closest to Vic Orena. Andrew Orena told Peter Lance that "Larry Lamps barely knew my father."[334] As it turned out, the two most often recounted reasons for the Lampasi hit had nothing to do with the third Colombo war.

Another version of Scarpa's rationale for killing Lampasi has Scarpa once again trying to prevent being outed as an FBI informant while insisting on full payment of an outstanding debt. According to this version, Lampasi, on behalf of an associate who disputed the amount of a loan he had with Scarpa, included with a loan payment to Scarpa a note that stated the following: there would be no further payments on the loan, and Lampasi was not willing to sit down with Scarpa to discuss the loan balance because "there was talk that Scarpa was an informant."[335] Carmine Sessa testified that Scarpa showed him the note,[336] and that Scarpa asked acting boss Joe Tomasello for permission to kill Lampasi.[337] According to Sessa, Tomasello gave Scarpa the requested permission, and Lampasi's home address and work schedule.[338] Scapa took it from there. Later that year, Scarpa showed the letter to Larry Mazza. Included with the letter was $5,000 of the $7,500 outstanding debt. The note stated that Lampasi "had paperwork proving that Greg was a rat!"[339] So, according to this version of the rationale for shooting Larry Lampasi four times—once by Scarpa with a rifle, twice by Mazza with a shotgun, and once by Delmasto with a handgun—was Lampasi's threat to tell the truth about Scarpa, and/or his refusal to pay a debt of $2,500, about $6,000 less than the average used car price for 1992.[340]

A third version of the rationale for murdering Lampasi came from Linda Schiro. According to Schiro, Scarpa's niece Rosemarie was a Lampasi employee. She drove a school bus for Lampasi's company. At Thanksgiving dinner in 1991, she complained to Scarpa about Lampasi's treatment of her. She "had a lousy route and wasn't allowed to drive her bus home while other drivers were. This was interpreted as disrespect directed at Scarpa."[341] Schiro went on to claim that "Greg's attitude at this time was that he was going to fuck everybody. He don't [sic] give a fuck who he kills."[342] So he killed Larry Lamps.

Finally, it is worth noting that the Lampasi murder took place *after* Scarpa was reopened as a TECI. Furthermore, it was one of the killings that Lin DeVecchio was indicted for by the Brooklyn DA's office in 2006. The crux of the allegation was that DeVecchio provided Scarpa with information about Lampasi's address and work routine that Scarpa used to hunt down and murder Lampasi. However, Linda Schiro, in an interview with Jerry Capeci and Tom Robbins in 1997, exonerated DeVecchio in the Lampasi case, saying, "'When Lin is right, I give him right. He didn't tell Greg about Larry Lampasi.'"[343] Schiro's statement about DeVecchio "definitively cleared him in the May 1992 murder of Lorenzo 'Larry Lamps' Lampasi."[344]

The Lampasi murder was the last murder in the third Colombo war carried out by Greg Scarpa, Larry Mazza, and Jimmy Delmasto. Although Scarpa discussed plans for murdering "Wild Bill" Cutolo and Joey Ambrosino's mother, after Ambrosino's arrest, neither of those plans came to fruition.[345] Law enforcement was closing in on the Colombo borgata in general, and on the "deadly trio" in particular.

CLOSURE

The dominos started to fall in the late spring of 1992. With the assistance of cooperating witness Carmine Imbriale,[346] the FBI planted a bug in Joseph "Joey Brains" Ambrosino's car on June 3.[347] It was operational the next day.[348] The FBI also tapped his phone.[349] Special agents gathered information via the bug for the next six days and on June 10, Ambrosino was arrested. He flipped almost immediately.[350] On June 14, Larry Mazza and Jimmy Delmasto were indicted on weapons charges.[351] With the heat turned up, Scarpa urged Carmine Sessa to go into hiding, and he tried to reassure Mazza and Delmasto that the entire matter "would blow over if [the two of them] stayed out of 'their' faces."[352]

But the summer brought no relief. On July 9, Scarpa informed DeVecchio that Carmine Sessa was indeed in hiding and likely to remain so.[353] Due to the increased pressure from law enforcement, the two sides declared an indefinite ceasefire, a temporary truce.[354] Scarpa informed SA DeVecchio of the truce on July 13.[355] "The shooting was over… The indefinite ceasefire was too late. The insanity that should never have been, was definitely over. [para.] The war was finally over and no one had won."[356]

The man who had spent only thirty days in jail[357] in three decades as an FBI informant, while he committed murder over and over again, was finally arrested, and his status as a Top Echelon Criminal Informant was closed for good.

> "On September 1, 1992, captioned source was arrested by New York Office agents on charges of conspiring to murder in connection with Colombo LCN family investigation. In view of the above, and until this matter is resolved, this source is being closed."[358]

The New York Times reported in late October of 1992 "that a year of Mafia infighting… [had] left at least 13 people dead and 23 injured across south Brooklyn."[359] That death toll likely included the October 7, 1992 murder of Steven Mancusi, a "Colombo family associate,"[360] but not the shooting death of Joe Scopo a little more than a year later.[361]

Scarpa personally participated in four murders, and at least three attempted murders, during the third Colombo war. One would assume that his arrest in September of 1992 for conspiring to commit murder would have meant an end to his engaging in shootouts on Brooklyn's streets, particularly given that he had less than two years to live. But assuming anything about Greg Scarpa, particularly when it came to his ability and willingness to visit violence on others, had been a losing proposition for decades. It would prove to be so one more time.

CHAPTER ELEVEN: A BANG AND A WHIMPER[1]

The last twenty-two months of Gregory Scarpa Sr.'s life were characterized in large measure by more of what had already made him infamous: crime, violence, and betrayal. However, the context within which he continued his brazen lawlessness and disloyalty overshadowed everything he did. His imminent death from AIDS became an obvious certainty that eluded accurate prediction. Nonetheless, his deteriorating physical and mental states seemed to heighten his recklessness to such a degree that people feared his penchant for murder even as he was lying in a hospital bed, days from dying. The final chapter of his ignominious life began in the summer of 1992, when he shamelessly sought a measure of justice from a judicial system that had for so long failed his long line of victims.

CHUTZPAH

On August 19, 1992, Gregory Scarpa, who "had been in virtual hiding since March,"[2] walked into a Brooklyn courtroom and took the stand to testify under oath before a jury and New York Supreme Court Justice Joseph Levine.[3] His sworn testimony that day was not about his uninterrupted string of criminal acts going back at least four decades, nor was it about the four murders he had recently committed during the third Colombo war, nor was it about the millions of dollars he had derived over the years from his illegal activities, nor was it about the mountain of information, both true and false, he had surreptitiously provided the FBI for twenty-five out of the previous thirty years, nor was it about any of his accomplices, coconspirators, or accessories in any of the above. Instead, Scarpa testified in a $1.5 million civil lawsuit he had filed against Victory Memorial Hospital and surgeon Dr. Angelito Sebollena for negligence and malpractice stemming from the HIV-tainted blood he had received during his emergency hiatal hernia operation in 1986.[4] The essence of the complaint was that the defendants "should not have allowed untested blood to be used no matter what the patient and family wanted, since the prescreened blood was readily available."[5] Of course, as detailed earlier, some of the blood he insisted on using came from a donor who was unknown to anyone to be HIV positive.

By the time Scarpa testified that summer, he was down to 150 pounds,[6] having been without much of his stomach since 1986, and suffering from AIDS, a diagnosis he had finally revealed to his daughter Linda after hiding the truth about his declining health from her for six years.[7] Trial of the lawsuit involved three weeks of testimony, including Scarpa's. His four hours on the stand[8] were particularly compelling, causing "one female juror to weep,"[9] and another juror to refer to him as a "'noble man.'"[10] After Scarpa's testimony, "Linda Schiro ran from the courtroom in tears."[11] The tactic worked and within a few days, the hospital agreed to an out-of-court settlement that would pay Scarpa $300,000.[12] Scarpa insisted that payment be made in cash and immediately.[13] Additionally, DeVecchio alleged that Scarpa "sent a crew member to the bank with a duffel bag to pick it up,"[14] whereas Harmon claimed that "Linda Schiro and Larry Mazza picked up $350,000 [sic] at the bank—in cash—and dumped it into canvas bags."[15]

Scarpa's celebrity-like appearance in court to testify, and his crowing about the settlement to reporters afterward,[16] not surprisingly, caught the attention of local and federal law enforcement.[17] The Brooklyn D.A. struck first. Scarpa's response, through his lawyer, was to agree to turn himself in to the local authorities on a pending state weapons possession charge. What he did not know as he entered a New York courtroom was that the FBI planned to arrest him at the courthouse on federal charges, including conspiracy to commit murder.[18] Special Agent Lin DeVecchio, angry that he had been left out of the loop on the pending arrest of Scarpa by the feds, tried to call him to warn him when he learned of the Bureau's intention to finally charge and arrest Scarpa.[19]

Linda Schiro's recollection of the sequence of events does not coincide with DeVecchio's. According to Schiro, DeVecchio had told Scarpa not to worry about the state court appearance. "'You're going to pay a fine and then you're going to get right back out.'"[20] However, again according to Schiro, when she and Scarpa were at the hearing in state court, they spotted federal agents waiting for him. Scarpa told her to call DeVecchio "to find out what was going on."[21] DeVecchio was caught off guard. He "seemed surprised to hear about the agents and promised to learn more and call back."[22]

At the conclusion of the hearing in state court, Scarpa was arrested, put in handcuffs, and taken before federal Magistrate John Caden. He was charged with "conspiracy to murder and carrying and using a firearm in connection with a violent crime, 18 U.S.C. §§ 924(c) and 1959(a)."[23] The magistrate determined that "defendant was a danger to the community 'based on the nature of the charges against him and evidence proffered by the government at the hearing concerning the defendant's prior violent acts.'"[24] Scarpa was immediately taken into custody. However, a little more than two weeks later, on September 16, Magistrate Caden "found that conditions were available that would 'reasonably assure the appearance of the defendant and the safety of the community.'"[25] As Judge Weinstein later noted, Scarpa's release was predicated on

> "the inability of the local prison system to meet defendant's medical needs, the small probability of defendant living long enough to stand trial, and the restrictive terms of his house arrest which, in connection with his medical condition, would effectively incapacitate defendant to the same extent as incarceration."[26]

Scarpa was released to his home as Magistrate Caden concluded that, otherwise, he would "face… an unacceptably high risk of infection and death on a daily basis inside the MCC."[27] The conditions of his release

> "included posting a bond of $1.2 million of equity, that he not leave his home except for necessary medical treatment, that he subject himself to monitoring by wearing an electronic bracelet at all times and that he not communicate with persons designated in a list submitted by the government."[28]

For Scarpa, who had just received a $300,000 cash payout, his monitored release to his home meant he was open for business, and it was business as usual. As Larry Mazza stated, "The Grim Reaper was back on the street. [para.] The new club was Greg's house. There, he would run his various rackets as if he had a license."[29] However, the fact that Scarpa's physical and mental health were in an inevitable state of serious decline, coupled with the realization that at some point in the near future he would be held to answer in federal court for some of the mayhem he had caused meant that the final months of his "home life" would be characterized by bouts of morose anxiety, unpredictable outbursts, near senility, and, one final time, deadly violence.

TWO SCARPAS

While on house arrest, Scarpa predictably continued to conduct his illegal businesses, which by then consisted primarily of loansharking and drug dealing. "[B]usiness went on as usual, with visitors sneaking across a neighbor's lawn and entering a house through a back door."[30] Customers who had outstanding loans were brought directly to the house on 82nd Street, where they could be threatened by The Grim Reaper himself.[31] Mazza and Delmasto alone had over $700,000 in loanshark money outstanding. Their sports book business, which had brought in about $150,000 a week, was down to about $30,000 per week. Collecting on debts of any kind was proving to be increasingly difficult. "Even friends were using the war and the legal problems to wiggle out of their debt to us."[32] In spite of the obvious financial difficulties Mazza and Delmasto were experiencing, Scarpa expected to keep receiving weekly interest payments from Mazza on outstanding loans. "[N]ot a semblance of a break. Nothing for our loyalty to him and the Family."[33] The two men who together with Scarpa made up the deadly trio that had been so tight during the darkest days of the third Colombo war were once again nothing more than a stream of income to The Grim Reaper.

Scarpa was incapable of keeping a low profile as DeVecchio had advised. He could not alter his lifelong habits that comprised the day-to-day operation of an illicit money-making machine. To make matters worse, "dementia was making him more hardheaded, comically at times.... Greg could not bear the thought of the profits going anywhere but directly to him at his dining room table."[34]

While Scarpa attempted to conduct business as usual, there was, of course, nothing "usual" about the circumstances in the Scarpa household in the latter months of 1992. As his disease progressed, "AIDS-related dementia began to affect him,"[35] so much so that he was often confused about where he was.[36] His medications, both physician-prescribed and self-prescribed, precipitated wild mood swings, causing his doctor to tell Linda Schiro that Scarpa was a danger to his own family.[37] At one point, in a rage at how she had addressed him, he struck his daughter Linda in the head with his closed fist, something he had never done before.[38] His doctor and Linda Schiro tried to convince Scarpa to enter a hospital, but he refused. He wanted to spend Christmas at home with his family.[39]

At times, he seemed to realize the end of everything he had known was near. He told Larry Mazza he wanted to step away from "the life," that he would talk to recently appointed consigliere Richie Fusco about having Larry represent him until Gregory Jr. got out of prison.[40] That fall, Scarpa came to understand he would not be alive when his son got out of prison, so he decided to make a video for him.[41] He never got around to it,[42] and, as noted above, Gregory Jr. did not get out of prison until more than twenty-six years after his father's death.

AULD LANG SYNE

Scarpa's criminal habits were not the only ones that remained strong even as he withered away from full-blown AIDS. After nearly a dozen years, he had become habituated to communicating with Special Agent DeVecchio and feeding him self-serving information. In the last months of 1992, even though he had been closed for a third and final time as a TECI in September, he took one last shot at planting exculpating allegations with the FBI Special Agent. By DeVecchio's own account in his book *We're Going to Win this Thing*, Scarpa's blatant manipulation hit its mark.

In November of 1992, while Scarpa was under house arrest, Linda Schiro contacted DeVecchio. "'Lin,' [she] said. 'Greg really needs to see you about something. He's in bad shape. He was hoping you'd stop by the house. It would mean a lot to him.'"[43] DeVecchio, with two FBI agents in tow, showed up on November 17, 1992, as requested. Rather than attending a brief final reunion between old friends,[44] one of whom was dying of AIDS, DeVecchio was being set up once again by the master manipulator. DeVecchio immediately danced to Scarpa's tune as he had less than a year before under nearly identical circumstances. First, he once again "parked" the other two agents "in front of the TV in the living room,"[45] thereby assuring they would not be able to corroborate or dispute DeVecchio's version of his ensuing conversation with Scarpa. Then he let Scarpa convince him that Frank Sparaco had been behind a plan to kill Joey Ambrosino's mother after Ambrosino flipped. DeVecchio "carefully analyzed" the information Scarpa allegedly provided that day. His conclusion would be laughable were it not so utterly predictable.

> "Was Scarpa telling me this as a way to send a threat through me to Ambrosino that if he didn't stop cooperating and recant his statements thus far, his mother would be hit? Or was it a warning to get his mother into Witness Protection along with her son? Or was it something that was already under control?

[para.] I sized it up as truthful and something that Scarpa had already handled."[46]

If the possibility that Scarpa was, as was his habit, shifting blame for something he had either done or planned occurred to DeVecchio, he did not say so either at the time of the meeting or in the book he wrote after having had nearly two decades to think about it. In this particular case, as Larry Mazza testified at Theodore Persico's trial in 1997, Scarpa, not Frank Sparaco, was the origin of "the plan to kill [Ambrosino's] mother."[47]

DeVecchio went on to recall, without comment, that "Scarpa added [at the same meeting] that the 'PERSICOs now feel that the ORENA faction will come over to their side since VIC ORENA is on trial.'"[48] This prediction echoed Scarpa's earlier claim about Orena defections made immediately after Orena's arrest. And once again, Scarpa was intimating that what was bad for Vic Orena was good for law enforcement's efforts to end the violence of the Colombo family's internecine contest for power. What DeVecchio never seemed to grasp fully, even after nearly a dozen years as Scarpa's handler, was that Scarpa viewed everything solely through a lens of what was best for Greg Scarpa. The perceived options of that profoundly personal calculus narrowed as the consequences of contracting AIDS further warped Scarpa's already sociopathic predilection.

BLIND RAGE

"Business as usual" during Scarpa's house arrest included a heavy dose of drug dealing. Much of that activity was being conducted by Scarpa's and Linda Schiro's son Joey. As Larry Mazza described, "Joey would also come and go all day long with several different dealers, old ones and new ones. He wanted them all to meet The Grim Reaper. It added to his own bravado."[49] As detailed above in chapter six, on December 29, 1992, Joey's interaction with rival drug dealers led to one more shootout for Greg Scarpa and one final shooting death connected to him.

That evening, Joey came home after having temporarily surrendered the field to a pair of antagonistic competitors, Ronald "Messy Marvin" Moran and Michael "Mikey Flattop" DeRosa. According to Joey, he and his friend Joe Randazzo got into an argument with Moran and DeRosa that quickly resulted in weapons being brandished. Joey and Joe, who were armed with baseball bats, wisely retreated in the face of handguns carried by DeRosa and his crew.[50] When Joey returned home, with Randazzo still in tow, Joey complained to his parents that he had been insulted by the other two men.[51] DeRosa, however, later stated that the genesis of the dispute had nothing to do with Joey. According to DeRosa, an acquaintance of Joey's, also a drug dealer, owed DeRosa some money.[52] DeRosa tried to collect the debt by taking some cash from the debtor's pocket. The man claimed the money was Joey Scarpa's and demanded its return. DeRosa refused. The debtor then let Joey Scarpa know what DeRosa had done.[53] That prompted Joey and Randazzo to come after DeRosa with baseball bats, which proved inadequate under the circumstances.[54]

The Scarpa household's reaction to Joey's version of the confrontation constituted, at least initially, less than a full escalation of hostilities between the two sides. With Scarpa ailing and restricted by an ankle bracelet, Linda Schiro once again turned to Larry Mazza for help. As always, the loyal Mazza obliged. When he arrived at the Scarpa/Schiro home shortly after getting Linda's phone call, Greg asked him to go talk to Moran and DeRosa. "Although I hated like hell getting involved in this drug shit, I agreed to go talk to the dealer."[55] When Larry, Joey, and Joe Randazzo got into

Scarpa's car to look for DeRosa and Moran, Mazza snatched a handgun Joey brought along for the "talk." Mazza did not approve. "'Give me that fuckin' thing,' I snapped, as I took it from his hand and locked it in the glove compartment."[56] Mazza, who at the time was doing everything he could to avoid any interaction with law enforcement, was not interested in a violent confrontation on Joey's behalf.

The three men drove around the neighborhood for about half an hour but could not find DeRosa or Moran. They returned and reported their lack of luck to Scarpa. Mazza then counseled, "Why not let everybody cool down a bit and we can see this guy in the morning?"[57] Scarpa astonished Mazza by agreeing. Mazza drove home thinking that was that and he would deal with it again come morning. But after Mazza left, all hell broke loose. Scarpa suddenly broke into a rage, insisting that they retaliate for the perceived disrespect aimed at his youngest son. Linda once again suggested letting Larry and Scarpa's crew take care of the matter,[58] and Joey may have tried to talk his father out of taking any violent action.[59] Mazza, however, suspected "Joey had nagged his father until Greg couldn't take it anymore."[60]

Whatever the catalyst, this time, Scarpa took the lead instead of insisting his son mete out punishment to the offenders as he had in the past with both Joey and Gregory Jr. The ensuing mele, as chronicled earlier, left Randazzo dead. He was killed by Moran who emptied a clip of sixteen rounds into Scarpa's car.[61] DeRosa was wounded, having been shot in the neck by Scarpa as he walked away from that same car. Scarpa was somehow still alive after having a bullet enter his face, take out his left eye, and leave "another hole near his nose."[62] And, remarkably, he drove home[63] in that condition after Joey fled on foot.[64]

Having just returned home, Mazza got another phone call from Linda Schiro. This one was a frantic plea for help. In near hysterics, she reported that Scarpa and his son had gone after DeRosa and Moran, that she thought Joey was dead, and that her long-time partner was in their kitchen, bleeding profusely from the socket where moments earlier his left eye had been.[65] Mazza got back in his car and drove to the Scarpa/Schiro home for the second time that night. The first sight Mazza encountered was eighteen-year-old Joe Randazzo clinging to life with a bullet in his head, slumped over and in extreme distress in the back seat of a bullet-riddled car.[66] Randazzo would die two days later.[67] When Mazza entered the house, he came upon Scarpa sitting in his kitchen, holding a bloody towel over the wound to his left eye socket and drinking a glass of scotch. Scarpa's ankle bracelet had gone off when he left the house for the showdown.[68] During a phone call from his probation office, Scarpa tried to blame the ankle bracelet alarm on a malfunction caused by water from a shower.[69]

Meanwhile, Linda Schiro had convinced Scarpa to get medical treatment for his wounds. Mazza, once again, was his chauffeur. He drove Scarpa to the Mount Sinai Hospital in Manhattan, where he was admitted. Mazza made up a story about Scarpa falling in his back yard, but when a nurse started getting too nosy for comfort, he took off. He drove away just as the police were arriving.[70] For Scarpa, December 29, 1992, was his last moment of relative freedom. He would spend the rest of his life in custody, either in a jail or in a hospital.

Much to the surprise of the doctors at Mount Sinai, Scarpa survived the bullet to his face. However, it was clear to members of his crew that this time he would not be released back onto the streets or even back to in-house arrest.[71] Ronald "Messy Marvin" Moran, a twenty-year-old, low level drug dealer associated with the Lucchese family,[72] did "what none of the Orena soldiers could do. A lowly drug dealer did what the law couldn't or wouldn't. [para.] The Grim Reaper was put out of commission."[73]

On January 14, 1993, sixteen days after the shootout, Scarpa's bail was predictably revoked "upon a finding that there was clear and convincing evidence that he violated the terms of his home detention...."[74] Once he was released from the hospital for treatment for his gunshot wound, he was remanded to MCC, the Metropolitan Correctional Center in Manhattan. His condition at MCC deteriorated rapidly. Linda Schiro visited him at MCC and described what she saw.

> "'I noticed his skin was turning purple and black. So I got in touch with his AIDS doctor, Dr. Jeffrey Gumprecht, on Park Avenue and I told him what was happening. He got in touch with the doctor at MCC and they brought him to another hospital. He was bleeding internally.'"[75]

After a stay of several days, during which he received treatment to stop the internal bleeding, he was transferred back to MCC. On February 4, 1993, while he was in MCC, he was indicted for "racketeering, racketeering conspiracy, murders, conspiracy to murder, and carrying and using a firearm in connection with a violent crime."[76] The murders he was indicted for were those of Vincent Fusaro, Nicholas Grancio, and Lorenz Lampasi.[77] He entered a plea of not guilty at his arraignment on February 18 and reapplied for bail.[78] Scarpa's physical appearance at his bail hearing figured heavily in Judge Weinstein's decision to allow Scarpa to be transferred from MCC to Beekman Downtown Hospital in Manhattan, where he could be treated by Dr. Gumprecht. "Observed in court, his skeletal-like frame, shuffling gait,

AIDS-related dementia, and scab-covered face confirm this diagnosis."[79] As the court further described,

> "The gunshot sustained by defendant destroyed his left eye and the surrounding area of his face and skull, leaving only soft tissue between his skin and brain. He has an infection on his face that threatens to spread to his brain. Intravenous antibiotics must immediately be administered. Defendant also has been suffering from AIDS-related dementia which has loosened his grip on reality. Defendant requires treatment in a hospital with AIDS specialists and access to his treating doctor. [para.] Defendant had visible difficulty walking and standing at the arraignment. He has fallen on more than one occasion at the MCC and bled as a result thus endangering fellow inmates who volunteer to assist him in moving about. He requires basic nursing care which is unavailable at the MCC. The prevalence of tuberculosis and flu viruses at the MCC gravely threatens defendant in view of his incapacitated immune system."[80]

Judge Weinstein then ordered Scarpa's release to Beekman Downtown Hospital,[81] conditioned in part on his paying for at two least two guards from the U.S. Marshals Service on a round-the-clock basis, and the posting of a $1.2 million equity bond.[82] Scarpa met the conditions for transfer to Beekman, where the infection of his "left orbit"[83] was treated quickly and successfully, after which he was returned to MCC. Scarpa then applied to be admitted to Cabrini Hospice, which at the time was "the oldest and largest hospital-based hospice program in New York City."[84] Judge Weinstein granted Scarpa's request on March 5, 1993.[85] In doing so, he noted Cabrini's ability to provide "terminally ill individuals with highly personalized palliative and supportive care during the final stages of illness."[86] Scarpa lived for more than a year after this transfer. To a certain extent, considering how close to death he appeared when he went before Judge Weinstein in February, he thrived at Cabrini.

Once again, Scarpa was required to pay for two guards from the U.S. Marshals Service twenty-four hours a day to qualify for being housed in a hospital rather than incarcerated in a jail. Cabrini was convenient for Linda Schiro, so she visited him often, so often that she felt like she was there "twenty-four/seven."[87] She brought Scarpa and the marshals food and liquor, and "cookies and other food for the other patients." Scarpa asked her to see if some of the young guys in the unit with AIDS who were in particularly bad shape needed anything that she could get them. His daughter enjoyed visiting him at Cabrini. She found the atmosphere to be "relaxed," and "more of homelike setting" in spite of being under constant guard.[88] At the end of six weeks, Scarpa, who most thought would be dead by then, "looked great."[89]

After spending $50,000 to pay for the guards at Cabrini Hospice, Scarpa was moved to Rikers Island as part of a plea bargain on a state charge of attempted criminal possession of a weapon entered into on Friday, April 23, 1993.[90] The expectation was that Scarpa would "spend the last months of his life in a special ward for AIDS patients on Rikers Island."[91] His personal physician, Dr. Gumprecht, "knew the AIDS doctor at Rikers and [Scarpa] would be put in that unit."[92] The plea bargain included Scarpa's agreeing to plead guilty in federal court to racketeering charges after which he would be sentenced to life in prison. After his sentencing in federal court, he would serve a year on the state weapons charge. He was "not expected to survive the year" according to the Brooklyn DA's spokesman Patrick Clark.[93] As detailed below, Scarpa was not sentenced to life in prison even though he admitted killing three men, and he lived for more than another year.

Two weeks after pleading guilty to the New York state weapons charge, Scarpa was once again in federal court. This time, he would plead guilty to only three of the murders he had committed in more than forty years. While Scarpa committed all three of those killings—Fusaro, Grancio, and Lampasi—during the third Colombo war, he was never charged for a fourth murder he perpetrated during that conflict, that of Gaetano "Tommy Scars" Amato. Furthermore, other than the three killings he admitted to on May 6, 1993, he would never be held to answer for any of the other murders he either personally carried out or ordered. Having entered his plea of guilty to three murders and effectively avoiding responsibility or at least some sort of official condemnation for four decades of criminal mayhem, Scarpa had one last goal left—to die at home.

Scarpa's first instinct was to once again contact Special Agent Lin DeVecchio and provide him with information as he had in the past. Scarpa was planting the seed for a request made by his attorney Steven Kartagener for Scarpa's release in return for his cooperation. At that point, Valerie Caproni was the Assistant U.S. Attorney handling the cases generated by the third Colombo war. Caproni already had her hands full. She was supervising "seventy-five [Colombo] war prosecutions,"[94] while the number of arrested Colombo family members or associates who agreed to flip and become cooperating witnesses for the prosecution was constantly growing and would continue to grow.

Joeseph Ambrosino, Carmine Imbriale, Alan Quattrache, Christopher Libertore, Anthony Libertore, Salvatore Miciotta, and, perhaps the biggest fish, Carmine Sessa had all agreed to cooperate with the feds with more to come. "Sessa was a huge catch, one of the highest-ranking mafia members ever to cooperate. He knew where all of the Scarpa Crew's bodies were buried. When he flipped, four other crew members realized the jig was up." [95] All in all, "[t]en turncoats undermined the family by defecting into the Witness Protection Program."[96] Others scrambled for favorable deals, hoping to avoid life sentences in exchange for information. It was in this context that Scarpa contacted his FBI handler one last time.

Scarpa was at Rikers when he telephoned DeVecchio in late August of 1993.[97] Scarpa provided some information about "Wild Bill" Cutolo, a club Cutolo was operating, and members of Cutolo's crew. [98] As Lance pointed out, DeVecchio considered the information to be "stale," and Scarpa, who "was well out of the loop by this point," "had nothing left."[99] Scarpa's next move, through his attorney, was to request a meeting with Caproni. The seed was planted and the request for a meeting was granted.

A month after contacting DeVecchio, Scarpa and his attorney Steven Kartagener met with Caproni, DeVecchio, FBI Special Agents Chris Favo and James Brennan, and Assistant U.S. Attorney George Stamboulidis.[100] Scarpa had yet to be sentenced in federal court for the murders he admitted committing. Caproni, who would be present at the sentencing hearing, was the natural point of contact for Scarpa at this point. Her recommendation would likely carry a good deal of weight with the sentencing judge.

Scarpa, who was emaciated and wore an eye patch to the meeting,[101] offered through his attorney to become a cooperating witness. His price? "In exchange he wanted a sentence that would allow him to die at home."[102] While DeVecchio felt that Scarpa, given his short life expectancy at that point, would have little value as a cooperating witness, he did believe that Scarpa might be able to "provide a lot of useful information, including a burial site or the likely location of a fugitive."[103] Caproni wasn't buying what Scarpa was selling and, wisely, turned down his offer. Having failed to convince Caproni that he should be allowed to die at home, Scarpa was running out of options. His final official opportunity to make his audacious request was his upcoming sentencing hearing scheduled for December 15, 1993. On that date, Scarpa would appear one last time before Judge Jack Weinstein. He would have to spend the next three and a half months in the Rikers Island AIDS ward, defying expectations by simply surviving until the hearing. During that time, he would have his last visit from his daughter Linda.[104] And although the conditions in the Rikers AIDS ward were, per Linda, a substantial downgrade from what Cabrini Hospice provided,[105] Scarpa once again managed to prove the prognosticators wrong by surviving.

THE BIG REVEAL

Sentencing hearings are usually routine matters. Unless the opposing sides have agreed on a recommended sentence in advance, defense counsel will typically argue for leniency while the prosecutor will urge the court to impose a sentence near or at the maximum allowed under the relevant sentencing guidelines. There are rarely any surprises as the presiding judge states his or her reasons on the record for imposing sentence after listening to the arguments of counsel. Once again, however, there would be little that was routine about Greg Scarpa's final court appearance.

From the outset of the hearing, Judge Weinstein made it clear that the clock had run out on Scarpa's attempts to avoid returning to prison. After his attorney, Steven Kartagener, asked the judge to consider allowing Scarpa to die at home, the judge replied, "That's impossible." Scarpa did not give up and said, "I expect go to home." The judge's response was succinct. "You're not going home. You're going to prison."[106] When asked if he had anything further to say, Scarpa responded with surprise number one: he admitted in open court and on the record that he had been an informant for the FBI. "I tried to help, Your Honor, I'm sure you're aware of that... I thought there was a possibility of me going home."[107]

Later in the hearing, AUSA Caproni confirmed Scarpa's admission. "In all fairness to Mr. Scarpa, he has been quite an asset to the Federal Bureau of Investigation over the years."[108] What some in the New York Mafia had suspected for years, going back at least to Carlo Gambino's 1973 admonition "to 'stay away' from GREGORY SCARPA... as [he has] a 'big mouth,'"[109] was now a matter of public record, a matter Scarpa freely admitted. And while Scarpa's status as an FBI informant for twenty-five of the previous thirty years was not a surprise to the primary participants in his sentencing hearing, confirmation of that fact had an immediate impact on those men he had betrayed for so many years. Larry Mazza, who was in custody at the Metropolitan Correctional Center in Manhattan at the time, flew into a rage when confronted with the news by fellow MCC inmate Vic Orena, who was accompanied by Mike DeSantis and Frank Lastorino.[110]

Mazza's loyal reaction was to try to beat to a pulp the men who, in his view, had just slandered his boss and mentor of a dozen years. Mike DeSantis calmed him down and asked Mazza to hear them out, but he was still not convinced.[111] During a visit from the two Lindas the next day, Mazza learned that Scarpa was having talks with Assistant U.S. Attorney George Stamboulidis. He was stunned. "I ended the visit. That was the last time that I would see either of them for some twenty years."[112] The day after that visit, Mazza was still struggling to come to grips with what he had learned about Scarpa, not knowing who or what to believe, when Vic Orena showed him the explosive *New York Daily News* story of the sentencing hearing. Orena read Scarpa's words from the hearing confirming his status as an informant.[113] Eventually, particularly as he looked back on the events of the third Colombo war, Mazza began to understand how thoroughly duped he had been by the man he thought embraced the core values of the Mafia brotherhood, a man he could not have conceived of as a turncoat, let alone an informant for the very institution intent on destroying that brotherhood.

Surprise number two at Scarpa's sentencing hearing came directly from Judge Weinstein. As noted above, Scarpa had entered a plea bargain that would, in exchange for his admitting to three murders, result in a life sentence in federal prison. After referring to Scarpa's "dreadful murderous conduct,"[114] and having committed "acts worse than a wild animal," Judge Weinstein backed off of the life sentence, instead choosing a ten-year term, which meant that Scarpa was eligible to spend the last days of his life in a correctional facility that could treat his deteriorating condition rather than in a maximum security institution "where he probably would have been denied what would be essential to his medical and other treatment during this terminal period."[115] The ten-year sentence would allow Scarpa to "stay in a prison hospital,"[116] an "act of mercy by a sitting federal judge for a Mafia killer who had been merciless over the years with dozens of his own victims."[117]

The sentence, which included a fine of $250,000, seemed to take Scarpa and his lawyer by surprise. "Scarpa then thanked Weinstein and Kartagener praised the judge for his 'great humanity.'"[118] However, Vic Orena's defense attorney Flora Edwards, whose client received three concurrent life terms in prison, an additional sixty-five years in prison, and a fine of $2,250,000,[119] decried Scarpa's sentence as being "'beyond belief… Scarpa was given the federal equivalent of a love tap at this late stage, and by the same judge who showed absolutely no mercy to Vic Orena Sr.'"[120] Love tap or otherwise, what was clear at this point was that Greg Scarpa would die in federal prison.

PERMISSION DENIED

Scarpa's next stop on his final journey would be to a federal facility near Pittsburgh, Pennsylvania. When Linda Schiro visited him, she was shocked by his condition. "'His hair was down to his shoulders, his nails were not cut, he wasn't shaved—I went nuts.'"[121]Those on staff whose responsibilities required attending to Scarpa with any sharp instrument feared accidentally cutting him and exposing themselves to AIDS-tainted blood. Schiro, together with Scarpa's physician Dr. Gumprecht and some AIDS activists, managed to get Scarpa transferred "to the Federal Medical Center (FMC) in Rochester, Minnesota."[122]

By June of 1994, a month after Scarpa reached the age of sixty-six, professionals had been predicting his demise for years. As detailed above, Scarpa's disposition within the criminal justice system was often based on those predictions. In early 1992, Scarpa's T-cell count fell into the single digits, from which it was concluded that his life expectancy was measured not in years, but in months.[123] He lived for more than two years after that prediction. His personal physician testified at the trial of Scarpa's negligence claim in August of 1992 that Scarpa had six months to live.[124] Even Scarpa predicted that same month that "he'd be dead by Christmas."[125] He outlived both predictions by about a year and a half despite getting in a gun battle and having one of his eyes shot out in the process.

U.S. District Court Judge Jack B. Weinstein wrote in March of 1993, that "[a]ccording to his treating physician [Dr. Jeffrey Gumprecht] Defendant Gregory Scarpa Sr. is terminally ill with AIDS. Observed in court, his skeletal-like frame, shuffling gait, AIDS-related dementia and scab-covered face confirm this diagnosis. He will shortly die, never to be tried for his alleged heinous crimes as a murderous mafia captain."[126] Judge Weinstein, later in the same order, more precisely estimated that Scarpa's "life expectancy is now only a month or two."[127] He lived for another fifteen months. A spokesman for the Brooklyn DA's office predicted in April of 1993 that Scarpa would not be alive a year from April 1993.[128] Even he missed the mark by two months.

It was not until about a month before Scarpa died that a prosecutor at long last asked the right question when evaluating Scarpa's health and how it might affect decisions about his incarceration. Linda Schiro was once again trying to get Scarpa released so that he could die at home.

> "'I was trying to get him home because he didn't have very long to live…. [para.] About a month after his birthday I was visiting Greg and I got a call from the doctor who said because Greg was bedridden and couldn't move, the judge was going to allow him to go home. But then I got another call and the doctor said he couldn't come home. He said the prosecutor had called him and asked if Greg could move the finger he pulled the trigger with, and the doctor said he could move it. So I asked if he told the DA that Greg weighed only, like, fifty pounds. The doctor said he did tell him that. The prosecutor was worried that Greg would go out and kill somebody if he was allowed to go home. I said, "You have to be kidding me." But I thought

that if he did go home, he probably would have killed someone.'"[129]

The question was the one that prosecutors and judges should have been asking at least since September of 1992: If Scarpa is not incarcerated, given his history, what he might he do right up until the moment of his death? Linda Schiro's frank admission about Scarpa's penchant for killing, even on his deathbed, is particularly chilling. No one knew Scarpa better than she did, and in her view, it is fair to say that his willingness to kill survived until the moment he drew his last breath.

THE LAST WORD

On June 7, 1994, Scarpa, if he was cognizant of what he was doing, committed one last act of disloyalty and deceit, one he may have thought was going to secure Linda Schiro's future. According to Gregory Scarpa Jr., at some point prior to that date, Alphonse "Little Allie Boy" Persico had reached out to Schiro with a message for Scarpa Sr. The message was simple: the family would take care of Linda after Scarpa's death if Scarpa would clear Allie Boy with a confession.

> "But anyway, Allie Boy now reaches out to, to Linda. He said, 'Listen, I want you to go back to Greg and tell him that we got your back. Whatever you need, whatever, you know, he, he has nothing to worry about, we need him to write this, uh, deathbed confession.' And he did. He wrote it all out, [unintelligible] and the guy, Allie, that he did that for, he walked!" [130]

According to the document's date, Scarpa appears to have executed it the day before he died. In this author's view, given the deterioration of Scarpa's physical and mental condition by June 7, 1994, and the facts surrounding the document's execution, it should have been of no legal value. First, as to Scarpa's mental condition, it was noted by Judge Weinstein in early 1993, more than a year before the statement was executed, that Scarpa had "been suffering from AIDS-related dementia which has loosened his grip on reality."[131] That evaluation is consistent with a number of observations about Scarpa's steadily declining cognitive abilities made by those close to him months before he purportedly executed the statement.[132]

As to the document itself, it is often referred to as a "dying declaration" for the purpose of arguing its admissibility into evidence as an exception to the hearsay rule during Little Allie Boy's trial in the summer of 1994.[133] For instance, "The Dying Declaration" is the name of the chapter in Lance's book which examines the document.[134] However, as a matter of hornbook law, and as reflected in rule 804(b)(2) of the Federal Rules of Evidence, the dying declaration exception to the hearsay rule is limited to allowing into evidence a decedent's out-of-court statement *about the cause or circumstance of his imminent death*, and for no other purpose.[135] The June 7, 1994, statement from Scarpa does nothing of the sort. The relevant portions attempting to absolve Little Allie Boy of any wrongdoing have nothing to do with the cause or circumstances of Scarpa's death. Instead, the document has all the hallmarks of being prepared by Alphonse Persico's attorney in a transparent and ham-handed attempt to exonerate Persico from any criminal liability for the events of the third Colombo war. Paragraph 6 of the statement is particularly egregious, given what is and was widely known about Carmine Persico's desire to have his son, Little Allie Boy, take control of the Colombo family upon his release from prison.

"6. Carmine Sessa never once mentioned Allie Persico to me. Allie Persico was of no concern to anybody. Allie Persico is a friend who was not going to and who had no intentions of taking over the leadership of the Colombo family.... Allie was never earmarked to take on any position in the family at all."[136]

Contrary to paragraph 6 of Scarpa's statement, "[f]rom an early age, Little Allie Boy, the eldest of Carmine's sons, was destined to follow in his father's footsteps."[137] And in fact, he became the acting boss of the Colombo family during the mid-1990s, exactly as his father had contemplated.[138] Paragraph 6 of Scarpa's statement may as well have read, "Allie Persico? Never heard of the guy."

Additionally, according to Lance and the statement Scarpa signed, Scarpa was not "deposed" on May 20, 1994, as Judge Sifton of the Eastern District of New York the court had apparently permitted.[139] Indeed, Scarpa's June 7, 1994, statement indicates the anticipated deposition never took place. "I am giving this sworn and truthful statement in the event of my demise so that the court will have the benefit of my testimony in the event a deposition is not held in time."[140] Instead of a deposition, Scarpa was "interviewed by Margaret D. Clemons, an investigator representing the offices of Barry Levin, an attorney representing Alphonse Persico."[141] Nothing in the reproduced sections of the affidavit indicates any attorneys were present during that interview, that Scarpa was subjected to any cross-examination during that interview by any of the parties or their representatives who might have had an interest in what Scarpa had to say, or that Scarpa's mental acuity was tested by the interviewer.[142]

Scarpa's "sworn affidavit"[143] of June 7 attempted to absolve Little Allie Boy Persico of responsibility for any acts during the third Colombo war. And it may have played a role in the jury's not guilty verdict in Persico's 1994 trial.[144] However, in his last days, Scarpa failed to provide any absolution for either Larry Mazza or Jimmy Delmasto, the two men who arguably risked the most on his behalf and who were almost pathetically loyal to him throughout the darkest and most dangerous days of the war. Quite the opposite, in fact. He instead signed a document that threw both men under the bus, as the saying goes. Paragraph 9 of the statement reads, in part, as follows:

> "9. The war began at this point in time and plans were made to kill Orena faction members. Prior to November, 1991, there were no meetings or agreements to engage in a war. This war began with Lawrence Mazza, James Del Masto and myself in the forefront."[145]

Nor, as he lay dying, did he attempt to provide anything of substance that might have assisted his incarcerated son, Gregory Jr. His last act, while it may have been part of an effort to see to Linda Schiro's long-term security, was one final betrayal of the men he led in the life he had chosen.

Schiro had visited Scarpa nearly every weekend when he was in Rochester. His weight got down to around eighty pounds and he could only get around in a wheelchair.[146] His condition resulted in his being prohibited from entering the visiting room due to fear of his possibly infecting the other inmates and their visitors. Schiro was only allowed to take him outside and to spend time with him in his own room, both of which she did on each visit.[147] According to Schiro, Scarpa expressed regret for what he had put his family through during one of those visits.[148] He also claimed to regret killing Gaetano Amato and Joe Brewster. "Those were the only regrets he really had of the people he murdered."[149]

Joey Scarpa came to see him once in Rochester but after that visit found he could no longer bear to see his father in his wretched condition.[150] Toward the end, Scarpa "had sores all over his body, in his mouth, everywhere. He was about fifty pounds because he couldn't eat."[151] His daughter Linda had not been able to get to Rochester as of June 8, 1994, a Wednesday, the day he died. Earlier in the day, she spoke to him on the phone telling him she was scheduled to visit him that weekend.[152] He did not make it to the weekend or even to the end of the day.

A LEGACY OF MISERY

It has been estimated that Scarpa received at least $158,000 from the FBI over the years for his services as an informant.[153] However, what the FBI directly paid him was only part of the financial incentive that motivated Scarpa to inform on his fellow mafiosi. As Anthony Villano explained, informants "worked with agents because it was profitable for them: They... picked up informers fees and some very substantial funds in the way of rewards by insurance companies delighted to refund five percent in return for saving the other ninety-five percent liability."[154] Villano estimated the insurance proceeds Scarpa was paid while Villano was his handler were four times greater than the informant's fees the FBI paid him during the same period.[155] If Villano's account is accurate and if it held for Scarpa's entire career as a Top Echelon Criminal Informant, then it is conceivable that Scarpa made at least $750,000, before converting to present-day dollars, over the years by working with the FBI.[156]

Besides the fact that he was able to pick up a considerable amount of money from the federal government and insurance companies, Scarpa was also motivated by his ability to avoid prison by virtue of his value to the FBI. As noted earlier, before his arrest in August of 1992 when he was no longer officially an informant, Scarpa spent a total of thirty days in jail over a span of three decades.[157] In short, Scarpa not only achieved his twin goals of financial enrichment and personal freedom by betraying those to whom he had sworn a blood oath of loyalty, but he did so in spectacular fashion while leaving a trail of death and misery in his wake.

For nearly half of his lucrative FBI career, Scarpa worked side-by-side with FBI Special Agent Lin DeVecchio. How did DeVecchio view his prized informant? DeVecchio made his opinion of Scarpa clear when, nearly twenty years after the fact, he reflected on Scarpa's reaction to being shot in the face during his final gun battle, a shootout Scarpa likely initiated and one that left Joe Randazzo mortally wounded with a bullet in his brain. "Before he went to the hospital, he returned home and had a glass of Scotch. [para.] Come on, loosen up, you've got to admire the man."[158] By the time DeVecchio wrote that sentence, Scarpa had been dead for more than fifteen years. In short, DeVecchio had had plenty of time to think about the kind of man deserving of his admiration and, in his view, deserving of ours. It is astonishing that a federal law enforcement officer would admire such a man and, frankly, perplexing that he would explicitly state his admiration in print for posterity. So, what kind of man did FBI Special Agent Roy Lindley DeVecchio admire? The record is clear.

Scarpa was a bigamist. Both of his marriages failed while he lived and had children with a long-time mistress who was a half his age and a teenager, a minor, in fact, when they began their affair. His mistress, as of this writing, has spent thirty years grieving the murder at the age of twenty-three of their only son, a boy who followed his gangster father into "the life." His namesake son by his first wife spent more than half of his adult life in federal prison for doing the same. His daughter by his mistress lost her only brother to murder. She and Scarpa's grandson were nearly caught in the crossfire of a gang war he actively promoted. And that same daughter's close friend was beaten to a pulp on Scarpa's orders for having supplied her with pot one night.

Scarpa murdered or ordered the murder of anyone, including a young woman who was desperate for a job and a young man he claimed to love like a son, he thought might reveal his double life. We will likely never know how many men and women he murdered in total. He spent twenty-five years betraying and manipulating those closest to him who, for whatever reason, admired and respected him and many of whom desperately sought his approval. He lived a life full of murder, violence, theft, coercion, deceit, and betrayal. He violated every oath he ever took, and in doing so made it clear that to him words like "family" and "loyalty" were useful only as tools of manipulation for his own advancement, his own protection, his own greed.

Perhaps DeVecchio admired Scarpa for what he viewed as his toughness, his courage in the face of fire. As dangerous as Scarpa was, it is a stretch to say he was a brave man. It does not take courage to shoot a man in the back as he hangs up his Christmas lights and wreath, to shoot a young man in the neck as he walks away, to shoot a woman in the head while she is pinned to the floor by a much larger and stronger man, to order a crew of full-grown men to beat a teenager senseless, to order his sons to commit murder, or to pull a pistol out of a desk drawer and shoot an unarmed man point blank in the face. It takes something other than courage, or something most of us have must be lacking in such a man.

The traits which constrain most of us in our day-to-day interactions with our fellow human beings were missing in Scarpa. For nearly all of his life he seemed incapable of empathy, compassion, sorrow, guilt, regret, or shame. He had little to no need for genuine fellowship based on something other than a cold-blooded cost/benefit calculus. Whatever he did, he had the cost to, and benefit of one person in mind to the exclusion of all others—Greg Scarpa. Even his most treasured personal relationships—the beautiful, devoted mistress, the daughter he showered with gifts, the compliant gangster sons—were trophies he valued primarily for what their possession represented, what their presence in his life said about him.

The last, agonizing months of Scarpa's life were no doubt miserable. Gregory Scarpa Jr. ascribed his father's long, slow, losing battle with AIDS to karma, adding, "He felt like he was God."[159] He was neither God nor devil. He was, like the rest of us, mortal, distinguished from most of his fellow human beings by his unlimited capacity for evil. His existence was terrifying during his life, and the story of his life is a frightening reminder of the human capacity for betrayal and deceit, for duplicity and greed, for violence and death.

The End

Georgetown, Texas
March 20, 2024

BIBLIOGRAPHY

1. "60 Minutes - The FBI and the Grim Reaper May 22, 2011." Amazon.com, Inc. June 7, 2011. www.youtube. com/watch?v=btQkfCyd6Lw.

2. Altheimer, I., D'Angelo, A., Rodriguez, L. (2023). "2022 Homicide Statistics for 24 U.S. Cities." https:// www.rit.edu/liberalarts/sites/rit.edu.liberalarts/files/ docs/SOC/CLA_CPSI_2023_WorkingPapers/CPSI%20 Working%20Paper%202023.02_2022%20US%20 City%20Homicide%20Stats.pdf. Rochester Institute of Technology, College of Liberal Arts, Center for Public Safety Initiatives.

3. Ancestry.com. 1940 U.S. Census. "Enumeration District 24-1894. Supervisor's District No. 8. Sheet No. 8A." www.ancestry.com/discoveryui-content/ view/9335602:2442.

4. Ancestry.com. 1940 U.S. Census. "Enumeration District 24-1004. Supervisor's District No. 8. Sheet No. 2A." www.ancestry.com/imageviewer/collections/2442/ images/m-t0627-02572-00195?ssrc=&backlabel=Retur n&pId=7642359.

5. Anzalone, Grace. (Spring 2013). "Identity, Therapy, and Womanhood: Humanity in the Mafia." NYU Applied Psychology OPUS.

6. Associated Press. (June 14, 1986). "Jury Convicts N.Y. Mafia Boss, His Son, 7 Others." *Los Angeles Times*.

7. Associated Press. (December 12, 1991). "Mob Wars. Crime Bosses' Feud is Turning N.Y.C. into a Shooting Gallery." *The Times Leader*. Wilkes-Barre, PA.

8. Associated Press. (June 6, 1998). "METRO NEWS BRIEFS: NEW YORK; 4 Men Are Indicted in March 1995 Murder." *The New York Times*.

9. Arrington, Derrion. (April 21, 2020). "Vernon Dahmer 1908-1966." www.blackpast.org/african-american-history/vernon-dahmer-1908-1966/. Black Past.

10. Bamford, Tyler. (2020). "The Points Were All That Mattered: The U.S. Army's Demobilization After World War II." www.nationalww2museum.org/war/articles/points-system-us-armys-demobilization.

11. Baram, Marcus. (2007). "The Gumar, The Fed, and the Mobster." abcnews.go.com/TheLaw/story?id=3794178&page=1. ABC News.

12. *Barrett v. United States* (2d Cir. 1997) 105 F.3d 793.

13. Behar, Richard. (January 20, 1992). "Organized Crime: A Gang the Still Can't Shoot Straight." *Time Magazine*.

14. Berkery, Marilyn. (December 18, 1987). "'Allie Boy' Persico Gets 25 years." UPI.

15. Berkery, Marilyn. (April 24, 1988). "Opening Statements Were Presented Tuesday in Trial of…" UPI.

16. *Berkman v. City of New York* (E.D.N.Y. 1982) 536 F. Supp. 177.

17. Bet-David, Patrick. (October 13, 2021), "Former Mafia Hitman Opens up About Dark Side of Greg

Scarpa & His 20 Hits." https://www.youtube.com/watch?v=BxSBN0y-mkc. Valuetainment.

18. Beyer, Gregory. (October 8, 2010). "Living in Borough Park, Brooklyn." *The New York Times*.

19. Buder, Leonard. (March 11, 1983). "New York Police Say Crime Fell 5.1% in '82; How the Precincts Tally, page B3." *The New York Times*.

20. Brick, Michael. (June 6, 2006). "Brooklyn: Fisherman Charged with Murder." *The New York Times*.

21. Brick, Michael. (October 21, 2007). "The Mafia, an F.B.I. Agent and Murder: Mr. Scorsese, Your Next Film Awaits." *The New York Times*.

22. Brick, Michael and O'Connor, Anahad. (November 1, 2007). "Charges Dropped in F.B.I. Murder Case." *The New York Times*.

23. Brooklyn Public Library Blog. (2009). "Regina Pacis and the Case of the Missing Crowns." www.bklynlibrary.org/blog/2009/08/05/regina-pacis-and-case. The Brooklyn Public Library.

24. Bruno, Anthony. "Married to the Mob: Mafia Wives and Mistresses." https://www.crimelibrary.org/gangsters_outlaws/mob_bosses/wives/1.html. Crime Library: Criminal Minds and Methods.

25. Bruno, Anthony. "The Colombo Family: Junior's War." https://web.archive.org/web/20080913194219/http://www.trutv.com/library/crime/gangsters_outlaws/family_epics/colombo/7.html. TruTV Crime Library.

26. Burns, James MacGregor and Burns, Stewart. (1991). *A People's Charter: The Pursuit of Rights in America*. Alfred A. Knopf.

27. *Byrd v. State of Mississippi* (1969) 228 So.2d 874.

28. Capeci, Jerry. (September 10, 1999). "Capo's Son Gets 6 yrs. in Plea Deal." *New York Daily News*.

29. Capeci, Jerry. (February 16, 2006). "From 'Drop-Dead Gorgeous' to DOA." *The New York Sun*.

30. Capeci, Jerry. (August 23, 2007). "Alleged FBI Hit Man Hit Banks, Too, Mobster Says." *The New York Sun*.

31. Capeci, Jerry. (November 4, 2007). "Twisted Tale of the Moll Linda Schiro and her Men." *New York Daily News*.

32. Capeci, Jerry and O'Shaughnessy, Patrice. (December 6, 1991). "New Rubout in Mafia War." *New York Daily News*.

33. Capeci, Jerry and Robbins, Tom. (August 16, 1992). "Blood's Hounding Mobster." *New York Daily News*.

34. Capeci, Jerry and Siemaszko, Corky. (March 21, 1995). "Mob Son Iced in B'klyn." *New York Daily News*.

35. Cates, Ellan. (October 24, 1984). "The Chieftains of the Colombo Organized Crime Family." UPI.

36. Celona, Larry and Golding, Bruce. (December 13, 2017). "The Reign of Terror When Murder was King of New York in the '80s and '90s." *New York Post*.

37. Celona, Larry and O'Shaughnessy, Patrice. (May 23, 1992). "Mob War." *New York Daily News*.

38. *Clemente v. FBI* (D.C. Cir. 2017) No. 16-5067.

39. Cohen, Stefanie. (June 5, 2008). "Goodbye Colombos." *New York Post*.

40. Coletti, J. (2022). "J. Coletti's Racket Reviews, ep. 86." www.youtube.com/watch?v=0P9OSdfeMj4.

41. Cook, Fred. (June 4, 1972). "A Family Business: Hijacking, Bookmaking, Policy, Dice Games, Loan-sharking, and Special Contracts." *The New York Times*.

42. Coppola, F. F. (1972). *The Godfather*. Paramount Pictures.

43. Cornell Law School, Legal Information Institute. "U.S. Code: Title 18." https://www.law.cornell.edu/uscode/text/18.

44. Cornell Law School, Legal Information Institute. "Dying Declaration." https://www.law.cornell.edu/wex/dying_declaration.

45. Dahlke, Arnold. (2012). *Business Succession Planning for Dummies*. John Wiley & Sons, Inc.

46. Daly, Michael. (November 1, 2007). "For a Victim's Family, it's the Cruelest Halloween Trick." *New York Daily News*.

47. Daniels, Lee A. (December 8, 1991). "Brooklyn Slaying Tied to Mob Feud." *The New York Times*.

48. Daniels, Lee A. (January 8, 1992). "Brooklyn Slaying May Be 6th in Mob Families' 2-Month Feud." *The New York Times*.

49. Dannen, Fredric. (December 16, 1996). "The G-man and the Hit Man." *The New Yorker Magazine*.

50. de Szigethy, J.R. (January 2004). "MOB WAR! Murder, Deception, and Intrigue Inside New York's Colombo Mafia Family." http://www.americanmafia.com/Feature_Articles_9.html. AmericanMafia.com.

51. de Szigethy, J.R. (January 2004). "MOB WAR! Part II Anatomy of a Frame-up." http://www.americanmafia.com/Feature_Articles_260.html. AmericanMafia.com.

52. DeVecchio, Lin and Brandt, Charles. *We're going to win this thing: the shocking frameup of a Mafia crime buster*. The Berkley Publishing Group, 2011.

53. Digital History. (2021). "The New Immigrants." www.digitalhistory.uh.edu/disp_textbook.cfm?smtid=2&psid=3289.

54. Dillon, Sam. (October 25, 1992). "Brooklyn's Neighbors to the Mob." *The New York Times*.

55. Dow, Harold. (November 12, 1992). "Greg Scarpa Interview with Harold Dow from CBS 'Street Stories.'" www.youtube.com/watch?v=gfYXZuZ7qB4. CBS News.

56. Duffy, Peter. (January 20, 2009). "Banned Sport Gains Fans and Seeks More in Albany." *The New York Times*.

57. Dunleavy, Steve. (October 31, 2007). "She's Paying the Price for a Lifetime of Vice." *New York Post*.

58. Dunleavy, Steve. (November 5, 2007). "I Loved a 'Cute' Killer; Moll Tells of Brutal Scarpa's 'Sensitive Side.'" *New York Post*.

59. Farber, M.A. (November 7, 1985). "Tax Agent Tells of Bribe for a Persico Visit Here." *The New York Times*.

60. FBI.gov. "Mississippi Burning." www.fbi.gov/history/famous-cases/mississippi-burning.

61. FBI History. "Directors, Then and Now. L. Patrick Gray." www.fbi.gov/history/directors/l-patrick-gray.

62. FBI Carmine John Persico Jr. Documents Set 1 – 50 Pages https://vault.fbi.gov/Carmine%20John%20Persico%2C%20Jr./Carmine%20John%20Persico%2C%20Jr.%20Part%201%20of%202/view.

63. FBI Carmine John Persico Jr. Documents Set 2 – 36 Pages https://vault.fbi.gov/Carmine%20John%20Persico%2C%20Jr./Carmine%20John%20Persico%2C%20Jr.%20Part%202%20of%202/view.

64. FBI Mississippi Burning (MIBURN) Case Documents Set 1 – 129 Pages https://vault.fbi.gov/Mississippi%20Burning%20%28MIBURN%29%20Case/Mississippi%20Burning%20%28MIBURN%29%20Case%20Part%201%20of%209/view.

65. FBI Mississippi Burning (MIBURN) Case Documents Set 7 – 112 Pages https://vault.fbi.gov/Mississippi%20Burning%20%28MIBURN%29%20Case/Mississippi%20Burning%20%28MIBURN%29%20Case%20Part%207%20of%209/view.

66. FBI Scarpa Documents Set 1 – 249 Pages vault.fbi.gov/gregory-scarpa-sr/gregory-scarpa-sr-part-01-of-01/view.

67. FBI Scarpa Documents Set 2 – 73 Pages vault.fbi.gov/gregory-scarpa-sr/gregory-scarpa-sr-part-02-of-08/view.

68. FBI Scarpa Documents Set 3 – 164 Pages vault.fbi.gov/gregory-scarpa-sr/gregory-scarpa-sr-part-03-of-08/view.

69. FBI Scarpa Documents Set 4 – 249 Pages vault.fbi.gov/gregory-scarpa-sr/gregory-scarpa-sr-part-04-of-08/view.

70. FBI Scarpa Documents Set 5 – 160 Pages vault.fbi. gov/gregory-scarpa-sr/gregory-scarpa-sr-part-05-of-08/ view.

71. FBI Scarpa Documents Set 6 – 80 Pages vault.fbi.gov/ gregory-scarpa-sr/gregory-scarpa-sr-part-06-of-08/ view.

72. FBI Scarpa Documents Set 7 – 113 Pages vault.fbi. gov/gregory-scarpa-sr/gregory-scarpa-sr-part-07-of-08/ view.

73. FBI Scarpa Documents Set 8 – 161 Pages vault.fbi. gov/gregory-scarpa-sr/gregory-scarpa-sr-part-08-of-08/ view.

74. Federal Rules of Evidence, rule 804(b)(2).

75. Fermino, Jennifer. (March 26, 2006). "Nail Him! Kin Cry – Indict vs. 'Mob Spy' Fed Thrills Family of Slain Moll." *New York Post*.

76. Feuer, Alan. (June 30, 2013). "The Mob and Angela Clemente." *The New York Times*.

77. Feuer, Alan. (June 22, 2017). "Appeals Court Reinstates 40-Year Sentence for Brooklyn Mobster." *The New York Times*.

78. Feuer, Alan. (November 3, 2017). "A Mafia Turncoat, Facing Life, is Sentenced to 11 Years." *The New York Times*.

79. FindAGrave.com. Headstone of Family of Rosario Nastasa. https://www.findagrave.com/ memorial/200822879/rosario-nastasa.

80. Fold3.com. 1930 U.S. Census. "Enumeration District 24-1197. Supervisor's District No.

31. Sheet No. 25B." https://www.fold3.com/image/264604161?rec=264828975.

81. Francescani, Christopher. (September 29, 2000). "Murderous Mob Canary Sprung." *New York Post.*

82. Fried, Joseph. (January 11, 1973). "$100,000 in Gems Stolen from a Brooklyn Church." *The New York Times.*

83. Fried, Joseph P. (March 6, 1982). "Women Win Ruling on Fire Dept. Test." *The New York Times.*

84. Fried, Joseph P. (January 30, 2019). "Charles J. Hynes, Brooklyn DA in a Tumultuous Era, Dies at 83." *The New York Times.*

85. Gage, Nicholas. (September 1, 1971). "Yacovelli Said to Succeed Colombo in Mafia Family." *The New York Times.*

86. Gage, Nicholas. (June 5, 1977). "Colombo 'Family' Underboss Flees after Failure to Overthrow Chief." *The New York Times.*

87. Getty Images, www.gettyimages.ie/detail/news-photo/vincent-emmino-18-year-old-brother-of-ralph-buck-emmino-news-photo/514952526.

88. Gevirtz, Leslie. (April 11, 1989). "Mobster Fingers Brother as Murderer." UPI.

89. Goldberg, Noah. (May 27, 2022). "Violent NYC Mobster Released from Prison Because Feds Didn't Take Care of his Health Problems: Judge." *New York Daily News.*

90. Golding, Bruce. (March 19, 2019). "A Ranking of the Most Notable Mob Funerals in NYC History." *New York Post*.

91. Goldman, John J. (February 4, 1989). "7-Year-Old AIDS Patient Shares Hug with Princess." *Los Angeles Times*.

92. "Gregory Scarpa Sr." NNDB 2019. www.nndb.com/people/434/000024362/. Soylent Communications.

93. Guzman, Pablo. (Archived October 31, 2007). "Squeeze Puts Squeeze on G-Man." WCBS.

94. Hamilton, Brad. (May 27, 2012). "Mafia Daughter Says Dad was Grim Reaper." *New York Post*.

95. Hamilton, Brad. (June 10, 2021). "G-mom's New Target: Mob Rats Who Killed While on the FBI Payroll." *New York Post*.

96. Hass, Nancy. (June 26, 2011). "Married to the Mob." https://www.newsweek.com/real-mob-wives-scarpa-widow-linda-schiros-lonely-life-68007. newsweek.com. *Newsweek*.

97. Harmon, Sandra. *Mafia Son: The Scarpa Mob Family, the FBI, and a Story of Betrayal.* St. Martin's Press, 2009.

98. Hays, Tom. (October 29, 2007). "Mob Moll Says Mafiosi Helped FBI." Associated Press.

99. HIV.gov "A Timeline of HIV and AIDS." https://www.hiv.gov/hiv-basics/overview/history/hiv-and-aids-timeline/.

100. Holloway, Lynette. (February 20, 1997). "Convictions of 3 in Mob Overturned in Slayings." *The New York Times*.

101.   Holusha, John and Rashbaum, William K. (March 30, 1996). "Ex-F.B.I. Agent Accused of Role in Four Organized Crime Killings." *The New York Times.*

102.   Hornblower, Margot. (September 19, 1986). "Mafia 'Commission' Trial Begins in New York." *The Washington Post.*

103.   Hunt, Thomas (2023) "The American Mafia: The History of Organized Crime in the United States. Mafia Morality: Church Theft Requires Murder." mafiahistory. us/a042/f_buckyemmino.html.

104.   *In the Matter of The Estate of Jacob Benjamin* (1974) 34 NY2d 27.

105.   Italian American Civil Rights League. www. italianamericanleaguenyc.org/.

106.   James, George. (April 20, 1988). "Murders in Queens Rise 25%; Crack is Key Factor." *The New York Times.*

107.   James, George. (April 23, 1991). "New York Killings Set a Record, While Other Crimes Fell in 1990." *The New York Times.*

108.   James, George. (December 6, 1991). "Killing in Brooklyn Social Club is Linked to Mob Power Struggle." *The New York Times.*

109.   James, George. (December 9, 1991). "Killing is Tied to Mafia War in Brooklyn." *The New York Times.*

110.   James, George. (October 22, 1993). "Man Tied to Crime Family is Shot to Death in Queens." *The New York Times.*

111. Johnson, Rudy. (June 18, 1974). "13 Indicted on Stock Theft and Counterfeit Counts." *The New York Times*.

112. Kerr, Peter. (April 14, 1986). "Car Bomb Kills the No. 2 Man in Crime Family." *The New York Times*.

113. Kroger, John. *Convictions: A Prosecutor's Battles Against Mafia Killers, Drug Kingpins, and Enron Thieves.* Farrar, Straus and Giroux, 2009.

114. Lance, Peter. *Deal with the Devil: The FBI's Secret Thirty-Year Relationship with a Mafia Killer.* William Morrow Publishing, 2013.

115. Lance, Peter. (June 27, 2016). "DOJ Report on MISSBURN Case Leaves out Key Detail: I.D. of the Mafia Killer Who Broke the Case for Hoover's FBI." peterlance.com/wordpress/?p=9083. HuffPost.

116. Later Days Podcast with Joe Poletto. "Greg Scarpa Jr. Interview Part 1, Episode 4." www.asterlight.com/work/laterdayspodcast.

117. Later Days Podcast with Joe Poletto. "Greg Scarpa Jr. Interview Part 2, Episode 5." www.asterlight.com/work/laterdayspodcast.

118. Later Days Podcast with Joe Poletto. "Larry Mazza - Wiseguys, Hollywood, and Sport Betting, Episode 3." www.asterlight.com/work/laterdayspodcast.

119. Later Days Podcast with Joe Poletto. "Larry Mazza - Greg Scarpa Sr. and Relationship with Greg, Episode 4." www.asterlight.com/work/laterdayspodcast.

120. Later Days Podcast with Joe Poletto. "Larry Mazza – Greg Scarpa Sr., Episode 5." www.asterlight.com/work/laterdayspodcast.

121.   Later Days Podcast with Joe Poletto. "Larry Mazza – Prison Time, Episode 6." www.asterlight.com/work/laterdayspodcast.

122.   LCN Bios (May 12, 2022). "Bio of Dominic [sic] Somma." lcnbios.blogspot.com/2022/05/dominic-somma-colombo.html.

123.   Le Carré, John. *Tinker, Tailor, Soldier, Spy*. Hodder & Stoughton, 1974.

124.   Liddick, Don. *The Mob's Daily Number: Organized Crime and the Numbers Gambling Industry.* University Press of America, 1999.

125.   Lubasch, Arnold H. (October 25, 1984). "11 Indicted by U.S. as the Leadership of a Crime Family." *The New York Times.*

126.   Lubasch, Arnold H. (February 27, 1985). "U.S. Indictment Says 9 Governed New York Mafia." *The New York Times.*

127.   Lubasch, Arnold H. (June 14, 1986). "Persico Convicted in Colombo Trial." *The New York Times.*

128.   Lubasch, Arnold H. (November 18, 1986). "Persico, His Son and 6 Others Get Long Terms as Colombo Gangsters." *The New York Times.*

129.   Lubasch, Arnold H. (November 20, 1986). "U.S. Jury Convicts Eight as Members of Mob Commission." *The New York Times.*

130.   Lubasch, Arnold H. (January 14, 1987). "Judges Sentences 8 Mafia Leaders to Prison Terms." *The New York Times.*

131.   Lubasch, Arnold H. (December 22, 1992). "Acting Crime Boss is Convicted of Murder and Racketeering." *The New York Times*.

132.   Lydgate, Chris and Bryan, Miles. (September 1, 2012). "Professor. Scholar. Attorney General. John Kroger Brings a Wealth of Experience—and Energy—to Eliot Hall." *The Advocate – Reed Magazine*. Reed College.

133.   MacAskill, Ewan. (October 31, 2007). "FBI Used Mafia Capo to Find Bodies of Ku Klux Klan Victims." *The Guardian*.

134.   Maddux, Mitchel. (April 12, 2012). "Mafia to Pothead: 'Kill or be Killed Next.'" *New York Post*.

135.   Martinez, Jose and Sherman, William. (January 7, 2006). "Hitman Singing FBI Song: Sez Agent Closely Tied to 1992 Slaying of Mob Rival." *New York Daily News*.

136.   Marzulli, John. (January 8, 2004). "My Father: the Killer Gangster: Dad Did it, Framed 2." *New York Daily News*.

137.   Mazza, Larry. *The Life: A Brooklyn Boy is Seduced into the Dark World of the Mafia*. Digital Publishing of Florida, Inc., 2017.

138.   McFadden, Robert D. (December 17, 1985). "Organized-Crime Chief Shot Dead Stepping from Car on E. 46th Street." *The New York Times*.

139.   McFadden, Robert D. (November 13, 1987). "8 Charged with Mafia Drug Plot, Including Murders and Extortion." *The New York Times*.

140.   McFadden, Robert D. (December 17, 1991). "Brooklyn's Mob War Interrupted with a Quiet Day in Court." *The New York Times*.

141.   McGraw, Seamus. (June 16, 2006). "Suspect Extradited to N.Y." *The Forward*.

142.   McGuire, Craig and Imbriale, Carmine. *Carmine and the 13th Avenue Boys: Surviving Brooklyn's Colombo Mob*. Kindle ed. WildBlue Press, 2022.

143.   Miller, Tracey L. (May 10, 1995). "Informant Testifies in NY Mob Trial." UPI.

144.   Mitchell, Chris. (January 4, 2008). "The Killing of Murder." *New York Magazine*.

145.   Mohr, Holbrook. (2010). "Ex-Klansman Convicted in '64 Slayings Sues FBI." *Memphis Daily News*. Associated Press.

146.   Mooney Dash Cam. (September 4, 2021). "Greg Scarpa Colombo Hitman: Gets Sons [sic] Friend Killed and Eye Shot Out while on House arrest" [Video]. YouTube. https://www.youtube.com/watch?v=byNTt_Yt9KM.

147.   Muckrock. Document 1470141-0 Section 6. cdn.muckrock.com/foia_files/2020/08/27/1470141-0_-Section_6_-_no_descriptionMedi.PDF.

148.   MyHeritage. https://www.myheritage.com/names/gregory_scarpa.

149.   NAACP.org. Empowerment Programs. "Medgar Evers." https://naacp.org/find-resources/history-explained/civil-rights-leaders/medgar-evers.

150. New York City Department of Parks and Recreation. "Freshkills Park." https://www.nycgovparks.org/park-features/freshkills-park/about-the-site.

151. New York City Police Department, Office of Management Analysis and Planning, Crime Analysis Unit. (1983). "Homicide Analysis 1983."

152. New York City Police Department, Office of Management Analysis and Planning, Crime Analysis Unit. (1984). "Homicide Analysis 1984."

153. New York Daily News. (May 25, 1996). "Judge Frees Mob Canary's Files." *New York Daily News*.

154. New York Daily News. (December 21, 1997). "Feds Have a New Canary." *New York Daily News*.

155. New York Daily News Staff. (June 14, 1995). "Mob Man's Saved by the Cell." *New York Daily News*.

156. New York Daily News Staff. (May 3, 1995). "Dad & Son to Sing in Mob Trial." *New York Daily News*.

157. New York Daily News Staff. (August 2, 1995). "A Father's Calm Gives Way at Trial of His Son's Killer." *New York Daily News*.

158. New York Daily News Staff. (September 4, 1995). "Innocent Victim's Dad Rages." *New York Daily News*.

159. New York Daily News Staff. (June 4, 2008). "'Tommy Shots,' Reputed Colombo Boss, Arrested in 3 Slayings from Early '90s." *New York Daily News*.

160. New York Domestic Relations Law §11.

161. New York State Archives. Coxsackie Correctional Facility, Greene County, N.Y. www.archives.nysed.

gov/research/series-overview-W0061?order=field_last_name&sort=desc&page=183.

162.   New York State Penal Law, Part 3, Title G, Article 105, §105.20.

163.   NYC Health + Hospitals/South Brooklyn Health, Ruth Bader Ginsburg Hospital. https://www.nychealthandhospitals.org/locations/south-brooklyn-health/.

164.   Notes provided to the author by Gregory Scarpa Jr. on July 12, 2023.

165.   Obituary of Connie Scarpa www.demarcofuneralhome.com/obituaries/Concetta-Connie-Scarpa?obId=27856274.

166.   Odd Stops. Tali's Restaurant: Sammy the Bull Gravano's Headquarters. https://oddstops.com/location.php?id=518. Double You Media. Wexford, Ireland.

167.   Onion, A., Sullivan, M., Mullen, M., Zapata, C. (Eds.). (June 14, 2021). "AIDS Crisis Timeline." https://www.history.com/topics/1980s/hiv-aids-crisis-timeline. HISTORY. A&E Television Networks.

168.   *Orena v. United States* (E.D.N.Y. 1997) 956 F. Supp. 1071.

169.   Orlando Sentinel. (January 9, 1992). "Organized Crime Figure Shot to Death in Brooklyn." *Orlando Sentinel.*

170.   Orlando Sentinel. (December 30, 1992). "Gunman Wounds 3 Men of Organized Crime Family." *Orlando Sentinel.*

171. Outskirts Press. (2007) "New Book by Mississippi Judge Exposes FBI Tampering in Civil Rights Cases." www.prweb.com/releases/2007/11/prweb570844.html.

172. Papers of John F. Kennedy. Pre-Presidential Papers. Presidential Campaign Files, 1960. Speeches and the Press. Speeches, Statements, and Sections, 1958-1960. Crime and legal ethics: The Fight Against Crime. Speech of April 1, 1960, given at Dodgeville, Wisconsin.

173. Parish History. "The Basilica of Regina Pacis." basilicaofreginapacis.org/parish-history.

174. Pashigian, B. Peter. (March 2001). "The Used Car Price Index: A Checkup and Suggested Repairs." U.S. Department of Labor, Bureau of Labor Statistics, Office of Prices and Living Conditions.

175. *People v. DeVecchio* (October 10, 2007) NY Slip Op 27440 [17 Misc 3d 990]. Reichbach, J. Supreme Court, Kings County.

176. *People v. DeVecchio* (October 12, 2007) NY Slip Op 51962(U) [17 Misc 3d 1114(A)] Supreme Court, Kings County.

177. *People v. Sinagra* (June 11, 2007) 2007 NY Slip Op 51180(U) [15 Misc 3d 1146(A)] Supreme Court, Kings County.

178. *People v. Velasquez* (N.Y. Sup. Ct. 1988) 139 Misc.2d 822; 528 NYS2d 502.

179. Pettus, Emily Wagster and Santana, Rebecca. (January 12, 2018). "Man Convicted of Killing 3 Civil Rights Workers Dies in Jail." Associated Press.

180. Phone interview with Gregory Scarpa Jr. on July 26, 2023.

181.   Phone interview with Larry Mazza on July 26, 2023.

182.   Phone interview with Melanie M. Dyer, MA, LPC on November 10, 2023.

183.   Piasini, Eugenio, Liu, Shuze, Chaudhari, Pratik, Balasubramanian, Vijay and Gold, Joshua I. (February 8, 2023). "How Occam's Razor Guides Human Decision Making." https://doi.org/10.1101/2023.01.10.523479.

184.   Puparo. (November 25, 2010). "Puparo Presents: The Roaring 1980s (Part I)." https://gangstersinc.org/profiles/blogs/puparo-presents-the-roaring-6. Gangsters Inc.

185.   Purdum, Todd. (March 9, 1986). "New York Crime Steady in 1985 Despite Rise in Last Half of Year." *The New York Times*.

186.   Raab, Selwyn. (September 11, 1987). "Queens Barber Shot to Death by 3 in Masks." *The New York Times*.

187.   Raab, Selwyn. (December 30, 1992). "Top Member of Colombo Crime Family is Ambushed in Brooklyn." *The New York Times*.

188.   Raab, Selwyn. (November 20, 1994). "The Mobster Was a Mole for the FBI; Tangled Life of a Mafia Figure Who Died of AIDS is Exposed." *The New York Times*.

189.   Raab, Selwyn. (July 2, 1995). "The Thin Line between Mole and Manager." *The New York Times*.

190.   Raab, Selwyn. *The Five Families: The Rise, Decline & Resurgence of America's Most Powerful Mafia Empire*. St. Martin's Press, 2005.

191.   Raab, Selwyn. (March 8, 2019). "Carmine Persico, Colombo Crime Family Boss, is Dead at 85." *The New York Times*.

192.   Rabinovitz, Jonathan. (October 19, 1992). "2 Men Slain in Brooklyn Said to Have Ties to Mob." *The New York Times*.

193.   Raper, Sarah. (November 12, 1987). "Eight, Including Colombo Capo, Named in Racketeering Complaint." UPI.

194.   Reilly, William M. (November 20, 1986). "Eight Convicted in Mafia 'Commission' Trial." UPI.

195.   Robbins, Tom and Capeci, Jerry. (June 21, 1994; updated January 24, 2015). "Mobster's Crime Helped FBI Find Slain Activists Civil Rights Struggle." *New York Daily News* via *Greensboro News & Record*.

196.   Robbins, Tom. (October 23, 2007). "Tall Tales of a Mafia Mistress." *The Village Voice*.

197.   Rose, Charlie. (1991). "Colombo Family Mob War in Brooklyn – Discussion." www.youtube.com/watch?v=GCvOJZmSCr8&t=872s.

198.   Salvatore Sammy The Bull Gravano. "Greg Scarpa Sr Shot Her Right After She Gave Him a Hug." YouTube. www.youtube.com/watch?v=Dd7H-ca3X_I.

199.   Salvatore Sammy The Bull Gravano. "Larry Mazza Grabbed a Shotgun and Shot Him in the Face." YouTube. https://www.youtube.com/watch?v=9_PWK7ItdPY.

200.   Salvatore Sammy The Bull Gravano. "My Sit Down with The Grim Reaper." YouTube.www.youtube.com/watch?v=tPaKfuPSXZU.

201. Sampson, Robert J., Ph.D. (June 1986) "The Contribution of Homicide to the Decline of American Cities." Bulletin of the New York Academy of Medicine (Vol. 62, No. 5).

202. Santayana, George. *The Life of Reason: Or The Phases of Human Progress*. 2nd ed. Scribner's, 1905.

203. Scarpa, Linda and Rosencance, Linda. *The Mafia Hit Man's Daughter*. Kindle ed. Kensington Publishing Corp., 2016.

204. Scarpo, Ed. (June 26, 2021). "Violent Crew Ready to Follow Huck's Orders if the Gambino Soldier is Released, Sources Say." https://www.cosanostranews.com/2021/06/violent-crew-would-follow-huck.html#google_vignette.

205. Scarpo, Ed. (November 16, 2021). "The Mob's Underground Railroad: How Allie Boy Persico Survived on the Lam for Seven Years." https://www.cosanostranews.com/2021/11/the-mobs-underground-railroad-how-allie.html. Cosa Nostra News.

206. Seigel, Max H. (March 12, 1976) "Scarpa, Reputed Colombo Aide, Indicted in Gambling Inquiry." *The New York Times*.

207. Shifrel, Scott. (October 30, 2007) "Court Hears Inside Story of FBI Agent, Mobster, and his Moll." *New York Daily News*.

208. *Sinagra v. City of New York* (October 18, 2012). NY Slip Op 22304 Supreme Court, Kings County.

209. Smith, Kati Cornell (January 10, 2006) "Dad's 'Hit' Order; Mob Big's Son Killed Buddy after G-Man's Tip: Affidavit." *New York Post*.

210.   "Special Report: Chapter Three: The Attorney General's Guidelines Regarding the Use of Confidential Informants." (September 2005). Office of the Inspector General U.S. Department of Justice.

211.   Spencer, Kyle. (April 20, 2014). "A Catholic High School Abruptly Loses its Fight to Stay Open." *The New York Times*.

212.   *State of New Jersey v. Aurelio Ray Cagno* (Superior Court of New Jersey Appellate Division 2009) 978 A.2d 921, 409 N.J. Super. 552.

213.   Tabor, Mary B. W. (April 2, 1992). "Man Accused as Colombo Chief is Held in Slaying of Ex-Member." *The New York Times*.

214.   Tabor, Mary B. W. (August 30, 1992). "Settlement in Lawsuit on H.I.V.-Tainted Blood." *The New York Times*.

215.   "The FBI's Lin DeVecchio and 'The Grim Reaper.'" (May 22, 2011). CBS News Staff. https://www.cbsnews.com/news/the-fbis-lin-devecchio-and-the-grim-reaper/. CBS Interactive Inc.

216.   "The Grim Reaper | Evil Lives Here." (September 24, 2018). investigationdiscovery.com. https://www.investigationdiscovery.com/video/evil-lives-here-investigation-discovery/the-grim-reaper. Discovery Communications, LLC.

217.   The New York Times. (October 11, 1974). "Mafia Discipline Linked to Killing." *The New York Times*.

218.   The New York Times. (April 29, 1975). "Police Ask a Witness in Slaying to Phone." *The New York Times*.

219.   The New York Times. (September 18, 1989). "Alphonse Persico, 61, is dead; Leader of Colombo Crime Family." *The New York Times*.

220.   The New York Times. (February 27, 1992). "Suspected Mob Capo, 51, Shot in Brooklyn." *The New York Times*.

221.   The New York Times. (February 23, 1993). "Reputed Mobster Sent to Hospital by Judge." *The New York Times*.

222.   The New York Times. (April 25, 1993). "Mobster with AIDS Gets Special Sentence." *The New York Times*.

223.   The New York Times. (November 2, 1989). "Brooklyn Youth Slain after Halloween Fight." *The New York Times*.

224.   The New York Times. (October 7, 2008). "Body Identified as Missing Mobster's." *The New York Times*.

225.   The Statue of Liberty-Ellis Island Foundation, Inc. heritage.statueofliberty.org/passenger-result.

226.   The United States Attorneys Office, Eastern District of New York. Press Release (December 28, 2007). "Colombo Organized Crime Family Acting Boss Alphonse T. Persico and Administration Member John J. Deross Convicted of Murder in Aid of Racketeering and Witness Tampering." https://www.justice.gov/archive/usao/nye/pr/2007/2007dec28.html.

227.   Thorton, Mary. (February 27, 1985). "9 Charged with Mafia Activities." *The Washington Post*.

228.   Torro, Kenny. "GREG SCARPA SNR. Part Two." Archived from the original on May 14, 2013. web.

archive.org/web/20120114091800/http://realdealmafia. com/scarpa2.html. Mafia-International.com.

229.   Torro, Kenny. "GREG SCARPA SNR. Part Three." Archived from the original on January 14, 2012. https://web.archive.org/web/20120114060251/http:/ realdealmafia.com/scarpa3.html.   Mafia-International. com.

230.   Torro, Kenny. "GREG SCARPA SNR. Part Four." Archived from the original on October 29, 2013. web. archive.org/web/20120113013017/http://realdealmafia. com/scarpa4.html. Mafia-International.com.

231.   "Traum; Lili Dajani." Redaktion. (September 17, 2021) *Tachles, Das jüdische Wochenmagazin* 21 Jahrgang, Ausgabe 37 www.tachles.ch/epaper/ tachles/17-september-2021-21-jahrgang-ausgabe-37.

232.   Tsiantar, Dody. (January 14, 1987). "3 Mafia Bosses Ordered to Prison for 100 Years." *The Washington Post*.

233.   Turning Point, Using Intel to Stop the Mob, Part 2 (August 9, 2007) FBI Stories. archives.fbi.gov/archives/ news/stories/2007/august/mobintel2_080907.

234.   University of Washington, Human Resources. (2016) Succession Planning Toolkit. hr.uw.edu/pod/wp- content/uploads/sites/10/2018/08/Succession-Planning- Toolkit.pdf.

235.   USAFacts. "Average Number of People in a Family." usafacts.org/data/topics/people-society/population-and- demographics/population-data/average-family-size/.

236.   U.S. Constitution amend. V.

237.   U.S. Constitution art. VI, § 1.

238. U.S. Department of Justice, Office of Justice Programs, Virtual Library. "Mob's Daily Number: Organized Crime and the Numbers Gambling Industry" Abstract. www.ojp.gov/ncjrs/virtual-library/abstracts/mobs-daily-number-organized-crime-and-numbers-gambling-industry.

239. U.S. Department of Health and Human Service, Office of the Assistant Secretary for Planning and Evaluation. "Poverty Guidelines." https://aspe.hhs.gov/topics/poverty-economic-mobility/poverty-guidelines.

240. U.S. Department of Labor Inflation Calculator. www.dol.gov/general/topic/statistics/inflation.

241. United States Senate. (April 1988). "Organized Crime: 25 Years after Valachi." Hearings Before the Permanent Subcommittee on Investigations of the Committee on Governmental Affairs United States Senate 100th Congress Second Session.

242. *United States v. Amato* (2d Cir. 1994) 15 F.3d 230.

243. *United States v. Bellomo, et al.* (2d Cir. 1999) 176 F,3d 580.

244. United States v. *Brady, et al.* (2d Cir. 1994) 26 F.3d 282.

245. *United States v. Cutolo* (E.D.N.Y. 1994) 868 F. Supp. 39.

246. *United States v. Gioeli* 08-cr-240 (BMC) (E.D.N.Y. May. 21, 2020).

247. *United States v. Langella and Persico* (2d Cir. 1986) 804 F.2d 185.

248. *United States v. Malpeso* (2d Cir. 1997) 115 F.3d 155.

249. *United States v. Monteleone, et al.* (2d Cir. 2001) 257 F.3d 210.

250. *United States v. Orena and Amato* (2d Cir. 1993) 986 F.2d 628.

251. *United States v. Orena* (2d Cir. 1994) 32 F.3d 704.

252. *United States v. Orena* (2d Cir. 1998) 145 F.3d 551.

253. *United States v. Orena (Sessa)* (2d Cir. 2013) No. 11-611.

254. *United States v. Persico* (E.D.N.Y. 1972) 339 F. Supp. 1077.

255. *United States v. Persico* (E.D.N.Y. 1981) 520 F. Supp. 96.

256. *United States v. Persico* (E.D.N.Y. 1986) 646 F. Supp. 752.

257. *United States v. Persico* (2d Cir. 1999) 164 F.3d 796.

258. *United States v. Salerno, et al.* (2d Cir. 1989) 868 F.2d 524.

259. *United States v. Scarpa* (E.D.N.Y. 1988) 691 F. Supp. 635.

260. *United States v. Scarpa* (E.D.N.Y. 1988) 701 F. Supp. 379.

261. *United States v. Scarpa* (E.D.N.Y. 1993) 815 F. Supp. 88.

262. *United States v. Scarpa* (2d Cir. 1990) 897 F.2d 63.

263. *United States v. Scarpa* (2d Cir. 1990) 913 F.2d 993.

264. *United States v. Scarpa* (2d Cir. 2017) No. 16-303.

265. *United States v. Scarpa* 94-cr-1119-1 (ERK) (E.D.N.Y. Nov. 11, 2020).

266. *United States v. Scopo* (2d Cir. 1994) 19 F.3d 777.

267. *United States v. Sessa* (E.D.N.Y. 1993) 821 F. Supp. 870.

268. *United States v. Sessa* (2d Cir. 1997) 125 F.3d 68.

269. *United States v. Sessa* (E.D.N.Y. Jan. 25, 2011) Opinion and Order 97-CV-2079 (ARR).

270. UPI. (May 15, 1981). "Convicted Mobster Carmine Persico Jr. has Surrendered to U.S." UPI.

271. UPI. (December 8, 1991). "Two Brooklyn Shootings May Be Linked to Mob Feud." UPI.

272. UPI. (January 8, 1992). "Brooklyn DA Vows Crackdown on Warring Mobsters." UPI.

273. UPI. (December 29, 1992). "Gunmen Wound AIDS-Stricken Mobster, 2 Others." UPI.

274. Vecsey, George. (January 19, 1973). "3 Held in Brooklyn Church-Jewels Theft." *The New York Times*.

275. Villano, Anthony and Astor, Gerald. *Brick Agent: Inside the Mafia for the FBI*. Ballantine Books, 1977.

276. Vlad, DJ (Vladimir Lyubovny). (June 22, 2020). "Michael Franzese on Gregory Scarpa aka 'The Grim Reaper' Allegedly Killing 120 People (Part 7)." www.youtube.com/watch?v=59PsN7FKXCg. VladTV.

277.   Vlad, DJ (Vladimir Lyubovny). (January 18, 2021). "Larry Mazza on Him & Grim Reaper Doing Over 20 Mafia Hits (Full Interview)." www.youtube.com/watch?v=lQGnpyaobnk.

278.   Wilkerson, Isabel. (January 15, 1987). "Urban Homicide Rates in U.S. up Sharply in 1987." *The New York Times*.

279.   Zelizer, Julian E. *The Fierce Urgency of Now: Lyndon Johnson, Congress, and the Battle for the Great Society.* Penguin Press, 2010.

280.   Zimring, Franklin E. (2011). "The City that Became Safe: New York and the Future of Crime Control." Strauss Institute Working Paper 09/2011.

ENDNOTES

CHAPTER ONE: WHAT LIES WITHIN HIM

1   Gregory Scarpa Jr., notes, transcribed July 12, 2023. *See*, also, Kroger, John. *Convictions: A Prosecutor's Battles Against Mafia Killers, Drug Kingpins, and Enron Thieves.* Farrar, Straus and Giroux, 2009, at pp. 129-130.

2   Phone interview with Larry Mazza on July 26, 2023.

3   Except as otherwise noted, the above description is derived from notes provided to the author by Gregory Scarpa Jr. on July 12, 2023.

4   Phone interview with Larry Mazza, *supra*.

5   Lance, Peter. *Deal with the Devil: The FBI's Secret Thirty-Year Relationship with a Mafia Killer.* William Morrow Publishing, 2013, at p. 504.

6   Harmon, Sandra. *Mafia Son: The Scarpa Mob Family, the FBI, and a Story of Betrayal.* St. Martin's Press, 2009, at p. 241. (Harmon's book is a biography of Gregory Scarpa Jr. He has described the book, without particulars, as "inaccurate and 'sensationalized'" (Lance, *supra*, at p. 496). Unless otherwise noted, this author has cited Harmon's book and all listed sources when he has found them credible. Harmon, who passed away in December of 2018,

is no longer in a position to defend her account of Gregory Jr.'s life, if she so desired); Dunleavy, Steve. (November 5, 2007). "I Loved a 'Cute' Killer." *New York Post.*

7   Scarpa, Linda. *The Mafia Hit Man's Daughter.* Kindle ed. New York. Kensington Publishing Corp., 2016, at pp. 21-23.

8   Ibid., at p. 216.

9   Lance, *supra,* at p. 503.

10   Later Days Podcast with Joe Poletto, Greg Scarpa Jr. Interview Part 2, Episode 5; Mazza, Larry. *The Life: A Brooklyn Boy is Seduced into the Dark World of the Mafia.* Digital Publishing of Florida, Inc., 2017, at p. 40.

11   Later Days Podcast with Joe Poletto, Larry Mazza - Greg Scarpa Sr. Episode 5.

12   McGuire, Craig and Imbriale, Carmine. *Carmine and the 13th Avenue Boys: Surviving Brooklyn's Colombo Mob.* Kindle ed., WildBlue Press, 2022, at p. 191 (quoting Tommy Dades).

13   Lance, *supra,* at p. 491; Mazza, *supra,* at p. 37. According to Lawrence Mazza Sr., Josephine Maniscalco, Mazza's maternal grandmother, called Scarpa "the fucking devil" (Mazza, *supra,* at p. 37).

14   Lance, *supra,* at p. 357 (quoting Judge Jack B. Weinstein).

15   Scarpa self-reported to the FBI that he earned his button in 1951 (FBI Files set 1, at pp. 33); Linda Scarpa, his daughter, claimed he earned it in 1950 (Scarpa, *supra,* at p. 20).

16   FBI Files, set 4, at p. 28.

17   Lance, *supra,* at pp. 372-373.

CHAPTER TWO: IMMIGRANTS, INFANTS, INFORMANTS & INFIDELITY

1   Golding, Bruce. (March 19, 2019). "A Ranking of the Most Notable Mob Funerals in NYC History." *New York Post.*

2   Scarpa, *supra,* at p. 173; Lance, *supra,* at p. 374; Dannen, Fredric. (December 16, 1996). "The G-man and the Hit Man," *New Yorker Magazine.* Sandra Harmon wrote that Scarpa died on June 4, 1994 (Harmon, *supra,* at p. 169). However, his daughter stated that he died on June 8 (Scarpa, *supra,* at p. 173), and as Lance pointed out, Scarpa executed a statement on June 7, 1994, and died the next day (Lance, *supra,* at pp. 372-374).

3   Mazza, *supra,* at p. 380.

4   Ibid.

5   As of this writing, the FBI has eight sets of documents available online relating to Scarpa's role as an FBI informant (sets 1 through 6) and investigations into Scarpa's criminal activity (sets 7 and 8). The total number of pages in the eight sets is 1,250. Set 1 consists of 249 pages. The first entry in set 1 is dated 11/31/61, and the last entry in set 1 is dated 1/20/64. Set 2 consists of 73 pages. The first entry in set 2 is dated 1/20/64, and the last entry in set 2 is dated 9/21/64. Set 3 consists of 164 pages. The first entry in set 3 appears to be from August of 1967, and the last entry in set 3 is dated 1/18/68. Set 4 consists of 249 pages. The first entry in set 4 is dated 1/26/70, and the last entry in set 4 is dated 8/1/72. Set 5 consists of 160 pages. The first entry in set 5 is dated 3/1/81, and the last entry in set 5 is dated 4/5/89. Set 6 consists of 80 pages. The first entry in set 6

is dated 3/27/89, and the last legible entry in set 6 is dated 4/22/92. Set 7 consists of 113 pages and relates to the FBI's investigation of Scarpa's alleged participation in and arrest for counterfeiting IBM stock certificates. The first entry in set 7 is dated 3/30/73, and the last entry in set 7 is dated 2/8/77. Set 8 consists of 162 pages and relates to the anti-racketeering file compiled by the FBI on Scarpa. The first entry in set 8 is dated 4/11/63, and the last entry in set 8 is dated 4/21/76. The documents, as of this writing, were located online at vault.fbi.gov/gregory-scarpa-sr. When reference is made in these endnotes to such a document or documents, the reference will be to "FBI Files," followed by the set the document or documents appeared in when accessed along with the page number or numbers of the document or documents within that set. *See, e.g.,* chapter one, endnote 16, *supra.*

6   FBI Files, set 1, at p. 2. Scarpa is often referred to as "Informant" throughout the FBI documents. At times he is referred to by name. Two possible explanations exist for referring to Scarpa by name. On the one hand, the information about Scarpa could be coming from another informant the FBI developed and was handling. On the other hand, use of Scarpa's name in certain instances may have been to provide clarity in the reported matter which came from Scarpa himself.

7   Lance and DeVecchio both reported that Scarpa was down to 150 pounds, from a previous weight of 220 pounds, by August of 1992 (Lance, *supra,* at p. 319; DeVecchio, Lin and Brandt, Charles. *We're Going to Win This Thing: The Shocking Frameup of a Mafia Crime Buster.* The Berkley Publishing Group, 2011, at p. 181). Lance also wrote that Scarpa weighed 116 pounds in early 1994, shortly before his death (Lance, *supra,* at p. 370). Mazza wrote that he "heard through the grapevine that Scarpa weighed about

80 pounds when he succumbed to the AIDS virus" (Mazza, *supra*, at p. 380). Harmon wrote that "Scarpa weighed just fifty-six pounds at the time of his death" (Harmon, *supra,* at p. 169). Linda Scarpa quoted her mother as saying that Scarpa weighed "like fifty pounds" shortly before his death (Scarpa, *supra*, at p. 173 (quoting Linda Schiro)).

8   Lance, *supra,* at p. 355; Mazza, *supra,* at p. 423; DeVecchio, supra, at p. 367.

9   Lance, *supra,* at pp. 372-373.

10   Scarpa, *supra*, at p. 176; Lance, *supra*, at p. 377.

11   Harmon, *supra,* at p. 169.

12   Ibid.

13   Digital History. "The New Immigrants."

14   Lance, *supra,* at p. 178.

15   The Statue of Liberty-Ellis Island Foundation, Inc.

16   Ancestry.com. 1940 U.S. Census. "Enumeration District 24-1004. Supervisor's District No. 8. Sheet No. 2A," "Supplementary Questions," at column 41, line 1.

17   Ancestry.com. 1940 U.S. Census. "Enumeration District 24-1004. Supervisor's District No. 8. Sheet No. 2A."

18   Fold3.com. 1930 U.S. Census. "Enumeration District 24-1197. Supervisor's District No. 31. Sheet No. 25B," at column 18, line 94.

19   Ancestry.com. 1940 U.S. Census. "Enumeration District 24-1004. Supervisor's District No. 8. Sheet No. 2A," at column 16, lines 3, 5, 6 & 7.

20   Fold3.com. 1930 U.S. Census. "Enumeration District 24-1197. Supervisor's District No. 31. Sheet No. 25B," at column 10, line 91.

21   Ancestry.com. 1940 U.S. Census. "Enumeration District 24-1004. Supervisor's District No. 8. Sheet No. 2A," at column 14, line 1.

22   Fold3.com. 1930 U.S. Census. "Enumeration District 24-1197. Supervisor's District No. 31. Sheet No. 25B," at columns 25 & 26, line 91.

23   Scarpa, *supra,* at p. 19.

24   Ancestry.com. 1940 U.S. Census. "Enumeration District 24-1004. Supervisor's District No. 8. Sheet No. 2A," at column 32, line 1.

25   Ibid., at column 27, line 1.

26   Ibid., at column 32, line 2.

27   Ibid., at columns 28 & 29, line 2.

28   Ibid., at column 14, line 2.

29   U.S. Department of Health and Human Service, Office of the Assistant Secretary for Planning and Evaluation. "Poverty Guidelines."

30   Scarpa, *supra,* at p. 19.

31   Phone interview with Gregory Scarpa Jr. on 7/26/23.

32   Bamford, Tyler (2020). "The Points Were All That Mattered: The U.S. Army's Demobilization After World War II."

33   Ibid.

34   Scarpa, *supra*, at p. 20.

35   Hunt, Thomas (2023). The American Mafia: The History of Organized Crime in the United States. "Mafia Morality: Church Theft Requires Murder."

36   Gregory Scarpa Jr., notes, at page 5, transcribed July 12, 2023.

37   A button man, a made man, a soldier, a goodfellow, a wiseguy, and being straightened out all refer to the same status, i.e., a man is officially a member of a family and is no longer merely an associate.

38   Villano, Anthony and Astor, Gerald. *Brick Agent: Inside the Mafia for the FBI.* Ballantine Books, 1977, at pp. 42-43.

39   Lance, *supra,* at p. 6 (quoting Unger, Sanford J. *FBI: An Uncensored Look Behind the Walls.* Atlantic Monthly Press, 1975, at p. 392).

40   Turning Point, Using Intel to Stop the Mob, Part 2, FBI Stories August 9, 2007; Peter Lance wrote that the Top Hoodlum Program started "[t]wo weeks after the Apalachin arrests," which would have been in late November of 1957 (Lance, *supra,* at pp. 7-9).

41   NY Penal Law section 1897 was replaced by Article 265 of the Penal Law in 1965 (*People v. Velasquez* (N.Y. Sup. Ct. 1988) 139 Misc.2d 822, 824, fn. 3; 528 NYS2d 502).

42   The FBI's record of that arrest, which included Scarpa's having been sent to Rikers Island as a result, misspelled Scarpa's name twice, once as "Scarbo" and a second time as "Scarba" (FBI Files, set 1, at pp. 3 & 7). The two misspelled entries at page 3 of the FBI files appear to have been crossed out. This may indicate that these items relate to someone other than Gregory Scarpa. However, the listing indicated

that in both cases, fingerprints of the arrestee were supplied. Furthermore, FBI Files, set 7, p. 2, a document from 1973, lists "Gregory Scarba" and "Gregory Scarbo" as aliases for Gregory Scarpa.

43   FBI Files, set 1, at pp. 3 & 7.

44   Ibid., at p. 5.

45   Ibid., at pp. 3 & 7.

46   Papers of John F. Kennedy. Pre-Presidential Papers. Presidential Campaign Files, 1960. Speeches and the Press. Speeches, Statements, and Sections, 1958-1960. Crime and legal ethics: The Fight Against Crime. Speech of April 1, 1960, at p. 3.

47   FBI Files, set 1, at p. 5.

48   Ibid.

49   Lance, *supra*, at p. 10.

50   PC, in this context, likely stands for personal contact or point of contact. It often stands for "probable cause" in the FBI files.

51   FBI Files, set 1, at p. 5.

52   Ibid.

53   Ibid., at p. 1 (capitalization in the original).

54   Ibid., at p. 4.

55   Ibid.

56   Ibid., at p. 3.

57   Ibid., at pp. 3-4.

58   Ibid., at pp. 5.

59   Ibid., at pp. 8-13.

60   Ibid., at p. 34.

61   Ibid., at p. 43.

62   Ibid., at pp. 36-37.

63   Ibid., at pp. 37-38.

64   Ibid., at pp. 38-40.

65   Ibid., at p. 40.

66   Ibid., at pp. 41-43.

67   Ibid., at p. 42.

68   A *caporegime*, or capo, sometimes referred to as a captain, is a leadership position in a Mafia family. A capo usually has a crew of members, or button men, and associates who report directly to him and for whom he is responsible. A capo outranks members and is below the family leadership which is typically comprised of a consigliere, an underboss, and a boss.

69   FBI Files, set 1, at pp. 26 & 33.

70   Ibid., at p. 33 (capitalization in the original).

71   FBI Files, set 8, at p. 5 (capitalization in the original).

72   FBI Files, set 1, at pp. 25 & 26.

73   Ibid., at p. 25.

74   Ibid., at p. 26.

75   Ibid., at p. 35.

76   Raab, Selwyn. *The Five Families: The Rise, Decline & Resurgence of America's Most Powerful Mafia Empire.*

St. Martin's Press, 2005, at p. 32 (quoting Lucky Luciano). Presumably, the FBI was not aware of Luciano's directive as of 1962.

77   FBI Files, set 1, at p. 35 (emphasis added).

78   Ibid., at p. 45. In 1962 $3,000 was worth roughly $30,135 as of this writing in 2023.

79   Ibid.

80   Ibid., at p. 62. The memo's time stamp is 1:35 a.m. indicating its urgency.

81   Ibid.

82   Ibid.

83   Ibid., at p. 63.

84   Ibid., at p. 64.

85   Ibid., at pp. 65-66.

86   Ibid., at p. 66.

87   Lance, *supra*, at p. 95.

88   Villano, *supra*, at p. 112.

89   DeVecchio, *supra*, at p. 313.

90   Raab, *supra*, at p. 338.

91   *Gumar*, sometimes written as *gumare*, has its origins in the Italian *comare*. The formal definition of *comare* is "godmother," which is derived from the word's literal meaning of "co-mother." However, *comare* has taken on the vulgar definition of mistress, especially by those in the Italian Mafia, and is often written in its anglicized

form as gumar which closely approximates its common pronunciation.

92   *See* Lance, *supra*, at xii; *See* also Baram, Marcus (2007) "The Gumar, The Fed, and the Mobster."

93   New York Domestic Relations Law § 11; *In the Matter of The Estate of Jacob Benjamin* (1974) 34 NY2d 27.

94   U.S. Const. art. VI, § 1.

95   Scarpa Jr. notes, *supra*, at p. 6.

96   Harmon, *supra*, at p. 67.

97   Lance, *supra*, at p. 128.

98   Ibid.

99   Ibid., at p. 127.

100   Harmon, *supra*, at p. 40 et seq.

101   Scarpa, *supra*, at p. 15.

102   Scarpa Jr. notes, *supra*, at p. 6.

103   Lance, *supra*, at p. 127.

104   Capeci, Jerry (November 4, 2007). "Twisted Tale of the Moll Linda Schiro and her Men." *New York Daily News*.

105   In the "numbers" racket "bettors essentially wager relatively small sums of money, usually a dollar or less, on a three-digit number, with payout rates typically 500:1 or 600:1" (U.S. Department of Justice, Office of Justice Programs, Virtual Library. "Mob's Daily Number: Organized Crime and the Numbers Gambling Industry" Abstract; Liddick, Don. *The Mob's Daily Number: Organized Crime and the Numbers Gambling Industry.* University Press of America, 1999.). A random new three-digit number each

day, derived from a known source, is the winning number. For instance, as John Kroger explained, each day "at 5:00, the Aqueduct horse racing track announced the daily handle, the total amount of bets placed at the track that day. The last three digits of the handle became the winning number" (Kroger, *supra*, at p. 131).

106   Lance, *supra*, at p. 127.

107   Harmon, *supra*, at pp. 47-48.

108   Lance, *supra*, at p. 127; Baram, *supra*.

109   Lance, *supra*, at p. 127; Baram, *supra*.

110   Lance, *supra*, at p. 128; Harmon, *supra*, at p. 56. The number of murders Scarpa committed or was otherwise responsible for is no longer possible to ascertain. The number attributed by some to Scarpa, in excess of 120, is reasonably in dispute (*See* Vlad, DJ (Vladimir Lyubovny). (June 22, 2020). "Michael Franzese on Gregory Scarpa aka 'The Grim Reaper' Allegedly Killing 120 People (Part 7).").

111   Dunleavy, Steve. (November 5, 2007). "I Loved a 'Cute' Killer." *New York Post*.

112   Lance, *supra*, at p. 127; Baram, *supra*.

113   FBI Files, set 1, at pp. 26-31.

114   Ibid., at p. 5.

115   Ibid., at p. 12.

116   Raab, *supra*, at p. 193.

117   Coletti, J. (2022) J. Coletti's Racket Reviews, ep. 86. "The Colombo Family – Larry & Albert Gallo"; FBI Files, set 1, at p. 11.

118   FBI Files, set 1, at p. 10.

119   Ibid.

120   Ibid., at p. 34.

121   FBI Files, sets 1 & 2.

122   FBI Files, set 1, at p. 99.

123   Harmon, *supra*, at pp. 106-107.

124   Later Days Podcast with Joe Poletto, Larry Mazza – Greg Scarpa Sr., ep. 5.

125   DeVecchio, *supra*, at p. 154.

126   McGuire, *supra*, at p. 190.

127   Lance, *supra*, at pp. 15-16 & 406.

128   Dow, Harold, Greg Scarpa Interview with Harold Dow from CBS 'Street Stories' aired on 11/12/92.

129   Vlad, D.J. (Vladimir Lyubovny). (June 22, 2020). "Michael Franzese on Gregory Scarpa aka 'The Grim Reaper' Allegedly Killing 120 People (Part 7)."

130   FBI Files, set 1, at p. 48.

131   FBI Files, set 1, pp. 83-84.

132   *See,* e.g., FBI Files, set 1, p. 135.

133   Scarpa Jr. notes, *supra*, at p. 1.

134   FBI Files, set 8, at p. 5 (capitalization in the original).

135   FBI Files, set 1, at p. 47.

136   Ibid., at p. 46 (capitalization in the original).

137   Ibid., at pp. 50-51.

138   Ibid., at pp. 48-49.

139   Ibid., at p. 51.

140   Ibid., at p. 97.

141   Ibid., at pp. 47-48. Scarpa claimed that shortly after LoCicero's demotion Joe Magliocco made Scarpa a capo, most probably at the direction of Joe Profaci (Ibid., at p. 83).

142   Ibid., at p. 52.

143   Ibid., at p. 81.

144   Ibid., at p. 90. LoCicero felt he could rely on the Gallos and their followers to help him overthrow Magliocco (Ibid. at p. 92).

145   Ibid., at p. 88.

146   Ibid., at p. 86.

147   Ibid., at p. 119.

148   Ibid., at p. 16.

149   Ibid., at p. 172.

150   Ibid., at p. 204.

151   Ibid., at p. 205.

152   FBI Files, set 2, at p. 30.

153   LoCicero turned sixty in 1964 and his age may have been a factor in the Commission's decision to overlook him.

154   FBI Files, set 2, at p. 55.

155   FBI Files, set 1.

156   Scarpa. Jr. notes, *supra*, at p. 1.

CHAPTER THREE: GREGORY SCARPA, CIVIL RIGHTS ICON?

1   FBI Files, set 1, at p. 10.

2   Ibid., at p. 61.

3   Ibid., at pp. 144 & 160. The following simple and accurate description of how loansharking operates appears in *United States v. Amato* (2d Cir. 1994) 15 F.3d. 230, 234: "The cash capital for loansharking usually comes from the higher levels of command and is funneled down through the captain to his crew members. A crew member lends money to a customer at extortionate rates of interest, commonly three to five percent per week, and enforces repayment with violence or threats of violence. The crew member retains only part of the interest payment, known as vigorish, and the remainder flows back up the chain of command."

4   FBI Files, set 1 at p. 99.

5   Ibid., at p. 8.

6   Ibid., at pp. 111 & 236.

7   Ibid., at pp. 166-167.

8   Ibid., at pp. 167-169.

9   Ibid., at pp. 149 & 173.

10   Ibid., at pp. 182-184 & 192.

11   Ibid., at p. 118.

12   Ibid., at pp. 145 & 237.

13   Ibid., at pp. 8-9.

14   Ibid., at pp. 113 & 141.

15   NAACP.org. Empowerment Programs. "Medgar Evers."

16   Villano, *supra*, at pp. 98-100.

17   Ibid., at p. 99.

18   Ibid., at pp. 100-101

19   Ibid., at p. 101.

20   Scarpa, *supra*, at p. 70.

21   Ibid., at pp. 70-73.

22   Villano, *supra*, at p. 100.

23   Ibid., at p. 97.

24   At the risk of splitting hairs, a TECI *provides information* to a special agent handler, the substance of which is to be recorded in a form "209," while a CW, a cooperating witness, is *debriefed*, and that debriefing is recorded in a form "302" (DeVecchio, *supra*, at p. 94). That may be a distinction without a difference, as it is clear from Lin DeVecchio's book that the process that leads to a 209 involves more than a TECI simply talking while the handler records what the TECI says (Ibid., at pp. 94-100). The process involves a conversation, and in that sense is akin to a debriefing. At times, this book uses the terms debrief and debriefing to refer to exchanges between confidential informants and the FBI irrespective of the FBI's limitation of the use of those terms to its interaction with a cooperating witness.

25   Villano, *supra*, at p. 98.

26   Ibid.

27   Lance, *supra*, at p. 40.

28   This author was unable to locate a copy of Dillard's book. The search included, but was not limited to, correspondence via email on 6/26/23 with the book's publisher, Outskirts Press. The publisher responded to the author's request to purchase the book by writing, "Unfortunately, the book is no longer available."

29   Lance, *supra*, at p. 40.

30   Villano, *supra*, at pp. 97-100.

31   DeVecchio, *supra*, at pp. 82-83.

32   For excellent exposition about the political forces that supported and opposed civil rights legislation at the national level during the early 1960s, *see* Zelizer, Julian E. *The Fierce Urgency of Now: Lyndon Johnson, Congress, and the Battle for the Great Society.* Penguin Press, 2015.

33   Burns, James MacGregor and Burns, Stewart. *A People's Charter: The Pursuit of Rights in America.* Alfred A. Knopf, 1991, at p. 319.

34   FBI.gov. "Mississippi Burning." https://www.fbi.gov/history/famous-cases/mississippi-burning.

35   Burns, *supra*, at pp. 321-323.

36   FBI.gov. "Mississippi Burning," *supra*.

37   The FBI has released 1,049 pages of documents regarding the 1964 case of the three slain civil rights workers, a case the FBI designated as MIBURN. Those documents can be accessed at

vault.fbi.gov/Mississippi%20Burning%20%28MIBURN%29%20Case.

38   *Orena v. United States* (E.D.N.Y. 1997) 956 F. Supp. 1071, 1086.

39   Selwyn Raab, without providing any detail, wrote in November of 1994 that Scarpa purportedly had a "role in helping the F.B.I. solve the 1964 murders of three civil-rights workers in Mississippi. In the last years of his life, Mr. Scarpa claimed that at the behest of the F.B.I., he terrorized a Ku Klux Klan member to disclose where the bodies had been buried, according to lawyers and law-enforcement officials who spoke on the condition of anonymity" (Raab, Selwyn. (November 20, 1994). "The Mobster Was a Mole for the FBI; Tangled Life of a Mafia Figure Who Died of AIDS is Exposed." *The New York Times*).

40   As noted above, Sandra Harmon placed the first encounter between Scarpa and Linda Schiro in the summer of 1964.

41   Scarpa, *supra*, at pp. 67-70.

42   Ibid., at p. 68.

43   Ibid.

44   Ibid.

45   Ibid.

46   Ibid.

47   Mohr, Holbrook (2010). "Ex-Klansman Convicted in '64 Slayings Sues FBI." *Memphis Daily*. The Associated Press.

48   Robbins, Tom and Capeci, Jerry. (June 21, 1994; updated January 24, 2015). "Mobster's Crime Helped FBI Find Slain Activists Civil Rights Struggle." *New York Daily News* via *Greensboro News & Record*.

49   Those details generally coincide with Linda Schiro's claim that Mississippi was the third and final stop on their trip in the summer of 1964 (Scarpa, *supra*, at p. 68).

50   Ibid.

51   The FBI's released MIBURN files include descriptions of all who were arrested in connection with the civil rights workers case. None of those listed is stated as having the occupation of an appliance merchant or appliance store owner. However, two of the men who were arrested have their occupations redacted from their arrest reports, and nine of them have no occupation listed (Set 2 at pp. 4-111). None of them are named Lawrence Byrd.

52   Robbins, Tom and Capeci, Jerry. (June 21, 1994; updated January 24, 2015). "Mobster's Crime Helped FBI Find Slain Activists Civil Rights Struggle." *New York Daily News* via *Greensboro News & Record.*

53   Ibid.

54   Ibid.

55   Ibid.

56   Ibid.

57   Ibid.

58   FBI Mississippi Burning (MIBURN) Case Documents Set 1 at p. 66.

59   Ibid., at p. 76.

60   Ibid.

61   FBI Mississippi Burning (MIBURN) Case Documents Set 2 at pp. 4-111.

62   Harmon, *supra*, at p. 62

63   DeVecchio, *supra*, at p. 83.

64   Robbins, Tom and Capeci, Jerry. (June 21, 1994; updated January 24, 2015). "Mobster's Crime Helped FBI Find Slain Activists Civil Rights Struggle." *New York Daily News* via *Greensboro News & Record*.

65   Scarpa, *supra*, at p. 68.

66   DeVecchio, *supra*, at p. 83; Lance, *supra*, at p. 30 (quoting Robbins, Tom and Capeci, Jerry (1994) New York *Daily News*); Scarpa, *supra*, at p. 68. DeVecchio's version dropped an "f-bomb" into Scarpa's threat for good measure (DeVecchio, *supra*, at p. 83).

67   Harmon, *supra*, at p. 63.

68   Lance, *supra*, at p. 30 (quoting W.O. Dillard).

69   Harmon, *supra*, at p. 63.

70   Scarpa, *supra*, at p. 68.

71   Raab, *supra*, at p. 337.

72   DeVecchio, *supra*, at pp. 82-83.

73   Robbins, Tom and Capeci, Jerry. (June 21, 1994; updated January 24, 2015). "Mobster's Crime Helped FBI Find Slain Activists Civil Rights Struggle." *New York Daily News* via *Greensboro News & Record*.

74   Scarpa, *supra*, at p. 70.

75   Hays, Tom (October 29, 2007). "Mob Moll Says Mafiosi Helped FBI." Associated Press.

76   Scarpa, *supra*, at p. 70.

77   Lance, Peter. (June 27, 2016). "DOJ Report on MISSBURN Case Leaves out Key Detail: I.D. of the Mafia Killer Who Broke the Case for Hoover's FBI." *HuffPost*.

78   Lance, in "DOJ Report on MISSBURN Case Leaves out Key Detail: I.D. of the Mafia Killer Who Broke the Case for Hoover's FBI," referred to a book by Dillard entitled *Clearburning: Civil Rights, Civil Wrongs*.

79   "Outskirts Press Announces the Release of The Final Curtain, the Latest Highly-Anticipated Book from Author Judge W.O. Chet Dillard." (August 14, 2007).

80   https://www.legacy.com/us/obituaries/clarionledger/name/w-o-dillard-obituary?id=16575135.

81   Mazza, *supra*, at p. 431.

82   Later Days Podcast with Joe Poletto, Greg Scarpa Jr. Interview, *supra*.

83   Vlad, DJ (Vladimir Lyubovny). (June 22, 2020). "Michael Franzese on Gregory Scarpa aka 'The Grim Reaper' Allegedly Killing 120 People (Part 7)."

84   Salvatore Sammy The Bull Gravano. "My Sit Down with The Grim Reaper."

85   Dannen, *supra*.

86   Arrington, Derrion. (April 21, 2020). "Vernon Dahmer 1908-1966." Black Past.

87   Ibid.

88   Lance, "DOJ Report on MISSBURN Case Leaves out Key Detail: I.D. of the Mafia Killer Who Broke the Case for Hoover's FBI," *supra*.

89   Lawrence Byrd v. State of Mississippi (1969) 228 So.2d 874, 877.

90   Villano, *supra*, at p. 98.

91   Scarpa, *supra*, at p. 68.

92   Harmon, *supra*, at p. 62.

93   DeVecchio, *supra*, at p. 82.

94   Ibid., at p. 83. Frankly, DeVecchio's "confidential source" sounds like the Robbins and Capeci article from June of 1994.

95   New York Daily News. (March 25, 1996). "Judge Frees Mob Canary's Files." *New York Daily News*.

96   Lance, *supra*, at p. 31.

97   Outskirts Press. (2007). "New Book by Mississippi Judge Exposes FBI Tampering in Civil Rights Cases."

98   Lance, *Deal with the Devil*, *supra*, at p. 31, and Lance, "DOJ Report on MISSBURN Case Leaves out Key Detail: I.D. of the Mafia Killer Who Broke the Case for Hoover's FBI," *supra*.

99   Lawrence Byrd v. State of Mississippi, *supra*, at p. 877.

100   Dannen, Fredric. (December 16, 1996). "The G-man and the Hit Man." *New Yorker Magazine*.

101   Ibid.

102   Lance, "DOJ Report on MISSBURN Case Leaves out Key Detail: I.D. of the Mafia Killer Who Broke the Case for Hoover's FBI," *supra*.

103   FBI Files, set 4, at p. 28.

104   Ibid.

105   18 U.S. Code § 1951.

106   FBI Files, set 4, at p. 26.

107   Ibid.

108   Ibid.

109   Ibid.

110   FBI Files, set 8, at p. 51.

111   FBI Files, set 4, at p. 26.

112   Ibid., at p. 28.

113   Ibid., at p. 29.

114   Ibid., at pp. 27, 30–31, 40–42, 47, 53–55, 62, 66–67, 77, 84, 86, 88, 96 97, 106–109 & 117.

115   Ibid., at p. 73.

116   Ibid., at p. 51.

117   Ibid.

118   Ibid., at p. 46.

119   Ibid., at pp. 46 & 71.

120   Raab, *supra*, at p. 189.

121   FBI Files, set 4, at p. 71.

122   Ibid., at p. 85.

123   Ibid., at p. 53.

124   Ibid., at pp. 65 & 84.

125   Ibid., at p. 54.

126   Ibid., at p. 116 (capitalization in the original). Scarpa also reported on Colombo's personal life including his suspicion that Colombo "may in fact be a bigamist" (Ibid., at p. 103).

127   Ibid., at p. 73.

128   Ibid., at p. 34.

129   Ibid., at p. 113.

130   Ibid.

131   Ibid.

132   Ibid., at pp. 116-117 (capitalization in the original).

133   Raab, *supra*, at p. 191.

134   Ibid.

135   FBI Files, set 4, at p. 126.

136   Ibid., at p. 120 et seq.

137   Ibid., at p. 120.

138   Ibid., at p. 121.

139   Phone interview on July 26, 20123 with Gregory Scarpa Jr.

140   FBI Files, set 4, at p. 120.

141   A new version of the Italian American Civil Rights League was established in 1974 (Italian American Civil Rights League).

142   FBI Files, set 4, at p. 124.Persico, whose full name was Carmine John Persico Jr. was known by "contradictory nicknames: the affectionate 'Junior' from his charmed

supporters, and the derogatory 'the Snake' from his detractors" (Raab, *The Five Families*, *supra*, at p. 321).

CHAPTER FOUR: IT'S WHO YOU KNOW AND WHAT YOU KNOW

1   Dahlke, Arnold. *Business Succession Planning for Dummies*. John Wiley & Sons, Inc., 2012.

2   *See,* e.g., University of Washington, Human Resources (2016) Succession Planning Toolkit.

3   FBI Files, set 4, at p. 122 (capitalization in the original).

4   Gage, Nicholas (September 1, 1971). "Yacovelli Said to Succeed Colombo in Mafia Family." *The New York Times*.

5   FBI Files, set 4, at p. 122. *See* also Gage, *supra*. The Gage article is notable for, among other things, the close relationship between the information Scarpa was feeding the FBI and the information the FBI was giving the press. As a side note, Gage stated that Yacovelli was forty-two years old. However, he was born on January 1, 1928, which would have made him forty-three years old at the time of Gage's article. Additionally of note, an internal FBI memorandum from Special Agent Anthony L. Christy records the date of Yacovelli's being named acting boss as not occurring until April of 1972, a delay of nearly ten months that seems unlikely (Muckrock Document 1470141-0-Section 6, at p. 3).

6   FBI Files, set 4, at p. 122 (capitalization in the original).

7   Ibid.

8   Ibid., at pp. 116-117.

9   Raab, *supra*, at p. 197.

10   FBI Files, set 4, at p. 121.

11   Ibid., at p. 122.

12   Ibid., at p. 123.

13   Ibid., at pp. 122-123.

14   Ibid., at p. 123 (capitalization in the original).

15   Ibid.

16   Ibid. (capitalization in the original).

17   Ibid., at pp. 124 & 126-128.

18   Ibid., at p. 128.

19   Ibid., at p. 127.

20   Ibid., at p. 124.

21   Ibid., at pp. 128-129.

22   Ibid., at p. 133.

23   Ibid., at p. 142.

24   Ibid.

25   Ibid. (capitalization in the original).

26   Ibid., at p. 143 (capitalization in the original).

27   Ibid., at p. 148. *See* also ibid. at pp. 157-159.

28   *United States v. Persico* (E.D.N.Y. 1972) 339 F. Supp. 1077, 1079.

29   Ibid., at p. 1080.

30   Raab, *supra*, at p. 325.

31   Cook, Fred (June 4, 1972). "A Family Business: Hijacking, Bookmaking, Policy, Dice Games, Loansharking and Special Contracts." *The New York Times*.

32   FBI Files, set 4, at p. 162.

33   Ibid., at pp. 162-163 & 170.

34   Ibid., at p. 163.

35   Ibid.

36   Ibid., at p. 164.

37   Ibid., at p. 166 (capitalization in the original).

38   Ibid., at p. 168.

39   Ibid., at p. 192.

40   Ibid., at p. 195.

41   Ibid., at p. 170.

42   Ibid., at pp. 170-171.

43   Charles "Moose" Panarella even summoned Scarpa to a Colombo family "court" to respond to rumors that Scarpa was an FBI informant (FBI Files, set 4, at pp. 196-198).

44   Scarpa was also suspected by Carlo Gambino, as early as 1973, of being an informant. A notation In an FBI report dated March 29, 1974, as part of the Bureau's ongoing antiracketeering case against Scarpa, stated that in December of 1973 the FBI was advised that "CARLO GAMBINO has put out the word to 'stay away' from GREGORY SCARPA and 'BUTTER ASS' DE CICCO as they have a 'big mouth'" (FBI Files, set 8, at p. 135 (capitalization in the original)). Finally, a note with the name of the informant redacted in the "ADMINISTRATIVE" section of a Bureau report, also in Scarpa's antiracketeering case, dated 12/11/74, stated

that "on August 26, 1974, [name redacted] advised he heard that GREG SCARPA is an informant" (FBI Files, set 8, at p. 148 (capitalization in the original)).

45   FBI Files, set 4, at pp. 197.

46   Ibid., at p. 191.

47   Ibid., at pp. 141 & 147.

48   FBI Carmine J. Persico Jr. Documents set 1, at p. 11.

49   Ibid., at pp. 10-11.

50   Parish History. "The Basilica of Regina Pacis."

51   Ibid.

52   Ibid.

53   Brooklyn Public Library Blog (2009). "Regina Pacis and the Case of the Missing Crowns."

54   According to the U.S. Department of Labor's inflation calculator, $2,000,000 in June of 1951, when the church was completed, was the equivalent of $23,560,540.54 in June of 2023, shortly before this chapter was written.

55   Ibid.

56   Ibid.

57   Parish History. "The Basilica of Regina Pacis," *supra.*

58   Brooklyn Public Library Blog, *supra.*

59   Ibid. Peter Lance had the theft in January of 1952 shortly after the crowns were blessed by the pope (Lance, *supra*, at p. 67). However, as the Basilica of Regina Pacis web page states, the crowns were attached to the painting on May 24, 1952 (Parish History. "The Basilica of Regina

Pacis," *supra*). The Brooklyn Library notes the crowns were put in place during a "coronation" in May, and it was one week after the coronation that Father James Russo, during a wedding, noticed the crowns were missing (Brooklyn Public Library Blog, *supra*).

60   Brooklyn Public Library Blog, *supra*.

61   Hunt, *supra*.

62   Brooklyn Public Library Blog, *supra*.

63   Hunt, *supra*.

64   Ibid. *See* also 1940 United States Federal Census for Ralph Emmenio.

65   Hunt, *supra*.

66   FBI Files, set 1, at p. 77.

67   Villano, *supra*, at p. 121.

68   Ibid.

69   Lance, *supra*, at p. 67.

70   *See,* e.g., original caption of photo of Vincent Emmino identifying his brother's body at www.gettyimages.ie/detail/news-photo/vincent-emmino-18-year-old-brother-of-ralph-buck-emmino-news-photo/514952526.

71   *See, e.g.*, Brooklyn Public Library Blog, *supra*.

72   *See* also Hunt, *supra*.

73   Ancestry.com. 1940 U.S. Census. "Enumeration District 24-1894. Supervisor's District No. 8. Sheet No. 8A."

74   New York State Archives.

75   Santayana, George *The Life of Reason: Or, The Phases of Human Progress*. 2nd ed. Scribner's, 1905.

76   Lance, *supra*, at p. 67; Fried, Joseph (January 11, 1973). "$100,000 in Gems Stolen from a Brooklyn Church." The New York Times. Even the simple fact of the date of the theft is not stated with specificity in Villano's book. He dated the theft as taking place "in the winter of 1972" (Villano, *supra*, at p. 121).

77   FBI Files, set 4, at p. 177.

78   Ibid., at pp. 177-180.

79   Fried, *supra*.

80   Ibid. *See* also FBI Files, set 4, at p. 177.

81   Fried, *supra*.

82   FBI Files, set 4, at p. 177.

83   The memorandum uses the terms "source" and "informant" interchangeably. *See, e.g.*, paragraphs 6 and 7 of the memorandum (Ibid.).

84   Gevirtz, Leslie. (April 11, 1989). "Mobster Fingers Brother as Murderer." UPI.

85   Lance, *supra*, at p. 180.

86   FBI Files, set 4, at p. 177; *See* also FBI Files set 8, at p. 125.

87   FBI Files, set 4, at p. 17.

88   Ibid., at pp. 177-178.

89   Ibid., at p. 179.

90   Ibid.

91 Ibid.

92 Ibid.

93 Ibid., at pp. 179-180.

94 FBI History. "Directors, Then and Now. L. Patrick Gray."

95 Lance, *supra*, at p. 67.

96 Villano, *supra*, at p. 121.

97 Ibid., at p. 122.

98 Ibid., at p. 121.

99 Ibid., at p. 123.

100 Ibid., at p. 121.

101 FBI Files, set 4, at p. 177.

102 Lance, *supra*, at p. 68.

103 Ibid. Lance may well have had access to additional sources he decided he could not or did not need to reveal.

104 Vecsey, George (January 19, 1973) "3 Held in Brooklyn Church-Jewel Theft." *The New York Times*.

105 Lance, *supra*, at p. 68.

106 FBI Files, set 4, at p. 176.

107 FBI Files, set 7, at p. 1.

108 Ibid., at p. 14.

109 Ibid., at p. 7.

110 Ibid., at p. 17.

111   Ibid., at p. 4.

112   FBI Files, set 7, at p. 94.

113   Johnson, Rudy. (June 18, 1974). "13 Indicted on Stock Theft and Counterfeit Counts." *The New York Times*.

114   FBI Files, set 7, at p. 93.

115   Ibid., at p. 15.

116   Ibid.

117   Ibid., at p. 14.

118   Ibid., at p. 16.

119   Ibid.

120   Ibid., at p. 17.

121   Ibid.

122   Ibid., at p. 18.

123   Ibid., at p. 19.

124   Ibid., at p. 20.

125   Ibid., at pp. 21-22.

126   Ibid., at p. 23.

127   Ibid.

128   Ibid., at pp. 24-25.

129   Ibid., at p. 25.

130   Ibid., at p. 1.

131   Ibid., at pp. 10-12.

132   Ibid., at p. 4.

133   Ibid., at p. 7.

134   Ibid., at pp. 27-33.

135   Ibid., at pp. 33-42. It is worth noting that many of the memos discussing Scarpa and De Domenico contained the following, or similar, language: "CAUTION SHOULD BE EXERCISED IN THE EVENT ANY CONTACT IS MADE WITH SUBJECT SCARPA AND SUBJECT DE DOMENICO IN VIEW OF PREVIOUS ARREST FOR POSSESSION OF A DANGEROUS WEAPON" (Ibid., at p. 35 (capitalization and underline in the original); *See* also ibid, at pp. 7, 45, 53, 55, 61, 64, 94, 100, and 104). Similarly, a warning that "SUBJECTS ARE ARMED AND DANGEROUS" was included in a "Synopsis" of the arrest of all three men (Ibid. at p. 68). Scarpa was arrested without incident (Ibid., at p. 74), and De Domenico voluntarily surrendered, also without incident (Ibid., at p. 86). The warnings are based on Scarpa's two arrests in 1950 for possession of a firearm (Ibid., at p. 28) and De Dominico's arrest in 1966 for possession of a loaded gun (Ibid., at p. 31).

136   Ibid., at p. 48.

137   FBI Files, set 8, at p. 126.

138   FBI Files, set 4, at p. 208.

139   Ibid.

140   FBI Files, set 7, at p. 50.

141   FBI Files, set 4, at p. 206.

142   Ibid., at pp. 206-207.

143   Ibid., at p. 207.

144   FBI Files, set 7, at p. 50.

145   FBI Files, set 4, at p. 208.

146   Ibid.

147   Ibid., & FBI Files, set 7, at p. 50.

148   FBI Files, set 4, at p. 238.

149   FBI Files, set 7, at p. 63; FBI Files, set 8, at p. 14.

150   Ibid. Section 2 defines who is a principal in any crime committed against the U.S. Section 371 covers conspiracies to commit an offense against or to defraud the U.S. Section 1343 applies to fraud by wire, radio, or television. Section 2314 criminalizes the transportation of stolen goods, securities, moneys, fraudulent State tax stamps, or articles used in counterfeiting (Cornell Law School, Legal Information Institute. "U.S. Code: Title 18.").

151   FBI Files, set 7, at p. 94.

152   Ibid., at p. 64.

153   Ibid., at p. 74; FBI Files, set 8, at p. 145.

154   FBI Files, set 7, at p. 70.

155   A personal recognizance bond, unlike a surety bond, does not require the defendant to deposit a percentage of the bond with the court.

156   FBI Files, set 7, at p. 68.

157   FBI Files, set 7, at pp. 67-68.

158   Ibid., at p. 86.

159   Ibid., at p. 89.

160   Ibid., at pp. 101-102.

161   Ibid., at pp. 101 & 102.

162   Ibid., at pp. 103-104.

163   Ibid., at p. 109. The date in the file is given as January 19, 1975. This appears to be a typo, a common end-of-year error, as the memorandum references McCaffrey's communication about the upcoming hearing as occurring on December 18, 1975.

164   Ibid., at p. 112.

165   Ibid., at p. 111.

166   Ibid., at p. 112.

CHAPTER FIVE: A THIRD FAMILY

1   USAFacts. "Average number of people in a family."

2   Gregory Scarpa Jr., notes, *supra*, at p. 6.

3   Ibid.

4   As of this writing, Linda Schiro lives, to the best of the author's knowledge, on Staten Island.

5   Baram, *supra*.

6   Harmon, *supra*, at pp. 42-43.

7   Scarpa, *supra*, at pp. 15-16.

8   Ibid., at p. 18.

9   Harmon, *supra*, at p. 51.

10   Hays, *supra*; Baram, *supra*.

11   Dunleavy, "I Loved a 'Cute' Killer," *supra*.

12   Harmon, *supra*, at pp. 49-50.

13   Gregory Scarpa Jr., notes, *supra*, at page 6.

14   Scarpa, *supra*, at pp. 19 & 20.

15   Ibid., at p. 22.

16   Harmon, *supra*, at p. 55.

17   Scarpa, *supra*, at p. 22.

18   Harmon, *supra*, at p. 58.

19   Baram, *supra*. Unlike Scarpa's possible connection to the Mississippi civil rights worker case described in detail in chapter three, *supra*, no information about any of these other alleged missions has come to light during research for this book other than the following: "During Scarpa's final days in prison, his AIDS dementia took hold, and he was given to rambling. Occasionally, he spoke of the dirty work he claimed to have done for the government.... He also spoke about a secret assignment in Costa Rica for the United States government in the sixties that involved murder" (Dannen, *supra*). While the stories about these additional "missions" may be true, they strike this author as fabrications. It is not clear to this author whose fabrications they are.

20   Harmon, *supra*, at p. 58; Scarpa, *supra*, at p. 69.

21   Harmon, *supra*, at pp. 58-59.

22   Diana described in her daughter's book, without being specific as to time or place, a murder she witnessed Scarpa commit. "I heard '*boom, boom.*' He shot him in the head and just took the stamps and coins. He wasn't paying for them. Then he came back to the car like nothing happened. He was all smiles." (Scarpa, *supra*, at p. 22).

23   Ibid., at p. 23; Harmon, *supra*, at p. 66.

24   Harmon, *supra*, at p. 66; Baram, *supra*; Lance, *supra*, at p. 128; Scarpa, *supra*, at p. 23.

25   Harmon, *supra*, at pp. 66-68.

26   Linda Diana will be referred to throughout the remainder of this book as Linda Schiro.

27   Harmon, *supra*, at p. 67.

28   Ibid., at p. 68.

29   Lance, *supra*, at p. 128.

30   Harmon, *supra*, at p. 70.

31   Scarpa, *supra*, at p. 24.

32   Ibid.

33   Harmon, *supra*, at p. 71.

34   Ibid.

35   Scarpa, *supra*, at p. 24; Harmon, *supra*, at p. 72.

36   Harmon, *supra*, at p. 71.

37   Scarpa, *supra*, at p. 23.

38   Ibid.

39   Harmon, *supra*, at p. 12.

40   Ibid. Scarpa's youngest child with Connie, Frank, was not born until 1963 when Gregory Jr. was twelve years old (Ibid., at p. 14); *See* FBI Files, set 1, at p. 1 re: Scarpa's address in 1962 as 43 Marscher Place on Staten Island.

41   Gregory Scarpa Jr., notes, *supra*, at page 6.

42   Later Days Podcast with Joe Poletto, Greg Scarpa Jr. Interview Part 1, Episode 4.

43   Gregory Scarpa Jr., notes, *supra*, at page 3.

44   Ibid., at p. 6.

45   Ibid., at p. 4.

46   Ibid., at p. 3.

47   Later Days Podcast with Joe Poletto, Greg Scarpa Jr. Interview Part 1, Episode 4, *supra*. Scarpa's actions may be reflective of Scarpa's desire to control his son's behavior, or to get a leg up on the competition, or it may simply be reflective of an over-anxious "helicopter" parent trying to help his son succeed.

48   Harmon, *supra*, at p. 27.

49   Later Days Podcast with Joe Poletto, Greg Scarpa Jr. Interview Part 1, Episode 4, *supra*.

50   Ibid.

51   Ibid.; Harmon, *supra*, at p. 31.

52   Harmon, *supra*, at p. 12.

53   Ibid., at p. 10.

54   Ibid., at p. 12.

55   Later Days Podcast with Joe Poletto, Greg Scarpa Jr. Interview Part 1, Episode 4, *supra*.

56   Ibid.

57   Harmon, *supra*, at p. 13.

58   Later Days Podcast with Joe Poletto, Greg Scarpa Jr. Interview Part 1, Episode 4, *supra*.

59   Harmon, *supra*, at p. 15.

60   Later Days Podcast with Joe Poletto, Greg Scarpa Jr. Interview Part 1, Episode 4, *supra*.

61   Lance, *supra*, at p. 64.

62   Ibid.; Harmon, *supra*, at p. 30.

63   Harmon, *supra*, at p. 31.

64   Ibid.

65   Ibid., at pp. 33-34.

66   Later Days Podcast with Joe Poletto, Greg Scarpa Jr. Interview Part 1, Episode 4, *supra*.

67   Scarpa, *supra*, at p. 42. Little Linda was known as Linda Schiro for many years, given who she thought her father was. She now goes by Linda Scarpa.

68   Ibid., at pp. 25 & 28.

69   Ibid., at p. 30.

70   Ibid., at p. 87.

71   Ibid., at p. 91.

72   Ibid., at p. 87.

73   Ibid., at p. 32.

74   Ibid., at p. 33.

75   Ibid., at p. 34.

76   Ibid., at p. 25.

77   Ibid., at p. 216.

78   Ibid., at pp. 86-87.

79   Ibid., at p. 30

80   Harmon, *supra*, at p. 70; Mazza, *supra*, at p. 43.

81   Scarpa, *supra*, at p. 34.

82   Ibid., at p. 86.

83   Ibid., at p. 38.

84   Harmon, *supra*, at p. 92. *See*, however, endnote 31, chapter seven, *infra*, and Larry Mazza's allegation that Linda Schiro had a joint that she offered to Larry the first time she seduced him in Scarpa's home.

85   Scarpa, *supra*, at p. 39.

86   Harmon, *supra*, at p. 92.

87   Scarpa, *supra*, at p. 41.

88   Ibid., at p. 42.

89   Ibid., at p. 43.

90   Ibid., at p. 44.

91   Ibid.

92   Bishop Ford Central Catholic High School closed in 2014 (Spencer, Kyle (April 20, 2014). "A Catholic High School Abruptly Loses its Fight to Stay Open." *The New York Times*.

93   Lance, *supra*, at p. 115.

94   Scarpa, *supra*, at p. 9.

95   The entrance to Prospect Park is about half a mile from where Bishop Ford Central was located.

96   Scarpa, *supra*, at p. 10.

97   Ibid., at p. 11.

98   Ibid.

99   Ibid.

100   Ibid., at p. 12.

101   Harmon, *supra*, at p. 93.

102   Scarpa, *supra*, at p. 12.

103   Lance, *supra*, at p. 115.

104   DeVecchio, *supra*, at p. 176.

105   Mazza, *supra*, at p. 74.

106   Harmon, *supra*, at p. 93.

107   Scarpa, *supra*, at p. 13.

108   Mazza, *supra*, at p. 79; Lance, *supra*, at p. 116; Harmon, *supra*, at p. 93; DeVecchio, *supra*, at p. 176.

109   Mazza, *supra*, at p. 75.

110   Scarpa, *supra*, at p. 13.

111   DeVecchio, *supra*, at p. 176.

112   Lance, *supra*, at p. 116.

113   Mazza, *supra*, at p. 80.

114   Mazza, *supra*, at p. 81.

115   Scarpa, *supra*, at pp. 12-13; Mazza, *supra*, at p. 74; Lance, *supra*, at p. 116; Harmon, *supra*, at p. 93; DeVecchio, *supra*, at p. 176.

116   Scarpa, *supra*, at p. 78.

117   Joseph Scarpa is often referred to in print media and elsewhere as Joey Schiro. He will be referred to as Joseph Scarpa or Joey Scarpa throughout this book.

118   Scarpa, *supra*, at p. 80.

119   FBI Files, set 7, at pp. 30-31.

120   FBI Files, set 5, at p. 149. Peter Lance reproduced most of that set 5 entry, but he omitted the date of the murder, leaving only the date that Scarpa reported the murder, which was one day later. Two pagers earlier, Lance wrote, incorrectly, that Brewster was murdered on September 17, 1987 (Lance, *supra*, at pp. 170 & 172).

121   His sister recalled the event happened when Joey was approximately four years old (Scarpa, *supra*, at p. 25). Harmon wrote that the same event happened when Joey was five years old (Harmon, *supra*, at p. 91).

122   Harmon, *supra*, at p. 91.

123   Scarpa, *supra*, at p. 25; Harmon, *supra*, at p. 91.

124   Scarpa, *supra*, at p. 25.

125   Ibid.

126   Ibid., at p. 29.

127   Ibid.

128   Ibid.

129   Ibid., at p. 37.

130   Ibid., at p. 36.

131   Mazza, *supra*, at p. 360.

132   Scarpa, *supra*, at p. 36.

133   Mazza, *supra*, at p. 69.

134   Harmon, *supra*, at p. 142.

135   Mazza, *supra*, at p. 360.

136   Daly, Michael. (November 1, 2007). "For a Victim's Family, it's the Cruelest Halloween Trick." *New York Daily News*.

137   Ibid. But *see* Harmon, *supra*, at p. 142, Scarpa, *supra*, at p. 83, McGraw, Seamus. (June 16, 2006). "Suspect Extradited to N.Y." *The Forward*; Brick, Michael. (June 6, 2006), and *The New York Times* (November 2, 1989). "Brooklyn Youth Slain after Halloween Fight." *The New York Times*, Section B, page 6, who all reported that the egg fight and Masseria's murder happened on the same night, Halloween, a few hours apart.

138   The New York Times (November 2, 1989). "Brooklyn Youth Slain after Halloween Fight." *The New York Times*, Section B, page 6.

139   In 2006, Craig Sobel was located and arrested in Florida, extradited to New York, and made to stand trial for Masseria's murder (McGraw, *supra*; Brick, Michael. (6 June 2006). "Brooklyn: Fisherman Charged with Murder." *The New York Times*). He was found not guilty (Lance, *supra*, at p. 451).

140   Daly, *supra*; McGraw, *supra*.

141   The New York Times, (November 2, 1989). "Brooklyn Youth Slain after Halloween Fight." The New York Times, Section B, page 6.

142   McGraw, *supra*.

143   Ibid.

144   Lance, *supra*, at p. 477; Scarpa, *supra*, at p. 83.

145   Lance, *supra*, at p. 477.

146   Scarpa, *supra*, at p. 83.

147   Harmon, *supra*, at p. 143.

148   Scarpa, *supra*, at p. 84; Harmon, *supra*, at p. 143.

149   Scarpa, supra, at p. 84; Harmon, *supra*, at p. 143; *People v. Sinagra* (11 June 2007) 2007 NY Slip Op 51180(U) [15 Misc 3d 1146(A)].

150   Harmon, *supra*, at p. 178; Scarpa, *supra*, at p. 181.

151   FBI Files, set 4, at p. 103.

152   Lance, *supra*, at p. xii.

153   "Dream; Lili Dajani." Editorial staff. (September 17, 2021) Tachles, Das jüdische Wochenmagazin 21 Jahrgang, Ausgabe 37.

154   Ibid.

155   Ibid.

156   Harmon, *supra*, at p. 102.

157   "Dream," *supra*.

158   Gregory Scarpa Jr., notes, *supra*, at p. 2.

159   Ibid.

160   Mazza wrote that by March of 1979 he and Linda had been having sex for four months (Mazza, *supra*, at p. 30). Harmon did not specify the year in which the Mazza/Schiro affair began (Harmon, *supra*, at p. 86), nor did Baram (Baram, *supra*}. Lance wrote that their affair began in 1979 (Lance, *supra*, at p. 128).

161 Baram, *supra*; Mazza, *supra*, at pp. 30-33.

162 Harmon, *supra*, at p. 84.

163 Mazza, *supra*, at pp. 33-34.

164 Ibid., at p. 84.

165 MyHeritage. https://www.myheritage.com/names/gregory_scarpa.

166 Lance, *supra*, at pp. 163; Harmon, *supra*, at pp. 104-105.

167 Lance, *supra*, at p. 504.

CHAPTER SIX: MY THREE SONS

1 FBI Files, set 7, at p. 86.

2 Lance, *supra*, at p. 162.

3 Harmon, *supra*, at p. 73.

4 Mazza, *supra*, at p. 165.

5 Harmon, *supra*, at p. 73.

6 Lance, *supra*, at p. 164. The other was Linda Schiro.

7 Scarpa, *supra*, at p. 80.

8 McGuire, *supra*, at p. 193.

9 Harmon, *supra*, at p. 78.

10 Ibid.

11 Lance, supra, at p. 164.

12 Scarpa, *supra*, at p. 35.

13 Harmon, *supra*, at p. 127.

14 Mazza, *supra*, at p. 126.

15 DeVecchio, *supra*, at p. 234.

16 FBI Files, set 8, at p. 22.

17 Harmon, *supra*, at pp. 102-107; Lance, *supra*, at p. 111.

18 *United States v. Sessa* (2d Cir. 1997) 125 F.3d 68, 70.

19 Kroger, *supra*, at p. 135; Lance, *supra*, at p. 114; Mazza, *supra*, at pp. 130-131 & 136-139. Harmon diverged from the other authors claiming that the Longobardi hit was ordered by capo Anthony Scarpati (Harmon, *supra*, at pp. 82-83).

20 DeVecchio, *supra*, at pp. 1-8; Harmon, *supra*, at p. 221; Kroger, *supra*, at p. 135; Lance, *supra*, at pp. 118-121.

21 Harmon, *supra*, at p. 76.

22 Scarpa, *supra*, at p. 35.

23 FBI Files, set 4, at p. 71.

24 FBI Files, set 8, at p. 73. Although the *name* of the informant who gave the FBI that information on January 14, 1972, is redacted, the memo memorializing the exchange identifies the informant as "NY 3461-C-TE." That was Scarpa's TECI designation.

25 FBI Files, set 4, at p. 155.

26 FBI Files, set 4, at p. 139 (emphasis added).

27 Later Days Podcast with Joe Poletto, Greg Scarpa Jr. Interview Part 2, Episode 5.

28   Lance, *supra*, at p. 163.

29   Kroger, *supra*, at p. 136.

30   Harmon, *supra*, at p. 73.

31   Kroger, *supra*, at p. 131.

32   Ibid., at pp. 131-132.

33   FBI Files, set 5, at pp. 9-10.

34   Lance, *supra*, at p. 167.

35   FBI Files, set 4, at p. 204.

36   Coincidentally, an earlier botched burglary of the same bank may have been the motive for Scarpa's murder of Dominick "Donnie" Somma in August of 1980. That murder is alluded to without specificity by DeVecchio at p. 175 of *We're Going to Win this Thing*.

37   Mazza, *supra*, at p. 124.

38   Ibid.

39   Ibid., at p. 127.

40   Ibid.

41   Ibid., at p. 165.

42   Harmon, *supra*, at p. 126.

43   Shifrel, Scott. (October 30, 2007). "Court Hears Inside Story of FBI Agent, Mobster, and his Moll." *New York Daily News*.

44   McGuire, *supra*, at p. 202.

45   Lance, *supra*, at p. 170; DeVecchio, *supra*, at pp. 237-239.

46   DeVecchio, *supra*, at p. 238.

47   Ibid.

48   Harmon, *supra*, at pp. 126-127; McGuire, *supra*, at p. 202. *See* also DeVecchio, *supra*, at p. 238 in which it is alleged Gregory Scarpa Jr. shot Brewster "in the face and chest."

49   Kroger, *supra*, at p. 136.

50   Mazza, *supra*, at p. 165.

51   McGuire, *supra*, at pp. 201-203.

52   Lance, *supra*, at p. 171.

53   DeVecchio, *supra*, at pp. 233-239.

54   Harmon, *supra*, at p. 127.

55   FBI Files, set 5, at p. 149.

56   FBI Files, set 5, at pp. 149 & 151.

57   Coincidentally, the 200th anniversary of the signing of the U.S. Constitution.

58   FBI Files, set 5, at p. 149.

59   *See*, e.g., FBI Files, set 5, at pp.15, 27, 29, 48, 49, 112, 120 & 151.

60   DeVecchio, *supra*, at pp. 233-239.

61   Harmon, *supra*, at p. 125.

62   Ibid.

63   Ibid.

64   Ibid. DeVecchio was indicted on March 30, 2006, for Brewster's murder as well as three others (Lance, *supra*, at p. 441). Trial began on October 10, 2007 (Harmon, *supra*, at p. 236). On November 1, 2007, the case was dismissed mid-trial at the request of Brooklyn Assistant DA Michael Vecchione, who was trying the case, after it was revealed that the state's star witness, Linda Schiro, had given sworn testimony that was purportedly materially inconsistent with a version of events she had provided to veteran reporters Tom Robbins and Jerry Capeci a decade earlier (Brick, Michael and O'Connor, Anahad. (November 1, 2007). "Charges Dropped in F.B.I. Murder Case." *The New York Times*; Lance, *supra*, at pp. 242 & 482-483). That dismissal, as a matter of law, acted as an acquittal for DeVecchio barring prosecution under the U.S. Constitution's double jeopardy prohibition (U.S. Const. amend. V). For a full exposition of the murder allegations of DeVecchio's indictment and trial, the reader is directed to Peter Lance's detailed account in *Deal with the Devil*. DeVecchio's competing view of the accusations and his trial are set forth at length in his book, *We're Going to Win this Thing*.

65   Harmon, *supra*, at pp. 125-126.

66   Lance, *supra*, at p. 171.

67   Ibid.

68   Lance, *supra*, at pp. 172-173.

69   Scarpa, *supra*, at pp. 80-81.

70   McGuire, *supra*, at p. 201 (quoting Carmine Imbriale).

71   Mazza, *supra*, at p. 166.

72   Ibid.

73   McGuire, *supra*, at p. 201.

74   Joe Saponaro was part of Greg Scarpa's crew and was running numbers for him at least as early as 1963 (FBI Files, set 1, at p. 156).

75   DeVecchio, *supra*, at p. 237; McGuire, *supra*, at p. 202.

76   Mazza, *supra*, at p. 166.

77   DeVecchio, *supra*, at p. 236.

78   *United States v. Scarpa* (E.D.N.Y. 1988) 701 F. Supp. 379, 379.

79   *United States v. Scarpa* (E.D.N.Y. Nov. 11, 2020) 94-cr-1119-1 (ERK).

80   FBI Files, set 8, at p. 76.

81   Ibid., at p. 106.

82   Mazza, *supra*, at p. 130.

83   Harmon, *supra*, at p. 106.

84   Harmon stated that in early December in 2006, Gregory admitted to having committed more than twenty-five murders (Harmon, *supra*, at p. 235).

85   In the first racketeering case brought against Scarpa Jr. and several members of his crew, the government originally included an allegation that Peter Crupi was murdered as one of the underlying offenses supporting the racketeering count. However, the government moved to strike that allegation from the indictment before trial (*United States v. Scarpa, et al.* (2d Cir. 1990) 913 F.2d 993, fn. 3). Only Nunzio DeCarlo was convicted on the basis of the remaining murder alleged in that first racketeering case, that of Albert Nocha (*United States v. Scarpa, et al.* (2d Cir. 1990) 913 F.2d 993, 998). In a second racketeering case, Gregory Scarpa Jr. was

alleged to have participated in more than ten murders. He was convicted in late 1998 in that case of having conspired to commit four of those murders. (*United States v. Scarpa* (2d Cir. 2017) No. 16-303, at p. 5). In addition, Gregory has admitted killing Dr. Eliezer Shkolnik (Harmon, *supra*, at pp. 104-105). Finally, Larry Mazza alleged in some detail Gregory's retelling hours later of how he killed Jose Guzman (Mazza, *supra*, at p. 80), a story corroborated in part by Carmine Sessa (Lance, *supra*, at p. 116). Neither the Shkolnik murder nor the Guzman murder was alleged in either of the racketeering cases brought by the federal government against Scarpa Jr.

86   Raab, Selwyn. (November 20, 1994). "The Mobster Was a Mole for the FBI; Tangled Life of a Mafia Figure Who Died of AIDS is Exposed." *The New York Times*.

87   Kroger, *supra*, at p. 128.

88   Harmon, *supra*, at pp. 78-79.

89   Ibid., at pp. 79-80.

90   Ibid., at p. 80.

91   According to Linda Scarpa, Greg Scarpa Sr. told her that Lillian was Gregory's favorite wife of his three wives (Scarpa, *supra*, at p. 221).

92   Ibid., at pp. 80-82 & 110-114.

93   Harmon, *supra*, at p. 103.

94   Ibid.

95   Lance, *supra*, at p. 111.

96   Harmon quoted Gregory Jr. as alleging that DeVecchio provided Shkolnik's address to Scarpa to facilitate the hit (Harmon, *supra*, at p. 104). Gregory Scarpa Jr. has also

alleged that DeVecchio provided a picture of Shkolnik, since "nobody knew what the Dr. looked like," and the doctor's schedule. (Notes provided to the author by Gregory Scarpa Jr. on July 12, 2023). Lance, citing the work of Jerry Capeci, alleged that Gregory Jr. was willing to testify that DeVecchio had tipped off Scarpa to Shkolnik's cooperation with an IRS investigation into Scarpa (Lance, *supra*, at pp. 110-111). It is worth noting that DeVecchio was never charged in connection with the Shkolnik murder. The allegations that DeVecchio provided Scarpa with Shkolnik's address, photo, and schedule strike this author as questionable. It seems reasonable to assume that Dajani, who had had a romantic relationship and a years-long business partnership with Shkolnik, would have had a picture of him and known his address. In the alternative, the Genovese goodfellow who was a friend of Shkolnik's would have had his address. And either or both of them could have at least furnished a description of Shkolnik. Furthermore, Scarpa had been reopened less than six months earlier by DeVecchio and the FBI's New York Office (FBI Files, set 4, at pp. 243-245). While the relationship that Scarpa and DeVecchio eventually established lends credibility to allegations about DeVecchio's later behavior, particularly during the war between the Orena and Persico factions of the Colombo family, it seems unlikely that six months in, DeVecchio would already be providing Scarpa with information that might prove fatal to a citizen not otherwise associated with organized crime. The allegations also beg the question, "Why would Scarpa, so early in their relationship, turn to an FBI agent for assistance in carrying out a murder?" However, if Gregory Jr.'s allegation, as related to Peter Lance, that Scarpa "had been associating with DeVecchio since at least the mid-1970s—years before reopening hm" (Lance, *supra*, at p. 499) is true, then by 1980 DeVecchio would have conceivably been close enough to Scarpa to provide him with Shkolnik's address. Gregory's allegation raises an additional question. Why would an ambitious special agent, as undoubtedly DeVecchio was, wait five years to reopen such a valuable Top Echelon Criminal Informant? As Lance noted, "There is little doubt that tying his star to Scarpa helped DeVecchio's career take off" (Lance, *supra*, at p. 106). It seems unlikely that it would have taken DeVecchio five years to come to that conclusion. Readers will have to satisfy themselves on these points, one way or the other, as they will likely never be definitively resolved.

97   Lance, *supra*, at p. 111.

98   Harmon, *supra*, at p. 106.

99   Ibid., at p. 82.

100   Kroger, *supra*, at p. 135.

101   Lance, *supra*, at p. 114.

102   Mazza, *supra*, at p. 130.

103   Harmon, *supra*, at pp. 82-83; *See* also Lance, *supra*, at p. 114.

104   Kroger, *supra*, at p. 135.

105   Mazza, *supra*, at p. 130.

106   Ibid., at p. 131.

107   Ibid. (capitalization in the original).

108   *United States v. Sessa* (2d Cir. 1997) 125 F.3d 68, 70. Gregory, however, was not convicted of that murder. Lance named Scarpa Sr. as the shooter (Lance, *supra*, at p. 114), and Kroger claimed there were two shooters, Scarpa Sr. and Joe Brewster (Kroger, *supra*, at p. 135). Gregory's involvement in the murder, which would support criminal

liability if proven, was limited to being "the getaway driver" (Mazza, *supra*, at p. 138).

109   Lance, *supra*, at p. 114.

110   Ibid.; Kroger, *supra*, at p. 135.

111   Harmon, *supra*, at p. 221; Scarpa, *supra*, at p. 80.

112   Lance, *supra*, at pp. 118-119.

113   Lance, *supra*, at p. 123 (quoting the testimony of NYPD Detective Tommy Dades).

114   Later Days Podcast with Joe Poletto, Larry Mazza – Greg Scarpa Sr., Episode 5

115   Harmon, *supra*, at p. 221.

116   Krogcr, *supra*, at p. 135.

117   Lance, *supra*, at p. 120 (quoting the testimony of Carmine Sessa); DeVecchio, *supra*, at p. 5.

118   Salvatore Sammy The Bull Gravano. "Greg Scarpa Sr Shot Her Right After She Gave Him a Hug." YouTube.

119   DeVecchio, *supra* at p. 5.

120   DeVecchio, *supra*, at pp. 5-6. Frankly, the better part of DeVecchio's account of the Bari murder and the moments leading up to it are fantasy not to be taken seriously.

121   Scarpa, *supra*, at p. 79; Lance *supra*, at p. 120.

122   Lance, *supra*, at p. 120 (quoting the testimony of Linda Schiro).

123   Lance, *supra*, at p. 123 (quoting the testimony of NYPD Detective Tommy Dades).

124   Tommy Dades and Larry Mazza were boyhood friends who, according to Dades, met at Louis Neglia's gym when Dades was twelve years old (Mazza, *supra*, at pp. 26-27).

125   Lance, *supra*, at pp. 122-123.

126   The New York Times. (September 18, 1989). "Alphonse Persico, 61, is Dead; Leader of Colombo Crime Family." *The New York Times*, Section B, page 8.

127   Harmon, *supra*, at p. 221; Lance, *supra*, at p. 119; DeVecchio, *supra*, at p. 1.

128   Lance, *supra*, at pp. 119-120. Linda Scarpa claimed the murder took place at the Wimpy Boys Club (Scarpa, *supra*, at p. 80).

129   Lance, *supra*, at p. 119-120.

130   Lance, *supra*, at p. 120; Kroger, *supra*, at p. 135; DeVecchio, *supra*, at p. 1.

131   DeVecchio, *supra*, at p. 7; Lance, *supra*, at p. 120.

132   Lance, *supra*, at p. 120.

133   Bet-David, Patrick. *Valuetainment*, Former Mafia Hitman Opens up About Dark Side of Greg Scarpa & His 20 Hits, YouTube.

134   *United States v. Sessa* (2d Cir. 1997) 125 F.3d 68, 70.

135   McGuire, citing a Jerry Capeci New York Sun article from February 16, 2006, entitled "From 'Drop-Dead Gorgeous' to DOA," claimed that Carmine Sessa shot Bari. However, that article states, "'When [Bari] arrived, Scarpa Jr. grabbed her, and forced her to the floor, where Scarpa Sr. shot and killed her, Sessa told FBI agents....'" (emphasis added).

136   Lance, *supra*, at p. 121 (quoting the testimony of Larry Mazza).

137   DeVecchio, *supra*, at p. 8.

138   Lance, *supra*, at p. 121 (quoting the testimony of Carmine Sessa).

139   Kroger, *supra*, at p. 135; Capeci (February 16, 2006). "From 'Drop-Dead Gorgeous' to DOA," *supra*.

140   Lance, *supra*, at p. 121.

141   Ibid.

142   Lance, *supra*, at p. 119

143   Ibid., at p. 123.

144   FBI Files, set 1, at p. 124.

145   FBI Files, set 4, at p. 7.

146   FBI Files, set 4, at p. 189 (capitalization in the original).

147   FBI Files, set 4, at p. 221.

148   FBI Files, set 5, at p. 4.

149   Ibid., at p. 17.

150   FBI Files, set 6, at p. 10.

151   Harmon, *supra*, at pp. 111-112.

152   Mazza, *supra*, at pp. 129-130.

153   *United States. v. Gregory Scarpa Jr., et al.* (2d Cir. 1990) 913 F.2d 993, 999 (footnote omitted).

154   Kroger, *supra*, at p. 144.

155   Ibid.

156   "The indictment in this case was initially filed on November 24, 1987. Superseding indictments were filed on December 23, 1987, and January 27, 1988" (*United States v. Scarpa* (E.D.N.Y. 1988) 691 F. Supp. 635, 636.

157   McFadden, Robert D. (November 13, 1987). "8 Charged With Mafia Drug Plot, Including Murders and Extortion." *The New York Times*.

158   *United States. v. Gregory Scarpa Jr., et al.*, *supra*, 913 F.2d 993, 997-998 (affirming defendants' convictions).

159   Kroger, *supra*, at p. 144.

160   Mazza, *supra*, at p. 181. Mazza's speculation strikes this author as tinged with sarcasm.

161   Scarpa, *supra*, at p. 76.

162   Lance, *supra*, at p. 144.

163   Harmon, *supra*, at p. 128.

164   Ibid., at p. 130; *See* also Lance, *supra*, at p. 142.

165   DeVecchio, *supra*, at pp. 369-370.

166   Harmon, *supra*, at p. 131.

167   *United States v. Scarpa* (E.D.N.Y. 1988) 701 F. Supp. 379, 380.

168   FBI Files, set 5, at p. 152.

169   *United States v. Scarpa* (E.D.N.Y. 1988) 701 F. Supp. 379, 380.

170   That conversation was eventually the subject of an unsuccessful motion to suppress its introduction in evidence. (Ibid.).

171   *United States v. Scarpa* (2d Cir. 2017) No. 16-303, at p. 4.

172   Ibid., at pp. 4-5.

173   Ibid., at p. 2.

174   Harmon, *supra*, at p. 135.

175   Ibid., at p. 136.

176   Ibid.

177   Lance, *supra*, at p. 435.

178   Later Days Podcast with Joe Poletto, Greg Scarpa Jr. Interview Part 1, Episode 4.

179   Lance, *supra*, at p. 503.

180   Scarpa Jr. publicly renounced the Mafia life during his second racketeering trial. "'I'm washing my hands of everything,' he testified. 'I don't want to do nothing with nothing. I don't want to know nobody'" (Lance, *supra*, at p. 435 (quoting the testimony of Gregory Scarpa Jr.)).

181   Lance, *supra*, at p. 504.

182   Capeci, Jerry and Siemaszko, Corky. (March 21, 1995). "Mob Son Iced in B'klyn." *New York Daily News*; Associated Press. (June 6, 1998). "METRO NEWS BRIEFS: NEW YORK: 4 Men Are Indicted in March 1995 Murder." *The New York Times*; *People v. Sinagra* (11 June 2007) 2007 NY Slip Op 51180(U) [15 Misc 3d 1146(A)] Supreme Court, Kings County Reichbach, J. According to Lin DeVecchio, NYPD Detective Tommy Dades handled

the case against Joey Scarpa's killers (DeVecchio, *supra*, at p. 431).

183   Capeci and Siemaszko, *supra*.

184   Harmon, *supra*, at p. 141.

185   Scarpa, *supra*, at p. 38.

186   Harmon, *supra*, at p. 141.

187   Scarpa, *supra*, at p. 171.

188   Ibid., at p. 195.

189   Mazza, *supra*, at p. 185.

190   Scarpa, *supra*, at p. 227.

191   Mazza, *supra*, at p. 360.

192   Ibid.

193   Ibid. at p. 185.

194   Ibid., at p. 439.

195   The allegations are, therefore, classic hearsay which do not fit under any of the hearsay rule's exceptions, and, as a matter of law, are inadmissible at trial.

196   In this case, "Little Vic" refers to Vic Orena Sr. *See, e.g., United States v. Orena* (2d Cir. 1994) 32 F.3d 704). Given the naming habits of those in Orena's line of work, one would expect that "Little Vic" would refer to his son Vic Orena Jr. That, however, is not the case. In this instance, the appellation "Little Vic" is due to Vic Orena Sr.'s short stature.

197   Tabor, Mary B. W. (April 2, 1992). "Man Accused as Colombo Chief is Held in Slaying of Ex-Member." *The New York Times*.

198   *Orena v. United States* (E.D.N.Y. 1997) 956 F. Supp. 1071, 1078.

199   Ibid., at p. 1082.

200   Lance, *supra*, at pp. 226 & 236-237,

201   *See*, e.g., *Orena v. United States* (E.D.N.Y. 1997) 956 F. Supp. 1071, 1109. It may go without saying that simply because a judge finds an allegation unconvincing, or a rule of evidence precludes a jury or judge from considering it due to its legal incompetence does not necessarily mean that the allegation is not truthful. In the same sense, a "not guilty" verdict does not equal a finding of innocence.

202   DeVecchio, *supra*, at p. 357.

203   Harmon, *supra*, at p. 206.

204   *Orena v. United States* (E.D.N.Y. 1997) 956 F. Supp. 1071, 1083.

205   Tabor, Mary B. W. (April 2, 1992). "Man Accused as Colombo Chief is Held in Slaying of Ex-Member." *The New York Times*.

206   Ibid.

207   *Orena v. United States, supra*, at p. 1082.

208   Scarpa, *supra*, at p. 153.

209   Ibid.

210   Lance, *supra*, at p. 327; Scarpa, *supra*, at p. 153.

211   Harmon, *supra*, at p. 161.

212   Scarpa, *supra*, at p. 153.

213   Ibid.

214   Harmon, *supra*, at p. 161; Lance, *supra*, at p. 327. For a visual tour of the Brooklyn streets on which the hunt and shootout occurred, readers are directed to Mooney Dash Cam. (September 4, 2021). "Greg Scarpa Colombo Hitman: Gets Sons Friend Killed and Eye Shot Out While on House arrest" [Video]. YouTube.

215   Scarpa, *supra*, at p. 154.

216   Harmon, *supra*, at p. 161; Lance, *supra*, at p. 327.

217   Scarpa, *supra*, at pp. 163-164.

218   Raab, Selwyn. (December 30, 1992). "Top Member of Colombo Crime Family Is Ambushed in Brooklyn." *The New York Times*.

219   Lance, *supra*, at p. 328.

220   Scarpa, *supra*, at p. 161.

221   Capeci, Jerry. (September 10, 1999). "Capo's son gets 6 yrs. in plea deal." *New York Daily News*.

CHAPTER SEVEN: THE MAZZA, SCHIRO, SCARPA TRIANGLE

1   *Berkman v. City of New York* (E.D.N.Y. 1982) 536 F. Supp. 177, 216.

2   Mazza, *supra*, at p. 19.

3   Ibid., at pp. 165 & 230.

4   Ibid., at p. 20.

5   Ibid.

6   Ibid., at p. 21.

7   Ibid., at p. 25.

8   Ibid., at pp. 26-27.

9   Ibid., at pp. 26-28.

10   Ibid., at p. 24.

11   Duffy, Peter. (January 20, 2009). "Banned Sport Gains Fans, and Seeks More in Albany." *The New York Times*.

12   Mazza, *supra*, at p. 24

13   Ibid., at pp. 27-28.

14   Ibid., at p. 28.

15   Ibid.

16   Ibid.

17   Bet-David, Patrick. *Valuetainment*, *supra*.

18   Mazza, *supra*, at p. 34.

19   Fried, Joseph. (March 6, 1982). "Women Win Ruling on Fire Dept. Test." *The New York Times*.

20   *Berkman v. City of New York, supra*, at p. 200.

21   Ibid.

22   Ibid.; Fried, Joseph. "Women Win Ruling on Fire Dept. Test," *supra*.

23   Mazza, *supra*, at p. 34.

24   Ibid.

25   Mazza, *supra*, at p. 29.

26   Ibid.

27   Lance, *supra*, at p. 128.

28   Baram, *supra* (quoting testimony of Linda Schiro);
Lance, *supra*, at p. 129 (quoting testimony of Linda Schiro);
See, also, Mazza, *supra*, at p. 33. To the contrary, Harmon
wrote that "Greg Sr. initially disliked the idea" (Harmon,
supra at p. 86).

29   Mazza, *supra*, at p. 31.

30   Ibid.

31   Ibid. He did, however, appreciate the "little candy dish
with M&Ms and peanuts for [them] to snack on" (Ibid.).

32   Ibid., at p. 33.

33   Ibid., at p. 31.

34   Scarpa, *supra*, at p. 24; Harmon, *supra*, at p. 72;
Lance, *supra*, at p. 128.

35   *See* chapter two, endnotes 93-95, and accompanying
text, *supra*, for a brief overview of why the designation of
common-law husband and wife, often used to describe the
relationship between Grego Scarpa and Linda Schiro is
inapposite as a matter of law.

36   Mazza, *supra*, at p. 33.

37   Ibid., at p. 34.

38   Ibid., at p. 35.

39   Ibid. (italics in the original).

40   Harmon, without the benefit of attribution, places this meeting at Romano's, another Brooklyn restaurant particularly popular with Scarpa and his crew (Harmon, *supra*, at p. 87).

41   Mazza, *supra*, at pp. 35-36.

42   According to Lance, the name of the company was "Hewlett Supply, a legitimate fire-extinguisher company [Scarpa] reportedly controlled…" (Lance, *supra*, at p. 130).

43   Mazza, *supra*, at p. 36.

44   Ibid., at p. 36.

45   Ibid. (quoting Lawrence Mazza Sr.).

46   Ibid., at p. 37 (quoting Joan Mazza).

47   Ibid.

48   Ibid. (quoting Lawrence Mazza Sr.).

49   Mazza, *supra*, at p. 42. Harmon, again without the benefit of attribution, claimed that Mazza "lasted only a few weeks in the [sales] job. He was a restless kid, uncomfortable behind a desk or making sales calls" (Harmon, *supra*, at p. 88). The two main sources for the personal information in Harmon's book *Mafia Son, A Mafia Family, The FBI and a Story of Betrayal*, based on the book's Preface, appear to be Linda Schiro and Gregory Scarpa Jr. (Harmon, *supra*, at pp. xi-xv). Nothing in the book's Preface, Postscript, or Acknowledgements indicates otherwise (Ibid. & at pp. 250-256). The book is not annotated; it is therefore difficult to credit its uncorroborated accounts of events that are directly disputed by first-hand witnesses in other sources.

50   Bet-David, Patrick. *Valuetainment*, *supra*. In that interview, Mazza speculated that the fire resulted in a large insurance payout to Scarpa (Ibid.).

51   Mazza, *supra*, at p. 42.

52   Ibid., at p. 43.

53   Bet-David, Patrick. *Valuetainment*, *supra*; Mazza, *supra*, at p. 58.

54   Mazza, *supra*, at p. 44.

55   Vlad, D.J. (Vladimir Lyubovny). (January 18, 2021). "Larry Mazza on Him & Grim Reaper Doing Over 20 Mafia Hits (Full Interview)." VladTV.

56   Mazza, *supra*., at p. 44. Lance, *supra*, at p. 131.

57   Ibid.

58   Phone interview with Larry Mazza on 7/26/23. Mazza took the admonition to heart. The next time he went to the beach before work he wore long pants (Ibid.).

59   Vlad, DJ (Vladimir Lyubovny). (January 18, 2021). "Larry Mazza on Him & Grim Reaper Doing Over 20 Mafia Hits (Full Interview)." VladTV.

60   Lance, *supra*, at p. 130.

61   Scarpa would, at times, have a crew member hiding in the office's closet ready to come out and shoot whoever was in the chair on Scarpa's signal (Ibid.).

62   Mazza, *supra*, at p. 84 (ellipsis in the original).

63   Ibid.

64   Ibid. (ellipsis in the original); Bet-David, Patrick. *Valuetainment*, *supra*; Vlad, D.J. (Vladimir Lyubovny).

(January 18, 2021). "Larry Mazza on Him & Grim Reaper Doing Over 20 Mafia Hits (Full Interview)." VladTV.

65   Bet-David, Patrick. *Valuetainment, supra*; Mazza, *supra*, at p. 5. DeVecchio, *supra*, at pp. 181-182. Harmon's version of the conversation differs in the particulars of when and where it happened. However, it tracks the overall tenor of Mazza's version. "I know about you and Linda, and it's okay. Really, it's okay. See, whatever makes Linda happy, makes me happy" (Harmon, *supra*, at p. 88).

66   Phone interview with Melanie M. Dyer, MA, LPC on November 11, 2023.

67   Mazza, *supra*, at p. 31.

68   Bet-David, Patrick. *Valuetainment, supra*; Mazza, *supra*, at p. 43.

69   Mazza, *supra*, at p. 43.

70   Bet-David, Patrick. *Valuetainment, supra*; Mazza, *supra*, at p. 43.

71   Mazza, *supra*, at p. 82.

72   Ibid.

73   Ibid., at pp. 114-115.

74   Ibid., at p. 42.

75   Ibid., at p. 53.

76   Ibid., at p. 134.

77   Ibid.

78   Ibid., at pp. 167-168 & p. 230.

79   Ibid., at pp. 216-217.

80   Ibid., at p. 168.

81   Ibid., at p. 74.

82   Ibid., at p. 172.

83   Ibid., at p. 168.

84   Scarpa, *supra*, at p. 39.

85   Harmon, *supra*, at p. 162; Mazza, *supra*, at pp. 370-371; Scarpa, *supra*, at p. 157.

86   Mazza, *supra*, at pp. 422-424; Lance, *supra*, at pp. 354-356; DeVecchio, *supra*, at p. 367.

87   Mazza, *supra*, at p. 26.

88   Ibid., at p. 22.

89   Ibid.

90   Ibid.

91   Ibid., at p. 20.

92   Ibid., at p. 27.

93   Lance, *supra*, at p. 128; Harmon, *supra*, at p. 56.

94   Lance, *supra*, at p. 127; Baram, *supra*.

95   FBI Files, set 7, at pp. 28-29 & 67-68.

96   Cook, *supra*.

97   *United States v. Sessa* (2d Cir. 1997) 125 F.3d 68, 70.

98   Bet-David, Patrick. *Valuetainment, supra*; Later Days Podcast with Joe Poletto. "Larry Mazza - Greg Scarpa Sr. and Relationship with Greg, Episode 4."

99   Later Days Podcast with Joe Poletto. "Larry Mazza - Greg Scarpa Sr. and Relationship with Greg, Episode 4."

100   Bet-David, Patrick. *Valuetainment, supra.*

101   Lance, *supra*, at pp. 106-108.

102   *United States v. Bellomo, et al.* (2d Cir. 1999) 176 F.3d 580, 587; Lance, *supra*, at p. 107. Scarpa reported to the FBI on August 26, 1980, that the hit on Somma was ordered by Carmine Persico, not his brother, Allie Boy Persico. Not surprisingly, Scarpa makes no mention of who killed Somma (FBI Files, set 4, at p. 248). It is possible, of course, that Scarpa told his handler, Lin DeVecchio, that he killed Somma and that DeVecchio purposely omitted that information from his report. However, that strikes this author as unlikely.

103   Lance, *supra*, at p. 107.

104   Lance, *supra*, at p. 108; LCN Bios. (May 12, 2022). "Bio of Dominic [sic] Somma." Although Lance's account and the LCN Bios account refer to the landfill as the "Arthur Kill" landfill, its official name was the Fresh Kills Landfill (New York City Department of Parks and Recreation. "Freshkills Park").

105   Harmon, *supra* at p. 117.

106   Harmon's source for the details of Somma's murder appears to have been Gregory Jr. (Harmon, *supra*, at pp. 116-118). *See*, also, chapter seven, endnote 51, *supra*.

107   Harmon, *supra*, at p. 117.

108   Ibid. This author is unaware of any such conviction or sentence of probation for credit card fraud by Scarpa Sr. in 1980. Scarpa was arrested on November 5, 1985, by the Secret Service after he was indicted for alleged credit card

fraud (FBI Files, set 5, at pp. 92-101). In February of 1987, he pleaded guilty to one count of credit card fraud and was sentenced by Judge Glasser in Federal District Court to probation for five years and fined $10,000 (FBI Files, set 5, at p. 139). Harmon may have incorrectly conflated two events which occurred six and one-half years apart.

109   Harmon, *supra*, at p. 118.

110   Ibid.

111   DeVecchio, *supra*, at p. 175.

112   FBI Files, set 4, at p. 248.

113   Ibid.

114   Bet-David, Patrick. *Valuetainment*, *supra*; Mazza, *supra*, at p. 43.

115   Scarpa and Dajani were divorced in 1983 (MyHeritage. https://www.myheritage.com/names/gregory_scarpa).

116   Baram, supra; Harmon, *supra*, at p. 64.

117   Bet-David, Patrick. *Valuetainment*, *supra*.

118   Mazza, *supra*, at p. 32.

119   Ibid., at p. 138.

120   Anzalone, Grace. (Spring 2013). "Identity, Therapy, and Womanhood: Humanity in the Mafia." NYU Applied Psychology OPUS.

121   Baram, *supra*.

122   Mazza, *supra*, at p. 81.

123   Scarpa, *supra* at p. 80.

124   Mazza, *supra*, at p. 103.

125   Harmon, *supra*, at p. 55.

126   Scarpa, *supra*, at p. 69; Harmon, *supra*, at p. 58.

127   Scarpa, *supra*, at p. 75.

128   Ibid., at p. 67.

129   Anzalone, *supra*.

130   Scarpa, *supra*, at p. 19.

131   Ibid., at p. 22.

132   Baram, *supra*.

133   Scarpa, *supra*, at p. 21.

134   Harmon, *supra*, at p. 85.

135   Ibid., at p. 70.

136   Ibid., at p. 84.

137   Mazza, *supra*, at p. 41.

138   Dunleavy, "I Loved a 'Cute' Killer," *supra*.

139   Lance, *supra*, at p. 128.

140   Dunleavy, "I Loved a 'Cute' Killer," *supra*.

141   Lance, *supra*, at p. 370.

142   Harmon's idyllic description, if accurate, must be referring to non-school days.

143   Harmon, *supra*, at p. 85.

144   Bet-David, Patrick. *Valuetainment, supra*; Harmon, *supra*, at p. 70; Mazza, *supra*, at p. 43.

145   Mazza, *supra*, at p. 43.

146   Ibid.

147   Gregory Scarpa Jr., notes, *supra*, at p. 2.

148   Ibid.

149   Mazza, *supra*, at p. 43.

150   Harmon, *supra*, at p. 103

151   Bruno, Anthony. "Married to the Mob: Mafia Wives and Mistresses."

152   Lance, *supra*, at p. 128 (quoting Linda Schiro).

153   It is this author's view that Scarpa and Schiro may have conspired to bring Mazza into Scarpa's crew and that was the initial motivation for Schiro's seduction of Mazza. DeVecchio wrote, without attribution, that "Linda personally recruited Larry Mazza into Scarpa's crew" (DeVecchio, *supra* at p. 181). When asked about the possibility that Schiro and Scarpa conspired to bring him on board from the time Linda first noticed him, Mazza responded that perhaps later on, after his relationship with Schiro was underway, Scarpa and Schiro may have viewed Mazza through that lens, but not initially (Phone interview with Larry Mazza, *supra*.). Since no physical evidence or first-hand testimony has been uncovered to support the view that Scarpa and Schiro conspired before Schiro's seduction of Mazza, that theory is properly relegated to this endnote.

154   *See* e.g., Mazza, *supra*, at pp. 39-41, 54-56, 62, 64, 82-83 & 114-115.

155   Lance, *supra*, at p. 129 (quoting Linda Schiro).

156   Mazza, *supra*, at p. 35.

157   Ibid., at pp. 42. *See*, also, ibid. at pp. 56 & 64. Harmon, who dismissed the relationship between Mazza

and Schiro as nothing more than a "nice diversion in the bedroom" from Schiro's point of view, wrote that Schiro told Scarpa about Mazza's suggestion that he and Linda run away together. "Scarpa merely laughed. He knew Linda would never leave him—and certainly not for a lightweight like Larry Mazza" (Harmon, *supra*, at p. 90). Harmon also paints a markedly different picture of the early sexual escapades of Schiro and Mazza, generally placing Scarpa as listening to the two of them having sex from the next room and/or receiving detailed reports from Schiro about sex with Mazza as a bit of foreplay to their own lovemaking afterwards (Ibid., at pp. 86-87). It may go without saying that Harmon's second-hand narrative differs substantially from Larry Mazza's recollection.

158   Mazza, *supra*, at pp. 113-114.

159   Ibid., at p. 90.

160   Ibid., at p. 153.

161   Dunleavy, Steve. (October 31, 2007). "She's Paying the Price for a Lifetime of Vice." *New York Post*.

162   Mazza, *supra*, at pp. 41 & 113.

163   Ibid., at p. 138.

164   HIV.gov. "A Timeline of HIV and AIDS."

165   Ibid.

166   Onion, Amanda, et al. (Eds.). (June 14, 2021). "AIDS Crisis Timeline."

167   Ibid.

168   Indeed, it would be another three years before Princess Diana's world-famous, stigma-breaking hug of a young AIDS patient in a Harlem hospital (Goldman, John.

"7-Year-Old AIDS Patient Shares Hug with Princess" *Los Angeles Times*).

169   Vlad, D.J. (Vladimir Lyubovny). (January 18, 2021). "Larry Mazza on Him & Grim Reaper Doing Over 20 Mafia Hits (Full Interview)." VladTV.

170   Ibid.

171   Harmon, *supra*, at p. 119.

172   DeVecchio, *supra*, at p. 180.

173   Lance, *supra*, at p. 189 (quoting testimony of Gregory Scarpa Sr.).

174   Lance, *supra*, at p. 189.

175   Gregory Scarpa Jr., notes, at page 5.

176   Capeci and Robbins. (August 16, 1992). "Blood's Hounding Mobster." *New York Daily News*.

177   Lance, *supra*, at p. 190.

178   Ibid.; Mazza, *supra*, at p. 172.

179   Mazza, *supra*, at p. 172.

180   Harmon, *supra*, at p. 119.

181   Scarpa, *supra*, at p. 97.

182   Mazza, *supra*, at p. 175.

183   Scarpa, *supra*, at p. 97; Lance, *supra*, at p. 190.

184   DeVecchio, *supra*, at p. 180; Harmon, *supra*, at p. 120; Lance, *supra*, at p. 190; Mazza, *supra*, at p. 175.

185   Dannen, *supra*.

186   Vlad, DJ (Vladimir Lyubovny). (January 18, 2021). "Larry Mazza on Him & Grim Reaper Doing Over 20 Mafia Hits (Full Interview)." VladTV.

187   Harmon, *supra*, at p. 119.

188   Scarpa, *supra*, at p. 97.

189   Lance, *supra*, at p. 190 (quoting testimony of Gregory Scarpa Sr.)

190   DeVecchio, *supra*, at p. 180.

191   Lance, *supra*, at p. 191.

192   Harmon, *supra*, at p. 120.

193   Capeci and Robbins. "Blood's Hounding Mobster," *supra*.

194   Ibid.; Scarpa, *supra*, at p. 98; Lance, *supra*, at p. 191; Harmon, *supra*, at p. 121; DeVecchio, *supra*, at p. 180; Tabor, Mary B.W. (August 30, 1992) "Settlement in Lawsuit on H.I.V.-Tainted Blood." *The New York Times*.

195   Lance, *supra*, at p. 191; Harmon, *supra*, at p. 121.

196   Mazza, *supra*, at p. 176.

CHAPTER EIGHT: A GRIM HARVEST

1   Sampson, Robert J., Ph.D. (June 1986). "The Contribution of Homicide to the Decline of American Cities," at p. 563.

2   Zimring, Franklin E. (2011). "The City that Became Safe: New York and the Future of Crime Control," at p. 3.

3   Celona, Larry and Golding, Bruce. (December 13, 2017). "The reign of terror when murder was king of New York in the '80s and '90s." *New York Post.*

4   James, George. (April 23, 1991). "New York Killings Set a Record, While Other Crimes Fell in 1990." *The New York Times.*

5   Altheimer, I., D'Angelo, A., Rodriguez, L. (2023). "2022 Homicide Statistics for 24 U.S. Cities," at p. 3.

6   Celona and Golding, *supra.*

7   Chapter eight focuses on 1980 through 1987, while chapter ten will review the murders Scarpa was responsible for during the third Colombo war in the early 1990s.

8   FBI Files, set 4, at p. 238.

9   Ibid., at pp. 239-240 (capitalization in the original).

10   Lance, *supra*, at p. 88.

11   DeVecchio, *supra*, at p. 153.

12   FBI Files, set 4, at pp. 244-245.

13   DeVecchio, *supra*, at p. 153.

14   Ibid., at pp. 153-155.

15   Ibid., at pp. 155-156.

16   FBI Files, set 4, at p. 248.

17   For a more detailed discussion of the Somma murder, *see* chapter seven, endnotes 102-118, and accompanying text, *supra.*

18   FBI Files, set 6, at pp. 36-37.

19   FBI Files, set 4, at p. 247.

20   McGuire, *supra*, at p. 131.

21   Ibid.

22   DeVecchio, *supra*, at p. 175.

23   On May 6, 1993, in open court in front of Judge Jack Weinstein, Scarpa admitted his role in the murders of Fusaro, Grancio, and Lampasi (Lance, *supra*, at p. 348) after which he entered a guilty plea (Harmon, *supra*, at p. 164; DeVecchio, *supra*, at p. 362; Scarpa, *supra*, at p. 169).

24   FBI Files, set 5, at p. 4.

25   Ibid., at p. 2.

26   Ibid., at pp. 6-24.

27   Ibid., at p. 15.

28   Ibid., at pp. 13-14.

29   Ibid., at p. 17.

30   Lance and Kroger both spelled Robert "Bucky" DiLeonardo's last name as ending in an "i" rather than an "o," the same spelling used by the U.S. Court of Appeals for the Second Circuit in *United States v. Sessa* (2d Cir. 1997) 125 F.3d 68, 70. Carmine Imbriale spelled his brother-in-law's last name as DiLeonardo. Bucky's brother, Michael "Mikey Scars," who is still alive as of this writing, also spells his last name as DiLeonardo. Conceding that Imbriale and Mikey Scars would likely have been in the best position to know how their close relative's last name was spelled, this author has decided to use their version of Bucky's last name—DiLeonardo—rather than that which appears in Lance's book, Kroger's book, or the Second Circuit's opinion, throughout this book.

31   Lance, *supra*, at p. 165.

32   Lance, *supra*, chapter 16, endnotes 15 & 17.

33   Lance, *supra*, at p. 165; Koger, *supra*, at pp. 134-135.

34   Kroger, *supra*, at p. 134.

35   *United States v. Sessa* (2d Cir. 1997) 125 F.3d 68, 70.

36   Mitchell, Chris. "The Killing of Murder." *New York Magazine.*

37   Buder, Leonard. (March 11, 1983). "New York Police Say Crime Fell 5.1% in '82; How the Precincts Tally, page B3." *The New York Times.*

38   FBI Files, set 5, at pp. 53-54.

39   Ibid., at pp. 26-27.

40   Ibid., at p. 27.

41   Ibid., at pp. 27-28.

42   Ibid., at pp. 29-30, 31.

43   Ibid., at pp. 32-33.

44   Ibid., at p. 48.

45   Ibid., at p. 49.

46   Lance, *supra*, at p. 114. For a lively and informative take on life as a Brooklyn Mafia associate, *see* McGuire, Craig and Imbriale, Carmine, *supra*.

47   New York City Police Department, Office of Management Analysis and Planning, Crime Analysis Unit. (1983), Table 103, at p. 117.

48   Although DeVecchio became the supervisor of the New York Office's Bonanno Family squad during the summer of 1983, he was allowed to continue handling his Top Echelon

Criminal Informants, including Scarpa (DeVecchio, *supra*, at p. 207).

49   FBI Files, set 5 at pp. 60-77.

50   Ibid., at pp. 73-74.

51   Carmine Sessa earned his button in March of 1987 (Lance, *supra*, at p. 244).

52   Lance, *supra*, at pp. 117 & 246; Kroger, *supra*, at p. 135.

53   Kroger, *supra*, at p. 170; Lydgate, Chris and Bryan, Miles. (September 1, 2012). "Professor. Scholar. Attorney General. John Kroger brings a wealth of experience—and energy—to Eliot Hall." *The Advocate—Reed Magazine.*

54   Kroger, *supra*, at p. 170.

55   DeVecchio, *supra*, at p. 237.

56   *United States v. Sessa* (2d Cir. 1997) 125 F.3d 68, 70.

57   Lance, *supra*, at p. 206, fn. 20.

58   This author's online searches also revealed a 1975 *New York Times* article regarding the murder in Brooklyn of Albert Varriale. Obviously, the date and the spelling of the last name do not fit the parameters of the alleged 1983 murder of Albert Variale (The New York Times. (April 19, 1975). "Police Ask a Witness in Slaying to Phone").

59   Puparo. "Puparo Presents: The Roaring 1980s (Part I)."

60   *United States v. Scarpa* (2d Cir. 1990) 913 F.2d 993.

61   Scarpo, Ed. (June 26, 2021). "Violent Crew Ready to Follow Huck's Orders if the Gambino Soldier is Released, Sources Say." Scarpo wrote that "Scarpa Jr. took control of

his father's crew after he died. The Scarpa Crew, under Greg Junior, operated several lucrative marijuana sales locations in parts of Brooklyn and Staten Island from approximately July 1985 until the law shut them down" (Ibid.). Gregory Scarpa Jr. was incarcerated from the time of his arrest in August of 1988 (*United States v. Scarpa* (E.D.N.Y. 1988) 701 F. Supp. 379, 379) until his release in November of 2020 (*United States v. Scarpa* (E.D.N.Y. Nov. 11, 2020) 94-cr-1119-1 (ERK). He was in federal prison at the time of his father's death in 1994.

62   New York City Police Department, Office of Management Analysis and Planning, Crime Analysis Unit. (1984). "Homicide Analysis 1984." Table 103, p. 117.

63   DeVecchio, *supra*, at p. 9.

64   Lance, *supra*, at p. 120.

65   Scarpa, *supra*, at p. 65.

66   Lance, *supra*, at pp. 118-119.

67   Berkery, Marilyn. (December 18, 1987). "'Allie Boy' Persico Gets 25 years." UPI; Scarpo, Ed. (November 16, 2021). "The Mob's Underground Railroad: How Allie Boy Persico Survived on The Lam for Seven Years." *Cosa Nostra News*.

68   Capeci, Jerry. (February 16, 2006). "From 'Drop-Dead Gorgeous' to DOA," *supra* (quoting Deputy U.S. Marshall Victor Oboyski).

69   Purdum, Todd. (March 9, 1986). "New York Crime Steady in 1985 Despite Rise in Last Half of Year." The New York Times; Wilkerson, Isabel. (January 15, 1987). "Urban Homicide Rates in U.S. up Sharply in 1987." *The New York Times*.

70 FBI Files, set 5, at p. 85.

71 Ibid., at p. 90.

72 Ibid., at pp. 92-95.

73 Ibid., at p. 94.

74 *See*, e.g., Seigel, Max H. (March 12, 1976) "Scarpa, Reputed Colombo Aide, Indicted in Gambling Inquiry." *The New York Times*.

75 Mazza, *supra*, at p. 90.

76 Kroger, *supra* at p. 132.

77 Mazza, *supra*, at p. 90.

78 Ibid., at p. 150.

79 Ibid.

80 Lance, *supra*, at p. 152. *See* also Harmon, *supra*, at p. 115. Harmon's account segues into a retelling of the murder of Donnie Somma. According to Harmon, the deal Scarpa reached with the federal prosecutor caused suspicion to mount that he was an FBI informant. Scarpa, per Harmon, then demonstrated his Mafia *bona fides* by murdering Somma. However, Somma was murdered by Scarpa more than five years earlier. For a more detailed discussion of the Somma murder, *see* chapter seven, endnotes 102-118, and accompanying text, *supra*.

81 FBI Files, set 5, at pp. 97-98.

82 Kelleher was appointed to replace Scarpa's counsel Lou Diamond who, it was felt, could not be trusted to keep Scarpa's TECI status from other LCN members (Ibid., at p. 99).

83 Ibid., at p. 100.

84   Ibid., at p. 108.

85   Ibid., at pp. 109-112.

86   Ibid., at p. 110.

87   McFadden, Robert D. (December 17, 1985). "Organized-Crime Chief Shot Dead Stepping from Car on E. 46th Street." *The New York Times*.

88   FBI Files, set 5, at p. 112.

89   Ibid., at pp. 113 & 120-122.

90   Ibid., at p. 118.

91   Ibid., at p. 94.

92   Ibid., at p. 95.

93   Ibid., at p. 98 (quoting Ed McDonald).

94   Ibid., at p. 99.

95   Ibid., at pp. 99 & 105.

96   Ibid., at p. 105.

97   Ibid., at p. 102.

98   Ibid., at p. 105.

99   DeVecchio claimed in his book that his actions in the credit card fraud case constituted "the only time [Scarpa] got help from me" (DeVecchio, *supra*, at p. 165).

100   Ibid., at p. 139.

101   McGuire, *supra*, at p. 198 (italics in the original).

102   Lance, *supra*, at p. 71.

103   Lance dated the Guzman murder as happening in 1983 (Lance, *supra*, at p. 206). However, Guzman was killed after assaulting Scarpa's daughter Linda when she "wasn't quite sixteen yet" (Scarpa, *supra*, at p. 9). Linda's sixteenth birthday was on June 21, 1985.

104   DeVecchio, *supra*, at p. 176 (quoting Greg Scarpa).

105   Kroger, *supra*, at pp. 135-136; Lance, *supra*, at p. 206; *United States v. Sessa, et al.* (2d Cir. 1997) 125 F.3d 68, 70-71.

106   Odd Stops. Tali's Restaurant: Sammy the Bull Gravano's Headquarters. Double You Media. Wexford, Ireland.

107   Mazza, *supra*, at pp. 146-147.

108   Ibid., at pp. 147 & 149.

109   Ibid., at pp. 151-152

110   Ibid., at p. 147.

111   Ibid., at p. 152.

112   Kroger, *supra*, at p. 136.

113   Ibid.

114   Ibid.

115   *United States v. Scarpa, et al.* (2d Cir. 1990) 913 F.2d 993, fn. 3.

116   Mazza, *supra*, at p. 174.

117   Ibid., at p. 157.

118   Lance, *supra*, at p. 141.

119   FBI Files, set 5, at p. 124. The entry goes on to note that the four "hang out with Greg Scarpa Jr. because of similarity of ages" (Ibid.).

120   *United States v. Scarpa, et al.* (2d Cir. 1990) 913 F.2d 993, 998.

121   Ibid., at p. 1000. Leon testified at trial that DeCarlo claimed to have shot Nocha three times. "I shot him twice in the stomach and once in the face" (Ibid., at p. 1009).

122   James, George. (April 20, 1988). "Murders in Queens Rise 25%; Crack is Key Factor." *The New York Times*.

123   *United States v. Sessa* (2d Cir. 1997) 125 F.3d 68, 70.

124   Ibid., at pp. 70-71.

125   Those 1986 meetings took place on January 1, February 5, 10, 26 and 28, March 6 and 24, April 24, May 7, June 3 and 10, July 1 and 18, and December 15 (FBI Files, set 5, *supra*, at pp. 110-144). Notice the lack of meetings from August, when Scarpa underwent emergency surgery, until mid-December.

126   FBI Files, set 5, at pp. 113 & 121.

127   Ibid., at pp. 113-114.

128   Kerr, Peter. (April 14, 1986). "Car Bomb Kills the No. 2 Man in Crime Family." *The New York Times*.

129   Lubasch, Arnold H. (October 25, 1984). "11 indicted by U.S. as the Leadership of a Crime Family." *The New York Times*.

130   FBI Files, set 5, at pp. 135-136; Lubasch, Arnold H. (June 14, 1986). "Persico Convicted in Colombo Trial." *The New York Times*.

131   Lubasch, Arnold H. (June 14, 1986). "Persico Convicted in Colombo Trial" (quoting Rudolph Giuliani), *supra*.

132   James, George. (April 20, 1988). "Murders in Queens Rise 25%; Crack is Key Factor." *The New York Times*.

133   Scarpa, *supra*, at p. 19.

134   Mazza, *supra*, at p. 88.

135   Lance, *supra*, at p. 177.

136   Dannen, *supra*.

137   Ancestry.com. 1940 U.S. "Enumeration District 24-1004. Supervisor's District No. 8. Sheet No. 2A."

138   Those conclusions are buttressed by the information contained in the 1930 U.S. Census. In that census, Salvadore [sic] Scarpa is listed as thirty-six years old as of April 24, 1930, and a "World War" veteran. His wife, Mary, is listed as twenty-eight years old as of the same date. Five children are listed in birth order: Theresa (spelled without an "h" in the 1940 census), eleven years old, Vincenza, eight years old, Maria, five years old, Gradudy [sic], two years old, and Salvadore [sic], five months old. Gregory's name is obviously misspelled. Theresa and Vincenza are both listed as attending P.S. 169 at the time, and the three youngest children were not then in school. Vincenza's birthplace is listed in the 1930 form as "New London Con," which is consistent with the 1940 form which lists "Conn." as her birthplace. The 1930 form, unlike the 1940 form, does not indicate the source of the family's information. In addition to misspelling Gregory's name, the 1930 form lists his relationship "to the head of the family" as "daughter" (Fold3.com, *supra*). Despite the obvious errors, the 1930 census and 1940 census entries for the Scarpa family

reinforce each other, particularly when establishing the birth order of the Scarpa children. The 1930 Census form also indicates the family's poverty. One column on the form was used to indicate whether the family owned a radio. The entry for the Scarpa family is "no." Finally, Salvatore's occupation is listed in 1930 as "Laborer tending furnaces." That description is consistent with Gregory Scarpa's stories later in life about hauling coal with his father as a young child.

139   Lance, *supra*, at p. 178.

140   Dannen, *supra*.

141   FBI Files, set 1, at pp. 2-5.

142   Lance, *supra*, at p. 14.

143   Ibid., at p. 181 (quoting Joey Ambrosino).

144   Scarpa, *supra*, at p. 20.

145   Mazza, *supra*, at p. 92.

146   Ibid.

147   Scarpa, *supra*, at p. 101.

148   Ibid. (quoting Linda Schiro).

149   Lance, *supra*, at pp. 177-179.

150   Ibid. at p. 178,

151   Hamilton, Brad. (May 27, 2012). "Mafia Daughter Says Dad was Grim Reaper." *New York Post*. For some reason, Linda Scarpa's allegation about her father being responsible for her Uncle Sal's murder did not make it into her book.

152   McGuire, *supra*, at p. 193.

153   Mazza, *supra*, at p. 166.

154   McGuire, *supra*, at p. 202.

155   Ibid. at p. 203 (quoting Carmine Sessa).

156   Ibid.

157   Peter Lance also credited Scarpa with the murder of Ray Shapiro in 1987 based upon the Second Circuit's opinion in *United States v. Sessa* (2d Cir. 1997) 125 F.3d 68, 70-71. However, the opinion in that case ties Gregory Scarpa Jr. to the Shapiro murder rather than his father. Other than repeating the allegation of Junior's involvement, the opinion does not discuss any of the underlying facts of the Shapiro murder. There simply is not enough to go on in the public record to tie Greg Scarpa Sr. to that 1987 murder.

158   FBI Files, set 5, at p. 124.

159   DeVecchio, *supra*, at p. 413.

160   Lance, *supra*, at pp. 142-143.

161   New York Daily News Staff. (June 14, 1995). "Mob Man's Saved by the Cell."

162   As a general matter, the law of conspiracy requires an overt act in furtherance of the conspiracy as an element of the crime. For example, New York State's Penal Law section 105.20 states, "A person shall not be convicted of conspiracy unless an overt act is alleged and proved to have been committed by one of the conspirators in furtherance of the conspiracy." It is the author's view that digging a grave for the purpose of concealing the body of a target of a murder plot would fulfill that element of the crime of conspiracy.

163   Lance, *supra*, at p. 143.

164   McFadden, Robert D. (November 13, 1987). "8 Charged with Mafia Drug Plot, Including Murders and Extortion." *The New York Times*.

165   *United States v. Scarpa, et al.* (2d Cir. 1990) 913 F.2d 993, 1001.

166   *United States v. Sessa* (E.D.N.Y. Jan. 25, 2011) Opinion and Order 97-CV-2079 (ARR), at pp. 40-41.

167   New York Daily News Staff. (June 14, 1995). "Mob Man's Saved by the Cell."

168   McFadden, Robert D. "8 Charged with Mafia Drug Plot, Including Murders and Extortion." *The New York Times*. McFadden reported on the Scarpa crew's November 10, 1987, arrests for *The New York Times*. He stated that Granato and DeCarlo, who were part of that crew and were named in the indictment that led to those arrests, were already in jail on other drug charges. However, he did not indicate that Catanzano, who had been convicted along with Granato a month earlier, was also already in custody.

169   Gregory Scarpa Jr., during his 1998 trial, was accused of planning to kill Catanzano by Assistant U.S. Attorney John Kroger during some aggressive cross-examination (Kroger, *supra*, at p. 192). So far as this author has been able to determine, Scarpa Sr., who according to all subsequent accounts allegedly ordered Catanzano's murder, was never officially accused of doing so, most likely because he was dead before the "facts" about the planned execution were revealed.

170   New York Daily News Staff. (June 14, 1995). "Mob Man's Saved by the Cell." Of course, simply being in custody, even protective custody, was no guarantee of safety when it came to perceived enemies of Cosa Nostra families. (*See*, e.g., FBI Files, set 2, at pp. 22-23 re: murder for hire

by NYPD homicide squad captain of woman in protective custody who was suspected of testifying against Whitey Tropiana).

171   Scarpa met with his handler once each in January, February, March, April, August, October, and December, twice each in July and September, and three times in May.

172   FBI Files, set 5, at p. 149.

173   Ibid.; *See* also Raab, Selwyn. (September 11, 1987). "Queens Barber Shot to Death by 3 in Masks." *The New York Times*."

174   *United States v. Sessa* (2d Cir. 1997) 125 F.3d 68, 70-71.

CHAPTER NINE: A STORM GROWS IN BROOKLYN

1   The eight murders Scarpa had by then connected Persico to in his FBI debriefings were of Joey Gallo (FBI Files, set 4, at p. 162), Joe Mutoli (FBI Files, set 4, at p. 71), Joe Brewster (FBI Files, set 5, at p. 149), Donnie Somma (FBI Files, set 4, at p. 248), Nick Prospero (FBI Files, set 5, at p. 2), John Matera (FBI Files, set 5, at pp. 13-14), Joe Peraino Jr. (FBI Files, set 5, at pp. 27-28), and Joseph Rizzo (FBI Files, set 5, at pp. 29-30, 31).

2   *United States v. Persico* (E.D.N.Y. 1972) 339 F. Supp. 1077, 1079.

3   Raab, *The Five Families, supra,* at p. 325.

4   FBI Carmine J. Persico Jr. Documents Set 1, at pp. 10-11. Gage, Nicholas. (June 5, 1977). "Colombo 'Family' Underboss Flees after Failure to Overthrow Chief." *The New York Times.*

5   Raab, *The Five Families*, *supra*, at p. 326.

6   *United States v. Persico* (S.D.N.Y. 1986) 646 F. Supp. 752, 754-755; *See* also Farber, M.A. (November 7, 1985). "Tax Agent Tells of Bribe for a Persico Visit Here." The New York Times, and *United States v. Persico* (E.D.N.Y. 1981) 520 F. Supp. 96, 97-98.

7   Raab, *The Five Families*, *supra*, at p. 327.

8   UPI (May 15, 1981). "Convicted Mobster Carmine Persico Jr. has Surrendered to U.S."

9   Raab, *The Five Families*, *supra*, at p. 327.

10   Lubasch, Arnold H. (October 25, 1984). "11 Indicted by U.S. as the Leadership of a Crime Family." *The New York Times*.; Raab, *The Five Families*, *supra*, at p. 327.

11   Lubasch, Arnold H. (October 25, 1984). "11 Indicted by U.S. as the Leadership of a Crime Family." *The New York Times*; Cates, Ellan. (October 24, 1984). "The Chieftains of the Colombo Organized Crime Family." UPI.

12   This operation is also referred to as "Starchamber - Five Star" (*see*, e.g., United States Senate. (April 1988). "Organized Crime: 25 Years after Valachi" at pp. 290, 369 & 400).

13   For a brief review of both investigations, *see* United States Senate. (April 1988). "Organized Crime: 25 Years after Valachi," *supra*, at pp. 368-371.

14   FBI Files, set 5, at p. 106.

15   Ibid.

16   Ibid., at pp. 110-111.

17   *United States v. Persico* (S.D.N.Y. 1986) 646 F. Supp. 752; Associated Press. (June 14, 1986). "Jury Convicts N.Y. Mafia Bos, His Son, 7 others."

18   *United States v. Persico* (S.D.N.Y. 1986) 646 F. Supp. 752, 761; Lubasch, Arnold H. (June 14, 1986). "Persico Convicted in Colombo Trial," *The New York Times, supra.*; Associated Press. (June 14, 1986). "Jury Convicts N.Y. Mafia Bos, His Son, 7 others," *supra.*

19   *United States v. Persico* (S.D.N.Y. 1986) 646 F. Supp. 752, 754.

20   Ibid., at p. 761.

21   Lubasch, Arnold H. (November 18, 1986). "Persico, His Son and 6 Others Get Long Terms as Colombo Gangsters." *The New York Times.*

22   Raab, *The Five Families, supra*, at pp. 329-330.

23   FBI Files, set 5, at pp. 135-136.

24   United States Senate. (April 1988). "Organized Crime: 25 Years after Valachi," *supra*, at p. 448.

25   FBI Files, set 5, at p. 137.

26   Thorton, Mary. (February 27, 1985). "9 Charged with Mafia Activities." *The Washington Post*; Lubasch, Arnold H. (February 27, 1985). "U.S. Indictment Says 9 Governed New York Mafia." *The New York Times*; FBI Carmine J. Persico Jr. Documents Set 2, at p. 3. The "Commission Case" is at times referred to in the federal case reporters as the Salerno case given that Anthony Salerno was its first named defendant. *United States v. Salerno, et al.* (2nd Cir. 1989) 868 F.2d 524, 528.

27   FBI Carmine J. Persico Jr. Documents Set 1, at p. 49; FBI Carmine J. Persico Jr. Documents Set 2, at p. 3; *United States v. Langella and Persico* (2nd Cir. 1986) 804 F.2d 185, 187.

28   Ibid., at p. 20; Hornblower, Margot. (September 19, 1986). "Mafia 'Commission' Trial Begins in New York." *The Washington Post*.

29   FBI Carmine J. Persico Jr. Documents Set 2, at p. 20; Reilly, William M. (November 20, 1986). "Eight Convicted in Mafia 'Commission' Trial." UPI; Lubasch, Arnold H. (November 20, 1986). "U.S. Jury Convicts Eight as Members of Mob Commission." *The New York Times*.

30   FBI Carmine J. Persico Jr. Documents Set 2, at p. 20; Lance, *supra*, at p. 175; Tsiantar, Dody. (January 14, 1987). "3 Mafia Bosses Ordered to Prison for 100 Years." *The Washington Post*; Lubasch, Arnold H. (January 14, 1987). "Judge Sentences 8 Mafia Leaders to Prison Terms." *The New York Times*.

31   Tsiantar, *supra* (quoting U.S. Attorney Rudolph W. Giuliani).

32   Raab, Selwyn. (March 8, 2019). "Carmine Persico, Colombo Crime Family Boss, is Dead at 85." *The New York Times*.

33   FBI Files, set 5, at p. 149.

34   FBI Files, set 5, at p. 147.

35   FBI Files, set 6, at pp. 5-6.

36   Ibid., at p. 18.

37   Kroger, *supra*, at p. 144.

38   Lance, *supra*, at p. 249 (quoting defense attorney Flora Edwards).

39   FBI Files, set 5, at pp. 129-130.

40   Ibid., at p. 143.

41   Lubasch, Arnold H. (June 14, 1986). "Persico Convicted in Colombo Trial," *supra*.

42   FBI Files, set 5, at p. 143.

43   Ibid., at pp. 143-144.

44   Ibid., at p. 146.

45   Ibid., at pp. 154-155. Scarpa refers to Cacace as "Joseph," apparently assuming incorrectly that his nickname of "Joe Waverly" was in part a diminutive of Joseph.

46   Scarpa later refers to him as "James Angelinno" when reporting his murder in November of 1988 (FBI Files, set 6, at pp. 5-6). From a review of the decision in *State of New Jersey v. Aurelio Ray Cagno* (Superior Court of New Jersey Appellate Division 2009) 978 A.2d 921, 409 N.J. Super. 552 in which the court refers to a "Vincent 'Jimmy' Angellino," it would appear that James Angelinno, Vincent Angellino, and Vincent "Jimmy" Angelina are the same person.

47   FBI Files, set 5, at pp. 146 & 152.

48   Ibid., at pp. 149-150.

49   Ibid., at p. 150.

50   FBI Files, set 6, at pp. 6-7.

51   FBI Files, set 5, at p. 144; Lance, *supra*, at p. 244; But *see*, DeVecchio, *supra*, at p. 218, where he wrote that Sessa "was straightened out in 1988. In that same year he was upped to capo."

52   FBI Files, set 6, at pp. 3-4; Lance, *supra*, at p. 244.

53   FBI Files, ibid; Lance, ibid.

54   FBI Files, set 6, at p. 5.

55   Ibid., at p. 32. DeVecchio, *supra*, at pp. 218-219. Lance reported that Sessa was appointed consigliere in May of that year (Lance, *supra*, at p. 244), which may have been the case. Scarpa's report about the appointment is dated June 12, 1990 (FBI Files, set 6, at p. 32). He may have been reporting on an appointment that happened the previous month, although on May 2, 1990, Scarpa reported that Benny Aloi was the Colombo family's consigliere. (Ibid., at p. 32).

56   Raab, *The Five Families*, *supra*, at p. 6.

57   Ibid., at p. 32.

58   Mazza, *supra*, at p. 196.

59   Ibid.

60   FBI Files, set 6, at p. 18.

61   FBI Files, set 5, at p. 155 & set 6, at p. 3.

62   FBI Files, set 5, at p. 156.

63   FBI Files, set 6, at p. 17.

64   Ibid. at pp. 21-22.

65   Ibid., at p. 2.

66   FBI Files, set 5, at p. 147.

67   Lance, *supra*, at p. 219.

68   FBI Files, set 5, at p. 144.

69   Ibid., at pp. 148 & 153; *State of New Jersey v. Aurelio Ray Cagno, supra*, at pp. 927-928.

70   FBI Files, set 5, at p. 152.

71   FBI Files, set 6, at p. 9.

72   Mazza, *supra*, at p. 195.

73   FBI Files, set 5, at pp. 157-158; "During the captioned period [5/10/88 – 8/8/88] the source has provided a continuous update of the Colombo family structure noting that significant changes in assignments are being made on a monthly basis, and the source is providing singular information currently unavailable from any other source" (FBI Files, set 6, at p. 4).

74   FBI Files, set 6, at p. 21.

75   FBI Files, set 5, at p. 144.

76   Lance, *supra*, at p. 249.

77   Mazza, *supra*, at p. 211.

78   Ibid.

79   *Orena v. United States* (E.D.N.Y. 1997) 956 F. Supp. 1071, 1079 (quotation marks in the original).

80   Mazza, *supra*, at p. 195 (quotation marks in the original).

81   *State of New Jersey v. Aurelio Ray Cagno, supra*, at p. 926.

82   Ibid., at p. 928 (quoting Rocco Cagno).

83   Ibid.

84   Mazza, *supra*, at p. 196.

85   Lance, *supra*, at p. 249.

86   *State of New Jersey v. Aurelio Ray Cagno, supra*, at p. 928.

87   FBI Files, set 6, at pp. 5-6.

88   Ibid., at p. 18.

89   *United States v. Amato* (2d. Cir. 1994) 15 F.3d 230, 233; McGuire, *supra*, at p. 224.

90   *United States v. Orena, et al.* (2d. Cir. 1998) 145 F.3d 551, 555.

91   *Orena v. United States* (E.D.N.Y. 1997) 956 F. Supp. 1071, 1078.

92   *United States v. Amato, supra*; Lance, *supra*, at p. 221 (citing testimony of Joseph Ambrosino in *U.S. v. Victor J. Orena*, trial transcript, at p. 856, November 30, 1992); Tabor, Mary B. W. (April 2, 1992). "Man Accused as Colombo Chief is Held in Slaying of Ex-Member." *The New York Times*; McGuire, *supra*, at p. 224.

93   *United States v. Orena* (2d Cir. 1994) 32 F.3d 704, 708; Marzulli, John. (January 8, 2004). "My Father: the Killer Gangster: Dad Did it, Framed 2." *New York Daily News*.

94   Lance, *supra*, at 221, (citing opening statement of Assistant U.S. Attorney Andrew Weissmann in *U.S. v. Victor J. Orena*, trial transcript, at p. 37, November 19, 1992); *Orena v. United States, supra*, at p. 1110; *United States v. Orena, supra*, 32 F.3d 704, 715; *United States v. Amato, supra*, 15 F.3d 230, 233.

95   DeVecchio, *supra*, at p. 290.

96   *Orena v. United States, supra*, 956 F. Supp. at p. 1079; Lance, *supra*, at p. 221 citing testimony of Diane Montesano in *U.S. v. Victor J. Orena*, trial transcript, at pp, 1167-1169, December 2, 1992; *United States v. Amato, supra*, 15 F.3d 230, 233; McGuire, *supra*, at p. 224.

97   *United States v. Orena, supra* (2d Cir. 1994) 32 F.3d 704, 708; *Orena v. United States, supra*, at p. 1079; Lance, supra at p. 221 (citing testimony of Diane Montesano in *U.S. v. Victor J. Orena, supra*).

98   Lance, *supra*, at p. 221 (citing testimony of Diane Montesano in *U.S. v. Victor J. Orena, supra*).

99   *Orena v. United States, supra*, at p. 1080; *United States v. Amato, supra*, 15 F.3d 230, 233.

100   (Lance, *supra*, at p. 221 (citing testimony of Joseph Ambrosino in *U.S. v. Victor J. Orena*, trial transcript, at p. 856, November 30, 1992).

101   *United States v. Amato, supra*, 15 F.3d 230, 234.

102   Ibid., at p. 236.

103   Although indicted simultaneously, Amato and Orena were tried separately (*United States v. Amato, supra*, 15 F.3d 230, 232).

104   *United States v. Orena, supra* (2d Cir. 1994) 32 F.3d 704, 715.

105   *United States v. Amato, supra*, 15 F.3d 230, 236.

106   *United States v. Orena, supra* (2d Cir. 1994) 32 F.3d 704, 715.

107   Raab, *The Five Families, supra*, at p. 333.

108   *Orena v. United States, supra,* 956 F. Supp. at p. 1079.

109   Ibid.

110   Ibid., at pp. 1079-1080.

111   *Orena v. United States, supra,* 956 F. Supp. at p. 1084; *See,* also, *United States v. Amato, supra,* 15 F.3d 230, 233.

112   Lance, *supra,* at p. 223.

113   *Orena v. United States, supra,* 956 F. Supp. at p. 1084; Lance, *supra,* at p. 223.

114   *Orena v. United States, supra,* 956 F. Supp. at p. 1080. Lance, *supra,* at p. 223.

115   Lance, *supra,* at p. 223.

116   *Orena v. United States, supra,* 956 F. Supp. at p. 1080. Lance wrote that Montesano "could just make out his face. She later picked his picture out of a series of FBI surveillance photographs of Colombo family members. [para.] It was Gregory Scarpa Sr." (Lance, *supra,* at p. 224). However, the contention "that it was definitely Scarpa who stalked Montesano and Ocera shortly before Ocera's death… is not a fair characterization of the tenuous evidence to this effect at trial" (*Orena v. United States, supra,* 956 F. Supp. at p. 1106).

117   *United States v. Orena, supra* (2d Cir. 1994) 32 F.3d 704, 717.

118   *Orena v. United States, supra,* 956 F. Supp. at p. 1080.

119   *United States v. Orena, supra* (2d Cir. 1994) 32 F.3d 704, 717.

120   *Orena v. United States, supra*, 956 F. Supp. at p. 1071

121   *United States v. Amato, supra*, 15 F.3d 230, 233. Harmon wrote that Ocera was killed on a contract put out by Scarpa for spreading the rumor that Scarpa was an informant (Harmon, *supra*, at p. 146). That claim is consistent with Gregory Scarpa Jr.'s 2004 testimony in which he related a conversation he had with his father (Marzulli, John. (January 8, 2004). "My Father: the Killer Gangster: Dad Did it, Framed 2." *New York Daily News*). *See*, also, DeVecchio, *supra*, at p. 321.

122   McGuire, *supra*, at p. 225.

123   *Orena v. United States, supra*, 956 F. Supp. at p. 1079.

124   Ibid.; *United States v. Amato, supra*, 15 F.3d 230, 233; *United States v. Orena, supra* (2d Cir. 1994) 32 F.3d 704, 708.

125   *United States v. Amato, supra*, 15 F.3d 230, 233.

126   McGuire wrote that *Scarpa* killed Ocera at Amato's house (McGuire, *supra*, at p. 224). His authority for this appears to be *Orena v. United States* (E.D.N.Y. 1997) 956 F. Supp. 1071. However, when the decision in that case mentioned Scarpa in connection with Ocera's murder, the court was reciting an argument proffered by petitioner Orena and rejected by the court. "Orena and Amato were proven guilty of the Ocera murder by strong evidence that remains unaffected by the evidence newly discovered" (*Orena v. United States* (E.D.N.Y. 1997) 956 F. Supp. 1071, Section III C 1, at p. 1108, entitled "Ocera Murder"). The court specifically rejected the theory that Scarpa killed Ocera and reaffirmed the federal jury's convictions of Orena and Amato (Ibid.). McGuire may have simply decided that the federal district court got it wrong, and that Orena and Amato

correctly attributed Ocera's murder to Scarpa. It is worth remembering that Ocera was garroted, and the wire used to strangle him was still present when his body was recovered two years after his murder. Although not dispositive of the question, Scarpa's preferred method of execution was some sort of firearm, usually a snub-nosed .38 revolver. Furthermore, by the time Ocera was murdered in late 1989, Scarpa had been HIV-positive for more than three years and was likely no longer in the sort of physical condition needed to strangle a grown man without assistance. As a side note, Jack Leale was not prosecuted; he was "shot to death before he could stand trial" (Tabor, Mary B. W. (April 2, 1992). "Man Accused as Colombo Chief is Held in Slaying of Ex-Member." *The New York Times*). *See* also United States v. Sessa, et al. (E.D.N.Y. 1993) 821 F. Supp. 870 in which Orena and Amato were sentenced for, among other offenses, the murder of Tommy Ocera.

127   Ibid.

128   *Orena v. United States, supra*, 956 F. Supp. at p. 1084.

129   *Orena v. United States, supra*, 956 F. Supp. at p. 1080 (quoting the trial testimony of Alphonse D'Arco).

130   *Orena v. United States, supra*, 956 F. Supp. at p. 1080.

131   FBI Files, set 6, at p. 22.

132   Ibid., at p. 31.

133   Ibid.

134   Ibid., at p. 32.

135   Ibid.

136   Ibid., at p. 40.

137   *Orena v. United States* (E.D.N.Y. 1997) 956 F. Supp. 1071, 1081.

138   Ibid.

139   Raab, *The Five Families*, *supra*, at p. 334.

140   Lance, *supra*, at p. 250; *See*, also, DeVecchio, *supra*, at p. 286 and Mazza, *supra*, at pp. 211-212.

141   *Orena v. United States* (E.D.N.Y. 1997) 956 F. Supp. 1071, 1081. *See* also Mazza, *supra*, at p. 208.

142   Carmine Persico's other brother, Alphonse, passed away in 1989 (*The New York Times*. (September 18, 1989). "Alphonse Persico, 61, is dead; Leader of Colombo Crime Family").

143   Lance, *supra*, at p. 250 (citing 1993 testimony of Carmine Sessa; capitalization in the original).

144   Ibid.

145   Mazza, *supra*, at p. 211.

146   Ibid., at p. 215; *See*, also, *United States v. Sessa* (E.D.N.Y. Jan. 25, 2011) Opinion and Order 97-CV-2079 (ARR), at pp. 13-14.

147   *United States v. Sessa* (E.D.N.Y. Jan. 25, 2011) Opinion and Order 97-CV-2079 (ARR), at p. 14.

148   Mazza, *supra*, at p. 216.

149   Harmon, *supra*, at p. 149; DeVecchio, *supra*, at p. 287; *Orena v. United States* (E.D.N.Y. 1997) 956 F. Supp. 1071, 1081.

150   Lance, *supra*, at pp. 253-254.

151   Mazza, *supra*, at p. 216.

152   *Orena v. United States* (E.D.N.Y. 1997) 956 F. Supp. 1071, 1081.

153   Ibid., at p. 254. *See* also FBI Files, set 6, at p. 45, and Mazza, *supra*, at p. 216.

154   FBI Files, set 6, at p. 45.

155   Lance, *supra*, at p. 255 (quoting Andrew Orena).

156   Mazza, *supra*, at p. 216.

157   FBI Files, set 6, at p. 38; Lance, *supra*, at p. 256.

158   Mazza, *supra*, at p. 219.

159   Ibid.

160   Ibid., at pp. 219-220. As Mazza noted, the Sessa Funeral Home owners/operators were not related to Carmine Sessa. According to the website of the McLaughlin & Sons, Inc. funeral home on 3rd Avenue in Bay Ridge, "The Sessa Family established their business in 1883 on President Street and in the early 1900's, moved their main office to Bay Ridge. In 1985 Joseph V. 'Jay' Sessa II merged with The McLaughlin and Sons, Inc. Funeral Homes..." https:// www.mclaughlinandsons.com/.

161   McGuire, *supra*, at p. 238.

162   Ibid. In spite of the presence of both the FBI and Scarpa, one of the FBI's prized Top Echelon Criminal Informants, the FBI's Scarpa files contain no mention of the wake/funeral.

163   Mazza, *supra*, at p. 219.

164   Imbriale made no mention of a meeting at Joe Saponaro's wake/funeral in his memoir. Harmon wrote

that Orena and Scarpa, who was accompanied by Linda Schiro, met briefly at the funeral of John Saponaro. "Orena approached Scarpa--and asked for his support in the family dispute. Greg Sr. looked at Orena and responded with three simple words: 'Go fuck yourself'" (Harmon, *supra*, at p. 146).

165   Mazza, *supra*, at p. 220.

166   Ibid.

167   Lance, *supra*, at p. 256-257 (quoting Ambrosino testimony in *U.S. v. Orena*, at pp. 896-897)

168   Mazza, *supra*, at p. 220.

169   That image Scarpa was hoping to project is consistent with Ambrosino's testimony (Ibid.).

170   Mazza, *supra*, at p. 220.

171   Ibid.

172   Scarpa, *supra*, at p. 103.

173   Ibid.

174   Ibid., at pp. 104-105.

175   Gregory Scarpa Jr., notes, *supra*, at page 2.

176   Ibid., at p. 3.

177   Scarpa, *supra*, at pp. 102, 106 & 172.

178   Gregory Scarpa Jr., notes, *supra*, at page 4; Scarpa, *supra*, at p. 153.

179   Gregory Scarpa Jr., notes, ibid; Scarpa, ibid.

180   Scarpa, *supra*, at p. 114.

181   Scarpa, *supra*, at p. 109.

182   Ibid.

183   Ibid., at p. 110.

184   Ibid.

185   Ibid., at p. 111.

186   Ibid., at p. 114.

187   *See* Harmon, *supra*, at p. 123.

188   FBI Files, set 6, at pp. 46-48.

189   Ibid., at p. 47.

190   Ibid., at p. 49.

191   Ibid.

192   Ibid., at p. 48.

193   McGuire, *supra*, at p. 224, et seq. According to Carmine Imbriale, at one point in the meeting, the issue of Joe Brewster's murder came up with "Bobby Zam sharing how we just lost a good guy in Joe Brewster" (Ibid. at p. 226). This is odd given that Brewster's death had occurred more than four years earlier. Imbriale is quoted as saying in the context of describing that same meeting that "'Carmine [Sessa] didn't want nothing to do with Greg [Scarpa] after that murder'" (Ibid.). That statement is difficult to reconcile with Sessa's own actions in the fall of 1991 and during the third Colombo war. *See*, e.g., Mazza's description of a meeting in Scarpa's home during the fall of 1991 when Sessa "literally begged Greg for his guidance, his help, his leadership" (Mazza, *supra*, at p. 225).

194   McGuire, *supra*, at p. 224.

195   Ibid., at pp. 226-227.

196   *Orena v. United States, supra*, 956 F. Supp. 1071, 1081.

197   Ibid.

198   Mazza, *supra*, at p. 223.

199   Ibid.,

200   Lance, *supra*, at p. 256 (quoting Carmine Sessa in Tomlinson & Leadbetter II, FBI 302 memo re: Carmine Sessa, April 7 – May 10, 1993, 2).

201   FBI Files, set 6, at p. 48.

202   Ibid., at pp. 47-48.

203   Ibid., at p. 54.

204   Ibid., at p. 53.

205   Ibid., at p. 54.

206   Ibid., at pp. 52-53.

207   Ibid., at p. 52.

208   Ibid.

209   Ibid. at p. 53.

210   Ibid.

211   Mazza, *supra* at p. 251.

212   Ibid., at p. 252.

213   Ibid., at p. 253.

214   Ibid.

215   Ibid., at p. 249.

216   Ibid., at p. 256

217   Ibid.

218   Ibid., at pp. 209 & 256.

219   Ibid., at pp. 256-257.

220   *Orena v. United States, supra*, 956 F. Supp. 1071, 1080 (quoting the trial testimony of Alphonse D'Arco).

221   *Orena v. United States* (E.D.N.Y. 1997) 956 F. Supp. 1071, 1080; Associated Pess. (December 12, 1991). "Mob Wars. Crime Bosses' Feud is Turning N.Y.C. into a Shooting Gallery." *The Times Leader*. Wilkes-Barre, PA.

222   FBI Files, set 6, at p. 54.

CHAPTER TEN: WAR!

1   Kroger, *supra*, at p. 145.

2   Harmon, *supra*, at p. 146.

3   James, George. (December 6, 1991). "Killing in Brooklyn Social Club is Linked to Mob Power Struggle." *The New York Times*.

4   Raab, Selwyn. (March 8, 2019). "Carmine Persico, Colombo Crime Family Boss, is Dead at 85." *The New York Times*.

5   Raab, Selwyn. (December 30, 1992). "Top Member of Colombo Crime Family is Ambushed in Brooklyn." *The New York Times*.

6   Dannen, *supra*.

7   Tabor, Mary B. W. (April 2, 1992). "Man Accused as Colombo Chief is Held in Slaying of Ex-Member." *The New York Times*.

8   Raab, Selwyn. (July 2, 1995). "The Thin Line between Mole and Manager." *The New York Times*.

9   DeVecchio, *supra*, at p. 314.

10   Raab, Selwyn. (November 20, 1994). "The Mobster Was a Mole for the FBI; Tangled Life of a Mafia Figure Who Died of AIDS is Exposed." *The New York Times*.

11   The statement and its attribution to Scarpa have been generally accepted and retold by the media and respected Mafia experts for years (*See*, e.g., Raab, *The Five Families*, *supra*, at p. 343). It has even appeared in the federal case law (*See*, e.g., Grancio v. DeVecchio (E.D.N.Y. 2008) 572 F.Supp.2d 299). All one need do is enter "This one's for Carmine" into a Google search to see how generally accepted the story has become. However, Larry Mazza was a first-hand witness to the shooting having personally killed Nicky Black. Scarpa was in the car with Mazza at the time. Mazza, in his book *The Life*, makes no reference to Scarpa saying anything during the Nicky Black hit (Mazza, *supra*, at pp. 313-316), and Mazza specifically denied that Scarpa made the statement during the hit when he was interviewed by Peter Lance (Lance, *supra*, at pp. 289-290).

12   Lance, *supra*, at p. 258.

13   *United States v. Malpeso* (2d Cir. 1997) 115 F.3d 155, 159.

14   FBI Files, set 6, at p. 37.

15   *United States v. Malpeso* (2d Cir. 1997) 115 F.3d 155, 159.

16   *Orena v. United States* (E.D.N.Y. 1997) 956 F. Supp. 1071, 1079 (quoting Lucchese family acting boss Alphonse D'Arco).

17   *United States v. Malpeso* (2d Cir. 1997) 115 F.3d 155, 159.

18   Scarpa, *supra*, at p. 119. Larry Mazza, who was not present during the shooting, reported that three men were with Scarpa that morning, "Danny," who was driving his Lincoln, Joe Fish and "Dean," who were in the back seat of the Lincoln (Mazza, *supra*, at p. 260). "Danny" likely refers to Danny Capaldo, and "Dean" likely refers to Dean Pirra [sic] (*See*, Mazza, *supra*, at p. 456). Linda Schiro testified in 2007 that the crew members with Scarpa that day were Larry Sessa, Joe Fish, and Dean Capiri (Lance, *supra*, at p. 262 (citing testimony of Linda Schiro in *People v. R. Lindley DeVecchio*, October 29, 2007, transcript at pp. 1662-1663)).

19   Scarpa, *supra*, at p. 117.

20   FBI Files, set 6, at p. 55.

21   Scapa, *supra*, at p. 117.

22   Ibid.

23   Ibid., at pp. 117 & 119.

24   Ibid., at p. 118; DeVecchio, *supra*, at p. 296; Mazza, *supra*, at p. 261.

25   Scarpa, *supra*, at p. 118.

26   Ibid.

27   Mazza, *supra*, at p. 262.

28   Scarpa, *supra*, at p. 118; DeVecchio, *supra*, at p. 296; Mazza, *supra*, at p. 261.

29   Scarpa, *supra*, at pp. 118 & 119; DeVecchio, *supra*, at p. 296.

30   Scarpa, *supra*, at p. 118.

31   Ibid., at p. 119.

32   DeVecchio, *supra* at p. 296.

33   Mazza, *supra*, at p. 261.

34   Ibid.

35   Ibid.

36   Scarpa, *supra*, at p. 119.

37   Ibid.

38   Mazza, *supra*, at p. 261.

39   Scarpa, *supra*, at p. 119.

40   Ibid., at p. 119.

41   Mazza, *supra*, at p. 261.

42   Ibid.

43   Scarpa, *supra*, at p. 120.

44   Ibid., at p. 119.

45   Ibid., at pp. 120-122.

46   Ibid., at p. 122.

47   Ibid.

48   Ibid.

49   Mazza, *supra*, at p. 262.

50   FBI Files, set 6, at p. 59.

51   Scarpa, *supra*, at p. 123.

52   Mazza, *supra*, at p. 261.

53   Ibid.; McGuire, *supra*, at p. 239.

54   Mazza, *supra*, at p. 262.

55   Ibid., at pp. 263-264.

56   Ibid., at p. 264.

57   Ibid.

58   Ibid., at pp. 263-264.

59   *Orena v. United States* (E.D.N.Y. 1997) 956 F. Supp. 1071, 1099. Similarly, Peter Lance suggests, after reviewing the lack of direct evidence linking Orena to the November 18, 1991, attack on Scarpa, that it may have been a hoax (Lance, *supra*, at pp. 375-376). However, Lance earlier quoted Vic Orena Jr. who stated that shortly before the November 18th attack, Scarpa had been spotted in a car with a gun chasing Cutolo who managed to get away (Lance, *supra*, at p. 258). Lance also quoted John Orena's allegation that Scarpa similarly harassed Cutolo's driver before the November 18 shooting "two or three times." John Orena's conclusion? "So now Billy [Cutolo] is thinkin' to himself that if he doesn't stop Scarpa, Scarpa's gonna stop him" (Ibid., at p. 258 (quoting John Orena)). John Orena, according to Scarpa, was a capo (FBI Files, set 6, at p. 54). In this author's view, these statements lend further credibility to the conclusion that the November 18, 1991, attack was not a hoax but was rather ordered by Orena and engineered by Cutolo. The law of parsimony, also known as Occam's razor, is "the principle that, all else being equal, simpler explanations should be preferred over more complex ones" (Piasini, et al. "How Occam's Razor Guides Human Decision Making"). That principle militates in favor

of the view that an attack perpetrated by forces loyal to Vic Orena rather than an elaborate hoax orchestrated by Greg Scarpa is the more reasonable description of what happened on November 18, 1991.

60   *Orena v. United States* (E.D.N.Y. 1997) 956 F. Supp. 1071, 1076.

61   Ibid., at p. 1101.

62   FBI Files, set 6, at p. 57.

63   McFadden, Robert D. (December 17, 1991). "Brooklyn's Mob War Interrupted with a Quiet Day in Court." *The New York Times*.

64   Mazza, *supra*, at p. 264.

65   DeMartino was convicted in 2001 of twice wounding Joseph Campanella in a failed hit attempt. While in prison he developed serious health problems and was granted a compassionate release to home detention in 2022 having served more than twenty-two years of his twenty-five-year sentence (Goldberg, Noah. (May 27, 2022). "Violent NYC Mobster Released from Prison Because Feds Didn't Take Care of his Health Problems: Judge." *New York Daily News*).

66   Ibid., at p. 264.

67   Ibid., at p. 266.

68   Ibid.

69   Ibid.

70   Ibid., at p. 267.

71   Ibid.

72   Lance, *supra*, at 265-266 (citing *U.S. v. Victor Orena*, Testimony of Joseph Ambrosino, transcript, 910-912).

73   Mazza, *supra*, at p. 277.

74   Ibid., at p. 276.

75   Ibid.

76   McBride, *supra* at p. 240 (quoting Carmine Imbriale).

77   Ibid.

78   Ibid.

79   Lance referred to Smurra's murder as the "second murder in the third Colombo war, following the hit on Jack Leale, who was killed on November 4" (Lance, *supra* at p. 267). However, if as Scarpa opined, both sides wanted Leale dead, it is fair to say his killing was not related to the third Colombo war. *See* FBI Files, set 6, at p. 54.

80   Mazza, *supra*, at p. 276.

81   Lance, *supra*, at p. 266 (citing Special Agents Jeffrey W. Tomlinson and Howard Leadbetter II, FBI 302 memo re: Carmine Sessa, May 17, 1993).

82   McBride, *supra*, at p. 25.

83   Mazza, *supra*, at pp. 276-277.

84   James, George. (December 6, 1991). "Killing in Brooklyn Social Club is Linked to Mob Power Struggle." *The New York Times*.

85   Lance, *supra*, at p. 266.

86   Mazza, *supra*, at p. 277.

87   Ibid.

88 Ibid.; Lance, *supra*, at p. 266.

89 McBride, *supra*, at p. 240.

90 Lance ascribed the intelligence to Scarpa's moles in the Orena camp (Lance, *supra*, at p. 267). Linda Scarpa ascribed the intelligence to Lin DeVecchio (Scarpa, *supra*, at p. 125).

91 Mazza wrote that it was Cutolo's girlfriend who lived there (Mazza, *supra*, at p. 270). Lance and Scarpa wrote that Cutolo's girlfriend's grandmother lived there (Lance, *supra*, at p. 263 (citing *U.S. v. Victor Orena*, testimony of Joseph Ambrosino, transcript, 908); Scarpa, *supra*, at p. 125).

92 *See* Beyer, Gregory. (October 8, 2010). "Living in Borough Park, Brooklyn." *The New York Times*.

93 DeVecchio, *supra*, at pp. 297-298; Lance, *supra*, at p. 267.

94 DeVecchio, *supra*, at p. 298; Mazza, *supra*, at p. 270; Lance, *supra*, at p. 267; Scarpa, *supra*, at p. 125.

95 DeVecchio, *supra*, at p. 298.

96 Mazza, *supra*, at p. 270.

97 Lance, *supra*, at p. 267.

98 Larry Mazza's close friend Jimmy Delmasto's last name appears in the sources variously as Delmasto, Del Masto, DelMasto, and Del'Masto. The version "Delmasto," used by the federal district court in Orena v. U.S. (E.D.N.Y. 1997) 956 F. Supp. 1071, has been adopted for use in this book.

99 Mazza, *supra*, at p. 270.

100   DeVecchio, *supra*, at p. 298; Scarpa, *supra*, at p. 125; Lance, *supra*, at p. 268; FBI Files, set 6, at p. 59.

101   *United States v. Monteleone* (2d. Cir. 2001) 257 F.3d 210, 220; DeVecchio, *supra*, at p. 298.

102   Scarpa, *supra*, at p. 125.

103   Lance, *supra*, at p. 268.

104   Mazza, *supra*, at p. 289. Mazza also put Sessa's weight at "easily between 360 and 380 pounds," and "pushing 400 pounds" (Ibid., at pp. 295 & 297).

105   Lance had the attack occurring on November 28, which was Thanksgiving (Lance, *supra*, at p. 269). Linda Scarpa had the attack occurring on November 29. On the Friday after Thanksgiving, businesses like a men's hair salon and a pizza parlor would have been open, and the sidewalks would have been crowded with holiday shoppers (Scarpa, *supra*, at p. 131); George James also had the attack happening on November 29 (James, George. "Killing in Brooklyn Social Club is Linked to Mob Power Struggle." *The New York Times*).

106   Mazza, *supra*, at p. 296.

107   Ibid.

108   Ibid.

109   Ibid.

110   Ibid., at p. 297.

111   James, George. "Killing in Brooklyn Social Club is Linked to Mob Power Struggle." *The New York Times*.

112   Mazza, *supra*, at p. 297; Lance, *supra*, at p. 269.

113   Lance, *supra*, at p. 269; James, George. "Killing in Brooklyn Social Club is Linked to Mob Power Struggle." *The New York Times*.

114   Mazza, *supra*, at p. 298; Lance, *supra*, at pp. 269-270.

115   Scarpa, *supra*, at p. 131; Dillon, Sam. (October 25, 1992). "Brooklyn's Neighbors to the Mob." *The New York Times*.

116   Mazza, *supra*, at p. 298.

117   Ibid.

118   Ibid.

119   Ibid. (capitalization in the original).

120   Mazza, *supra,* at p. 280.

121   Mazza was likely referring to Pasquale "Fat Patty" DiMatteo.

122   Joel Cacace's pseudonym.

123   Mazza, *supra,* at p. 280.

124   Ibid., at p. 279.

125   Ibid., at p. 280.

126   Ibid., at p. 281.

127   Ibid., at p. 282.

128   James, George. "Killing in Brooklyn Social Club is Linked to Mob Power Struggle." *The New York Times*.

129   Lance, *supra*, at p. 269.

130   Mazza, *supra*, at p. 283.

131   Ibid.

132   James, George. "Killing in Brooklyn Social Club is Linked to Mob Power Struggle." *The New York Times*.

133   Mazza, *supra*, at p. 283.

134   DeVecchio, *supra*, at p. 305; James, George. "Killing in Brooklyn Social Club is Linked to Mob Power Struggle." The New York Times; Lance, *supra*, at p. 269; McGuire, *supra*, at p. 24; UPI (December 8, 1991). "Two Brooklyn Shootings May Be Linked to Mob Feud."

135   Mazza, *supra*, at p. 285.

136   DeVecchio, *supra*, at p. 306.

137   Mazza, *supra*, at p. 285.

138   Ibid.

139   Scarpa, *supra*, at p. 132.

140   Ibid.

141   The fact of the meeting and the participants in that meeting strike this author as the sort of information officials at USP Lompoc would have, as a matter of policy, automatically relayed to the FBI's New York Office, or at a minimum to the FBI's headquarters in Washington, D.C.

142   DeVecchio, *supra*, at p. 306.

143   McGuire wrote that Nastasi was killed on December 6 (McGuire, *supra*, at p. 25). Additionally, although McGuire later referred to his last name as "Nastasi" (Ibid., at p. 228), during the reference on page 25 of the same book, McGuire wrote his last name as "Nastasa" (Ibid., at p. 25). "Nastasa" is the spelling on the family headstone over Rosario's grave in Saint John Cemetery and Mausoleum, Middle Village,

Queens County, New York (FindAGrave.com. Headstone of Family of Rosario Nastasa).

144   Lance, *supra*, at p. 270.

145   Capeci, Jerry and O'Shaughnessy, Patrice. (December 6, 1991). "New Rubout in Mafia War." *New York Daily News*; *See*, also, James, George. "Killing in Brooklyn Social Club is Linked to Mob Power Struggle." *The New York Times*, and Associated Pess. (December 12, 1991). "Mob Wars. Crime Bosses' Feud is Turning N.Y.C. into a Shooting Gallery." *The Times Leader*. Wilkes-Barre, PA; Scarpa, *supra*, at p. 133.

146   Lance, *supra*, at p. 270; Scarpa, *supra*, at p. 133.

147   Mazza, *supra*, at p. 294.

148   Ibid.

149   DeVecchio, *supra*, at p. 306.

150   Mazza, *supra*, at p. 294.

151   Ibid., at p. 293.

152   Mazza wrote, without further identifying information, that "Cousin Joe" was riding shotgun, and "Tommy" was in the second row of seats with Greg (Ibid., at pp. 291-292).

153   Daniels, Lee A. (December 8, 1991). "Brooklyn Slaying Tied to Mob Feud." *The New York Times*. Lance wrote the murder occurred at 3:35 p.m. (Lance, *supra*, at p. 270); Daniels's reporting for *The New York Times* two days after the murder had it at 3:55 p.m. (Daniels, *supra*).

154   Dillon, *supra*.

155   Mazza, *supra*, at p. 291; Harmon, *supra*, at p. 147; DeVecchio, *supra*, at pp. 306-307; Lance, *supra*, at p. 270;

Dillon, *supra*; Daniels, *supra*; UPI (December 8, 1991). "Two Brooklyn Shootings May Be Linked to Mob Feud."

156 Mazza, *supra*, at p. 292.

157 Lance, *supra*, at p. 271 (citing Gregory Scarpa Sr., sworn affidavit, June 7, 1994, and *People v. R. Lindley DeVecchio*, testimony of Larry Mazza, October 18, 2007, 698). Lance wrote that Scarpa's rifle was an M1 carbine (Ibid.). McGuire wrote that, according to Mazza, Scarpa used an M52, a sniper rifle, to kill Fusaro (McGuire, *supra*, at p. 228). It is worth noting that the "affidavit" Lance relied on was executed the day before Scarpa died. That document s discussed at length in chapter eleven, *infra*.

158 Daniels, *supra*.

159 Mazza, *supra*, at p. 292.

160 Ibid., Mazza, *supra*, at p. 292. *See*, also, Scarpa, *supra*, at p. 133.

161 Daniels, *supra*; Dillon, *supra*; UPI (December 8, 1991). "Two Brooklyn Shootings May Be Linked to Mob Feud."

162 Daniels, *supra*; UPI (December 8, 1991). "Two Brooklyn Shootings May Be Linked to Mob Feud."

163 Dillon, *supra*.

164 James, George. "Killing in Brooklyn Social Club is Linked to Mob Power Struggle." *The New York Times*.

165 Coney Island Hospital is now South Brooklyn Health (NYC Health + Hospitals/South Brooklyn Health, Ruth Bader Ginsburg Hospital. https://www.nychealthandhospitals.org/locations/south-brooklyn-health/).

166   Mazza wrote that James Malpeso was shot in the stomach (Mazza, *supra*, at p. 324).

167   Libertore was noted as being 23 years old during his trial in an article dated May 10, 1995 (Miller, Tracey L. (May 10, 1995). "Informant Testifies in NY Mob Trial." UPI).

168   *United States v. Malpeso* (2d Cir. 1997) 115 F.3d 155, 159.

169   Ibid.

170   Ibid.

171   Ibid.

172   Dillon, *supra*.

173   Lance, *supra*, at p. 273; *United States v. Malpeso* (2d Cir. 1997) 115 F.3d 155, 159.

174   *United States v. Malpeso* (2d Cir. 1997) 115 F.3d 155, 159.

175   Ibid.; UPI (December 8, 1991). "Two Brooklyn Shootings May Be Linked to Mob Feud." UPI.

176   *United States v. Malpeso* (2d Cir. 1997) 115 F.3d 155, 159.

177   Miller, *supra*; New York Daily News Staff. (May 3, 1995). "Dad & Son to Sing in Mob Trial." *New York Daily News*; *United States v. Malpeso* (2d Cir. 1997) 115 F.3d 155, 161.

178   *United States v. Malpeso* (2d Cir. 1997) 115 F.3d 155, 159.

179   Miller, *supra*.

180   *United States v. Malpeso* (2d Cir. 1997) 115 F.3d 155, 159; McGuire alleged that "two gunmen entered Wanna Bagel" and killed Speranza (McGuire, *supra*, at p. 234). McGuire's source for that allegation is the George James December 9, 1991, article in the New York Times, "Killing is Tied to Mafia War in Brooklyn," which alleged that "one or more men walked… into the bagel shop where Mr. Speranza was working. They shot him numerous times in the head and body." That nearly contemporaneous account is the only account of the shooting this author found alleging that anyone other than Christopher Libertore entered the store by himself and shot Speranza that morning.

181   UPI (December 8, 1991). "Two Brooklyn Shootings May Be Linked to Mob Feud." UPI.

182   Six sources reported Speranza's age as being eighteen at the time of his murder (Behar, Richard. (January 20, 1992). "Organized Crime: A Gang the Still Can't Shoot Straight." *Time Magazine*; Lance, supra, at p. 273; Miller, *supra*; *New York Daily News* Staff. (May 3, 1995). "Dad & Son to Sing in Mob Trial." *New York Daily News*; Dillon, *supra*; Mazza, *supra*, at p. 324). Three sources reported Speranza's age as being seventeen at the time of his murder (New York Daily News Staff. (September 4, 1995). "Innocent Victim's Dad Rages." *New York Daily News*; *United States v. Malpeso* (2d Cir. 1997) 115 F.3d 155, 158; UPI. (January 8, 1992). "Brooklyn DA Vows Crackdown on Warring Mobsters." UPI.).

183   *United States v. Malpeso* (2d Cir. 1997) 115 F.3d 155, 159.

184   *United States v. Malpeso* (2d Cir. 1997) 115 F.3d 155, 159; Miller, *supra*.

185   *United States v. Malpeso* (2d Cir. 1997) 115 F.3d 155, 159; Miller, *supra*.

186   Miller, *supra*.

187   *United States v. Malpeso* (2d Cir. 1997) 115 F.3d 155, 159-160.

188   Miller, *supra*; Lance, *supra*, at pp. 273-274.

189   New York Daily News Staff. (May 3, 1995). "Dad & Son to Sing in Mob Trial." *New York Daily News*.

190   New York Daily News Staff. (September 4, 1995). "Innocent Victim's Dad Rages." *New York Daily News*. *See*, also, Mazza, *supra*, at p. 324.

191   UPI (December 8, 1991). "Two Brooklyn Shootings May Be Linked to Mob Feud." UPI.

192   Dillon, *supra*. For a graphic view of the interior of the Wanna Bagel shop after the Speranza murder, the reader is directed to Dow, Harold. (November 12, 1992). "Greg Scarpa Interview with Harold Dow from CBS 'Street Stories.' www.youtube.com/watch?v=gfYXZuZ7qB4.

193   Scarpa, *supra*, at p. 134.

194   McGuire, *supra* at p. 234.

195   Ibid.

196   Ibid.

197   McGuire, *supra*, at p. 235 (quoting Carmine Imbriale).

198   Lance, *supra*, at p. 274.

199   McGuire, *supra*, at p. 234 (quoting NYPD Detective Thomas Dades).

200   Hynes "took Joseph as his confirmation name and was called Joe by all who knew him" (Behar, *supra*).

201   Behar, *supra*. McGuire, *supra*, at p. 235. See, also, Rose, Charlie. (1991). "Colombo Family Mob War in Brooklyn – Discussion" in which Hynes stated his office had issued more than 100 subpoenas.

202   Mazza, *supra*, at p. 299.

203   Behar, *supra*; Rose, *supra*.

204   Behar, *supra*; *see* also Dow, *supra*.

205   UPI. (January 8, 1992). "Brooklyn DA Vows Crackdown on Warring Mobsters." UPI.

206   Lance, *supra*, at p. 294.

207   Mazza, *supra*, at p. 310.

208   Ibid.

209   Ibid.

210   Ibid.; Lance, *supra*, at p. 294.

211   Mazza, *supra*, at pp. 310-311.

212   Mazza, *supra*, at p. 311; Lance, *supra*, at p. 294.

213   Mazza, *supra*, at p. 311; Lance, *supra*, at p. 294.

214   Mazza, *supra*, at p. 311.

215   DeVecchio, *supra*, at p. 307; Lance, *supra*, at p. 275. DeVecchio's account stated the meeting took place on December 11. Lance's account quotes a "302" of the meeting dated December 10, and a "209" of the meeting dated December 11 (Lance, *supra*, at pp. 275 & 276).

216   DeVecchio, *supra*, at p. 307; Lance, *supra*, at p. 275.

217   Lance, *supra*, at p. 275.

218   Lance, *supra*, at p. 276; *See* also DeVecchio, *supra*, at pp. 307-308 re: Amato and Fusaro murders.

219   Lance, *supra*, at p. 278; DeVecchio, *supra*, at p. 308.

220   DeVecchio, *supra*, at p. 313.

221   Mazza, *supra*, at p. 300

222   Ibid., at pp. 322-323; Vlad, D.J. (Vladimir Lyubovny). (January 18, 2021). "Larry Mazza on Him & Grim Reaper Doing Over 20 Mafia Hits (Full Interview)." VladTV; Later Days Podcast with Joe Poletto. "Larry Mazza – Greg Scarpa Sr., Episode 5."

223   Mazza, *supra*, at pp. 300 & 323.

224   Mazza, *supra*, at p. 323.

225   Ibid., at pp. 302 & 323.

226   Ibid., at pp. 302-303 & 323.

227   Ibid.; at p. 323. Vlad, D.J. (Vladimir Lyubovny). (January 18, 2021). "Larry Mazza on Him & Grim Reaper Doing Over 20 Mafia Hits (Full Interview)." VladTV.

228   FBI Files, set 5, at p. 9.

229   Ibid., at p. 48.

230   Ibid., at p. 50.

231   FBI Files, set 6, at p. 39.

232   Ibid., at pp. 45 & 52.

233   Mazza, *supra*, at p. 317.

234   Lance, at p. 243.

235   Ibid.

236   Mazza, *supra*, at p. 315.

237   Ibid.

238   Ibid.

239   DeVecchio, *supra*, at p. 201.

240   UPI. (January 8, 1992). "Brooklyn DA Vows Crackdown on Warring Mobsters." UPI.

241   Daniels, Lee A. "Brooklyn Slaying May Be 6th in Mob Families' 2-Month Feud." *The New York Times*.

242   Ibid.; Orlando Sentinel. (January 9, 1992). "Organized Crime Figure Shot to Death in Brooklyn." Orlando Sentinel.

243   Mazza, *supra*, at p. 314-315.

244   Ibid., at p. 314.

245   Ibid., at pp. 312-315.

246   Lance, *supra*, at p. 283.

247   Mazza, *supra*, at p. 313.

248   Lance, *supra*, at p. 283 (quoting Larry Mazza).

249   Vlad, DJ (Vladimir Lyubovny). (January 18, 2021). "Larry Mazza on Him & Grim Reaper Doing Over 20 Mafia Hits (Full Interview)." VladTV.

250   Bet-David, Patrick. (October 13, 2021), "Former Mafia Hitman Opens up About Dark Side of Greg Scarpa & His 20 Hits." *Valuetainment*.

251   Vlad, D.J. (Vladimir Lyubovny). (January 18, 2021). "Larry Mazza on Him & Grim Reaper Doing Over 20 Mafia Hits (Full Interview)." VladTV.

252   Lance, *supra*, at p. 284 (quoting NYPD Detective Joe Simone).

253   Ibid., at p. 283 (quoting NYPD Detective Joe Simone).

254   Ibid., at p. 283.

255   Ibid. (quoting NYPD Detective Joe Simone).

256   Lance, *supra*, at p. 286 (quoting testimony of Larry Mazza in *People v. R. Lindley DeVecchio*, October 18, 2007, transcript pp. 114 & 113).

257   Lance, *supra*, at pp. 285-286 (quoting Flora Edwards and Dr. Stephen Dresch).

258   Scarpa, *supra*, at p. 134 (quoting Linda Schiro).

259   Ibid.

260   DeVecchio, at p. 393.

261   Ibid.

262   Mazza, *supra*, at p. 314.

263   Ibid.

264   Ibid.

265   Lance, *supra*, at p. 284 (quoting Larry Mazza).

266   Lance, *supra*, at p. 284; Mazza, *supra*, at p. 314.

267   DeVecchio wrote that Scarpa declared "This one's *from* Carmine," adding, for dramatic purposes no doubt, that Scarpa made the statement "to the accompaniment of a hail of bullets" (DeVecchio, *supra*, at p. 201).

268   DeVecchio, *supra*, at p. 200. DeVecchio apparently forgot about the subsequent murder of capo John Minerva. *See* endnote 298 and accompanying text, *infra*.

269   Scarpa, *supra*, at p. 134 (quoting Linda Schiro).

270   Mazza, *supra*, at p. 317.

271   Ibid.

272   Ibid.

273   Lance, *supra*, at p. 289 (quoting DeVecchio memo of January 1, 1992, capitalization in the original).

274   The "Colombo Family Strike Force ('CFSF'), which was comprised of Federal Bureau of Investigation Agents ('FBI') and New York City Police Detectives" (*United States v. Scopo* (2d Cir. 1994) 19 F.3d 777, 779).

275   Ibid.

276   *Orena v. United States* (E.D.N.Y. 1997) 956 F. Supp. 1071, 1077.

277   Ibid.

278   Mazza, *supra*, at p. 318.

279   Ibid., at p. 319

280   Ibid.

281   Ibid., at p. 346.

282   Lance, *supra*, at p. 295. Lance referred to Scarpa as an "expert marksman" when describing the shootout with Cacace (Ibid.). However, as *The New York Times* pointed out the next day, the street on which the gun battle took place was narrow, and Scarpa and Mazza between them got off as many as fourteen shots, which seems excessive for

an expert under the circumstances. When asked, Gregory Scarpa Jr. stated that his father was not an expert marksman, but he was a "good shot" with both a revolver and a rifle as a result of experience and practice. (Notes provided to the author by Gregory Scarpa Jr. on July 12, 2023).

283   Mazza, *supra*, at p. 346.

284   The New York Times. (February 27, 1992). "Suspected Mob Capo, 51, Shot in Brooklyn." *The New York Times*. *The Times* reported, consistent with Mazza's recollection, that the shots were fired from a "white station wagon" (Ibid.). Linda Scarpa wrote that the hit team was in Scarpa's black Mercedes (Scarpa, *supra*, at p. 137). She may have confused the details of the third attempt on Cacace's life with the second attempt.

285   Mazza, *supra*, at pp. 322-323.

286   Mazza, *supra*, at p. 323.

287   Ibid.

288   Ibid., at p. 347.

289   Ibid.

290   Lance, *supra*, at p. 296; FBI Files set 6, at pp. 61-62.

291   Lance, *supra*, at p. 295.

292   Ibid., at p. 296; McGuire, *supra*, at p. 261.

293   McGuire, *supra*, at pp. 260-261

294   Lance, *supra*, at p. 296.

295   FBI Files, set 6, at p. 62.

296   DeVecchio, *supra*, at p. 317 (quoting Greg Scarpa; capitalization in the original).

297   Ibid., at pp. 317-318.

298   *United States v. Monteleone* (2d. Cir. 2001) 257 F.3d 210, 213.

299   Ibid.; Lance, *supra*, at p. 297; DeVecchio, *supra*, at p. 318; Maddux, Mitchel. (April 12, 2012). "Mafia to Pothead: 'Kill or be Killed Next.'" *New York Post*; New York Daily News Staff. (June 4, 2008). "'Tommy Shots,' Reputed Colombo Boss, Arrested in 3 Slayings from Early '90s." *New York Daily News*.

300   Lance, *supra*, at p. 297 (capitalization in the original); DeVecchio, *supra*, at p. 318.

301   Holloway, Lynette. (February 20, 1997). "Convictions of 3 in Mob Overturned in Slayings." *The New York Times*.

302   Their original conviction was overturned by the U.S. District Court which granted them a new trial due to the failure of the government the first time around to disclose the relationship between Scarpa and DeVecchio and Scarpa's practice of blaming others for murders he had committed (Holloway, *supra*). The government appealed, and the District Court's order for a new trial was reversed by the Second Circuit (*United States v. Orena* (2d Cir. 1998) 145 F.3d 551). The defendants then appealed their convictions, and those convictions were upheld on appeal by the Second Circuit in *United States v. Monteleone* (2d. Cir. 2001) 257 F.3d 210.

303   Lance, *supra*, at p. 298 (citing testimony of Gregory Scarpa Jr., in *Pasquale Amato and Victor Orena v. U.S.*, hearing before Hon. Jack B. Weinstein, January 7, 2004, transcript at pp. 57-58).

304   Cohen, Stefanie. (June 5, 2008). "Goodbye Colombos." *New York Post*.

305 *United States v. Gioeli* 08-cr-240 (BMC) (E.D.N.Y. May. 21, 2020).

306 Maddux, Mitchel. (April 12, 2012). "Mafia to Pothead: 'Kill or be Killed Next.'" *New York Post*.

307 Feuer, Alan. (November 3, 2017). "A Mafia Turncoat, Facing Life, is Sentenced to 11 Years." *The New York Times*.

308 Lance, *supra*, at p. 225; DeVecchio, *supra*, at p. 320; McGuire, *supra*, at p. 265; *Orena v. United States* (E.D.N.Y. 1997) 956 F. Supp. 1071, 1082.

309 Tabor, Mary B. W. (April 2, 1992). "Man Accused as Colombo Chief is Held in Slaying of Ex-Member." *The New York Times*.

310 This plastic bag has been the subject of a good deal of controversy since its discovery during the April 1, 1992, search and seizure. For additional exposition on the subject of the bag, *see* chapter six, endnotes 206-219, *supra*.

311 *Orena v. United States* (E.D.N.Y. 1997) 956 F. Supp. 1071, 1082; *See* also *United States v. Orena* 32 F3d 704, 708. The Orenas' claim the fact that Vic Orena possessed only defensive weapons (Lance, *supra*, at pp. 299-300) demonstrated he posed no threat and was therefore not interested in a shooting war with supporters of Carmine Persico ignores the firepower capabilities of the dozens of men who supported Orena and who were subject to his direction. Mazza's recounting of the formidable arsenal of Orena supporters at a fall of 1991 meeting between the two sides is more indicative of how the Orena side was outfitted and operating than the small cache of weapons seized from inside the home of Vic Orena's girlfriend in the April 1, 1992, raid. The numbers on the Orena side in the street during that meeting approached 100 heavily armed men including rooftop snipers, two men with Uzis in full view,

and a machine gun sitting on top of "Wild Bill" Cutolo's Lincoln and leveled squarely at Scarpa's crew (Mazza, *supra*, at pp. 252). At the risk of being flippant, the Orenas' argument is akin to saying that General George S. Patton posed no threat to the Germans given that he was only armed with two revolvers. The Orenas' characterization of Vic Orena Sr., also ignores sworn testimony about Ocera's murder (*Orena v. United States, supra*, 956 F. Supp. at p. 1080 (quoting the trial testimony of Alphonse D'Arco), and Vic Orena's tendency to leave the dirty work to others (Raab, *The Five Families, supra*, at p. 333). His sons' portrayal of Orena as a "nonviolent money-maker" (Lance, *supra*, at p. 249), as not much more than a successful businessman (*see*, Lance, *supra*, at pp. 214-220), when in reality he was a capo and then an acting boss of a violent, extensive criminal enterprise, who managed to rake in "millions a year for the borgata" (Lance, *supra*, at p. 216) is at best disingenuous.

312　For a first-hand account from FBI Special Agent Joe Fanning of the April 1, 1992, search of Gina Reale's Long Island home, the reader is directed to DeVecchio, *supra*, at pp. 509-510.

313　DeVecchio, *supra*, at p. 324.

314　Ibid.

315　FBI Files, set 6, at pp. 66-68.

316　FBI Files, set 6, at p. 64.

317　Ibid., at pp. 64-65.

318　DeVecchio, *supra*, at p. 324.

319　FBI Files, set 6, at p. 71.

320　Lance, *supra*, at p. 304.

321   Celona, Larry and O'Shaughnessy, Patrice. (May 23, 1992). "Mob War." *New York Daily News*.

322   Lampasi's last name is often spelled Lampesi in various accounts (*See*, e.g., *Orena v. United States* (E.D.N.Y. 1997) 956 F. Supp. 1071, 1086; Dannen, *supra*; Mazza, *supra*, at pp. 348-351).

323   Mazza, *supra*, at p. 349.

324   Ibid.

325   Ibid.

326   Ibid.

327   Ibid.

328   Ibid.

329   Ibid., at p. 348.

330   Ibid., at p. 350.

331   *See*, e.g., Celona and O'Shaughnessy, *supra*.

332   Fermino, Jennifer. (March 26, 2006). "Nail Him! Kin Cry – Indict vs. 'Mob Spy' Fed Thrills Family of Slain Moll." *New York Post*.

333   *Orena v. United States* (E.D.N.Y. 1997) 956 F. Supp. 1071, 1088.

334   Lance, *supra*, at p. 307.

335   DeVecchio, *supra*, at p. 338; *See*, also, Lance, *supra*, at p. 305 & McGuire, *supra*, at pp. 243-244.

336   DeVecchio, *supra*, at p. 339.

337   Ibid., at p. 339; Lance, *supra*, at p. 305.

338   DeVecchio, *supra*, at p. 339; Lance, *supra*, at p. 305.

339   Mazza, *supra*, at p. 367.

340   Pashigian, B. Peter. (March 2001). "The Used Car Price Index: A Checkup and Suggested Repairs." U.S. Department of Labor, Bureau of Labor Statistics, Office of Prices and Living Conditions. Table 7, at p. 34.

341   DeVecchio, *supra*, at p. 486.

342   Ibid. (quoting Linda Schiro).

343   Lance, *supra*, at p. 305 (quoting Linda Schiro). Sandra Harmon wrote that DeVecchio and Scarpa met at Scarpa's home on May 15, 1992. At that meeting, according to Harmon, Scarpa let DeVecchio know that he wanted to kill Lampasi, and he asked DeVecchio for assistance in providing Lampasi's address and work schedule. DeVecchio, again according to Harmon, agreed to provide the information (Harmon, *supra*, at p. 153). That allegation is contrary to the statement of Linda Schiro to Jerry Capeci and Tom Robbins as noted above.

344   Lance, *supra*, at p. 484. Mazza's first-hand account of the hit contains two sarcastic references to Scarpa's "crystal ball" both as to Lampasi's work schedule and where he parked his car (Mazza, *supra*, at p. 348). Mazza did not make any specific reference to either DeVecchio or Tomasello regarding this "crystal ball." He did, however, mention Scarpa's eagerness to report the hit to Tomasello after the fact (Mazza, *supra*, at p. 349).

345   Lance, *supra*, at pp. 310-311; McGuire, *supra*, at p. 259.

346   McGuire, *supra*, at pp. 258-259.

347 DeVecchio, *supra*, at p. 331. Lance wrote that the bug was planted the next day, on June 4, 1992 (Lance, *supra*, at p. 310).

348 DeVecchio, *supra*, at p. 334.

349 DeVecchio, *supra*, at p. 310.

350 Ibid., at p. 335; Lance, *supra*, at p. 311; Mazza, *supra*, at pp. 353-354.

351 Lance, *supra*, at pp. 311-312; Mazza, *supra*, at p. 354.

352 Mazza, *supra*, at p. 354; Lance, *supra*, at p. 312. Mazza eventually made his way to Florida with his wife and son. He was arrested on February 9, 1993, when he and his family were on their way to a day at Disney World (Mazza, *supra*, at p. 381; Lance, *supra*, at p. 312).

353 Lance, *supra*, at p. 317; DeVecchio, *supra*, at p. 337.

354 Lance, *supra*, at p. 317; DeVecchio, *supra*, at p. 337; Mazza, *supra*, at p. 355.

355 Lance, *supra*, at p. 317; DeVecchio, *supra*, at p. 337.

356 Mazza, *supra*, at p. 355.

357 Raab, Selwyn. (November 20, 1994). "The Mobster Was a Mole for the FBI; Tangled Life of a Mafia Figure Who Died of AIDS is Exposed." *The New York Times*.

358 FBI Files, set 6, at p. 71. Lance wrote that Scarpa's arrest occurred on August 31, 1992, the date of his arrest which is set forth in *United States v. Scarpa* (E.D.N.Y. 1993) 815 F. Supp. 88, 89.

359 Dillon, *supra*.

360 Rabinovitz, Jonathan. (October 19, 1992). "2 Men Slain in Brooklyn Said to Have Ties to Mob." *The New York Times.*

361 James, George. (October 22, 1993). "Man Tied to Crime Family is Shot to Death in Queens." *The New York Times.* Peter Lance attributes both the Mancusi and the Scopo killings to the violence of the third Colombo war (Lance, *supra*, at p. 354).

CHAPTER ELEVEN: A BANG AND A WHIMPER

1 The final stanza of T.S. Eliot's poem "The Hollow Men" is:

This is the way the world ends

This is the way the world ends

This is the way the world ends

Not with a bang but a whimper.

2 Lance, *supra*, at p. 318.

3 Lance, *supra*, at p. 319; Capeci, Jerry and Robbins, Tom (August 16, 1992). "Blood's Hounding Mobster." *New York Daily News.*

4 Capeci, Jerry and Robbins, Tom (August 16, 1992). "Blood's Hounding Mobster." *New York Daily News*; Harmon, *supra*, at pp. 155-156; Lance, *supra*, at pp. 318-219.

5 Capeci, Jerry and Robbins, Tom (August 16, 1992). "Blood's Hounding Mobster." *New York Daily News*; Harmon, *supra*, at pp. 155-156.

6 Lance, *supra*, at p. 319.

7   Scarpa, *supra*, at p. 143.

8   Lance, *supra*, at p. 319.

9   Ibid., at p. 319.

10   Harmon, *supra*, at p. 156.

11   Lance, *supra*, at p. 319.

12   Tabor, Mary B. W. (August 30, 1992). "Settlement in Lawsuit on H.I.V.-Tainted Blood." *The New York Times*.

13   DeVecchio, *supra*, at p. 181; Lance, *supra*, at p. 319.

14   DeVecchio, *supra*, at p. 181.

15   Harmon, *supra*, at p. 156.

16   Lance, *supra*, at p. 320.

17   Ibid.

18   *United States v. Scarpa* (E.D.N.Y. 1993) 815 F. Supp. 88, 89. Scarpa was also charged with "carrying and using a firearm in connection with a violent crime" (Ibid.).

19   DeVecchio, *supra*, at p. 350.

20   Scarpa, *supra*, at p. 146 (quoting Lin DeVecchio).

21   Harmon, *supra*, at p. 157.

22   Ibid. *See*, also, Scarpa, *supra*, at p. 146.

23   *United States v. Scarpa* (E.D.N.Y. 1993) 815 F. Supp. 88, 89.

24   Ibid.

25   Ibid. DeVecchio, when writing about Scarpa's arrest on August 31, 1992, stated that "Scarpa went home that day

with an anklet" (DeVecchio, *supra*, at p. 352). However, in Judge Weinstein's supplementing order of March 5, 1993, he pointed out that Scarpa was not released and allowed to return home with an "electronic bracelet" until September 16, 1992 (*United States v. Scarpa* (E.D.N.Y. 1993) 815 F. Supp. 88, 89). It would appear from Weinstein's order that Scarpa was initially incarcerated for a little over two weeks before being allowed to go home as noted after a second detention hearing.

26   *United States v. Scarpa* (E.D.N.Y. 1993) 815 F. Supp. 88, 89.

27   Ibid.

28   Ibid., at p. 90.

29   Mazza, *supra*, at p. 359.

30   Harmon, *supra*, at p. 159.

31   Ibid., at p. 161.

32   Mazza, *supra*, at p. 358.

33   Ibid.

34   Ibid., at p. 363.

35   Lance, *supra*, at p. 326.

36   Harmon, *supra*, at p. 159.

37   Scarpa, *supra*, at p. 146.

38   Ibid., at p. 147.

39   Ibid.

40   Mazza, *supra*, at p. 367.

41   Scarpa, *supra*, at p. 148.

42   Ibid.

43   DeVecchio, *supra*, at p. 357 (quoting Linda Schiro).

44   In his book, DeVecchio referred to himself as Scarpa's friend (*See*, e.g., DeVecchio, *supra*, at p. 422).

45   DeVecchio, *supra*, at p. 358.

46   Ibid.

47   Lance, *supra*, at pp. 310-311 (citing *U.S. v. Persico*, Mazza testimony, 3845).

48   Ibid., at pp. 358-359 (capitalization in the original).

49   Mazza, *supra*, at p. 363.

50   Scarpa, *supra*, at pp. 153 & 163; Mazza, *supra*, at p.368.

51   Lance, *supra*, at p. 327.

52   Scarpa, *supra*, at p. 163.

53   Ibid.

54   Ibid.

55   Mazza, *supra*, at p. 368.

56   Ibid., at p. 368-369.

57   Ibid., at p. 369.

58   Scarpa, *supra*, at p. 153.

59   Harmon, *supra*, at p. 161.

60   Mazza, supra, at p. 369.

61   Moran pleaded guilty to the murder of Randazzo in 1997 and became a cooperating witness for the FBI (*New*

York Daily News (December 21, 1997). "Feds Have a New Canary." *New York Daily News*).

62   Harmon, *supra*, at pp. 161-162.

63   Ibid., at p. 161.

64   Lance, *supra*, at p. 327; Mazza, *supra*, at p. 371.

65   Mazza, *supra*, at p.370.

66   Ibid., at p. 369.

67   Lance, *supra*, at p. 328; Mazza, *supra*, at p. 371; *New York Daily News* (December 21, 1997). "Feds Have a New Canary." *New York Daily News*.

68   Mazza, *supra*, at p. 370.

69   Harmon, *supra*, at p. 161.

70   Mazza, *supra*, at p. 371.

71   Ibid., at p. 372.

72   Scarpa, *supra*, at p. 153.

73   Mazza, *supra*, at p. 371.

74   *United States v. Scarpa* (E.D.N.Y. 1993) 815 F. Supp. 88, 90.

75   Scarpa, *supra*, at p. 165 (quoting Linda Schiro).

76   *United States v. Scarpa* (E.D.N.Y. 1993) 815 F. Supp. 88, 89.

77   Lance, *supra*, at p. 345.

78   Ibid. Scarpa, *supra*, at p. 165. Lance, *supra*, at p. 346.

79   *United States v. Scarpa* (E.D.N.Y. 1993) 815 F. Supp. 88, 89.

80   *United States v. Scarpa* (E.D.N.Y. 1993) 815 F. Supp. 88, 90.

81   Beekman Downtown Hospital was located at 170 William Street. It is, as of this writing, New York-Presbyterian Lower Manhattan Hospital.

82   *United States v. Scarpa* (E.D.N.Y. 1993) 815 F. Supp. 88, 93-94. The full terms of Scarpa's transfer to Beekman Hospital were as follows: "1. Upon the defendant's satisfaction of the conditions set forth below, the defendant shall be released from custody to Beekman Downtown Hospital in Manhattan (the "Hospital"). 2. Defendant will be required to obtain a private room at the Hospital.3. The defendant shall be guarded by the United States Marshal's Service twenty-four hours per day, seven days per week. At least two Marshals or other guards selected by the Marshal's Service shall guard the defendant at all times. 4. The cost of paying for the guards shall be borne entirely by the defendant and his family at the rate of $15.00 per hour, per guard. Payment for the guard service must be made in advance to the Marshal's Service each week and if it is not done, the defendant is to be remanded to the custody of the Metropolitan Correctional Center (the "MCC"). 5. The cost of hospitalization shall be borne by the defendant and his family and any insurer that they may have. 6. The defendant shall be allowed personal visits by the doctors and medical staff of the Hospital, the defendant's treating physician Dr. Gumprecht, his attorney of record in this case and those members of his immediate family whose names appear on the attached list. No other people are to be allowed to visit or communicate with the defendant. Visitors are to present identification to establish their identity to the Marshal's Service. 7. The Marshal's Service will have the

sole discretion to determine the frequency and length of visits as well as the number of people who may visit the defendant at any one time. They may search any visitor and must be present during all such visits. In particular, the Marshal's Service will carefully monitor any visits or communications with Frank Scarpa and Joseph Schiro. All visitors must disclose to the guards any items that they are bringing in to the defendant. 8. The above-mentioned visitors may go directly to the Hospital without first going to the Marshal's office in the Eastern District of New York to obtain an individual pass. 9. The defendant is not to have access to or possession of any firearms. If any visitor brings a firearm or any other weapon to the Hospital, the defendant shall be immediately remanded by the Marshal's Service to the MCC. 10. The defendant will be allowed one phone call per day, which may only be made to the people referred to in paragraph 6, above. However, during business hours, he may also make telephone calls to his attorney of record in this case.

11. The defendant will not otherwise have access to a telephone and no telephones will be present in the defendant's room other than when needed to make the calls noted in paragraph 10, above. 12. The Marshal's Service is to monitor all telephone calls. 13. The defendant is not to discuss any criminal activity on the telephone or with any visitor. 14. If the defendant is not admitted to the Hospital or is discharged from the Hospital at any time, he is to be remanded directly to the MCC by the Marshal's Service. 15. The defendant is not to leave the Hospital for any reason except for court appearances. The defendant shall be transported to court appearances by the Marshal's Service in the manner it deems appropriate. Marshals are authorized to use handcuffs and other security devices at any time. 16. The Marshal's Service shall immediately remand the defendant to the MCC if in its sole judgment any of the conditions of

his release are violated. Specifically, and without limitation, if the defendant attempts to leave the Hospital, other than in the custody of the Marshal's Service for court appearances, he is to be remanded to the MCC. 17. Marshals shall have the authority to take all steps that in their judgment are required to assure their own safety, the safety of the defendant and the safety of the community in carrying out this Order. 18. The defendant shall sign a bond of $1.2 million of equity secured by real property, as was previously done pursuant to Magistrate Judge Caden's Order dated September 16, 1992. A violation of any of the conditions of release will result in the forfeiture of these assets." (Ibid.)

83 *United States v. Scarpa* (E.D.N.Y. 1993) 815 F. Supp. 88, 94.

84 Ibid.

85 Ibid., at p. 95.

86 Ibid.

87 Scarpa, *supra*, at p. 168.

88 Ibid.

89 Ibid.

90 The New York Times. (April 25, 1993). "Mobster with AIDS Gets Special Sentence." *The New York Times*; Lance, *supra*, at p. 348.

91 The New York Times. (April 25, 1993). "Mobster with AIDS Gets Special Sentence." *The New York Times*.

92 Scarpa, *supra*, at p. 168.

93 The New York Times. (April 25, 1993). "Mobster with AIDS Gets Special Sentence." *The New York Times*; Lance, *supra*, at p. 348.

94   Lance, *supra*, at p. 353.

95   Kroger, *supra*, at p. 145.

96   Raab, *The Five Families, supra*, at p. 344.

97   Lance, *supra*, at p. 350; DeVecchio, *supra*, at p. 364.

98   Lance, *supra*, at p. 350; DeVecchio, *supra*, at p. 364.

99   Lance, *supra*, at p. 350; DeVecchio, *supra*, at p. 364.

100   Lance, *supra*, at p. 351.

101   DeVecchio, *supra*, at p. 365.

102   Ibid.

103   Ibid.

104   Scarpa, *supra*, at p. 168.

105   Ibid.

106   Judge Jack Weinstein to Greg Scarpa on December 15,1993 (Dannen, *supra*; Lance, *supra*, at p. 355).

107   *United States v. Sessa* (E.D.N.Y. Jan. 25, 2011) Opinion and Order 97-CV-2079 (ARR), at p. 31. DeVecchio, *supra*, at p. 367; Lance, *supra*, at p. 355.

108   Lance, *supra*, at p. 356.

109   FBI Files, set 8, at p. 135 (capitalization in the original).

110   Mazza, *supra*, at p. 422.

111   Ibid.

112   Ibid., at p. 423.

113   Ibid.

114   Lance, *supra*, at p. 357.

115   Ibid.

116   DeVecchio, *supra*, at p. 367.

117   Lance, *supra*, at p. 357.

118   Ibid.

119   *Orena v. United States* (E.D.N.Y. 1997) 956 F. Supp. 1071, 1083.

120   Lance, *supra*, at p. 357 (quoting Flora Edwards).

121   Scarpa, *supra*, at p. 170 (quoting Linda Schiro).

122   Scarpa, *supra*, at p. 170.

123   *United States v. Scarpa* (E.D.N.Y. 1993) 815 F. Supp. 88, 90.

124   Lance, *supra*, at p. 319.

125   Ibid., at p. 326.

126   *United States v. Scarpa* (E.D.N.Y. 1993) 815 F. Supp. 88, 89.

127   Ibid., at p. 90.

128   The New York Times. (April 25, 1993). "Mobster with AIDS Gets Special Sentence." *The New York Times*; Lance, *supra*, at p. 348.

129   Scarpa, *supra*, at p. 173 (quoting Linda Schiro).

130   Later Days Podcast with Joe Poletto, Greg Scarpa Jr. Interview Part 2, Episode 5 (starting at about the 15:34 mark).

131   *United States v. Scarpa* (E.D.N.Y. 1993) 815 F. Supp. 88, 90.

132   *See*, e.g., Scarpa, *supra*, at p. 146; DeVecchio, *supra*, at p. 486; Mazza, *supra*, at p. 363; Lance, *supra*, at p. 326; Harmon, *supra*, at pp. 164 et seq.

133   Lance, *supra*, at p. 375.

134   Lance, *supra*, at p. 370 et seq.

135   Cornell Law School, Legal Information Institute. "Dying Declaration"; Federal Rules of Evidence, rule 804(b)(2).

136   Lance, *supra*, at p. 372.

137   Raab, *The Five Families, supra*, at p. 344.

138   *See*, The United States Attorneys Office, Eastern District of New York. Press Release (December 28, 2007). "Colombo Organized Crime Family Acting Boss Alphonse T. Persico and Administration Member John J. Deross Convicted of Murder in Aid of Racketeering and Witness Tampering."

139   Coincidentally, Sifton is also the judge who ruled on the claim of sexual discrimination by the FDNY in its hiring practices.

140   Lance, *supra*, at p. 373.

141   Ibid., at pp. 371-372.

142   One final note about Scarpa's June 7, 1994, statement: the Orenas' theory that Scarpa and DeVecchio engineered the November 18, 1991, attack on Scarpa and his daughter to foment an internecine Colombo family war was emphatically not supported by the document. In fact, the document noted that the November 1991 attack was

the primary if not the sole motivation for Scarpa's hunting and killing Orena supporters starting in late 1991 (Lance, *supra*, at pp. 372-373). It is of course conceivable that such a statement was as lacking in factual accuracy as the rest of the document. It is not advisable to overlook Scarpa's capacity for deception right up until the moment of his death.

143　Nothing in the text of the document that Lance reproduced indicates anyone with the power to swear a witness was present. Investigator Clemons may have been so empowered, but that is not clear from the reproduction (*See*, Lance, *supra*, at pp. 372-373).

144　Lance, *supra*, at p. 375.

145　Ibid., at p. 373.

146　Scarpa, *supra*, at p. 171.

147　Ibid., at p. 171.

148　Ibid.

149　Ibid., at p. 172.

150　Ibid., at p. 171.

151　Ibid.

152　Ibid., at p. 173.

153　Lance, *supra*, at p. 45; Raab, *The Five Families, supra*, at p. 338; *New York Daily News*. (May 25, 1996). "Judge Frees Mob Canary's Files." *New York Daily News*; Dannen, *supra*, estimated the amount to have been at least $150,000.

154　Villano, *supra*, at p. 112.

155   Ibid., at p. 114; *See* Villano at pp.114-115 for a brief description of how the insurance proceeds made their way to an FBI informant such as Scarpa.

156   Lance estimated a much lower figure for insurance payouts given to Scarpa. According to Lance, Scarpa received approximately $52,000 in "reward money from insurance companies anxious to recover a portion of the millions of dollars he stole in precious gems, furs, liquor, cigarettes, antiques, negotiable securities, and bonds" (Lance, *supra*, at p. 45).

157   Raab, Selwyn. (November 20, 1994). "The Mobster Was a Mole for the FBI; Tangled Life of a Mafia Figure Who Died of AIDS is Exposed." *The New York Times*.

158   DeVecchio, *supra*, at p. 182.

159   Later Days Podcast with Joe Poletto, Greg Scarpa Jr. Interview Part 2, Episode 5.

INDEX

Symbols

A

415, 428, 429, 430, 456, 461, 462, 463, 464, 465, 466, 467, 468, 469, 470, 471, 472, 474, 477, 484
Brooklyn Hospital   154
Brown Street   153
Brown v. Board of Education   49
burglar   124, 125
Byrd   54, 55, 57, 58, 59, 60, 62, 327. *See* Lawrence Byrd
Byron De la Beckwith   45, 49

C

Cabrini Hospice   307, 308, 311
Cacace   228, 249, 275, 276, 278, 284, 285, 286, 443, 465, 476, 477
Cafe on N   255
Calla   264
Calogero "Charlie the Sidge" Lo Cicero   19, 26, 70
Calogero "Charlie the Sidge" LoCicero   36
Cantalupo Realty   104
Capeci   47, 51, 52, 53, 55, 148, 198, 292, 327, 343, 362, 369, 370, 371, 373, 400, 403, 406, 407, 409, 410, 412, 424, 425, 430, 467, 482, 484
Cape Cod   121
capo   25, 36, 38, 41, 56, 76, 77, 83, 120, 126, 127, 130, 132, 133, 134, 136, 142, 155, 162, 169, 189, 202, 206, 225, 226, 227, 231, 234, 235, 239, 242, 246, 247, 252, 277, 278, 282, 286, 360, 365, 397, 443, 460, 476, 480
Caproni   309, 310, 311, 312

Cardaci   194, 195
Carlo "Collie" Di Pietro   189
Carlo Gambino   73
Carmine Imbriale   37, 126, 131, 187, 192, 204, 214, 242, 247, 258, 263, 274, 285, 293, 309, 400, 427, 454, 462, 471
Carmine Persico   24, 35, 37, 68, 72, 75, 77, 123, 128, 130, 132, 140, 169, 187, 188, 189, 191, 192, 196, 210, 219, 221, 222, 223, 224, 225, 226, 228, 229, 230, 231, 232, 233, 238, 242, 243, 246, 248, 249, 251, 252, 253, 254, 270, 277, 282, 285, 288, 290, 317, 343, 350, 419, 440, 442, 451, 456, 479
Carmine Sessa   110, 122, 125, 127, 138, 141, 168, 169, 170, 190, 194, 198, 205, 214, 226, 227, 228, 232, 233, 238, 239, 242, 244, 246, 247, 248, 253, 255, 259, 262, 263, 269, 278, 291, 293, 309, 318, 402, 405, 406, 407, 429, 437, 451, 452, 455, 462
Carmine "The Snake" Persico   68, 71, 72, 138, 197, 252, 254
Carmine Tramunti   73
Catanzano   215, 216, 438
Catskills   155
CDC   179
Census   18, 81, 324, 331, 356, 357, 380, 435
Center for Disease Control   179
Charles Hynes   37, 272
Charles Lo Cicero   24
Charles "Moose" Panarella   76,

H

382

Lucchese   151, 226, 231, 237, 247, 277, 306, 458
Lucchese crime family   237
Lucchese family   151, 231, 277, 306, 458
Luke Spann   89
Lyndon Johnson   50, 351, 368

M

MacAskill   55, 337
Madison Square Garden   63
Mafia   13, 14, 15, 16, 19, 20, 24, 25, 26, 27, 28, 42, 54, 63, 64, 70, 79, 81, 86, 87, 97, 99, 100, 103, 104, 105, 123, 125, 142, 145, 161, 171, 172, 175, 185, 210, 221, 224, 227, 294, 312, 313, 324, 325, 326, 327, 328, 329, 331, 332, 333, 334, 335, 336, 337, 342, 343, 344, 345, 346, 347, 350, 351, 352, 353, 355, 358, 360, 361, 369, 372, 373, 376, 402, 406, 408, 409, 415, 416, 417, 420, 422, 424, 425, 428, 431, 436, 438, 441, 442, 457, 467, 470, 473, 474, 478, 479, 483, 496
Magistrate John Caden   297
Magliocco   28, 29, 34, 35, 37, 38, 39, 40, 41, 70, 253, 365
Magliocco family   37
Manhattan   116, 164, 166, 174, 220, 261, 262, 280, 281, 305, 306, 312, 489
Manor Restaurant   234
Margaret D. Clemons   318
Maria Palmetta   17

Mario Parlagreco   127, 194, 206, 208
Mary Bari   122, 137, 138, 139, 141, 142, 196, 197, 198, 199, 205
Mary Scarpa   18, 211
Massapequa   286
Masseria   114, 394
Matteo Speranza   272, 273, 274, 275
Mazza   56, 110, 113, 117, 118, 127, 131, 132, 133, 137, 141, 149, 154, 155, 156, 157, 158, 159, 160, 161, 162, 163, 164, 165, 166, 167, 168, 169, 171, 172, 175, 176, 177, 178, 180, 181, 205, 206, 207, 227, 233, 239, 242, 243, 247, 249, 250, 257, 258, 259, 261, 262, 264, 267, 268, 269, 271, 275, 277, 278, 279, 280, 281, 284, 290, 291, 293, 299, 303, 304, 305, 312, 319, 337, 353, 354, 355, 356, 372, 391, 392, 393, 394, 395, 396, 397, 398, 399, 400, 401, 402, 404, 405, 406, 407, 408, 410, 412, 413, 414, 415, 416, 417, 418, 420, 421, 422, 423, 424, 425, 431, 433, 435, 436, 437, 444, 445, 451, 452, 453, 454, 455, 457, 458, 459, 460, 461, 462, 463, 464, 465, 466, 467, 468, 469, 470, 471, 472, 473, 474, 475, 476, 477, 479, 481, 482, 483, 486, 487, 488, 492, 494
Mazzola   191
MCC   298, 306, 307, 312, 489,

490

McCaffrey 91, 93, 386

McDonald 142, 203, 268, 279

McDonald Avenue 142, 268, 279

McFadden 260, 337, 338, 408, 432, 438, 461

McGuire 126, 127, 130, 338, 353, 364, 396, 398, 399, 400, 401, 406, 427, 428, 432, 436, 437, 446, 447, 449, 452, 454, 460, 466, 468, 470, 471, 472, 477, 479, 481, 482

Meadowlands Racetrack 277

Medgar Evers 43, 44, 45, 46, 48, 49, 56, 58, 61, 338, 367

Merchant Marines 18

Merrick 234, 237

Metropolitan Correctional Center 166, 220, 306, 312, 489

MIBURN 50, 53, 330, 368, 370

Michael "Black Mike" Calla 263

Michael DeRosa 152

Michael Franzese 37, 56, 350, 363, 364, 372

Michael Imbergamo 286

Michael Maffatore 237, 251

Michael "Mickey Boy" Paradiso 82

Michael "Mikey Flattop" DeRosa 152, 303

Michael Paradiso 82

Michael Schwerner 50

Michael Yodice 209

Miciotta 250, 251, 309

Mike DeSantis 312

Mikes Candy Store 194

Minerva 286

Mississippi 43, 44, 45, 46, 48, 50, 51, 52, 53, 54, 55, 56, 57, 58, 59, 60, 61, 62, 99, 109, 172, 327, 329, 330, 341, 368, 369, 370, 373, 387

Mississippi Freedom Democratic Party 50

Montgomery Bus Boycott 49

Monticello Raceway 155

Mooney Cutrone 73, 74, 77

Moose Panarella 76

Moran 152, 303, 304, 305, 487

Morris "Moe" Terzi 244

Mossad 99

Mother Cabrini social club 268

Motta di Livenza 16

Mount Sinai Hospital 305

MTA 261

Mt. Sinai Hospital 181

murder 10, 12, 20, 24, 28, 29, 43, 45, 46, 49, 50, 55, 56, 58, 60, 61, 77, 79, 82, 87, 107, 110, 111, 114, 115, 117, 118, 119, 122, 126, 127, 128, 129, 130, 131, 132, 134, 136, 137, 138, 140, 141, 142, 143, 145, 146, 148, 149, 150, 168, 169, 170, 173, 178, 182, 183, 184, 187, 188, 190, 191, 192, 193, 194, 195, 196, 198, 202, 204, 205, 206, 208, 209, 210, 211, 213, 214, 215, 216, 217, 224, 227, 231, 232, 233, 236, 238, 265, 267, 269, 272, 274, 275, 276, 278, 279, 282, 285, 286, 288, 289, 290, 292, 293, 294, 295, 297, 306, 309, 321, 322, 387, 393, 394, 398, 400, 401, 403, 404, 405, 406, 419, 426, 429, 431,

Turquoise   240

U

Uncle Albert   155, 160
United States Marshal   93, 489
United States Penitentiary   220, 270
United States Senates Committee on Governmental Affairs Subcommittee on Investigations   222
United States v. Michael Sessa   215
United States v. Sessa, et al.   195, 433, 450
Unity Day   63, 66, 67
University of Mississippi   44
U.S. Army   18, 105, 325, 357
U.S. Attorney General John Mitchell   64
U.S. Constitution   31, 347, 399, 400
U.S. District Court for the Eastern District of New York   154
U.S. District Court in Newark   93

V

Valerie Caproni   145, 309
Venice   16
Venus II diner   271, 272, 273
Vernon Dahmer   43, 47, 49, 54, 56, 57, 58, 60, 61, 325, 372
Vic Orena   149, 150, 166, 225, 226, 227, 228, 229, 230, 231, 232, 233, 234, 235, 236, 237, 238, 239, 241, 242, 243, 246, 247, 249, 252, 254, 255, 258, 259, 262, 269, 276, 278, 287, 288, 290, 302, 312, 313, 410, 460, 479
Vic Orena, Jr.   228, 278, 410, 460
Victor Oboyski   197, 430
Victory Memorial Hospital   180, 296
Villano   30, 45, 46, 47, 48, 49, 52, 56, 58, 61, 80, 81, 82, 85, 86, 104, 185, 320, 350, 358, 361, 367, 368, 373, 380, 381, 382, 495, 496. *See* Anthony VIllano
Vincent "Chickie" DeMartino   261, 264
Vincent "Chin" Gigante   226, 263
Vincent Emmino   79, 380
Vincent Fusaro   256, 272, 276, 286, 306
Vincenza   17, 212, 435
Vinnie Aloi   243, 246
Vinnie Venus   259, 271
Vinny Rizzuto   115, 153
Vito Corleone   13, 14, 15
Vito Scaglione   217
Vittorio "Little Vic" Orena   150, 235
Voting Rights Act in 1965   57

W

Wall Street   33, 97
Wanna Bagel   273, 470, 471
Washington, D.C.   28, 29, 63, 203, 466
West Hartford, Connecticut   141, 198
White Citizens Council   58
Wild Bill   227, 249, 255, 258, 264, 276, 292, 310, 480
William Kelleher   201, 202
William "Wild Bill" Cutolo   227
Wimpy Boys   103, 104, 107,

*For More News About Jonathan Dyer,
Signup For Our Newsletter:*

http://wbp.bz/newsletter

Word-of-mouth is critical to an author's long-term success. If you appreciated this book please leave a review on the Amazon sales page:

https://wbp.bz/gsler

ALSO AVAILABLE FROM WILDBLUE PRESS

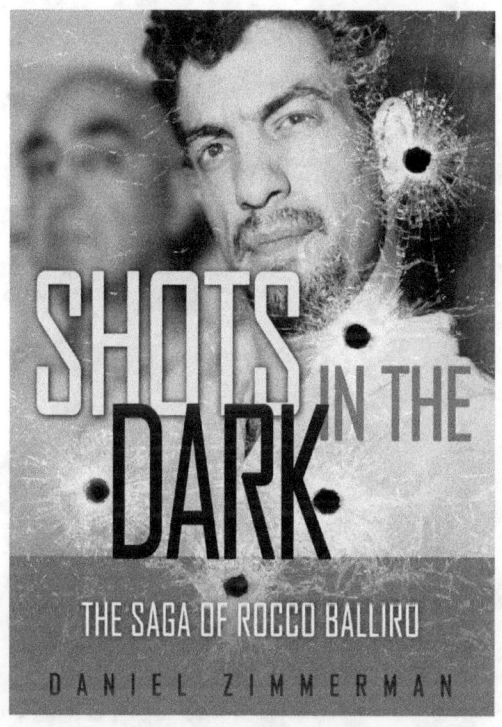

http://wbp.bz/sitda

"The fascinating story of the 1963 deaths of Boston mobster Rocco Balliro's girlfriend and her son in a police shootout . . . a real page-turner."—**Dennis N. Griffin, bestselling author of** *The Rise and Fall of a "Casino" Mobster*

www.ingramcontent.com/pod-product-compliance
Lightning Source LLC
Chambersburg PA
CBHW061130120626
46546CB00005B/1724